PROPHECY

Prophecy
© 2012 by Gloria Daulton

Published by Insight Publishing Group
4739 E. 91st Street, Suite 210
Tulsa, OK 74137
918-493-1718

Unless otherwise noted, all Scripture quotations are taken from the Holy Bible: King James Version. N.T. Greek, 1958. Landon S. Bagster, 1958.

ISBN: 978-1-932503-25-8

Library of Congress catalog card number: 2011940247

Printed in the United States of America

Prophecy
The
Word
of the Spirit
Of God

Recorded
by
Sister Gloria
Servant of the Lord

These words from God
though dated ten years ago are
released now as God speaks
ongoing of the same jurisdictions,
governments and judgments.
All of these prophecies were sent
to Washington Officials and to
Spiritual Leaders when God
spoke them.

Dedication

To my precious darling Mother, Ilena Saylor Ward, Sanctified, Holy, Set Apart and Full of Joy, a Soldier of the Cross, an Epistle of Righteousness, full of Good Works, without partiality and without hypocrisy, a Proverbs 31 Saint of The Lord, who fasted three days every week for decades while working full time in a factory and keeping a ten-room home, still found time to visit and pray for the sick and cook glorious, wonderful meals daily! Home-cooked Birthday Dinners for each child and grand-child! Faithful and True. How great is our God manifested in you, Dear Mother! Thank you for <u>all</u> your service, suffering, courage, and perseverance! This book is a product of your faithfulness!!!

IN MEMORIAM

MY PRECIOUS DARLING MOTHER, KNOWN AND LOVED BY MANY AS SISTER WARD, WENT HOME TO BE WITH JESUS SEPTEMBER 15, 2010 AND AT AGE NINETY-TWO WAS STILL GOING TO CHURCH FOUR TIMES A WEEK! SECRETARY-TREASURER OF HER CHURCH FOR FORTY YEARS. PRAYER WARRIOR. SINGER. LOVER OF SOULS. SMILED IN ADVERSITY. STAYED SWEET AND KIND THROUGH AFFLICTION AND SORROW. CARRIED HER CROSS WITH PEACE AND SPUNK. IN EARLIER YEARS TAUGHT SEWING AND COOKING IN 4H. BAKED WEDDING CAKES FOR GRAND-CHILDREN. SHE WAS OF GREAT GOODNESS AND GLORY. SHE MADE THE ROOM SMILE WHEREVER YOU WERE. SHE WAS JESUS WITH WORK CLOTHES ON. COULD BEAT ANYONE AND EVERYONE AT CHECKERS. MOTHER OF THREE, GRAND-MOTHER OF THIRTEEN, GREAT GRAND-MOTHER OF TWENTY-EIGHT AND MANY GREAT, GREAT GRAND-CHILDREN STILL BEING BORN. LOVING DAUGHTER OF JOHN P. AND FLORA BELLE SAYLOR. BELOVED SISTER TO DELPHINE FUGATE AND ZENA ELLIS. BROTHERS EMANUEL AND DEWARD SAYLOR, DECEASED. SISTER-IN-LAW KATIE SAYLOR, BROTHER-IN-LAW JOSEPH ELLIS. MANY, MANY NIECES AND NEPHEWS. MY MOTHER WAS A NATIONAL TRAVELER, STILL GOING TO MORRIS CERULLO MEETINGS WHILE IN HER EIGHTIES. DEVOTED WIFE OF FIFTY-SEVEN YEARS TO THOMAS W. WARD, MY STEP-FATHER. THEY ARE NOW WITH OUR LOVING LORD. HALLELUJAH! AND GLORY TO GOD! THANK YOU JESUS!

Contents

> What is the stand of our Constitution?
> What holds it firmly in place?
> Opinions of one ... or many?
> Or just plain ... Truth and Grace

> Little bitty babies ... Torn from limb to limb ...
> Because mothers Want to get rid of them.
> Others ... chemically cremated. Their very
> Existence ... hated. Make a baby and then kill it.
> Our National Sin!

> The Holy One
> Babies see the great good force ... Amor.
> Filtering every facet of the abundant activity,
> Parcels of impregnated ... Odes of Love.

To die true ... is to just begin to live. Wonder
fare waging war on greed! Starlight humanity
embracing the Embryo ... World System seed!
Bubble bath of bestial bloodletting Severing our
progeny ... Where is destiny? ... Triumphant seed
of Provocative shrouds. Negating man's Eternal
Treasures. Speak forth, O Truth! ... The World is
in need.

Nations move to the beat of now. What is
programmed in youth will be the future how!

Prayers are people turned prostrate
Laying down their lives ... giving time to eternity.

Power is word strategy!
Making mountains bow! Words! True Wonders
of the world! Epitome Of Creation! Power in
progression. Capability of the Gods. Monarchy
Of magical movement of matter. Missions of
creativity ... crying out To you and me. Speak
forth, O Truth, Our Leasehold of legacy!

> Play the part, Little Unknown.
> Though the script be incomplete.
> Let a moment of magic fill thy spirit to overflow
> Coursing the pages of the Greatest Age!

> Can God?
> Where is the Lord, right now? Does he really
> know how to bind and Loose? Make sane the
> gristled minds ... shrapnel riddled with dope,
> Divorce, death and demons? Can he recreate the
> pieces that have Been torn out? Scraps of ... "Who
> Am I?" Broken bits of ... "It Doesn't really matter
> anyhow!" Gnarled proclivity of, "My life ain't
> Much. Who cares? Can this Jesus really ... ?"

> Speak boldly ... Servants ... of Power!
> Just ahead ... our finest hour! Let not fear of pain
> Thrust thee sore. For justice prevailing ... will
> open The door ... to expose the evil report ... to be
> the right! Giving grace and credence to the light!

> Love is a matchless gram of gold and diamonds.
> Ruby-redness perches ... on luster-laden prayers.
> Bloodstains of countless martyrs ... paint the stars
> To heaven's glory!

Preface

This printing of The Testimony of Our Lord and Savior Jesus Christ should be self-explanatory. As John the Revelator wrote in Revelation 19:10, I AM THY FELLOW SERVANT AND OF THY BRETHREN THAT HAVE THE TESTIMONY OF JESUS: WORSHIP GOD: FOR THE TESTIMONY OF JESUS IS THE SPIRIT OF PROPHECY! The Apostle Paul wrote in I Thessalonians, QUENCH NOT THE SPIRIT! DO NOT REJECT PROPHECIES!

The instruction he gave to the Church in I Corinthians 14:12, 4 is, "FORASMUCH AS YOU ARE ZEALOUS OF SPIRITUAL GIFTS SEEK THAT YOU MAY EXCEL TO THE EDIFYING OF THE CHURCH! PROPHECY EDIFIES THE CHURCH!" If the church is edified by being built up, encouraged, enlightened, improved, educated, comforted and equipped, the community can be reached, by being edified, built up, encouraged, enlightened, improved, educated, comforted and equipped. If the communities are equipped, by each church reaching their own, the world can be reached by each heart touching another heart through the heart of Our Lord's Love and Comfort. Prophecy.

Prophecy is divinely inspired utterance. Some prophecies are spoken to or about individuals. Other prophecies are to the masses. Let the Lord Minister to your heart as He may be attempting to speak to you, as well. Let the Spirit minister, Hope, Healing, Edification, Deliverance and Comfort as you receive His Testimony.

Acknowledgement and Blessing

To My God, That is More than Enough, I give Glory and Honor and Praise! For you are The Everlasting One! The All-Existent One! I Magnify you above <u>All</u> Things, and Glory in Your Holy Presence! I Stand in Awe of All Your Creation, Your Love, Your Forgiveness, Your Magnificence and Your Grandeur!

To my Darling Daughters and to my Splendid Sons, I, again, give glory to God for you! For your love, caring, long-suffering, I say thank you, Shari, Vicki, Rick, Tabitha, Tamah and Nate! What a wonder you are to me! To Sherry, Tim, and John, spouses and parents of love to my children, I love you! Great is your faithfulness! And to my children's children, who are grand, indeed, I speak success and fortitude into your future! Power and faith into your present! May the Love of God <u>always</u> surround you with <u>His</u> Purpose! And may you feel His Presence under-girding you daily, hourly, minute by minute! Sarah, Tracy, Jason, Samantha, Kelsey, Jessica, Abbey, Craig, Andrew, Courtney, Be Released into your Destiny!

A special tribute to <u>all</u> my family and friends, my sister Betty L. Stratton, my brother Edgar E. Saylor, and to <u>all</u> Ministers, to The Five-Fold Ministry of Apostles, Prophets, Evangelists, Pastors and Teachers, to Intercessors and Saints everywhere who have prayed, plowed, planted, purified and positioned themselves in lighting a candle, I say Thank you! Thank you! Thank you!!!

Office of Prophet: Introduction

PROPHETS RECEIVE THEIR CALL OR APPOINTMENT FROM GOD. A PROPHETIC CALL IS A CALL TO LIBERTY AND FREEDOM TO BE WHO YOU ARE IN GOD. WHO GOD MADE YOU TO BE! IT ENABLES THE PROPHETS TO BE UNMOVED BY HUMAN BIAS AND CRITICISM. THE CALL OF THE PROPHETS REQUIRES THEY NOT BE INTIMIDATED BY REJECTION OR CONFRONTATION. MANY TIMES THE PROPHETS STAND ALONE, MUST SPEAK TO UNSYMPATHETIC OR EVEN ANTAGONISTIC AUDIENCES. PROPHETS ARE NOT PEOPLE OF ROUTINE TASKS. THEY CHART NEW PATHS. ACTUALLY CALLING THE PEOPLE BACK TO THE OLD PATHS OF THE TRUTH OF GOD'S WORD WHICH AT TIMES APPEARS TO BE NEW. PROPHETS SPEAK FOR GOD AND COMMUNICATE GOD'S MESSAGE TO THE PEOPLE, SPEAKING THE WILL OF THE LORD FOR THE PURPOSE OF REPROOF, INSTRUCTION, CORRECTION, TRAINING IN RIGHTEOUSNESS. WHETHER WARNING, OF PROCLAMATION OF IMPENDING DANGER, JUDGMENT OR OF BLESSING. A PROPHET SPEAKS WITH THE AUTHORITY OF THE HOLY SPIRIT, PROCLAIMING GOD'S WORD AND NOT THEIR OWN, FAITHFULLY REPEATING GOD'S WORD TO THE PEOPLE. GOD HAS USED PEOPLE DOWN THROUGH THE AGES TO FULFILL THE PROPHETIC ROLL OF PROCLAIMING HIS TRUTH. THE OFFICE OF PROPHET IS A SPECIFIC DISTINCT CALL NOT ENMESHED AND SUBDUED! WITH GREAT COURAGE AND INDEPENDENCE OF SPIRIT, DEPENDING ON GOD'S SPIRIT! PROPHETS ARE TO EXALT GOD'S WORD AND NOT TO SEEK THEIR OWN GLORY.

DEBORAH WAS A PROPHET, A JUDGE AND A WARRIOR! Judges Chapters Four and Five. EVERYONE WHO PROPHESIES IS NOT A PROPHET! THE APOSTLE PAUL SAID, YOU MAY ALL PROPHESY. BUT ALL ARE NOT PROPHETS. THE CALL OF THE PROPHET IS AN OFFICE, ONE OF THE FIVE MINISTERIAL OFFICES OF APOSTLES, PROPHETS, EVANGELISTS, PASTORS, AND TEACHERS. THE SCRIPTURES STATE, AND GOD HAS SET SOME IN THE CHURCH, FIRST APOSTLES, SECONDARILY PROPHETS, THIRDLY TEACHERS,

AFTER THAT MIRACLES, THEN GIFTS OF HEALING, HELPS, GOVERNMENTS (CHURCH ORDER!), DIVERSITIES OF TONGUES. AND YOU BETTER START RELEASING THEM AND ALLOWING THEM TO ABIDE IN THEIR OWN CALLING. GOD DOES NOTHING WITHOUT A PURPOSE! HE PURPOSES HIS BODY, THE BODY OF CHRIST, THE CHURCH, TO MANIFEST HIS LOVE AND PRESENCE TO THE WORLD! IF YOU THINK YOU ARE GOING TO MANIFEST THE LOVE AND PRESENCE OF OUR PRECIOUS LORD WITHOUT LOVING AND ALLOWING ALL OF THE LORD'S BODY PARTS TO OBEY THE SPIRIT OF GOD, YOU ARE DECEIVED.

I Corinthians Chapters Twelve, Thirteen and Fourteen
The First Epistle of John

Introduction

HE THAT DESCENDED IS THE SAME ALSO THAT ASCENDED UP FAR ABOVE ALL HEAVENS, THE CHRIST, THAT HE MIGHT FILL ALL THINGS! HE CAN FILL ANYTHING AND EVERYTHING EXCEPT SOMEONE WHO IS FULL OF HIMSELF. THAT IS WHY HE GAVE SOME APOSTLES AND SOME PROPHETS AND SOME EVANGELISTS AND SOME PASTORS AND TEACHERS! THERE IS A DEFINITE PURPOSE FOR EVERYTHING GOD DOES! WHAT ARE THESE FIVE OFFICES OF THE CHURCH? WHAT IS THEIR PURPOSE? THE HOLY WRIT SAYS, FOR THE PERFECTING OF THE SAINTS, FOR THE WORK OF THE MINISTRY (SIGNS ARE SUPPOSED TO FOLLOW THEM THAT BELIEVE!) FOR THE EDIFYING (MY BIBLE STILL SAYS, COVET TO PROPHESY. PROPHECY EDIFIES THE CHURCH) OF THE BODY OF CHRIST: TILL WE ALL COME INTO THE UNITY OF THE FAITH (WE ARE NOT THERE AS YET, OTHERWISE, INSTANT, VISIBLE MIRACLES WOULD BE TRANSPIRING CONSTANTLY!) AND OF THE KNOWLEDGE OF THE SON OF GOD, INTO A PERFECT MAN (WE ARE NOT THERE, AS YET, BECAUSE THERE IS NOT DISCIPLINE, CORRECTION AND CHECKS AND BALANCES!) UNTO THE MEASURE OF THE STATURE OF THE FULLNESS OF CHRIST! THE LAME WALK, THE DUMB TALK, THE BLIND SEE, AND DEVILS ARE CAST OUT! UNTIL GOD ALWAYS MOVES MIGHTILY WITHOUT FORM OF TRADITION AND CEREMONY!!!!!

I WON'T SAY CHRISTIANS, 'CHRISTIAN' MEANS CHRIST-LIKE, PURPORT TO HAVE A BETTER WAY. IF IT IS NOT BASED, FUNDAMENTALLY ACCURATE ON THE WORD OF GOD, CAST IT OUT! IT IS STILL WRITTEN, ALL LIARS WILL HAVE THEIR PART IN THE LAKE WHICH BURNS WITH FIRE AND BRIMSTONE. SOME THINK IT NO INFRINGEMENT TO LIE AGAINST THE HOLY GHOST! WHEN YOU WANT TO DO IT YOUR WAY INSTEAD OF GOD'S WAY, THAT IS A LIE! WHOSOEVER LOVES AND MAKES A LIE IS LISTED WITH THE SORCERERS AND WHOREMONGERS AND MURDERERS AND IDOLATERS! Revelation 22:15. Verse 12 of Ephesians 4, THE GREEK WORD 'RELIOS' THAT IS TRANSLATED PERFECTING MEANS 'TO

BRING YOU TO YOUR INTENDED PURPOSE!' GOD IS GETTING READY TO SET THE CHURCH IN DIVINE ORDER! NOT MAN'S.

Ephesians Four

FOR WHO HAS STOOD IN THE COUNSEL OF THE LORD AND HAS PERCEIVED AND HEARD HIS WORD? WHO HAS MARKED HIS WORD AND HEARD IT? THE PROPHET THAT HAS MY WORD, LET HIM SPEAK MY WORD FAITHFULLY. WHAT IS THE CHAFF TO THE WHEAT? SAITH THE LORD!!! TOUCH NOT MINE ANOINTED AND DO MY PROPHETS NO HARM!

Jeremiah 23:28
I Chronicles 16:22
Psalms 105:15

It is Written

HE THAT PROPHESIES SPEAKS UNTO MEN TO EDIFICATION, AND EXHORTATION AND COMFORT! HE THAT PROPHESIES EDIFIES THE CHURCH! I WOULD THAT YOU ALL SPOKE WITH TONGUES, BUT RATHER THAT YOU PROPHESIED!!! FOR GREATER IS HE THAT PROPHESIES THAN HE THAT SPEAKS WITH TONGUES, EXCEPT HE INTERPRET, THAT THE CHURCH MAY RECEIVE EDIFYING!!! LET THE PROPHETS SPEAK TWO OR THREE, AND LET THE OTHER JUDGE! IF ANYTHING BE REVEALED TO ANOTHER THAT SITS BY, LET THE FIRST HOLD HIS PEACE! FOR YOU MAY ALL PROPHESY ONE BY ONE, THAT ALL MAY LEARN AND ALL MAY BE COMFORTED! WHEREFORE, BRETHREN, COVET TO PROPHESY, AND FORBID NOT TO SPEAK WITH TONGUES!!! BRETHREN, BE NOT CHILDREN IN UNDERSTANDING! IN UNDERSTANDING BE MATURE! EVEN SO, FORASMUCH AS YOU ARE ZEALOTS OF SPIRITUAL THINGS, SEEK, IN ORDER THAT YOU MAY ABOUND IN THE EDIFICATION OF THE CHURCH!!!

FOLLOW THE WAY OF LOVE, BUT DESIRE EARNESTLY THE SPIRITUAL THINGS SO THAT YOU MAY PROPHESY. PROPHECY IS GOD SPEAKING TO HIS PEOPLE TO BUILD THEM UP, TO ENCOURAGE THEM, TO INCREASE THEIR FAITH, TO INSPIRE THEM, TO INSTRUCT THEM, TO CONSOLE THEM, TO EXPRESS HIS LOVE TO THEM.

I Corinthians 14 New Testament of the Holy Scriptures

He that has an ear
Let him hear
What the Spirit speaks

F L A S H P O I N T

GOD 2004

THE GONG HAS STRUCK. THE HOUR IS FAST APPROACHING. I WILL HAVE NO MERCY FOR THIS NATION THAT HAS SHOWN NO MERCY TO THE BABIES GROWING IN THE WOMB! I WILL STRIP THE LAURELS FROM THE GOVERNMENT! I WILL BREAK THE BACK OF INDIGNITY TO HUMAN LIFE! I STAND READY TO ENFORCE THE JUDGMENTS I HAVE SPOKEN. THEY ARE FOR AN APPOINTED HOUR. I GIVE LIFE. WHEN MAN PRESUMES TO PLAY GOD. TO TAKE LIFE. THERE ARE CONSEQUENCES TO FACE. THE JUDGMENTS THAT ARE BRINGING WRATH UPON THIS NATION SHALL COMMENCE AT THE APPOINTED HOUR. GEORGE BUSH KNOWS NOT THE FURY BY WHICH I SPEAK. HE TAKES MATTERS INTO HIS OWN HANDS IF HE DISREGARDS THE URGENCY OF THIS DECREE!

THE WORD BY WHICH THESE JUDGMENTS ARE BEING SPOKEN IS BY THE SAME WORD THAT WAS SENT TO WASHINGTON ON NOVEMBER 10, 2000, "MURDER IS STILL MURDER EVEN IN THE WOMB! YOUR GROWTH OF DEGRADATION HAS REACHED ITS PINNACLE! YOUR HIGH SEAT PINNACLED ON THE SOULS OF THE DEAD AND DYING SHALL TOPPLE SOON FOR JUDGMENT HAS COME TO AMERICA FOR HER NATIONAL SIN OF ABORTION!" THE SAME WORD THAT IS SPEAKING OF JUDGMENTS TO COME IN THE COMING MONTH SPOKE, TO WASHINGTON IN OCTOBER, 2001, THREE DAYS BEFORE THE ANTHRAX ATTACK THAT THERE WOULD BE AN ATTACK IN THREE DAYS! THE SAME WORD THAT IS WARNING OF MASS DESTRUCTION ON EVEN A GREATER SCALE THAN 9/11, FAXED TO WASHINGTON, THREE DAYS BEFORE THE RICIN WAS DISCOVERED IN FEBRUARY, 2004 AND THREE SENATE OFFICE BUILDINGS HAD TO CLOSE FOR DAYS AND FORTY PLUS PEOPLE HAD TO BE DECONTAMINATED, "PESTILENCE IS COMING TO WASHINGTON!" THIS WORD WAS FAXED TO BUSH, FRIST, WHOSE OFFICE THE RICIN WAS DISCOVERED IN, AND FIVE

OTHER OFFICIALS!!! THE SAME WORD THAT SPOKE TO WASHINGTON ON JANUARY 21, 2003, TEN DAYS BEFORE THE SPACE SHUTTLE WENT DOWN THAT, "DESTRUCTION AND DEATH ARE IMMINENT AND IMPENDING! NO DESTRUCTION COMES TO AMERICA EXCEPT WHAT I ALLOW! I AM GIVING AMERICA SPACE TO FULLY REPENT OF HER ATROCITIES AND MALIGNITIES, TO AVERT THE NEXT WAVE OF DESTRUCTIONS THAT ARE ALREADY IN THE MAKING!!! I CAN NO LONGER HOLD BACK THE JUDGMENTS! I AM A GOD OF MY WORD! MY HONOR IS TRUTH! DENY TRUTH AND SUFFER THE CONSEQUENCES OF YOUR DECEITS AND MALIGNITIES!!!" I HAVE HELD BACK MANY DEATHS FROM THIS NATION BUT THEY REFUSE TO REPENT AND TO CHANGE! I SPEAK THESE THINGS FOR THE SOLE PURPOSE: IF THERE IS ANYONE WHO IS ABLE TO COMPREHEND THE DISASTER THAT IS COMING TO AMERICA AND CAN COUNSEL THIS PRESIDENT TO AVERT THIS "HELL" (THAT IS THE ONLY WORD THAT CAN COME CLOSE TO DESCRIBING A 911 MAGNIFIED MANY TIMES) TO SPEAK NOW, WHILE THERE IS YET TIME TO STOP A HOLOCAUST OF MASS MURDER AND PAIN!!!

JOB SECURITY IS NOT A DEFINING FACTOR! THE EMPIRE IS AT STAKE! HUMANITY IS WEIGHED IN THE BALANCES! AMERICA HAS THE DEFINING MOMENT! "YOU CANNOT STAKE A PRESIDENCY, GEORGE BUSH, ON NOT "ROCKING THE BOAT!" THE BOAT IS ABOUT TO BE OBLITERATED!!! I CALLED YOU, GEORGE BUSH, TO BRING AN END TO CRUCIFYING BABIES IN THEIR SAFE HAVEN! I COUNSEL YOU TO STRIP THE ABORTION DECREE FROM THE NATIONAL SECURITY OF THESE UNITED STATES OF AMERICA!!! EXCEPT YOU DO THIS EXPEDIENTLY, THE NEXT WAVE OF MANY 9/11'S WILL BE EXCLUSIVELY YOURS BY CHOICE! YOU ARE THE ONLY ONE WHO CAN STOP AMERICA FROM FALLING BY DEFAULT!!! A PRESIDENTIAL DECREE AGAINST ALL ABORTION IS YOURS TO MAKE! IT WILL STOP THE HOLOCAUST THAT IS EARMARKED TO BEGIN IN APRIL! I WILL MAKE YOU TO KNOW THE WORDS THAT ARE BEING SPOKEN HERE ARE TRUTH AND NO LIE! YOU WILL KNOW WITHOUT ANY DOUBT, I WILL MAKE PLAIN TO YOU THE ACTION YOU MUST TAKE TO SAVE THIS NATION!!!

CORPORATE AMERICA HAS BEEN SERVED NOTICE! RELIGIOUS AMERICA HAS BEEN SERVED NOTICE! EDUCATIONAL AMERICA HAS BEEN SERVED NOTICE! EXECUTIVE, JUDICIAL AND LEGISLATIVE AMERICA IS BEING SERVED NOTICE! YOU HOLD AMERICA'S BALANCE IN THE PALM OF YOUR HAND, GEORGE BUSH! I SERVE YOU NOTICE AGAIN, THAT IF YOU CHOOSE TO NOT BRING ABORTION TO A HALT AT THIS TIME, I WILL BREAK AMERICA, FOR SHE IS NO LONGER MY NATION FOUNDED ON TRUTH AND FREEDOM!!!!!"

March 7, 2004

I SHALL STRIP MANY OF THEIR SEATS IN CONGRESS. I WILL RESTORE RIGHTEOUSNESS TO AMERICA. SHE SHALL SEE THE DEMISE OF ABORTION AND SEXUAL SATURATION. I CAN NO LONGER PROTECT DEVIATES AND MASS MURDERERS! AMERICA MURDERS HER OWN AND TEACHES HER LITTLE ONES TO BE SEX-POTS! AMERICA IS DIVIDED! THAT IS WHY SHE IS BEING ATTACKED. YOU CANNOT CONQUER IF YOU ARE NOT UNITED! YOU ARE NO LONGER THE UNITED STATES! YOU HAVE ALLOWED GREED AND GLAMOUR TO BECOME YOUR GODS! NOW YOU SHALL REAP DESTRUCTION! YOU SHALL GIVE UP MANY DEAD TO YOUR GODS OF GREED, ABORTION AND LUST!!! YOU SHALL REAP INCREDULOUS BOMBINGS. MAIMINGS, CRUSHINGS. TORMENTINGS. AMERICA, O, AMERICA, WHERE ARE YOUR MEN OF FORTHRIGHTNESS AND RIGHTEOUSNESS??? WHERE ARE YOUR ABRAHAMS AND YOUR LINCOLNS? WHERE ARE THE MARTIN LUTHERS AND THE MARTIN LUTHER KINGS??? WHERE ARE THE JOANS AND THE JOSHUAS???

February 17, 2004

F L A S H P O I N T

GOD SPEAKS

THE MYSTERY OF MIRACLES THAT YOU HAVE RELEASED TO THE NATION IS IN EFFECT. THE MYSTERY OF MIRACLES IN YOU WILL ESTABLISH THE CHURCH. THIS DAY IS A MAGICAL DAY. THE WORDS THAT YOU HAVE SENT TO WASHINGTON AND TO SPIRITUAL LEADERS THROUGHOUT THE LAND HAVE BROKEN SOIL FOR SEED TO BE PLANTED. I SHALL SOON TAKE THE MEN AND THE WOMEN WHO HAVE GUTS, TO THE LEADERS OF AMERICA. I SHALL SPEAK TO MEN IN AUTHORITY AND I SHALL BREAK THE BONDAGES OF THE ABORTION FIASCO. IT SHALL FALL BY THE WAYSIDE EVEN AS DID WOMEN NOT BEING ALLOWED TO VOTE AND BLACKS BEING BARRED FROM VOTING! MEN'S LAWS WILL ALWAYS BE DEFEATED, BUT MINE SHALL UTTERLY ENDURE! I WILL ATTEMPT ONE MORE TIME TO MAKE PLAIN TO THIS GOVERNMENT THAT I WILL SEND EVEN GREATER DESTRUCTIONS IF KILLING BABIES IS NOT RIPPED FROM THE LAW OF THIS NATION! I DO NOT QUAKE WHEN MY MEN AND WOMEN OF GOD ARE THREATENED BY MERE MEN.

I WILL ESTABLISH TRUE JUSTICE ONCE AGAIN IN THIS REPUBLIC THAT ONCE STOOD FOR FREEDOM FOR ALL PEOPLE! THAT INCLUDES THOSE PEOPLE IN THE WOMB AND IT SHALL YET BE A SAFE HAVEN FOR BABIES TO BEGIN LIFE AND MATURE. I GAVE IT TO THEM AND I SHALL RESTORE THE BLESSING TO THE WOMBS OF MANKIND. MY PEOPLE SHALL ONCE AGAIN BE HELD ACCOUNTABLE FOR WHAT THEY RESTRICT AND FOR WHAT THEY ALLOW! WHAT THEY ARE REFUSING TO ALLOW ... LIFE IN THE WOMB ... IS BEYOND THEIR BOUNDARIES OF AUTHORITY! THEY HAVE TAKEN MY RULE AND BROKEN MY BOUNDARIES! NOW I SHALL BEGIN TO BREAK THEIR PESTILENCE UPON THEIR OWN HEADS! THE MEN WHO CAN CHANGE THIS DESPICABLE ATROCITY CALLED 'LAW' SHALL BE DEALT WITH IN CHAMBERS.

I HOLD BACK THE MASS MURDER OF MANY NOW AS I KEEP THE TERROR FROM BEING EXECUTED, BUT TIME IS RUNNING OUT FOR MERCY! <u>THE ABORTION LAW MUST BE BROKEN AND STRICKEN FROM THE ROSTERS OF THIS REPUBLIC FOR CONTINUED PROTECTION AGAINST FOREIGN ATTACKS OF TERRORISM</u>! MY MERCY IS ABOUT TO END. DON'T BELIE SCRUTINY AND FORESIGHT. MAKE YOUR VOICES TO BE HEARD ON THE HILL! THE RESCUE OF MANY IS AT STAKE. I TRAMPLE SOON THIS LAW OF BLUDGEONING, BUT MAJOR DESTRUCTION LIES AT THE DOOR! HELPLESS, INNOCENT LIVES WILL AGAIN BE SACRIFICED ON YOUR ALTARS BECAUSE YOU REFUSE TO STOP THE KILLING FIELDS OF ABORTION! NAME YOUR PRICE. IS LIFE SO CHEAP AND DEATH SO DEAR THAT YOU CANNOT SEE THE PRECIPICE THAT AMERICA IS NOW HURLING HERSELF TOWARDS? STAND UP MEN, IF THAT'S WHAT YOU ARE! BE HEARD.

<u>ARE THERE REAL TRUE MEN OF INTEGRITY IN THIS GOVERNMENT OR HAVE THEY ALL SUCCUMBED TO GRABBING VOTES</u>? MY GOVERNMENT SHALL AGAIN BE THE LAW OF THE LAND. BUT MEN SHALL LOSE THEIR MORTAL SOUL! AND LIFE IS WEIGHED IN THE BALANCES. A VOTE. A VOTE. AND WHAT SHALL THE END BE OF THOSE WHO BECOME MY ENEMY? O, MY CHILDREN, BE ENCOURAGED FOR TRULY IT IS I THAT AM MAKING WAYS WHERE THERE SEEM TO BE NONE. TRULY IT IS I THAT AM OPENING DOORS THAT NO MAN CAN CLOSE. I SHALL ESTABLISH JUSTICE ONCE AGAIN IN THIS NATION THAT WAS FOUNDED UPON THE PRINCIPLES THAT <u>ALL</u> MEN ARE <u>CREATED</u> EQUAL! ALLOW ME TO ASK, O CONGRESSMEN. O CONGRESSWOMEN. O JUDGES OF THE COURTS, PRAY TELL ME WHERE ARE MEN CREATED AND PRAY TELL ME WHO CREATES THEM! NOT A FINGER OF A MAN OR WOMAN FORMS CREATED BEINGS IN THE WOMB OF THEIR MOTHER, BUT IT IS I BY THE POWER OF MY AUTHORITY THAT CREATES HUMAN BEINGS. AND IT IS I ALSO, THAT AM THE <u>SUPREME</u> JUDGE!

I WILL JUDGE THE SO-CALLED SUPREME COURT THAT HAS ALLOWED SUCH BLATANT DESPICABLE ATROCITIES TO BE DONE

TO MY CREATED HUMAN BEINGS! I WILL NOT TARRY MUCH LONGER WITH THIS GOVERNMENT! I SHALL SOON SEND MORE DESTRUCTIONS TO THE CAPITOL IN WASHINGTON THUS THE 'I AM' SPEAKS THIS TWENTIETH DAY OF DECEMBER, 2003. YOUR HIGH SEATS SEATED ON THE SOULS OF THE DEAD AND DYING SHALL BE BROUGHT TO DESOLATION. I AM WROTH WITH SUCH BLATANT EVIL THAT AMERICA PRACTICES IN HER ABORTION PARLORS. NOW SEE WHAT THIS ATROCITY BRINGS TO YOUR GOVERNMENT. I PROTECT THOSE WHO ALLOW ME TO BE GOD. I REFUSE TO PROTECT BABY BLUDGEONERS!

AMERICA, AMERICA, HOW OFTEN HAVE I PROTECTED YOU FROM FOREIGN POWERS. BUT YOUR HATRED OF MY LAWS NO LONGER ALLOWS ME TO KEEP YOU SAFE. BE NOT DECEIVED, AMERICA! JUDGMENTS IN WASHINGTON SHALL COMMENCE. INTERPRET WHAT YOU WILL. TO KILL IS MURDER! YOUR HANDS ARE BLOODY WITH YOUR OWN CHILDREN! THEIR BLOOD CRIES OUT FROM THE GORY GRAVES. NOW YOU SHALL REAP THE WHIRLWIND OF YOUR ABUSE TO MY PROGENY. ARISE, ARISTOCRATS! CAN YOU STILL NAME TRUTH IN YOUR LIPS??? WELL, RECEIVE THIS TRUTH SAITH THE 'I AM': JUDGMENTS ARE AT YOUR DOORS. BLAME NOT FOREIGN POWERS. YOUR SAFETY WAS REMOVED BECAUSE OF YOUR LAW. BABY KILLING IS MURDER!!! AMERICA, HOME OF MURDERERS.

December 20, 2003

NOTE: AND WHILE WE ARE ON THE SUBJECT OF FOREIGN POWERS, WHAT EVER HAPPENED TO THE THREE GIANT CARGO SHIPS THAT AMERICAN INTELLIGENCE WAS TRACKING ON SUSPICION THAT THEY WERE CARRYING IRAQI WEAPONS OF MASS DESTRUCTION? THE SHIPS WERE THOUGHT TO HAVE SET SAIL FROM A COUNTRY OTHER THAN IRAQ TO AVOID INTERCEPTION BY WESTERN NAVAL PATROLS IN THE GULF. THE SHIPS, SAID TO BE FLYING THE FLAGS OF THREE COUNTRIES, HAD BEEN SAILING FOR THREE MONTHS AFTER THEY REPORTEDLY

LEFT PORT IN LATE NOVEMBER, <u>SHORTLY AFTER THE U.N.</u> <u>WEAPONS INSPECTORS ARRIVED IN BAGHDAD</u>.

THEY WERE ALL REFUSING FREQUENT REQUESTS TO PROVIDE DETAILS OF THEIR CARGO OR DESTINATION AND OFFICIALS STATED THAT THE VESSELS WERE MAINTAINING RADIO SILENCE IN CLEAR CONTRADICTION OF INTERNATIONAL MARITIME LAWS.

DESPITE GRAVE SUSPICIONS OF WHAT IS ON BOARD, BRITAIN AND THE UNITED STATES WERE AFRAID TO ORDER INTERCEPTION BY NAVAL SHIPS BECAUSE OF FEAR THAT ANY INTERVENTION WOULD CAUSE THE CREWS TO SCUTTLE THE VESSELS, EACH BETWEEN 35,000 AND 40,000 TONS. IF THEY ARE CARRYING CHEMICAL, BIOLOGICAL OR NUCLEAR WEAPONS THIS COULD CAUSE CATASTROPHIC ENVIRONMENTAL DAMAGE. THE VESSELS HAVE CALLED BRIEFLY AT A HANDFUL OF ARAB COUNTRIES, INCLUDING YEMEN, BUT THEY HAVE BEEN RE-SUPPLIED AT SEA WITH FOOD, FUEL AND WATER BY OTHER SHIPS. ALL THREE WERE CHARTERED BY A SHIPPING AGENT BASED IN EGYPT. FOR A CONSIDERABLE TIME THEY HAVE BEEN STEAMING ROUND IN EVER-DECREASING CIRCLES.

THE VESSELS ARE BELIEVED TO BE CARRYING WEAPONS SMUGGLED OUT THROUGH SYRIA OR JORDAN.

THEY DID NOT DROP OFF THE FACE OF THE EARTH!!! ANYBODY?

Associated Press - February 19, 2003

GOD 2004

MY BEGINNING OF SORROWS HAS ALREADY BEGUN. TURMOIL
ON EVERY HAND. TAKE NO THOUGHT FOR THE MORROW.
SUFFICIENT UNTO THE DAY IS THE EVIL THEREOF. I WILL
CONTINUE TO RESOURCE MY INITIATIVES. I WILL MAKE
PROVISION FOR ALL MY DIRECTIVES. ESTABLISH JUSTICE!!!
INSURE DOMESTIC TRANQUILITY! AMERICA SHALL BE SET IN
ORDER IN GOVERNMENT AND IN CHURCH! I WILL REGAIN THE
RULE OF ORDER. I WILL SET IN MEN AND WOMEN OF INTEGRITY
IN MY HOUSES OF PRAYER AND IN MY HOUSES OF GOVERNMENT.
I WILL REGAIN ORDER. ORDER SHALL BE SET. IT'S NOT MY WILL
FOR YOU TO PONDER. I TAKE THE INITIATIVE IN ALL AREAS. I
GIVE THE ORDERS. I MAKE THE CROOKED PLACES STRAIGHT. I
BREECH THE GAPS. I THROW DOWN. I ROOT UP. I DESTROY. I
TEAR DOWN. I ROOT OUT. I BUILD AND I PLANT. SECURE THE
HOUSES OF PRAYER!!!!! MAKE SURE PRAYER IS SET IN ORDER.
INTERCESSION AND SPIRITUAL WARFARE!!!!! REMOVE
MOUNTAINS AND TEAR DOWN STRONGHOLDS! ESTABLISH
JUSTICE! DESTRUCTION SHALL PREPARE THE WAY FOR MEN AND
WOMEN OF MIGHT TO TAKE BACK THE REINS OF GOVERNMENT.
I WILL BREAK THE GODS, THE IDOLS OF THIS NATION!!! MY
WORD SHALL BE REINSTATED IN THIS GOVERNMENT!!! NO MAN
IS THE RULER OF AMERICA! I RULE BY MY MIGHTY RIGHT HAND
AND STRETCHED OUT ARM! I WILL RESTORE ORDER TO THE
UNITED STATES GOVERNMENT AND I WILL RESTORE ORDER TO
THE CHURCH GOVERNMENT!!! WILLINGNESS TO FIGHT FOR
TRUTH IS THE BACKBONE OF ESTABLISHING JUSTICE! JUSTICE
CAME FOR BLACKS WHEN KING TOOK HIS PLACE AND OBEYED IN
CIVIL DISOBEDIENCE!!!!!!! OTHERS STANDING AND SPEAKING
FOR TRUTH HAVE HELPED IN HALTING SLAVERY, GIVING
BLACKS AND WOMEN THE RIGHT TO VOTE AND TO HOLD OFFICE,
ALL OF WHICH WERE ILLEGAL ACCORDING TO THE STATUTES OF
MAN MADE LAW!!!!!! ABORTION IS ALSO A MAN MADE LAW THAT

IS ALSO CONTRARY TO THE LAWS OF GOD! STRIKE IT DOWN!!!!! GEORGE BUSH, THE JUDGMENTS THAT SOON SHALL COME TO AMERICA WILL BE UPON YOUR HEAD AND HANDS!!!!!! DEATHS, ATROCITIES, MAIMINGS, CRUSHINGS, CRIPPLINGS AND DECAPITATIONS, ALL OF WHICH COULD BE AVOIDED IF YOU WOULD RENOUNCE THE DEATHS, THE ATROCITIES, THE MAIMINGS, THE CRUSHINGS, THE CRIPPLINGS, THE DECAPITATIONS IN THE WOMB WHERE I CREATE HUMAN BEINGS!!!!! A PRESIDENTIAL DECREE TO STOP THE HOLOCAUST OF MURDERING LITTLE LIFE BEINGS! THEY HAVE HEARTS, HEADS, HANDS, FEET! AND YOU ALLOW THEM TO BE MURDERED BY THE THOUSANDS DAILY!!! UNDER YOUR WATCH! UNDER YOUR ORDERS! UNDER YOUR GOVERNMENT'S DECREE! AS HEAD OF STATE, AS PRESIDENT OF THE UNITED STATES, YOU PUT YOUR APPROVAL, YOUR SANCTION, YOUR AUTHORITY ON WHAT IS HAPPENING UNDER YOUR WATCH! AND YOU ARE HELD ACCOUNTABLE TO THE ALMIGHTY WHAT YOU ALLOW, STIPULATE AND CONDONE!!! THE DAYS ARE NUMBERED BEFORE THE JUDGMENTS BEGIN! HORRENDOUS WARHEADS ARE EAR-MARKED FOR THE UNITED STATES! STOP THE SUICIDE, GEORGE BUSH! AMERICA IS ON THE BRINK OF UTTER DISASTER AND CHAOS! YOU HOLD THE KEY TO PREVENT THE NEXT NATIONAL DISASTER! MANY TIMES WORSE THAN 9/11!!!!!

February 26, 2004

F L A S H P O I N T

GOD 2004

I HAVE HEARD YOUR CRIES FOR MY PEOPLE. I WILL STIPULATE SOON A REPRIEVE. ONLY FOR A SHORT SEASON. NO ONE CAN CONTINUE KILLING PEOPLE AND EXPECT A BLANKET MORATORIUM. I WILL SPEAK TO THIS NATION. I WILL CALL SOME TO TASK CONCERNING THEIR SUBVERSIVE ACTIVITIES. I WILL NOT RELENT BUT FOR A SHORT PERIOD. WHEN MY PLEAS ARE IGNORED I SHALL PRONOUNCE MY JUDGMENTS SWIFTLY WITHOUT DELAY. SUBSTANTIAL PORTIONS OF MEDIOCRITY SHALL BE EXPOSED. I DO NOT ALLOW JUDGMENTS WITHOUT GRAVE WARNINGS! PLEAD NO LONGER FOR MERCY FOR A BABY BLUDGEONING NATION! SPEAK TO THE SPIRITS!!! BIND THE STRONGMEN OF GREED, ABORTION, LUST!!! I CANNOT ALLOW MERCY FOR CRUELTY TO INFANTS AND CHILDREN!!! ABORTION IS CRUELTY TO INFANTS AND CHILDREN!!! ABORTION IS CRIME AT ITS MOST DEVIATE OF ALL INTENTIONS!!! PREMEDITATED MURDER!!! RENOUNCE AND EXTRICATE ABORTION – PREMEDITATED MURDER AND I SHALL STOP THE DESTRUCTION THAT IS EARMARKED FOR AMERICA!!!

BUSH, COME OUT OF THE BUSHES AND TELL IT LIKE IT IS AND STRIP THIS DIABOLICAL DECREE FROM THE LAWS OF THIS ONCE GREAT NATION, SO THAT SHE CAN BECOME GREAT ONCE MORE! A PRESIDENTIAL DECREE!!! ARE YOU A MAN OF INTEGRITY? THAT MEANS DO YOU ACTUALLY IN REAL TERMS DO ALL THAT IS POSSIBLE FOR YOU TO DO? NOT POLITICALLY, BUT FOR HUMANITY! ARE YOU HUMANE? CHARACTERIZED BY TENDERNESS AND COMPASSION FOR THE SUFFERING? FREE IRAQ. YES. STOP THE TORTURE. YES. WHAT ABOUT THE TORTURE AND THE KILLING OF AMERICANS IN THE WOMB??? WHAT ABOUT THAT FREEDOM, PRESIDENT BUSH??????? ARE YOU UP TO HUMANITY CORRECT OR TO JUST POLITICALLY CORRECT? ABRAHAM LINCOLN WAS A MAN OF INTEGRITY. HE STOOD UP

FOR WHAT HE KNEW TO BE RIGHT AND HUMANE!!! AS DIFFICULT AS IT WAS HE GAVE HIS LAST FULL MEASURE OF DEVOTION TO THAT WHICH HE KNEW TO BE HONEST AND TRUE!!!

EVERY TIME THE POLLS OR THE PUNDITS PRAISE A MAN I DON'T BAT AN EYE. MY WORD IS TRUTH IN SPITE OF WHAT IS SPOKEN, PRINTED OR PARADED OR PANDERED! AND MY WORD ALONE SHALL BE THE FINAL OUTCOME OF ALL INTEGRITY!!! WILL YOU STAND WITH ME, GEORGE BUSH???

February 15, 2004

F L A S H P O I N T

GOD 2004

I WILL NOT EXTEND THE REPRIEVE. THE DESTRUCTION WILL COME IN APRIL. THIS THE 'I AM' SPEAKS TO THE LEADERS OF THIS REPUBLIC. PRONOUNCE BREAKINGS AND TIME TABLES. I AM GETTING READY TO POUR OUT A CURSE WITHOUT HUGE CHANGES IN THE LAWS. I WILL NO LONGER PROTECT YOUR ASSETS, AMERICA. I DO NOT PARTAKE WITH ABORTIONISTS, HOMOSEXUALS, DRUGGIES, AND PORN DEVIATES. YOU WILL SUFFER MUCH DESTRUCTION IN THE DAYS AHEAD, AMERICA, EXCEPT DRASTIC CHANGES BE MADE IN THE LAWS OF YOUR GOVERNMENT! THE PEOPLE OF THIS GREAT EMPIRE SHALL BE DESTROYED EN MASSE WITH 40,000 KILLED IN ONE DAY. I DON'T PLAY, AMERICA. I HAVE LAWS AND WHEN YOU BREAK THEM AND LAUGH IN MY FACE, I SEND CORRECTION TO ALLOW YOU TO REPENT! WHEN YOU REFUSE TO CHANGE, YOU QUICKEN ME TO ALLOW GREATER DESTRUCTION. NO DESTRUCTION COMES TO AMERICA WITHOUT I ALLOW IT TO COME! WHEN I ALLOW DESTRUCTION TO COME TO THIS PEOPLE, IT HAPPENS BECAUSE YOU REFUSE MY PRECEPTS AND MY EXAMPLES. LAUGH IN MY FACE NO MORE, AMERICA! ROOT OUT THE EVIL OF YOUR SELF-WILL AND REMOVE FROM THE LAWS OF THIS LAND THIS ABORTION DECREE AND I SHALL REPENT OF THE DESTRUCTION THAT IS EARMARKED FOR WASHINGTON! THUS THE 'I AM' OF ALL DOMINION AND POWER AND MIGHT AND AUTHORITY SPEAKS TO THIS HIERARCHY THIS DAY OF JANUARY 1, 2004.

BE SWIFT, FOR THE DESTRUCTION IS AT THE DOOR, THE 'I AM' SPEAKS WITHOUT MALICE. I GRIEVE OVER MY PEOPLE WHO THWART THE AUTHORITY OF MY WORD. I WEEP OVER THE SLAIN. I GRIEVE BECAUSE YOU REFUSE TO HEAR MY WILL AND MY WORD. O, AMERICA, AMERICA, HOW OFT HAVE I PROTECTED YOU FROM YOUR EVIL ENEMIES. I HAVE KEPT YOU AS THE APPLE OF MY EYE, BUT NOW YOU THWART THE RIGHTEOUSNESS THAT

35

HOLDS THIS NATION IN PLACE. RIGHTEOUSNESS EXALTS A NATION, BUT SIN IS YOUR REPROACH, AMERICA! AND SIN SHALL BE THE DOOM BY WHICH YOU ALLOW THE JUDGMENT TO COME UPON YOUR OWN HEADS! THE CURSE CAUSELESS DOES NOT COME!!! AMERICA BRINGS JUDGMENT UPON HER OWN PEOPLE, UPON HER OWN CITIZENS, UPON THE INNOCENT, THOSE NOT EVEN PARTAKING OF ABORTION! O, AMERICA, SEARCH YOUR SOULS! IS KILLING BABIES IN THE WOMB WORTH THE ATROCITIES THAT ARE AT YOUR DOOR???

January 1, 2004

Note: The prophecies of this book, including all the Flash Points have been faxed to the Government and Spiritual Leaders of these United States of America. I am reminded in my spirit of what the American Soldiers spoke to their enemies as they thrust the bayonets into their bodies (as per training video), MAY GOD HAVE MERCY ON YOUR SOUL! I wept as I viewed the video. I yet weep for our soldiers and for our nation! IS ANYBODY OUT THERE? DOES ANYBODY TRULY CARE? DOES ANYBODY <u>HEAR</u> THE WORD OF THE LORD? IS ANYBODY DOING ANYTHING TO STOP THE MASSACRE OF OUR OWN CHILDREN, AND GRAND-CHILDREN? AS GOD HAS ALREADY SPOKEN: WHEN YOU SEE THEM COME HOME IN BODY BAGS, ASK YOURSELF THIS QUESTION, <u>WHAT LAW IS IT THAT AMERICA HAS MADE *LEGAL TO SLAUGHTER THEIR OWN BY THE MILLIONS*</u>???

F L A S H P O I N T

<u>GOD SPEAKS</u>

THE BRAVERY THAT IS BEING SHOWN BY MY TROOPS SENT FROM AMERICA TO THE MIDDLE EAST IS A REFLECTION OF MY LOVE FOR <u>ALL</u> PEOPLE. SOME ONLY THINK OF THEMSELVES WHEN DISCUSSING CONFLICT AND WAR. AMERICA STANDS FOR TRUTH AT THE TIME OF CRISIS. SHE KNOWS THE HURDLES, THE HOOPS AND THE HELLS. SHE SUFFERED THE LOSSES IN OBTAINING HER OWN FREEDOM. SHE KNOWS THAT IF ALL MEN ARE NOT FREE, ALL FREEDOM IS JEOPARDIZED AND THREATENED. AS HAS BEEN SAID, THE ONLY THING NECESSARY FOR EVIL TO TRIUMPH IS FOR GOOD MEN TO DO NOTHING.

I SHIFT MY COURSE NOW TO OBLITERATE THE EVIL DESTRUCTIONS THAT WOULD HAVE COME AT THE HANDS OF SADDAM HUSSEIN HAD IT NOT BEEN THWARTED. YES, STOPPING EVIL <u>IS</u> PART OF ESTABLISHING JUSTICE AND INSURING DOMESTIC TRANQUILITY, AS WELL AS, PROVIDING FOR THE COMMON DEFENSE. FORCE IS THE ONLY LANGUAGE TYRANTS KNOW. BE NOT DECEIVED! THIS CONFLICT WILL STOP AN EVEN GREATER ONE FOR THE TIME BEING. THE END IS NOT YET. THIS BUILDUP IN IRAQ OF WEAPONS OF MASS DESTRUCTION IS BEING SQUELCHED AT <u>MY</u> DIRECTION. I AM THE GENERAL OF THIS GREAT UNIVERSE! I BOW TO NO OTHER GOD. I AM THE MOST HIGH GOD! AND AMERICA IS IN THE HANDS OF THE ALMIGHTY! I SHALL LEAD THIS GOVERNMENT BACK TO RIGHTEOUSNESS! STOP PLAYING GAMES, SENATORS! YOU ARE NOT ON THE BATTLEFIELD! AND WAR GAMES ARE OUT OF ORDER ON THE SENATE FLOOR! YOU ARE <u>ALL</u> AMERICANS, RIGHT? STOP YOUR HARASSING OF GOODLY CANDIDATES FOR BENCH SEATS!!! I CAN MOVE YOU RIGHT OUT OF YOUR SEAT. I SIT IN THE <u>HIGHEST</u> COURT. <u>THE HEAVENLY SUPREME COURT. THAT SITS HIGH AND LOOKS LOW. YOUR ANTICS ARE NOT JUST. STOP IT, NOW, LEST YOU BRING DISGRACE UPON A PEOPLE AND A</u>

<u>NATION FOR WHICH GRACE WAS ONCE THE GREATEST ATTRIBUTE IN COMING TO THESE SHORES</u>.

LABEL NOT YOURSELF LIBERAL. LUSTFUL IS YOUR CATEGORY. TAKING SOMETHING FROM SOMEONE ELSE THAT IS THEIR RIGHT AND PRIVILEGE IS LUST! BUT YOU WILL NOT RALLY LONG IN THIS FIT OF TEMPER FOR I SHALL REMOVE MORE OF YOU IF NEED BE TO GET MY PRECEPTS AND STATUTES TO BE ENFORCED. RIGHTEOUSNESS IS RIGHT WHETHER YOU LIKE IT OR APPROVE OF IT OR NOT AND IN THE END IT SHALL WIN OUT!!! RIGHT <u>DOES</u> MAKE MIGHT! EVIL PRACTICES IN DOING BUSINESS IN GOVERNMENT SHALL BE BROUGHT TO A HALT. I WILL SECURE THE HOUSE OF REPRESENTATIVES AND THE SENATE. THEY SHALL KNOW JUSTICE AND JUDGMENT. MEN'S TITLES WILL BITE THE DUST AGAIN LEST TRUTH IS INSTITUTED IN POLICY MAKING AND CONFIRMATION HEARINGS.

March 7, 2003

SADDAM HUSSEIN IS COMING DOWN! HE IS COMING DOWN QUICKLY SAITH THE LORD. I SHALL STOP THIS ONSLAUGHT OF DEPRAVITY.

March 6, 2003

F L A S H P O I N T

GOD SPEAKS

I AM TELLING GEORGE BUSH TO REFURBISH HIS HOUSE. HIS TEMPLE. I AM GIVING HIM ORDERS TO CRY ALOUD AND TO WAIT UPON ME. I COUNSEL HIM IN THE NIGHT SEASONS. I SECURE HIS POSITION AND TELL HIM THE NEXT STEP OF ENFORCEMENT. I WILL GIVE HIM ONE MORE DAY TO DEAL WITH IRAQ BEFORE I TELL HIM TO ATTACK. IT IS NEBULOUS TO GO AROUND THE SAME MOUNTAIN. I AM AWARE OF ALL THE CONSEQUENCES THAT SHALL ERUPT BECAUSE OF THIS BREAKING FORTH OF UNILATERAL FORCES. I WILL GIVE SADDAM HUSSEIN ONE MORE CHANCE TO RECANT OF HIS WEAPONS. THEN I SHALL SPEAK TO GEORGE BUSH ... ATTACK! NO MAN IS AN ISLAND. NO MAN LIVES OR DIES JUST UNTO HIMSELF. HIS LIFE REPROVES THE CULTURE, STAGNATES THE PROCESS, OR REPUDIATES THE PAIN. SADDAM HUSSEIN IS NEITHER GOD NOR GUARDIAN. HE IS REPROBATE. HIS EVIL REGIME IS DOOMED. WORLD WAR III LOOMS UPON THE HORIZON. TROUBLE NOT YOURSELF. IT IS INEVITABLE. BUT YOU MUST DO WHAT YOU HAVE TO DO. KNOWING WHAT IS TO COME MUST NOT STOP YOU FROM DOING ALL THAT YOU CAN TO AVERT IT! YOU WILL STOP FOUR KINGDOMS FROM AGGRESSION BEFORE IT IS TIME FOR THE FULFILLMENT OF THE END. I HOLD YOU ACCOUNTABLE TO TAKE THE INITIATIVE TO STRIKE THOUGH YOU ARE MISUNDERSTOOD AT HOME AND ABROAD. DESTINY DEPENDS NOT UPON POPULARITY. WAR IS NOT A GAME. BUT IT IS A REALITY. THE REALITY OF WHAT IS 'WORSE' IF AGGRESSION IS NOT THWARTED! THE BEST DEFENSE IS A GOOD OFFENSE. STRUGGLE NOT WITH SIGHT SEERS AND SATANISTS. STAMP YOUR SEAL OF APPROVAL FOR PEACE BY THWARTING THE RAGE OF DEMENTED MINDS. I CALL YOU FORTH TO DESTINY, BUSH! YOU ARE NOT YOUR OWN. I HAVE REVEALED THE TIME OF THE END. NOW STAND YOUR GROUND AND BE NOT WEARY. STAY FOCUSED ON THE TASK AT HAND AND BE NOT DISMAYED BY THE

CONSEQUENCES OF YOUR DECISION. I HAVE ALL THE PLAYERS IN MY HANDS. NO ONE WILL BE ABLE TO DISMANTLE WHAT I HAVE SPOKEN TO BE THE INTERIM OF INTELLIGENT ACTIVITY. I AM GIVING YOU YOUR MARCHING ORDERS. GREAT BREAKTHROUGHS, A MOVEMENT OR ADVANCE ALL THE WAY THROUGH AND BEYOND A DEFENSIVE SYSTEM INTO THE UNORGANIZED AREAS IN THE REAR, SHALL BE EVIDENT AS YOU FOREWARN YOUR TROOPS. MY WILL IS NOT ALWAYS EASY BUT IT MAKES TRUTH FOCAL INSTEAD OF FEAR. IT REMINDS THE SOULS OF MAN OF THE VERY PURPOSE OF THEIR EXISTENCE: TO FULFILL DESTINY, TO ESTABLISH RIGHTEOUSNESS, TO BRING DELIVERANCE, TO GIVE HOPE, TO ABOLISH EVIL!!! BE YE STRONG THEREFORE AND LET NOT YOUR HANDS BE WEAK: FOR YOUR WORK SHALL BE REWARDED. II CHRONICLES 15:7

February 11, 2003

F L A S H P O I N T

GOD SPEAKS

I WILL SPEAK TO YOU IN JUDGMENTS SAITH THE LORD. I SEND CORRECTIONS AND MALADIES. SOME SAY I DO NOT SEND EVILS. BE IT KNOWN UNTO YOU THIS DAY THAT NO EVIL COULD BEFALL YOU EXCEPT I ALLOW IT. WHETHER I SEND IT OR WHETHER I ALLOW IT, IT DOES COME UPON THE CHILDREN OF DISOBEDIENCE. IT WAS AN ANGEL OF THE LORD THAT SMOTE HEROD BECAUSE HE GAVE NOT GOD THE GLORY FOR HIS ACCOMPLISHMENTS AND BENEFITS! HOW MUCH GLORY DO YOU HOLD BACK FROM THE ALMIGHTY WHEN YOU ARE BRAGGING AND TOOTING YOUR OWN HORN ABOUT WHAT YOU HAVE ACCOMPLISHED AND WHAT YOUR EFFORTS HAVE DONE? WHO DO YOU THINK STRUCK SAUL WITH BLINDNESS? IT WASN'T THE DEVIL! NOR WAS IT THE DEVIL THAT CAUSED ANANIAS AND SAPPHIRA TO DROP DEAD IN CHURCH! I DID IT! I DO A LOT OF THINGS YOU GIVE THE DEVIL AND CHANCE THE CREDIT FOR. I ALLOW A LOT OF JUDGMENTS, CORRECTIONS AND YES, EVEN DISEASES. NO, OF COURSE, IT IS NOT MY PERFECT WILL! BUT MY PERFECT WILL DOES COME FORTH FROM CORRECTIONS AND CHASTISEMENTS! THE SON OF MAN WAS MADE PERFECT, MATURE AND SEASONED BY THE THINGS I ALLOWED HIM TO SUFFER. AND YOU THINK YOU ARE GOING TO BE MATURE AND EXCELLENT BY SOME OTHER METHOD??? READ THE BOOK! READ HEBREWS CHAPTER ELEVEN! READ DEUTERONOMY CHAPTER EIGHT! READ DEUTERONOMY CHAPTER TWENTY-EIGHT!

DISOBEDIENCE IS SIN AND SIN RECEIVES A JUST RECOMPENSE OF REWARD! NOW STOP SAYING I DON'T SEND JUDGMENTS!

February 1, 2003

Note: This Word of the Lord was given to me the morning of February 1. I knew nothing of the space shuttle disaster until late that day. Good men and women die before their time because governments and politicians deal in greed and power, disregarding creed and posterity!!!!! On January 21, I faxed to the White House and to the Senate and House Majority and Minority Leaders and to Spiritual Leaders across America This Word of The Lord: "DESTRUCTION AND DEATH ARE IMMINENT AND IMPENDING TO THIS UNITED STATES GOVERNMENT! STOP THE KILLING FIELDS OF ABORTION. WHEN I REMOVE THE HEDGE OF PROTECTION AMERICA WILL RECEIVE JUDGMENTS WITHOUT MERCY. NO DESTRUCTION COMES TO AMERICA EXCEPT WHAT I ALLOW. THE NEXT WAVE OF DESTRUCTIONS ARE ALREADY IN THE MAKING. I CAN NO LONGER HOLD BACK THE JUDGMENTS, FOR AMERICA REFUSES TO REPENT OF HER ATROCITIES AND MALIGNITIES. I AM A GOD OF MY WORD! MY HONOR IS IN TRUTH. DENY TRUTH AND SUFFER THE CONSEQUENCES." The full page of this prophecy was also faxed individually to NINETY-ONE of the United States Senators on January 28 and 29. GOD'S WORD IS TRUTH AND NO LIE!

F L A S H P O I N T

GOD SPEAKS

2:30 am GREAT DESTRUCTION IS COMING TO THIS NATION. I AM
CALLING FOR AN ALL OUT WAR AGAINST ABORTION! I HAVE
CALLED AND PLEADED, BEGGED AND BESEECHED! NOW I SHALL
CORRECT WITHOUT MERCY WHO HAS SHOWN NO MERCY.
CANDIDATES FOR ABORTION WILL CEASE AS WELL AS THE
ABORTIONISTS THEMSELVES. THEY WILL NO LONGER SUBPOENA
MY BABIES FOR BLUDGEONING!!! MY LITTLE ONES HAVE BEEN
MASSACRED AND MANGLED, DECAPITATED AND
DISEMBOWELED! BUT I SHALL SOON PLEAD WITH MY PEOPLE TO
PARALYZE LIES OF THE JURISTS THAT UNDER-GIRD MURDER!
THAT GIVE RIGHTS TO PEOPLE TO KILL THEIR OWN FLESH! I
SHOW MERCY TO REPENTANT. BUT CONTINUOUS MURDERERS
SHALL BE FORCED TO FORFEIT THEIR RIGHT. I WILL PLACE MY
MANTLE OF CORRECTION UPON THIS CONTINENT! IT SHALL
KNOW AGAIN THE BLOOD OF LOVED ONES SLAUGHTERED AND
MAIMED! MY COUNSEL HAS BEEN SET ASIDE, REFUSED, REJECTED!
MY WORDS WILL NOT RETURN VOID! I SHALL SEND A BITTER CUP
TO THE SHORES OF THIS ONCE GREAT NATION! I WILL NO
LONGER HEAR THEIR PLEAS FOR DELAY OF CORRECTIONS! THE
STENCH OF BLOODBATHS STINGS MY NOSTRILS! THE ENTRAILS
OF MY LITTLE ONES DECAY IN DUMPSTERS!!! MY POWER SHALL BE
RETURNED IN THE NOT TOO DISTANT FUTURE. MY AUTHORITY
HAS BEEN RIDICULED AND MALIGNED, BUT I MINCE NO WORDS
WHEN I SPEAK THIS MANDATE: DESTRUCTION AGAIN! AMERICA
DESCENDS. PITS OF PAIN PERMEATE THIS SHORE. RELY ON NO
ONE TO PROTECT YOUR ASSETS. WITHOUT MY BLESSING YOU ARE
DOOMED. MANY WILL DIE ONCE AGAIN. SHORE TO SHORE
MADNESS WILL INCREASE.

THE DOMINANT SPIRIT IN AMERICA IS PRIDE. THE LESSER ONE IS
DECEIT. I CANNOT PROTECT THE ARROGANT AND THE LIARS. I
WILL NO LONGER DEBATE YOUR CAUSES. YOU HAVE OFFENDED

ME BEYOND MEASURE. I CANNOT PROTECT YOUR OFFSPRING AND YOUR LOVED ONES. YOU DEAL IN GREED, CARNALITY, INCEST AND LEWDNESS! YOU ARE NOT A CHRISTIAN NATION. YOU HAVE BACKSLIDDEN AND PROSTITUTED MY NAME! I SHALL SO CLEANSE MY HANDS OF THIS DECEIT AND MALIGNITY! I WILL TURN MY BACK AND SEE IF YOU WILL BE CORRECTED UNTO TRUE REPENTANCE AND TO FULL SALVATION! NOT TEARS OF SORROW FOR YOUR PAIN AND WOE. BUT TEARS OF KNOWING YOU ARE PAYING THE PRICES OF THE SEEDS YOU HAVE SOWN. I SHALL CASTIGATE ONE SOON. I SHALL GIVE A CALL, "IT IS FINISHED!"

August 18, 2003

November 2000

What is the Stand of our Constitution?
  What holds it Firmly in Place?
Opinions of One ... or Many?
  Or just Plain ... Truth and Grace?

Part I

Judgment is Imminent

And the Lord said, My Spirit shall not always strive with man.

**Genesis Chapter Six
Verse Three**

Prophecy

THE TELEPHONE IS NOT YOUR GOD! OR IS IT? THE TELEVISION IS NOT YOUR GOD! OR IS IT? COMPUTERS AND GAMES ARE NOT YOUR GODS! OR ARE THEY? IF YOU ARE SPENDING MORE TIME IN PASTIMES AND PLEASURES THAN IN OBEDIENCE TO THE GOD OF <u>ALL</u> FORCES THE PLEASURES OF THIS LIFE HAVE BECOME YOUR GODS!!! IS IT NOT WRITTEN, THOU SHALL NOT BOW DOWN THYSELF TO THEM, NOR SERVE THEM FOR I THE LORD THY GOD AM A JEALOUS GOD!!! WHY CALL YOU ME LORD, LORD, AND DO NOT THE THINGS WHICH I SAY? HE THAT HEARS AND DOES NOT DO THE THINGS THAT I SAY IS LIKE A MAN THAT WITHOUT A FOUNDATION BUILT A HOUSE UPON THE EARTH AND THE RAINS DESCENDED, THE WINDS BLEW AND THE FLOODS CAME AND BEAT VEHEMENTLY UPON THAT HOUSE AND IMMEDIATELY IT FELL AND GREAT WAS THE FALL OF THAT HOUSE AND THE RUIN THEREOF!!!

November 2, 2000

Prophecy

MY SPIRIT MOVES ACROSS THIS NATION. I AM GIVING THE
LITMUS TEST OF TRUTH! WILL THIS NATION CONTINUE TO
STAND, OR SHOULD I SAY, WILL THIS NATION STAND FOR WHAT
THE FOREFATHERS STOOD??? WILL THIS NATION BE COUNTED
AMONG THE BRAVE, THE FREE, THE MORAL? TIME IS A DECIDING
FACTOR IN THE COURSE OF HEARTFELT FATE! TIME IS THE
DECIDING FACTOR IN THE TEST OF THE TRULY GREAT! WHY
STAND, OR SIT YOU HERE GAZING AS THOUGH SOME STRANGE
THING IS HAPPENING UNTO YOU? YOU ARE WEIGHED IN THE
BALANCES AND FOUND WANTING! YOU LACK INTEGRITY OF
SOUL! YOU HAVE MIXED AND MINGLED YOUR HONESTY AND
FORTHRIGHTNESS WITH THE COMPROMISE OF GREED! NOW WE
WILL SEE WHAT TESTING DOES TO THE HUMAN SPIRIT! WILL THE
GOVERNMENT OF THE PEOPLE AND BY THE PEOPLE AND FOR THE
PEOPLE BE SEGREGATED INTO THE LEGALITY OF THE COURTS?
<u>MANMADE SOLUTIONS CANNOT HOLD THIS UNION IN PLACE.</u>
<u>ONLY THE GOD WHO FOUNDED IT BY HIS REDEEMING GRACE.</u>
<u>LET THE SHAKING CONTINUE TO REVERBERATE IN THE HEARTS</u>
<u>OF MAN. LET THE SIMPLICITY OF THE CONSTITUTION REIGN</u>
<u>THROUGHOUT THIS LAND! LET THE JUDGMENT OF THE</u>
<u>CREATOR SETTLE INTO SEEKING HEARTS!</u> LET THE CONSCIENCE,
THE CANDLE OF THE LORD EXPLORE, PLACATE, AND RELEGATE
THE TRUE MEANING OF LIFE! O, GOD, THAT BREAD SHOULD BE SO
DEAR!!! AND FLESH AND BLOOD SO CHEAP!!! FAITH AND
INTEGRITY ARE HIGHER FACULTIES THAN NATURAL REASONING
AND LOGIC! TRUTH IS STILL THE HIGHEST ATTRIBUTE THAT
MAN CAN KEEP! LET IT BE SHOT INTO THE VEINS OF THE
FEARLESS AND THE FREE!!! LET US NOW SEE THAT THIS NATION,
UNDER GOD, ENDURES, AS THE PENALTIES OF PANDERING TO
LESSER GODS OF GAIN AND COMFORT, ARE DEFEATED IN THE
FIGHT FOR THE SECURITY OF THE SOUL AND THE MEANING OF
LIFE ITSELF BE NOT LOST IN THE MINDS OF MEN AND
SLAUGHTERED IN THE COURTS! HAIL, HAIL KING JESUS! THE
SLAUGHTERING OF INFANTS PRECEDES THE COMING OF A KING
OR THE ARRIVAL OF A SAVIOR! THE AUTHORITIES OF MAN

COULD NOT KILL ENOUGH BABIES TO SLAUGHTER INFANT MOSES AND HOLD BACK THE DELIVERANCE OF ISRAEL! NOR COULD A CORRUPT LEADER KILL ENOUGH BABIES TO SODDEN THE INFANT JESUS! THE SAVIOR OF THE WORLD! YET AMERICA IS OBLIVIOUS TO THE DUNGEONS OF THE DEAD! SHE HAS CREMATED THE CREATION OF GOD AND SUCKED OUT THE SOULS OF SANITY AS SHE HAS SUCKED OUT THE BRAINS OF THE HELPLESS, THE PROGENY OF DEITY! THEIR LIVES CRY OUT FROM THE GRAVES, EMBOLDENED IN THE TEST OF TIME! SPEAK FORTH AMERICA! WHAT SAYEST THOU? DO THE KILLING FIELDS CONTINUE? WEIGHED IN THE BALANCES! WHAT SAYEST THOU? DO YOU ACTUALLY, IN ALL BASTIANS OF THE SOUL, HAVE THE AUDACITY TO BELIEVE, THAT BUTCHERING OF BABIES, LIFE AND LIMB, WOULD NEVER BE CALLED TO TASK BY THE CREATOR OF THESE BEINGS? DECEPTIONS COME WHEN TRUTH IS REFUSED! YOU ARE HELD ACCOUNTABLE! MURDER IS STILL MURDER EVEN IN THE WOMB!!! YOUR GROWTH OF DEGRADATION HAS REACHED ITS PINNACLE!!! BUT YOUR HIGH SEAT PINNACLED ON THE SOULS OF THE DEAD AND DYING SHALL TOPPLE SOON FOR JUDGMENT HAS COME TO AMERICA FOR HER NATIONAL SIN OF ABORTION! WATCH AND WAIT, AMERICA!!! TRUTH DOES PREVAIL BECAUSE IT STANDS THE TEST OF TIME!!!

"LITTLE BITTY BABIES TORN FROM LIMB TO LIMB BECAUSE MOTHERS, SO-CALLED, WANT TO GET RID OF THEM! OTHERS CHEMICALLY CREMATED! THEIR VERY EXISTENCE HATED! ABORTION! AMERICA'S NATIONAL SIN! AND AS IF THAT WERE NOT ENOUGH ... NOW THEIR BRAINS ARE SUCKED OUT OF THEIR LITTLE HEADS ... ARE SUCTIONED OUT AS THEY COME FORTH FROM THE WOMB TO BREATHE LIFE AND FIND IMMEDIATE DEATH! THE SUCTION OF THEIR SOUL!"

November 10, 2000

NOTE: THIS WORD FROM THE LORD WAS E-MAILED TO THE SITTING VICE-PRESIDENT, TO THE MAJORITY LEADERS OF BOTH THE HOUSE AND THE SENATE ON NOVEMBER 10, 2000. IT

WAS THEN MAILED TO THE INCOMING PRESIDENT, VICE-PRESIDENT, TO EACH OF THE NINE UNITED STATES SUPREME COURT JUDGES, THE ATTORNEY GENERAL, VARIOUS CABINET, CONGRESSIONAL, AND SPIRITUAL LEADERS. BUT ALAS, A WORD FROM ALMIGHTY GOD THROUGH AN UNKNOWN HANDMAIDEN, NOT VERY IMPRESSIVE!

On November 17, the above mandate from our Lord with a handwritten plea was sent to Pat Robertson, Paul Crouch, Rod Parsley, Morris Cerullo, Marilyn Hickey, Jan Crouch, Matthew Crouch and The Christian Coalition.

I AM RELEASING MY PROPHETS UPON THIS NATION!

November 11, 2000

Prophecy

THE GRACE THAT I HAVE GIVEN TO YOU TO DO THIS WORK HAS BEEN TRANSMITTED TO YOUR SON. THIS GRACE IS GIVING HIM A NEW BEGINNING. HE WILL BEGIN TO DO THE WORK THAT IS REQUIRED. I HAVE CHOSEN HIM IN THE FURNACE OF AFFLICTION. I AM CALLING HIM FORTH TO PUT UP OR SHUT UP. TO BE A FAITHFUL WARRIOR WITH ALL REQUIREMENTS MET OR TO STEP ASIDE. THERE ARE NO FREELOADERS IN THIS ARMY. IT GOES BY THE BOOK!!! FASTING AND PRAYER HE WILL COMMENCE. I AM GIVING HIM AN INJECTION OF FORTITUDE TO BEGIN THE TASKS OF OBEDIENCE TO DETAIL AND TO FOLLOWING ORDERS. WITHOUT OBEDIENCE TO ALL SUPERIORS ONE IS NOT FIT FOR ADVANCEMENT OR PROMOTION!!! LAZINESS IS THE DOWNFALL OF MANY ... NOT LACK OF KNOWLEDGE! BUT TRUE WISDOM IS KNOWLEDGE WITH WORK CLOTHES ON. PUTTING INTO ACTION THE GROUND WORK PRINCIPLES OF LAYING THE FOUNDATION OF GREATNESS. DOING THE FUNDAMENTALS. THE REQUIREMENTS. FOLLOWING THROUGH ON BASIC ORDERS GIVEN. KEEPING EVERY COMMAND. NOT DISCARDING SOME THAT SEEM TO BE UNNECESSARY OR REPETITIOUS. A GREAT MAN IS MOLDED BY ONE OBEDIENCE AT A TIME. CHARACTER IS FORMED BY SUBMITTING TO AUTHORITY. YOU ARE KNOWN BY YOUR DEEDS. NOT YOUR I.Q. IF YOU CANNOT FAITHFULLY FOLLOW ORDERS, THOUGH SEEMINGLY BENEATH YOUR INTELLECT, YOU WILL NOT RISE TO YOUR POTENTIAL OR YOUR PURPOSE. THE CAPTAIN OF YOUR SALVATION LEARNED OBEDIENCE BY THE THINGS WHICH HE SUFFERED! BY THE THINGS THAT HE CONTINUOUSLY CHOSE TO FOLLOW THROUGH ON, RATHER THAN DISMISS AS UNIMPORTANT OR BENEATH HIS STATURE. MEN ARE MADE BY ONE CHOICE AT A TIME. THEY ARE FORMED OR DEFORMED BY ONE DECISION AT A TIME. MANY ARE MADE TOP HEAVY, ARROGANT, POMPOUS, BY NOT BEING DUG OUT DEEP BY THE HOLY GHOST, THUS HUMILITY, LONG-SUFFERING, PERSEVERANCE ARE UNLEARNED AND DEPTH OF CHARACTER IS LOST IN THE QUEST FOR IMMEDIATE COMFORT AND GRATIFICATION! MEN

OBEY! TURNING THE DISOBEDIENT HEART TO THE WISDOM OF THE JUST! TO MAKE READY A PEOPLE PREPARED FOR THE LORD! THE END OF THE COMMANDMENT IS LOVE OUT OF A PURE HEART, AND OF A GOOD CONSCIENCE, OF UNFEIGNED FAITH!!! THUS SAITH THE LORD!

November 13, 2000

NOBODY STOPS ME SAITH THE LORD! IF ONE REFUSES TO OBEY ME I WILL RAISE UP ANOTHER! I AM GETTING READY TO STOP ABORTION IN THIS NATION! THIS NATION HAS PERVERTED MY NAME! IT HAS SET ASIDE MY LAWS AND MY LOVE! HOW CAN YOU SAY YOU LOVE ME AND KILL MILLIONS OF MY PROGENY EACH YEAR? I CAST MY VOTE FOR LIFE! MY VOTE IS THE DECIDING FACTOR! I AM IS THE MAJORITY! I AM NOT AGAINST BIRTH CONTROL! ABORTION IS NOT BIRTH CONTROL! ABORTION IS THE SLAUGHTER OF THE INNOCENTS!!! GET YOUR PRIORITIES IN ORDER! HEADS ARE ABOUT TO ROLL! I PULL DOWN ONE AND SET UP ANOTHER! YOU CHOOSE TO DEFY ME??? THE ONLY TRUE LIVING GOD! THE GOD OF ALL LIFE! THE GOD OF ALL LIVING!!! YOU CALL YOURSELVES PRO CHOICE! THE CHOICE TO CHOOSE TO SLAUGHTER OR NOT TO SLAUGHTER! THE CHOICE TO TAKE A HUMAN LIFE OR NOT TO TAKE A HUMAN LIFE!!! THAT CHOICE IS NOT YOURS TO MAKE!!!

November 14, 2000

Prophecy

STOP PONDERING THINGS AS THOUGH I HAVE NOT SPOKEN ABOUT THEM. THE REALITY OF THINGS IS WHAT I SPEAK ABOUT THEM, NOT WHAT YOU THINK ABOUT THEM! IT IS NOT MY WILL FOR YOU TO JUDGE OR CONTEMPLATE AS THOUGH I HAVE NOT ALREADY SAID WHAT TRUTH IS CONCERNING THEM! LET MY THOUGHTS BE YOUR THOUGHTS AND MY JUDGMENTS YOUR JUDGMENTS. AS YOU ARE CONFORMED TO MY IMAGE, SPEAK PEACE TO TRUTH AND LET MY SAYINGS BE YOUR FINAL SAY! SUBMIT YOUR FEELINGS TO MY AUTHORITY AND LINGER NO LONGER UPON MATTERS AS THOUGH THE DECISIONS HAVE NOT ALREADY BEEN MADE! MY PARTNERING IN YOUR PLANNING FREES YOU FROM ERROR AND MISCONCEPTION. I AM THE SENIOR PARTNER! MY THOUGHTS HAVE MORE WEIGHT, IMPORTANCE THAN YOURS. BUT YOU ARE NOT A ROBOT, OR "YES" PERSON, FOR IT IS STILL YOUR CHOICE TO BELIEVE AND ACCEPT MY COUNSEL!!! HAVE I NOT SHOWN YOU BY EXAMPLE THE IMPORTANCE OF BEING LED BY MY SPIRIT? HOW WALKING IN MY SPIRIT PROMOTES VICTORY, SUCCESS, PEACE, ON-GOING MATURITY, AND PROGRESS IN YOUR PURPOSE! THINGS OF THE SPIRIT ARE SPIRITUALLY DISCERNED. ENTERING INTO THE REST, WHICH IS BEING LED BY MY SPIRIT IS THE MOST HOLY PLACE! IN MY PRESENCE IS FULLNESS OF JOY! AT MY RIGHT HAND THERE ARE PLEASURES FOREVERMORE! I PROMOTE GROWTH OF CHARACTER AND POSITION AS YOU WAIT TO KNOW MY WILL! AS YOU LISTEN INTENTLY TO MY WORDS, AS THEY IN TRUTH BECOME YOUR NECESSARY FOOD. NOT THE APPROVAL OF PEERS, BUT THE HEARING OF THE EAR.

November 15, 2000

THE LORD AWAKENED ME AT 6:00 A.M. WITH: IT IS FINISHED! GEORGE BUSH IS PRESIDENT OF THE UNITED STATES OF AMERICA!

November 21, 2000

Prophecy

MY SPIRIT SHALL NOT ALWAYS STRIVE WITH MAN! I AM GETTING READY TO DO A QUICK WORK IN THESE UNITED STATES OF AMERICA! TOO LONG HAS THE GOVERNMENT HELD BACK MY GLORY! I AM GOING TO REMOVE FROM OFFICE THE ONES WHO HAVE COMPROMISED THE HERITAGE OF THESE UNITED STATES! I HAVE GIVEN TO MAN THE TRUTHS OF MY WORD! I WILL NOT BE HELD BACK ANY LONGER FROM REIGNING RIGHTEOUSNESS UPON THIS LAND OF THE FREE, THE HOME OF THE BRAVE!

TAKE HEED THAT YOU DO YOUR FIRST WORKS! INTEGRITY, HONESTY, FORTHRIGHTNESS! TRUTH, REALITY OF DIGNITY AND HONOR! COMPEL PEOPLE EVERYWHERE TO SEE THAT WHAT ORIGINALLY MADE THIS NATION GREAT WAS MY GLORY! I AM TRUTH!!! WITHOUT IT YOU BECOME SOUNDING BRASS AND TINKLING SYMBOL! THE TRUE SYMBOLS OF AMERICA: RED FOR THE BLOOD THAT WAS SHED FOR FREEDOM! FREEDOM TO WORSHIP ME!!! WHITE FOR PURITY! NOTHING TAINTED, NOR UNRIGHTEOUS!!! BLUE FOR THE HONESTY OF THE HEART! SUCH TREASURES ARE NOT NOW MEASURED BY POLLS! THEY ARE THE UNSEEN GUIDES OF THE CHARACTER THAT THIS NATION WAS FOUNDED UPON!!! YOU WILL SEE THE OUTCOME OF DESTINY RESOLVED BY MAJOR CHANGES IN THIS GOVERNMENT OF THE PEOPLE, AND BY THE PEOPLE, AND FOR THE PEOPLE! THIS GOVERNMENT WAS ESTABLISHED THAT ALL MEN ARE CREATED EQUAL!!! IN THE WOMB! BECAUSE: GUESS WHAT? THAT IS WHERE THEY ARE CREATED! THAT THEY ARE ENDOWED BY THEIR CREATOR WITH CERTAIN INALIENABLE RIGHTS, NOT CAPABLE OF BEING GIVEN UP! AMONG THESE IS LIFE! AND TO SECURE THIS RIGHT, GOVERNMENTS ARE INSTITUTED AMONG MEN, DERIVING THEIR JUST POWERS FROM THE CONSENT OF THE GOVERNMENT. NO! BUT FROM THE CONSENT OF THE GOVERNED! THAT WHENEVER ANY FORM OF GOVERNMENT BECOMES DESTRUCTIVE TO THESE ENDS, IT IS THE RIGHT OF THE PEOPLE TO ALTER OR TO ABOLISH IT, AND TO INSTITUTE NEW GOVERNMENT, LAYING ITS FOUNDATION ON THESE

PRINCIPLES!!! WHAT PRINCIPLES? THE RIGHT TO LIFE, LIBERTY, AND THE PURSUIT OF HAPPINESS! THUS SAITH THE HIGH AND LOFTY ONE! IT IS WRITTEN! THIS IS YOUR DECLARATION OF INDEPENDENCE!!! AMERICA, WHERE WERE YOU WHEN I HUNG THE STARS IN SPACE? WHEN I SPOKE TO THE SUN AND TO THE MOON? IT IS TIME TO RESOLVE THIS MATTER OF BUTCHERING AND BLUDGEONING!!! IT IS MY CREATION THAT YOU ARE KILLING! CEASE NOW! CORPORAL PUNISHMENT IS AHEAD FOR THOSE WHO WILL NOT CEASE. I AM CALLING THIS NATION BACK TO RIGHTEOUSNESS. RIGHT STANDING. RIGHT THINKING.

November 23, 2000

YES, YES, MY CHILD! YOU ARE PERFECT BEFORE ME. I HAVE SEEN YOUR GLOWING HONESTY AND FORTHRIGHTNESS! I AM PLEASED TO BE YOUR FATHER! STAY HUMBLE AND THERE IS NOTHING THAT I WILL WITHHOLD FROM YOU! YOU ARE RIGHTEOUS. I AM CALLING YOUR SISTER AND BROTHER INTO OBEDIENCE!!! FAITH IS COMING TO THEM! THEY WILL BE OBEDIENT TO ME SAITH THE LORD!

November 24, 2000

Prophecy

MY SPIRIT IS GOING TO MOVE IN AMERICA IN SUCH A WAY THAT THE PEOPLE WILL KNOW THAT IT WAS ME THAT SETTLED THIS ELECTION DEBACLE! MILLIONS OF SOULS ARE AT STAKE! MY PEOPLE MUST HAVE A NEW BIRTH OF FREEDOM AND RIGHTEOUSNESS!!! A CLEANSING OF THEIR SOUL! TO KNOW AND UNDERSTAND THAT SODOMY: SAME SEX SEXUAL RELATION IS ABOMINATION TO ME! IS EVIL, VILE, WRETCHED! FROM THE PIT OF HELL! AND MUST BE EXTRICATED, CAST OUT, DELIVERED, HEALED, SET FREE FROM THIS CURSE OR JUDGMENT MUST COME TO AMERICAN SOIL TO CLEANSE AND ERADICATE THIS EVIL PRACTICE! DID I NOT DESTROY TWO ENTIRE CITIES, SODOM AND GOMORRAH, FOR THIS SAME EVIL? DO YOU THINK THAT IT IS LESS EVIL IN MY SIGHT NOW BECAUSE YOUR GOVERNMENT CONDONES THIS PRACTICE? NO, NOT ONLY CONDONES, BUT IS ACTUALLY IN THE PROCESS OF PROPAGATING THIS EVIL!!! I MADE MALE AND FEMALE TO DO THE PROPAGATING! BUT AS IT IS WRITTEN IN HOLY SCRIPTURE BY THE APOSTLE PAUL IN ROMANS ONE: BECAUSE WHEN THEY KNEW GOD, THEY DID NOT HONOR THE LAWS OF GOD, BUT BECAME FUTILE IN THEIR REASONING, AND THEIR FOOLISH HEARTS WERE DARKENED! CLAIMING TO BE WISE, THEY BECAME FOOLS!

THEY EXCHANGED THE GLORY OF THE IMMORTAL GOD FOR MORTAL HUMANS, AND BIRDS AND BEASTS, AND CREEPING THINGS! WHEREFORE, I GAVE THEM UP TO UNCLEANNESS, TO THE LUSTS OF THEIR OWN HEARTS TO DISHONOR THEIR OWN BODIES AMONG THEMSELVES!!! BECAUSE THEY EXCHANGED MY TRUTH INTO A LIE AND WORSHIPPED AND SERVED THE CREATURES RATHER THAN THE CREATOR WHO CREATED THEM!!! FOR THIS REASON, I GAVE THEM UP TO PASSIONS OF DISHONOR! FOR EVEN THEIR FEMALES CHANGED THE NATURAL USE INTO THAT WHICH IS AGAINST NATURE! LIKEWISE, ALSO, THE MALES LEAVING THE NATURAL USE OF THE FEMALES BURNED IN THEIR LUSTS ONE TOWARD ANOTHER, MALES AMONG MALES WORKING THAT WHICH IS LASCIVIOUS! AND SINCE THEY DID NOT THINK IT

WORTHWHILE TO RETAIN MY ORDINANCE, WHICH IS MALE AND FEMALE, I GAVE THEM OVER TO A DEPRAVED MIND TO DO THOSE THINGS WHICH ARE AGAINST NATURE! AND ALTHOUGH THEY KNOW MY RIGHTEOUS DECREE, YES, LAWS DO MATTER, THAT THOSE WHO DO SUCH THINGS ARE WORTHY OF DEATH, NOT ONLY DO THEM, BUT GIVE CONSENT TO THE ONES PRACTICING THEM!!! WHAT ARE YOU GIVING CONSENT TO, PERMISSION TO, THAT IS AGAINST MY LAWS??? LISTEN UP, AMERICA, JUDGMENT IS ONLY JUSTICE!!! JUSTICE IS WHAT I SAY IT IS!!! I AM JUDGE, JURY AND UNDERTAKER OR LIFE GIVER! THE CHOICE IS YOURS! CHOOSE LIFE! IF YOU CHOOSE MY WILL AND MY WORD YOU MAY LIVE! IF YOU REFUSE TO OBEY MY WILL AND MY WORD YOU CHOOSE DEATH! CHOOSE YOU THIS DAY WHOM YOU WILL SERVE! YOU HAVE NO PROMISE OF TOMORROW!!! YOU KNOW NOT WHAT A DAY MAY BRING FORTH! I AM THE ALMIGHTY! BESIDES ME THERE IS NONE OTHER! WHEN YOU CHOOSE LESSER GODS, YOU ARE ACTUALLY CHOOSING DEATH, BECAUSE WITHOUT ME YOU SHALL PERISH!!! I AM THE ONLY TRUE LIVING GOD!!! WHERE IS BUDDHA? WHERE IS MOHAMMED? I AM ALIVE AND WELL ... PUTTING UP KINGDOMS AND TEARING DOWN RITUALS AND TRADITIONS OF MEN! WHY CAST YOUR VOTE FOR THE DEMAGOGUES OF DEATH??? ABORTION IS DEATH! HOMOSEXUALITY IS DEATH! LESBIANISM IS DEATH! TAXATION WITHOUT REPRESENTATION IS DEATH! WITHHOLDING THE RIGHT TO BEAR ARMS AND TO PROTECT ONESELF IS DEATH! DOING AWAY WITH THE ELECTORAL COLLEGE IS DEATH! BEING AGAINST WHAT I AM FOR IS DEATH! BEING FOR WHAT I AM AGAINST IS DEATH! DEATH AND LIFE ARE IN THE POWER OF THE TONGUE!!! SPEAK FORTH AMERICA!!! THE WORLD IS IN NEED! IN NEED OF TRUTH! IN NEED OF A SAVIOR!!! THERE IS A NEW BIRTH OF FREEDOM IN THE ARMED FORCES OF THE UNITED STATES FOR I AM RESTORING DIGNITY TO THE PRESIDENCY! THE PRESIDENT WILL BE A LEADER OF MEN AND WOMEN! NOT MOGULS AND WATERSHEDS. HE IS TO BE WHAT RIGHTEOUSNESS IS TO A NATION. RIGHTEOUSNESS EXALTS A NATION! SIN IS A REPROACH. LET RIGHTEOUSNESS BEGIN TO ELEVATE AMERICA BACK TO ITS PROPER POSITION. STAYING IN MY WILL IS OF PRIME NECESSITY TO AMERICA'S FUTURE. NO ONE CAN TOPPLE A NATION THAT IS

BUILT UPON THE FOUNDATION OF GOD! YOUR SOURCE IS NOT MEN! YOUR SOURCE IS ME SAITH THE LORD! REESTABLISH PRAYER IN THIS NATION AS THE SOURCE OF STRENGTH! NOT LOBBYISTS! REESTABLISH STRENGTH OF CHARACTER AS THE SOURCE OF GREATNESS! NOT POLITICAL PUNDITS. STRENGTH OF CHARACTER, TRUTH, INTEGRITY, SINCERITY OF SOUL, HONESTY OF HEART IS THE APPLAUSE OF SUCCESS. POSITION WITHOUT INTEGRITY IS FUTILE. GRAVE CHANGES ARE FORTHCOMING TO MEN OF ILL REPUTE. MORE COVERS ARE TO BE TAKEN OFF OF SHAME AND DEGRADATION. NO LIE IS A GOOD LIE. ALL EVIL WILL BE UNCOVERED. BETTER IT IS TO BE WITH THE FEW WHO STAND FOR TRUTH THAN TO BE BUSTED WITH THE MIGHTY WHOSE MIGHT IS CRUMBLING.

November 25, 2000

I SEE EVERY CORPUSCLE IN YOUR BODY! I HAVE SPARED YOUR LIFE! I HAVE GIVEN YOU AN EDICT TO PROCLAIM THE MOORING OF MY COMING!!!

November 26, 2000

Submission

THE BRIDE OF CHRIST IS BEING FITTED FOR HER WEDDING GARMENTS! SHE WILL SOON BE CAUGHT UP TO MEET HER BRIDEGROOM! SHE WILL STAND BEFORE HER GOD BEFORE SHE IS RAISED UP TO MEET HER GROOM! SHE WILL NOT BE DECKED WITH JEWELS BUT WITH THE ROBE OF RIGHTEOUSNESS! SHE WILL BE SHEDDING ALL THE THINGS THAT SHE HAS NO NEED OF! SHE NEEDS ONLY TO BE CLEAN, HOLY, SPOTLESS! SHE NEEDS NO FANCY TITLES. NO RHYTHMS TO CHARM THE WORLD. NO MOVES TO SWAY THE OPPOSITION. SHE NEEDS ONLY TO SETTLE INTO HER PLACE. HER CALLING. HER PURPOSE. SHE STANDS ALONE. BUT SHE IS NEVER ALONE. SHE KNOWS TRUTH! AND STANDS FOR TRUTH ALONE! SHE CARES NOT WHAT OTHERS THINK, INTIMATE, OR FORMULATE. SHE IS SETTLED, PURE, CALM. SHE AWAITS HIS COMING! SHE HAS PREPARED HERSELF. SHE IS AT PEACE! PAINS OF DEATH BRING NO FEAR. SHE KNOWS THAT DEATH IS FRUITLESS IN THIS FINAL HOUR. DEATH IS SWALLOWED UP IN VICTORY!!!

November 28, 2000

Spiritual Warfare

WILL THE UNITED STATES OF AMERICA STILL PROPAGATE THE GOSPEL OF CHRIST??? CHRIST WILL NOT TOLERATE EVIL!!! EVIL IS WHAT GOD SAYS IT IS, NOT MAN'S OPINION! COME DOWN FROM YOUR THRONE, AMERICA!!! THERE IS ONLY ONE TRUE LIVING GOD!!! AND YOU ARE NOT IT! GOD CAN SAVE AMERICA IF SHE REPENTS AND TURNS FROM HER WICKEDNESS!!! IF!!!

November 19, 2000

I BREAK THE POWER OF DISCORD IN THESE UNITED STATES OF AMERICA! I CURSE TO THE ROOTS THE SPIRIT OF VICE IN THE COURTS OF AMERICA! I BREAK THE POWERS OF DARKNESS OVER THESE UNITED STATES OF AMERICA AND I CURSE TO THE ROOTS ALL EVIL PRIDE OF POSITION! I CASTIGATE THE EVILS IN THE JUDICIAL SYSTEMS IN THESE UNITED STATES! I CALL FORTH THE COURT-MARTIALS OF THE HEAVENLY SUPREME COURT TO BRING POWER BACK TO THE PEOPLE OF THESE UNITED STATES! TO BRING AUTHORITY BACK TO THE PEOPLE!!! TO SET IN ORDER THAT WHICH HAS PUBLICLY DENIED ... THE RIGHTS AND WISHES OF THE PEOPLE FOR WHICH THIS NATION WAS FOUNDED UNDER GOD! I BREAK THE SELF-WILL OF MAN THAT HAS BROUGHT IN KICKBACKS, PAY OFFS, GRAFT AND BRIBERY! I CURSE ALL POWERS THAT ARE NOT IN LINE WITH THE CONSTITUTION OF THE UNITED STATES OF AMERICA!!! I GIVE BACK GOVERNMENT TO THE PEOPLE FOR WHICH IT WAS ESTABLISHED!!! BE FREE TO PRESERVE YOUR CONSTITUTIONAL RIGHTS OF FREEDOM OF WORSHIP, FREEDOM OF SPEECH, FREEDOM OF PRESS, FREEDOM OF ASSEMBLY, FREEDOM TO BEAR ARMS, FREEDOM TO HAVE ONE'S VOTES COUNTED ACCORDING TO THE LAWS OF EACH STATE WITHOUT FEDERAL INTERVENTION!!! I BREAK THE CHAINS OF DARKNESS OFF OF THESE UNITED STATES! I PUT IN PLACE ORACLES OF EXPEDIENCY TO EXECUTE JUSTICE SAITH THE LORD!!!

November 26, 2000

Spiritual Warfare

I SPEAK UNTO THE POWERS OF THE DARKNESS OF THIS WORLD, BE THOU BROKEN AND CURSED IN THE NAME OF JESUS!!! I BREAK YOUR POWER OVER THIS NATION! I BREAK THE FETTERS OF DARKNESS OFF THE MINDS OF ALL LIVING ON THIS CONTINENT! I CURSE TO THE ROOTS ALL DIABOLICAL SCHEMES TO OVERTHROW THESE UNITED STATES OF AMERICA! AND THE POWER INVESTED TO THE GOVERNMENT BY THE ORIGINAL CONSTITUTION OF THE UNITED STATES! I BREAK ALL INSIDIOUS, UNDERHANDED PROGRAMS, PLANS AND PROVISIONS THAT SUBSTITUTE THE AUTHORITY OF OUR CONSTITUTION! I CALL FORTH WARRIORS OF RIGHTEOUSNESS INTO BATTLE EVEN NOW TO STRIP AWAY WHAT HAS TAKEN PLACE IN OUR JUDICIAL SYSTEM, TAKING AWAY THE RIGHTS THAT WERE GIVEN TO US BY THE CONSTITUTION! I BATTLE EVEN NOW THE PROVISIONS OF THE COURTS THAT HAVE SET ASIDE INDIVIDUALS' RIGHTS AND PROTECTIONS!!! I BREAK EVERY BONDAGE OF FILTH, PERVERSION, AND HOMOSEXUALITY THAT IS FLOODING OUR SCHOOLS AND OUR INSTITUTIONS WITH THESE THINGS THAT ARE ABOMINATION TO GOD! ABORTION CLINICS BE CLOSED IN THE NAME OF JESUS! PORN PARLORS BE CLOSED IN THE NAME OF JESUS! MOVIES OF FILTH AND SENSUALITY BE SHUT DOWN IN THE NAME OF JESUS! I CURSE THOSE NOW WHO ARE PERMITTING SUCH ATROCITIES TO BE MADE! SEX MURDERS AND CHILD PORNOGRAPHY, BE THOU CURSED IN THE NAME OF JESUS! CEASE PEDOPHILES! CEASE RAPISTS! CEASE MURDERERS OF FATHERS AND MURDERERS OF MOTHERS! CEASE THESE MADNESSES! I POUR OUT UPON THE WILLFUL AND THE DISOBEDIENT CURSES OF PENALTIES FOR PROMOTING THIS FILTH IN THE NAME OF JESUS! I CALL FOR THE RAPISTS OF LITTLE CHILDREN TO BE STOPPED IN THE NAME OF JESUS,

EITHER BY BEING SET FREE OR BY SUDDEN DEATH!!!
YOU WILL CEASE! THE LORD HAS SPOKEN IT!!! CEASE
THIS MADNESS OF ROLE PLAYING GAMES! HURLING
YOURSELVES INTO HELL! KNOW YOU NOT THAT YOU
ARE DOOMING YOUR DESTINY WITH CHARDS OF HELL
AND THERE WILL BE NO REMEDY FOR YOUR MADNESS
IF YOU CONTINUE TO PROPEL YOURSELF INTO THE
PITS OF THE ABYSS? YOU WILL NOT STAY MY HAND
SAITH THE LORD FOR I DELIVER WHOEVER WILLS TO
BE FREE OF SATANIC CONTROL! BUT IF YOU PERSIST IN
PURSUING THESE EVILS SAITH THE LORD I WILL DOOM
YOUR FUTURE FOR YOU WILL TORMENT THE
RIGHTEOUS NO LONGER ... YOUR TIME IS NUMBERED!
I WILL HAVE THE LAST WORD! I WILL SAY WHO GOES
FREE AND WHO IS CAST INTO OUTER DARKNESS
WHERE THERE IS WEEPING AND GNASHING OF TEETH!
AND THE AGONY OF TORMENT NEVER ENDS! THE
NERVE ENDINGS NEVER DIE, AND THE FIRE IS NEVER
QUENCHED! YOU CHOOSE POWER. BUT YOUR POWER
ULTIMATELY LEADS YOU TO NEVER ENDING PAIN! NO
END! DAY NOR NIGHT!

BE SET FREE IN THE NAME OF JESUS! THE NAME THAT IS
ABOVE EVERY NAME! I CANCEL YOUR DEBT AND CALL
YOU FORTH EVEN NOW!!! YOU WILL NO LONGER
WHOREMONGER AND ENGAGE IN ILLICIT SEX! YOU
WILL CEASE YOUR PERVERSIONS AND SEXUAL
PASTIMES! I CURSE EVEN NOW THE MEMORIES OF
YOUR PAIN! YOU ARE HEALED BY THE POWER OF
ALMIGHTY GOD! YOU WILL NO LONGER REMEMBER
THE AGONIES OF HUMAN SACRIFICES!!! YOU WILL
FORGET THE ATROCITIES OF MIND CONTROL, MURDER
ON DEMAND AND TORTURE CHAMBERS! YOU ARE SET
FREE! RECEIVE THE GRACE OF GOD AND THE POWER OF
THE HOLY GHOST OF GOD! BE MADE WHOLE BODY,
SOUL AND SPIRIT! BE RENEWED IN THE SPIRIT OF YOUR
MIND! BE SET FREE FROM ALL CARNALITY AND MIND

GAMES! BE NURTURED WITH THE WORDS OF GOD!!! RECEIVE THE PEACE OF GOD! BE RESTORED IN YOUR MIND AND IN YOUR WILL AND IN YOUR EMOTIONS! BE DELIVERED FROM FEAR AND PROCRASTINATION! BE OPEN TO THE LEADING OF THE SPIRIT OF GOD TO GUIDE YOU INTO THE TRUTH OF GOD'S WORD AND THE AUTHORITY OF HIS POWER!!! TO THE RIGHTEOUSNESS OF HIS DOMINION! TO WHOM BE ALL HONOR AND GLORY AND POWER! BE SURE OF THIS ONE THING ... THE PERVERTED WILL NOT INHERIT ETERNAL LIFE! THEY WILL HAVE THEIR PART IN THE LAKE OF FIRE! I CALL FORTH THE POWERS OF DARKNESS TO CEASE IN THESE UNITED STATES! I BREAK THE DOMINION OF BLUDGEONING THE CREATION OF GOD! ABORTIONISTS CEASE! CHILD ABUSERS CEASE!!! CHILD PORNOGRAPHY CEASE! I BREAK YOUR FETTERS EVEN NOW! STOP THE KILLING!!!

November 28, 2000

Wisdom

THE SAGES OF THE AGES ARE THE PUREST OF THE GOLD! TRUE TO SELF... THE UNSPEAKABLE TOLD. GRIEF AND GLORY, GRIT AND SHAME. COWERING ON THE PAGES OF WHO IS TO BLAME! SUNSETS LIE IN MOURNING. SUNRISES COME ADORNING. I CANNOT SEE WITH THE EYES OF THOSE WHO FLEE THE PAINS OF MENTAL AGONY. I CAN SEE ONLY WITH THE EYES OF THOSE WHO DOTH ACCOMPANY ME IN DREADED DARKNESSES AND DANK DOWN UNDERS. SADNESS FLEES WHEN BLACKNESS GIVES WAY TO THE CREDIBILITY OF GRANDEUR! THE HIGHEST POWER SETTLES EVERY ARGUMENT! I SEE THAT TRUTH IS NOT ALTERED BY ONE'S DESTINY!!! THAT PAIN, NOR POVERTY ... NOTHING CHANGES THE HIERARCHIES OF HEAVEN! THAT ONLY THE CHAIN OF COMMAND RULES THE BASTIANS OF ETERNITY! TO SEE THAT GOD IS IN CONTROL GIVES GRACE TO GAUNT. HOPE TO LACK, AND PEACE TO PAIN. OUR GOD DOES REIGN! LOVE IN THE HIGHEST GIVES MEANING TO THE MAZE. HIS PINIONS PARADE! HIS WORKS DO INVADE! AND THE LORDS OF HIM WHO RULES TAKE THEIR PLACES IN THE FRAY!!! THE GOD OF THE UNIVERSE DOTH GIVE POWER TO THE DAY!!! GLEAN YOUR DUTIES! GET THEM DONE! THE POWER OF ONE. GOD, IS STILL MAN'S MEASURE THRUST! SOW SEED ... SPEAR DRAGONS! GIVE MUCH! LOVE MEASURES LOST MAN AS DEATH UNREAPED. SORELY CORRUPT AS THE REAPERS SLEEP! STAY YOUR PLOW. BID THE HARVEST TO BEGIN. I PULL THESE CREATURES FROM THEIR SIN!!!

November 4, 2000

HOLINESS IS POWER!

November 5, 2000

PASSIONS OF YOUR PROVEN LIFE WILL POUR OUT TO THE PRODIGALS.

November 6, 2000

YOU ARE GOING TO NEED SUPERNATURAL LOVE IN ORDER TO LOVE YOUR BROTHERS AND YOUR SISTERS AS YOURSELF! WITHOUT SUPERNATURAL LOVE YOU WILL NOT BE ABLE TO FULFILL YOUR PURPOSE!

November 12, 2000

THE ELECTORAL COLLEGE IS THE CHECKS AND BALANCES THAT GOD SET IN ORDER IN THE UNITED STATES THROUGH OUR FOREFATHERS!!! THE BALLOTS ARE IN THE HANDS OF THE LORD!

November 19, 2000

Prophetic Teaching

GOD IS BLESSING YOU INTO OBEDIENCE! YOU HAVE ONLY ONE OBLIGATION! THAT IS TO <u>HEAR</u> THE VOICE OF GOD! WHEN YOU RELEASE, SET ASIDE, THROW OUT EVERYTHING ELSE IN ORDER TO OBTAIN THAT ... THE ULTIMATE ... HEARING GOD ... EVERYTHING ELSE IS A PIECE OF CAKE! EVEN AS A CHILD WHO REPEATS TO A SIBLING OR A FRIEND ... CAUSE MOMMA SAID! OR DADDY SAID SO! IN OTHER WORDS, THAT SETTLES IT! DADDY SAID SO! ABBA FATHER! DADDY GOD!!! DADDY SAID SO! HEAR GOD! IN ORDER TO REALLY FEAR GOD ... WHICH WE MUST DO IN ORDER TO KEEP HIS COMMANDMENTS ... WE MUST FIRST <u>HEAR</u> GOD! GUESS WHAT! IF YOU ARE NOT KEEPING HIS COMMANDMENTS ... YOU DO NOT FEAR GOD! HOW CAN WE KNOW WITHOUT DOUBT OR DENIAL WHAT IT IS WE ARE TO DO WITHOUT FIRST HEARING WHAT IT IS THAT GOD IS SPEAKING TO US, ABOUT US FOR OUR GOOD AND FOR HIS GLORY??? IF WE WILL ... YOU HAVE SOMETHING TO DO WITH WHETHER GOD SPEAKS TO YOU AND WHETHER HE CONTINUES TO SPEAK TO YOU ... FRIENDS DO SPEAK, YOU KNOW!!! ESPECIALLY FRIENDS THAT ARE CLOSER THAN BROTHERS! GET QUIET ENOUGH AND GIVE GOD A PLACE, SOME TIME! IF WE SET ASIDE TIME AND GIVE A PLACE TO GOD! GOD KNOWS MANY HAVE CERTAINLY GIVEN THE DEVIL A PLACE ... TO SPEAK, TO INFLUENCE! YOU KNOW WHY THE DEVIL MOVES, YOU GIVE HIM A PLACE! Ephesians 4:27 IF WE WILL GIVE GOD TIME AND A PLACE WHERE WE SUBMIT TO NOTHING ELSE BUT LISTENING TO HIS VOICE ... HE WILL SPEAK! MANY TIMES HE DOES NOT SPEAK BECAUSE WE HAVE DISMISSED, IGNORED, OR SET ASIDE HIS SPEAKING. WE HAVE REFUSED TO BE OBEDIENT TO HIS WORDS, THUS, HE STOPS SPEAKING. IF HE IS NOT SPEAKING TO US, THERE IS ONLY ONE REASON! WE DO NOT GIVE HIM A PLACE! OR HE STOPS SPEAKING BECAUSE WE DO NOT OBEY WHAT HE HAS ALREADY SPOKEN! EVEN, AGAIN, AS FRIENDS, WE MUST MEND OUR RELATIONSHIP TO HAVE ONGOING DIALOGUE! GOD DOES NOT HAVE DYSFUNCTIONAL RELATIONSHIPS! IF YOU DESIRE HIM, HE IS AVAILABLE! BUT HE IS NOT GOING TO BE ONE OF YOUR MANY LOVERS! WHERE YOU PUT JUST ENOUGH EFFORT IN THE RELATIONSHIP TO GET WHAT YOU WANT OUT OF IT AND DO

NOT WITH LOVE SEEK TO MEET YOUR PARTNER'S NEEDS AND CONCERNS! THE LORD IS A BRIDEGROOM! WHY DO YOU TREAT HIM AS IF HE WERE YOUR SURROGATE MOTHER OR YOUR PIMP? GET IN RIGHT RELATIONSHIP! YOU ARE THE BRIDE OF CHRIST! DO WHAT BRIDES DO WITH BRIDEGROOMS! MAKE LOVE!!! LET IT BUBBLE OUT OF YOUR INNERMOST BEING! REMINISCENCE OF WHAT HE REALLY DID FOR YOU!!! DID HE ACCEPT YOU JUST AS YOU ARE? OR ARE YOU TREATING HIM AS AN EARTHLY LOVER, WHO IS ON ONE DAY AND OFF THE NEXT??? DID HE REALLY MAKE YOU WHOLE AND GIVE YOU PEACE AND JOY? DID HE WASH YOUR SINS AWAY? GUESS WHO MOVED! HE HASN'T BUDGED!!! HE IS ALWAYS THE SAME! A READY LOVER! COME UNTO ME, ALL YOU THAT LABOR AND ARE HEAVY LADEN AND I WILL GIVE YOU REST! Matthew 11:28 REST IN THE ARMS OF JESUS! LET HIM WRAP YOU IN HIS EMBRACE! SUFFERING GOOD IS NOT DISGRACE! LET HIM BE THE KEEPER OF YOUR SOUL! SURRENDER YOUR THOUGHTS, FEELINGS, APPREHENSIONS, ANXIETIES, FEARS, DISTRESSES, AND TERRORS UNTO THE LOVER OF YOUR SOUL! CASTING ALL YOUR CARE UPON HIM FOR HE CARES FOR YOU! I Peter 5:1-11 YOU MAY HAVE A HUSBAND, WIFE, FRIEND. THEY CANNOT CARRY ALL YOUR BURDENS! GOD CAN!!! GIVE THEM TO HIM!!! BE RELEASED NOW FROM YOUR WORRY, FRUSTRATIONS, FINANCIAL CARES AND CONCERNS! THE LORD SAYS, I AM ABLE TO DO EXCEEDINGLY, ABUNDANTLY ABOVE ALL THAT YOU ARE ABLE TO ASK OR THINK, ACCORDING TO THE POWER THAT WORKS IN YOU! Ephesians 3:20 TAKE MY YOKE UPON YOU AND LEARN OF ME! I AM MEEK AND LOWLY IN HEART! FIND REST FOR YOUR SOUL … MIND, WILL, EMOTIONS, AS YOU YOKE YOURSELF TOGETHER WITH ME, SUBMITTING TO MY LOVE AND TO MY LEADING! I WILL GUIDE YOU AS YOU ALLOW ME TO MAKE A WAY, WHERE THERE SEEMS TO BE NONE! QUIT TRYING TO LEAD, MEN AND WOMEN OF THE GOSPEL, THE BRIDE OF CHRIST. SUBMIT YOURSELVES TO YOUR BRIDEGROOM! ENTER INTO THE BRIDE-CHAMBER! YOU ARE NOT GOING TO DO GREAT WORKS UNTIL YOU MINISTER TO YOUR BRIDEGROOM IN THE BRIDE-CHAMBER! UNTIL YOU RELEASE YOUR LOVE UPON THE CHRIST … YOU CANNOT BE FULLY RELEASED TO LOVE THE WORLD, THE LOST OF SOCIETY! AS THEY MINISTERED TO THE LORD AND FASTED, THE HOLY GHOST SPOKE! Acts 13:2 WHEN

YOU MINISTER TO THE LORD HE SPEAKS! WHEN YOU LOVE THE LORD, YOUR BRIDEGROOM, YOU TAKE TIME TO BE ALONE WITH HIM!!! YOU BASK IN HIS GLORY!!! IT DOES NOT MATTER ABOUT YOUR POSITION OR TITLE BECAUSE YOU KNOW YOU ARE UNDER HIS AUTHORITY!!! YOU HAVE YOUR MARCHING ORDERS!!! IF YOU LAY IN HIS PRESENCE AND HE MINISTERS HIS LIFE INTO YOUR OPEN SOUL, HIS GOODNESS COVERS YOUR GRIEF! HIS POWER IMPREGNATES YOUR WOMB, YOUR INNERMOST BEING, WITH POSSIBILITIES OF THE IMPOSSIBLE! HE WOOS YOU WITH HIS LOVE! YOU SUBMIT TO HIS AUTHORITY! YOU LOVE HIS TOUCH! HIS SPIRIT QUICKENS YOU TO PEACEFULNESS!!! HE WHISPERS SOOTHING COMFORTS! HE FILLS YOU TO OVERFLOWING AS YOU SURRENDER YOUR BODY TO HIS TOUCH! THIS JOY IS YOUR STRENGTH! THE STRENGTH THAT COMES FROM RELAXING IN HIS PRESENCE, AS HE MINISTERS HIS SPIRIT INTO YOUR OWN SPIRIT, THE OIL OF HIS SPIRIT INTO YOUR SIGHING SENSES. HIS LOVE DEEPENS INSIDE OF YOU AS YOU ALLOW HIM TO MINISTER TO THE DEPTHS OF YOUR NEEDS! READ THE SONG OF SOLOMON! THE BRIDEGROOM REPRESENTS GOD AND HIS CHRIST! GOD IS ENOUGH IF WE WILL LET HIM BE! EL SHADDAI! ACTUALLY, HE IS MORE THAN ENOUGH!!! BUT BECAUSE OF OUR LIMITED SURRENDER UNTO THE LOVER OF OUR SOUL, HE IS LIMITED IN PROCREATION, POWER AND PROVISION! ONLY BY OUR LACK OF SUBMISSION IS GOD LIMITED IN PROVIDING WHATEVER WE NEED! WHEN WE SUBMIT, GOD DOES HIS BEST WORK! WE ARE THEN OUT OF THE WAY SO THAT HE CAN RECEIVE THE GREATEST GLORY!!! WE ENVELOP GOD AS WE ALLOW HIM TO ENVELOP US! WE BECOME THE EPISTLE OF CHRIST, WRITTEN NOT WITH INK, BUT WITH THE SPIRIT OF THE LIVING GOD! NOT IN TABLES OF STONE, BUT IN FLESHLY TABLES OF THE HEART! NOT THAT WE ARE SUFFICIENT AS OF OURSELVES TO THINK ANYTHING AS OF OURSELVES, BUT OUR EFFICIENCY AND SUFFICIENCY IS OF GOD! WHO HAS MADE US ABLE MINISTERS OF THE NEW TESTAMENT. NOT OF THE LETTER, BUT OF THE SPIRIT: FOR THE LETTER KILLS, BUT THE SPIRIT GIVES LIFE!!! NOW THE LORD IS THAT SPIRIT AND WHERE THE SPIRIT IS LORD, <u>FINAL AUTHORITY</u>, THERE IS TOTAL LIBERTY! II Corinthians 3 A TEST OF THAT LIBERTY! ABOUT 35 YEARS AGO AFTER I WAS BERATED, VERBALLY ABUSED AND FALSELY ACCUSED OF

INFIDELITY, MY HUSBAND ASKED ME TO COME TO BED. AS I WAS STIRRING DINNER ON THE STOVE, I BEGAN TO POUR OUT MY HEART UNTO THE LORD TELLING HIM THAT I KNEW THAT HE WAS OFTEN MISUNDERSTOOD AND TREATED CRUELLY BY FRIENDS, COUNTRYMEN, AND FALSE BRETHREN, BUT SINCE HE WAS NEVER MARRIED HE COULD NOT POSSIBLY KNOW THE <u>DEPTH</u> OF MY SORROW AND GRIEF SINCE THE MARRIAGE RELATIONSHIP IS THE MOST INTIMATE OF <u>ALL</u> RELATIONSHIPS AND HE HAD NEVER EXPERIENCED THIS BETRAYAL AND DEGRADATION. I WAS CRYING FROM MY HEART, TEARS STREAMING DOWN MY FACE ... THIRTY-FIVE YEARS LATER I CRY AT THE THOUGHT OF IT, IT WAS SO DEEP A HURT. THE DEEPEST OF HURTS, TO BE SO TERRIBLY WOUNDED AND TORN APART BY THE VERY ONE WHO HAD LOVED YOU MORE DEEPLY AND THOROUGHLY THAN YOU THOUGHT POSSIBLE TO BE LOVED IN THE NATURAL. NOW THIS SAME LOVER WAS TEARING OUT MY SOUL AND SEEMINGLY CUTTING IT INTO PIECES. BECAUSE I BELONGED TO THE LORD, I MEAN I REALLY BELONGED TO THE LORD, THUS, I DID NOT HAVE RESENTMENT AND RETALIATION ON MY MIND. WHEN YOU REALLY BELONG TO THE LORD, HE LIVES INSIDE OF YOU AND YOU ARE NOT YOUR OWN. WHEN YOU SUBMIT YOUR FEELINGS TO THE LORD, YOUR FEELINGS BECOME LIKE HIS BECAUSE YOU ARE NO LONGER IN CHARGE! YOUR CHARGE IS TO BECOME ONE WITH HIM! A CHARGE TO KEEP HAVE I! WHEN I POURED OUT MY HEART TO THE LORD, I WAS NOT JUDGING ACCUSINGLY, "OH, YOU JUST DON'T UNDERSTAND!" I WAS EXPRESSING MY INNERMOST FEELINGS FROM THE DEPTH OF MY PAIN TO THE BEST FRIEND OF MY SOUL. KNOWING THAT HE WAS OF FAR GREATER KNOWLEDGE AND WISDOM THAN WHAT I POSSESSED. BUT TELLING MY BEST FRIEND WHAT I WAS FEELING! WHEN I FINISHED, THERE WERE NO WORDS, NO INNER PROMPTINGS, NO SCRIPTURE VERSES. JUST SILENCE. LOVE HIMSELF WAS THEN POURED OUT UPON ME FROM THE TOP OF MY HEAD TO THE SOLES OF MY FEET!!! LITERALLY, AS IF A BUCKET OF HONEY WAS POURED OUT UPON ME! I HAVE NOT HAD THAT SAME MANIFESTATION IN JUST THAT WAY SINCE THEN! GOD LET ME KNOW THAT HE KNOWS WHAT WE GO THROUGH! AND HE LET ME KNOW THAT LOVE COVERS!!! AND THAT HE HAS AMPLE, MORE THAN ENOUGH,

PROVISION FOR WHATEVER WE NEED!!! BECAUSE I WAS COVERED WITH LOVE, INSIDE AND OUT, I LOVED THAT MAN AS IF HE HAD BEEN PASSIONATELY PURSUING ME WITH TENDERNESS AND AFFECTION!!! WHAT A GOD! CAN GOD??? GOD CAN!!! WHEN WE ALLOW HIM TO OPEN US UP AND POUR INSIDE OF US WHAT WE NEED TO FULFILL THE NEEDS OF OTHERS AND OURSELVES!!!

OH, JUST GO AHEAD AND CRY OUT UNTO HIM NOW! COVER ME, LORD! COVER ME! I CAN'T MAKE IT UNLESS YOU DO!!! PLEASE LORD, JUST COVER ME WITH YOU! I AM CRYING UNCONTROLLABLY NOW AT JUST THE THOUGHT OF THE LORD'S PRESENCE THEN, HOW HE MET MY NEED! AND HE CAN DO IT AGAIN! WHATEVER YOU NEED ... REACH OUT AND TOUCH HIM! TOUCH HIM WITH YOUR HEART'S CRY! I BELIEVE THAT IS WHAT TOUCHED HIM FOR ME THAT DAY ... THE CRY OF MY HEART! THE SOBBING OF MY SOUL!

THE RELEASE OF POWER COMES TO YOU WHEN YOU ACKNOWLEDGE YOU CAN'T, BUT HE CAN! WHEN WE ACKNOWLEDGE OUR OWN INADEQUACY AND WHEN WE ACKNOWLEDGE HIS ABILITY, HE IS ABLE TO DO EXCEEDINGLY, ABUNDANTLY ABOVE ALL THAT WE CAN ASK OR EVEN THINK! LET HIM! ACCORDING TO THE POWER THAT WORKS IN US! BY SUBMITTING OUR WILL UNTO THE AUTHORITY OF HIS DOMINION!!! WHO IS GOD HERE, ANYWAY? YOUR EGO OR THE MAIN MAN? YOUR PRIDE OR THE ONE WHO DIED? YOUR GLORY OR THE ONE WHO MADE THE STORY? HISTORY! I'LL GO WITH THE ONE WHO HAS POWER OVER DEATH, HELL AND THE GRAVE!!! LET HIM OPEN YOUR HEART, HIS BLESSINGS TO IMPART! DON'T STUMBLE OVER RULES AND REGULATIONS! JUST LET THE CREATOR OF THE UNIVERSE GIVE YOU HIS INITIATIVES!!! HE HAS YOUR INTERESTS AT HEART! AND HE DOES KNOW BEST! OUR HEAVENLY, HOLY FATHER!!! Ephesians 4:14-21 I Corinthians 15:50-58 JEHOVAH ELOHIM!!! TO YOU WHO ARE ALONE IN YOUR WALK WITH THE LORD, THE LORD WOULD SAY UNTO YOU, THY MAKER IS THY HUSBAND, THY WIFE, THE LORD OF HOSTS IS HIS NAME: AND YOUR REDEEMER, THE HOLY ONE OF ISRAEL! THE GOD OF THE WHOLE EARTH!!! FOR THE LORD HAS CALLED YOU, FORSAKEN AND GRIEVED IN SPIRIT! O, THOU AFFLICTED, TOSSED AND TESTED, IN

RIGHTEOUSNESS SHALL YOU BE ESTABLISHED! NO WEAPON FORMED AGAINST YOU SHALL PROSPER!!! EVERY TONGUE THAT SHALL RISE AGAINST YOU IN JUDGMENT THOU SHALL CONDEMN! THIS IS THE HERITAGE OF THE SERVANTS OF THE LORD AND YOUR RIGHTEOUSNESS IS OF ME SAITH THE LORD OF HOSTS!!! WITH GREAT MERCIES SHALL I GATHER YOU. WITH EVERLASTING KINDNESS WILL I HAVE MERCY ON YOU! ALL OF YOUR CHILDREN SHALL BE TAUGHT OF THE LORD! AND GREAT SHALL BE THE PEACE OF YOUR CHILDREN!!! THUS SAITH THE HIGH AND LOFTY ONE THAT INHABITS ETERNITY, WHOSE NAME IS HOLY! I DWELL IN THE HIGH AND HOLY PLACE, WITH HIM ALSO THAT IS OF A CONTRITE SPIRIT, TO REVIVE THE SPIRIT OF THE HUMBLE, AND TO REVIVE THE HEART OF THE CONTRITE ONES!!! Isaiah 54 JEHOVAH-SHAMMAH … THE LORD IS PRESENT IN YOUR PAIN!!!

REFERRING BACK TO WHERE I CRIED UNCONTROLLABLY JUST AT THE THOUGHT OF WHAT HAPPENED 35 YEARS AGO, I WOULD LIKE TO EMPHASIZE THAT THE EMOTION I AM FEELING NOW IS NOT UNRESOLVED PAIN FROM THE PAST, BUT IT IS COMPASSION FOR YOUR PAIN, YOUR HELL, YOUR BETRAYAL, YOUR HEARTBREAK, YOUR LOSS, YOUR DEVASTATION, YOUR MISERY! THE MUTILATION OF YOUR MIND, YOUR WILL AND YOUR EMOTIONS, YOUR HOPES, YOUR DREAMS, YOUR REASON FOR LIVING! LET GOD GIVE YOU A REASON TO GO ON! HE IS THE PAIN KILLER! LET HIM ASSUAGE YOUR GRIEF! LET HIM BE THE DIAMOND SET IN YOUR SOUL! THE PEARL OF GREAT PRICE, THE LOVER OF YOUR GOAL! SEIZE THIS MOMENT AND SPEAK TO YOUR PAIN … "THE LORD WILL RENEW AGAIN!" GRIEF IS NOT FOREVER. LOSING PREPARES US FOR ANOTHER PURPOSE! ANOTHER PREREQUISITE! HIS PURPOSE! THE FASHIONING OF THE FATHER GIVES US GLORY IN OUR GRIEF! EVEN JESUS SOUGHT RELIEF WHEN HE SAID, "FATHER, LET THIS CUP PASS! NEVERTHELESS NOT MY WILL, BUT THINE BE DONE!" WHEN YOU ARE DUG DEEP, WHEN YOU THINK THAT YOU CANNOT ENDURE ANOTHER LOSS, NOT ANOTHER PAIN, GOD IS PURPOSING FOR A GREATER GAIN! ONE THAT SHINES OUT OF THE DARKNESS OF DESPAIR, THAT NO MATTER HOW UTTERLY HOPELESS … GOD IS THERE!!! HE RESURRECTS THE PIECES OF BROKEN HEARTS AND

LIVES!!! GIVING THEM NEW MEANING. HIS GLORY IN DISGUISE! YOUR CUP OF PAIN WILL BE USED FOR OTHERS TO RECEIVE GRACE AS YOU LIFT IT UP TO HONOR THE KING OF ALL GLORY!!! THAT YOU ARE COUNTED WORTHY TO SUFFER AND FROM THESE GLOWING EMBERS A BONFIRE ERUPTS, OF FAITHFULNESS, FORTITUDE, AND FRIENDSHIPS THAT CAN NEVER BE OBLITERATED!!! BECAUSE THROUGH THE PAINS OF OUR PAST WE ARE MADE TO COMPREHEND THAT LOVE DOES OUTLAST, THAT LOVE DOES CONQUER ALL THINGS, THAT LOVE DOES COVER A MULTITUDE OF SIN, THAT WE ARE MORE THAN CONQUERORS THROUGH HIM THAT LOVES US!!! THAT THE ALMIGHTY CAN TAKE THE CRUSHED, THE BRUISED, THE BROKEN, THE MISUSED AND THE ABUSED AND MAKE PINNACLES OF PRAISE, POWER SOURCES OF PRIDE ... GOOD PRIDE, A JOB WELL-DONE, AGAINST INSURMOUNTABLE ODDS, AGAINST CRUSHING DEFEATS, AGAINST PRISONS OF IMPOSSIBILITIES, GOD IS MANIFESTED AS GOD!!! EL ELYON, THE MOST HIGH GOD!!!

IT TAKES GOD TO RAISE A NATION! IT TAKES GOD TO FULFILL A DESTINY! IT TAKES GOD TO ESTABLISH A VILLAGE THAT IS WORTHY OF RAISING A CHILD!!! IS OUR NATION WORTHY OF RAISING A CHILD!!! IT TAKES GODLY PRINCIPLES TO PROVIDE A NATION WITH THE PROVISION TO RISE ABOVE THE VILE, THE WICKED, AND THE CONDEMNED! WHAT GOD SAYS IS VILE, IS VILE, WHETHER MAN SAYS SO OR NOT!!! WHAT GOD SAYS IS WICKED, IS WICKED, WHETHER MAN THINKS SO OR NOT! WHAT GOD CONDEMNS IS CONDEMNED ALREADY, WHETHER THE JUDGMENT HAS FALLEN UPON IT, YET, OR NOT!!! THE RIGHTEOUS HAVE HELD BACK THE JUDGMENTS OF THE LORD, BY THEIR VERY PRESENCE! BUT SOON JUDGMENTS SHALL BEGIN TO BE UNLEASHED, AS GOD PREPARES HIS BRIDE TO BE TAKEN OUT BEFORE THE WRATH OF GOD IS POURED OUT UPON THE CHILDREN OF DISOBEDIENCE!!! EL ROI!!!

November 3, 2000

Word of Faith

ONE CANNOT FOLLOW ON TO SUCCEED WITHOUT TRAINING ONE'S SPIRIT TO WAIT FOR THE INSTRUCTIONS OF WHAT IT IS YOU ARE TO DO NEXT! NOT WHAT SOUNDS LIKE A GOOD IDEA, A PROPER PLAN, OR THE THRUST OF THE MATTER, BUT WHAT IS MY SENIOR PARTNER SAYING AT THIS TIME! HE HAS THE EXPERIENCE OF COMPLETE VICTORY, UNBIASED KNOWLEDGE, THE GOD-KIND SUCCESS! WHAT I SUBMIT FULLY UNTO HIM BECOMES MY SEED! MY SEED IS THE ONLY THING THAT CAN MEET MY NEED! GROWTH OF CHARACTER COMES FROM WAITING UPON THE LORD! THE HEBREW MEANING OF "WAIT" IS TO TWIST, TO TURN AND TO STRETCH! THAT IS THE BIBLICAL AWAITING ON THE LORD!!! BEING TWISTED OUT OF MEASURE AND BEYOND ONE'S OWN STRENGTH! BEING TURNED ASIDE TO WAIT, TO LISTEN, TO DRAW FROM THE WELL OF THE MASTER! TURNING FROM ONE'S OWN PERCEPTION OF WHAT SUCCESS DEMANDS AND BEING LAID TO WASTE, SEEMINGLY, BUT ACTUALLY BEING PROCESSED, FILTERED, PURIFIED AND CONFORMED TO THE PATTERN OF THE SHEPHERD OF OUR SOUL! EVEN DESPAIRING OF LIFE, HAVING THE SENTENCE OF DEATH IN OURSELVES SO THAT WE WOULD NOT TRUST IN OURSELVES, BUT IN GOD!!! WHO RAISES THE DEAD, AND WHO RAISES US UP IN HIS LIKENESS BEING CONFORMED TO HIS IMAGE!!! AND READY TO EVERY GOOD WORD AND WORK NOT HAVING OUR OWN RIGHTEOUSNESS, BUT THE RIGHTEOUSNESS WHICH IS OF GOD BY FAITH! GRACE REIGNS THROUGH RIGHTEOUSNESS! Romans 5:21 RIGHTEOUSNESS IS A GIFT! Romans 5:17 IT COMES BY FAITH UNTO ALL AND UPON ALL THAT WILL BELIEVE! THERE IS NO DIFFERENCE! Romans 3:22

THE RIGHTEOUSNESS OF GOD IS REVEALED BY FAITH! IT IS THE POWER OF GOD UNTO SALVATION, TO EVERYONE WHO WILLS TO BELIEVE. TO EVERYONE WHO WILL SAY, "YES" TO TRUTH AND SURRENDER THEIR OWN RIGHTEOUSNESS UNTO THE RIGHTEOUSNESS OF GOD! Romans 1:16-17 OUR OWN RIGHTEOUSNESSES ARE AS FILTHY RAGS! Isaiah 64:6 WHAT SHALL

WE SAY THEN? THAT THE GENTILES, WHICH FOLLOWED NOT AFTER RIGHTEOUSNESS, HAVE ATTAINED TO RIGHTEOUSNESS, EVEN THE RIGHTEOUSNESS WHICH IS OF FAITH! BUT ISRAEL, WHICH FOLLOWED AFTER THE LAW OF RIGHTEOUSNESS, HAS NOT ATTAINED TO THE LAW OF RIGHTEOUSNESS! WHEREFORE? BECAUSE ... THERE IS ALWAYS A BECAUSE! BECAUSE THEY SOUGHT IT NOT BY FAITH, BUT AS IT WERE BY THE WORKS OF THE LAW! FOR THEY STUMBLED AT THAT STUMBLING-BLOCK! Romans 9:30-32 FOR THEY BEING IGNORANT OF GOD'S RIGHTEOUSNESS, AND GOING ABOUT TO ESTABLISH THEIR OWN RIGHTEOUSNESS, HAVE NOT SUBMITTED THEMSELVES TO THE RIGHTEOUSNESS OF GOD!!! FOR CHRIST IS THE END OF THE LAW FOR RIGHTEOUSNESS TO EVERYONE THAT BELIEVES! Romans 10:3-4

HAS GOD CAST AWAY HIS PEOPLE? GOD FORBID! GOD HAS NOT CAST AWAY HIS PEOPLE, WHICH HE FOREKNEW! AT THIS PRESENT TIME THERE IS A REMNANT ACCORDING TO THE ELECTION OF GRACE! I SAY THEN, HAVE THEY STUMBLED, SO THAT THEY SHOULD FALL? GOD FORBID! BUT THROUGH THEIR FALL, SALVATION IS COME UNTO THE GENTILES! NOW IF THEIR OFFENSE BE THE WEALTH OF THE WORLD, THEIR DEFAULT, THE RICHES OF THE NATIONS, HOW MUCH MORE THEIR FULLNESS? AND THEY ALSO, IF THEY ABIDE NOT STILL IN UNBELIEF, SHALL BE GRAFTED IN FOR GOD IS ABLE TO GRAFF THEM IN AGAIN! Romans 11 Philippians 3:9 FOR THE LAW WAS POWERLESS IN THAT IT WAS WEAK THROUGH THE FLESH, GOD SENT HIS OWN SON IN THE LIKENESS OF SINFUL FLESH, AND FOR SIN, CONDEMNED SIN IN THE FLESH! SO THAT THE REQUIREMENT OF THE LAW MIGHT BE FULFILLED IN US, WHO WALK NOT AFTER THE THINGS OF FLESH BUT AFTER THE SPIRIT! IF CHRIST DWELLS IN YOU, THE BODY IS DEAD BECAUSE OF SIN, BUT THE SPIRIT IS LIFE BECAUSE OF RIGHTEOUSNESS! Romans 8:3-4, 10

THE WORK OF RIGHTEOUSNESS IS PEACE!!! THE EFFECT OF RIGHTEOUSNESS IS QUIETNESS AND ASSURANCE! HE THAT FOLLOWS AFTER RIGHTEOUSNESS AND MERCY FINDS LIFE, RIGHTEOUSNESS AND HONOR!!! BREAK OFF YOUR SINS BY

RIGHTEOUSNESS AND YOUR INIQUITIES BY SHOWING MERCY TO THE POOR!!! Daniel 4:27 KNOW YOU NOT TO WHOM YOU YIELD YOURSELVES SLAVES TO OBEY ... YOUR BODY, SOUL AND SPIRIT, HIS SLAVES YOU ARE! WHETHER OF SIN UNTO DEATH OR OF OBEDIENCE UNTO RIGHTEOUSNESS!!! Romans 6:16

IF YOU ARE STILL SINNING, THE ANSWER TO YOUR DELIVERANCE IS VERY SIMPLE!!! YOU HAVE NOT BECOME A SLAVE TO RIGHTEOUSNESS! SERVANTS OBEY THEIR MASTERS! WHO IS YOUR MASTER? IF YOU ARE YIELDING YOUR MEMBERS, YOUR MORTAL BODY AND THE ACTIONS THEREOF UNTO CARNALITY, SENSE KNOWLEDGE, RATHER THAN SPIRITUALITY AND GOD-KIND KNOWLEDGE, WHO IS YOUR MASTER??? YOU CHOOSE EACH DAY WHOM YOU ARE SERVING BY WHICH MASTER YOU YIELD YOUR AFFECTIONS, PRIORITIES, AND MEMBERS TO!!! TO BE CARNALLY MINDED IS DEATH, BUT TO BE SPIRITUALLY MINDED IS LIFE AND PEACE!

THE CARNAL MIND, ONE THAT DOES NOT STAY SUBMITTED TO THE RIGHTEOUSNESS OF GOD, IS THE <u>ENEMY</u> OF GOD! WHAT IS GOD'S ENEMY? YOUR CARNAL MIND!!! WHY? BECAUSE ... THERE IS ALWAYS A BECAUSE ... "IT IS NOT SUBJECT TO THE LAWS AND LOVES OF GOD! IF YOU LIVE AFTER THE CARNAL MIND, YOU SHALL DIE SPIRITUALLY, BUT IF YOU THROUGH BEING LED BY THE SPIRIT, MORTIFY ... DIE OUT TO THE CARNAL DEEDS OF THE BODY ... YOU SHALL LIVE!" Romans 8:6-13 THE LITERAL TRANSLATION OF GREEK IN Romans 6:18 IS: AND HAVING BEEN SET FREE FROM SIN, YOU BECOME ENSLAVED (BONDMEN) TO RIGHTEOUSNESS! ARE YOU ENSLAVED TO RIGHTEOUSNESS OR ARE YOU JUST SKIPPING OVER THE FLAMES OF HELL BY DANCING ON THE BLOOD OF JESUS???

November 15, 2000

December 2000

Little bitty babies ... Torn from limb to limb,
Because Mothers ... Want To get rid of them.
Others chemically cremated. Their very existence hated.
Make a baby ... And then kill it ... Our National Sin!!!

Part II

Hear
the Word
of the
Lord

The fear of the Lord is the beginning of knowledge:
But fools despise wisdom and instruction.

Proverbs Chapter One Verse Seven

Insight

THE DEMOCRATS ARE STILL TRYING TO ACCOMPLISH WHAT THEY THINK THEY DO BEST. TAKING THE RIGHTS AND PRIVILEGES AWAY FROM THOSE WHO FOLLOW THE RULES AND HAVING THEM FOOT THE BILL ... PAY THE PRICE ... FOR THOSE WHO MARCH TO A DIFFERENT DRUMMER ... THEIR OWN DRUMBEAT ... ALL THE WHILE NOT SEEING OR REALLY NOT CARING TO SEE THAT WHILE THEY PURPORT TO GET THOUSANDS OF BALLOTS THAT WERE NOT PUNCHED AT ALL, AND/OR THAT HAVE ONLY A DIMPLE ... PROBABLY MEANING THAT MANY DID NOT WANT TO VOTE FOR EITHER PRESIDENTIAL CANDIDATE. SOME PEOPLE WANT TO ELECT THEIR OWN LOCAL OFFICIALS, YET DO NOT WANT EITHER PRESIDENTIAL CANDIDATE OR WERE NOT SURE, THUS DECIDING TO LEAVE THE OUTCOME TO FATE. IS IT NOT BIZARRE THAT THEY CAN DISCERN A MINUTE DIMPLE ON A PIECE OF PAPER, AND YET DO NOT KNOW A BABY WHEN THEY SEE ONE??? OR WORSE YET, THEY KNOW IT'S A BABY AND KILL IT ANYWAY!!! IT'S NOT BALLOTS, STUPID! IT'S BABIES! DIMPLES? PREGNANT CHADS? OH, MY GOD! AN OBSTACLE COURSE FROM GOD!!! YET THEY WILL NOT ADMIT THAT A PREGNANT WOMAN CARRIES A BABY AND NOT A BALLOT!!!

December 1, 2000

Prophecy

I AM GOING TO CATAPULT HIM INTO AN ARENA THAT IS FAR SUPERIOR TO HIS LIKING OR HIS INTELLECT! HE WILL BE STRETCHED TO THE LIMIT! I WILL REVIVE HIS SURVIVAL SKILLS AND HE WILL MATURE VERY QUICKLY FOR NECESSITY IS LAID UPON HIM. AND HE WILL RISE TO THE OCCASION!

December 2, 2000

I AM SHOWING MY POWER. I AM SHOWING MY AUTHORITY SAITH THE LORD. I AM PUTTING THIS NATION ON NOTICE!!! I AM GOING TO CLEAN OUT THE PUTRID-NESS OF GRAFT, BRIBERY, SEDITION, FORGERY, MAYHEM, AND MISUSE OF POWER! IT IS HIGH TIME THAT MY PEOPLE WHICH ARE CALLED BY NAME BE RELEGATED TO POSITIONS OF AUTHORITY AND NOT THE USERS OF MY NAME. BUT THE POWERS THAT BE ARE ORDAINED BY ME! I AM CALLING MANY TO STEP ASIDE AND LET ME LEAD THIS NATION BACK TO RIGHTEOUSNESS! ABORTION IS NOT RIGHT! SEX BETWEEN SAME SEX PARTNERS IS NOT RIGHT! PHILANDERING IS NOT RIGHT! FORNICATION IS NOT RIGHT! ADULTERY IS NOT RIGHT! THE DECISIONS IN THE COURTS THAT SHOW PREJUDICE AND TAMPERING ARE NOT RIGHT! THE JUSTICE SYSTEM WILL BE CLEANED OUT! I AM A GOD OF JUSTICE, INTEGRITY, HONESTY, AND WITHOUT RESPECT OF PERSONS! GIVING POSITIONS AND COURT DECISIONS TO THE HIGHEST BIDDER IS THE GALL OF BITTERNESS! YOU WILL SEE JUSTICE PREVAIL IN THIS NATION!

THIS NATION WAS FOUNDED ON GODLY PRINCIPLES AND THESE PRINCIPLES WILL BE REINSTATED IN THIS NATION UNDER GOD!!! TOO MANY TIMES MY PEOPLE REFUSE TO STAND UP FOR TRUTH AND TO FOLLOW THROUGH WITH THE COURSE OF ACTION THAT COULD LEAD TO REMEDIES. THIS MUST BE A QUEST FOR THE FINAL OUTCOME, THE END RESULT. NOT A QUICK FIX. NOR NO FIX AT ALL BECAUSE IT DOES NOT FULFILL ALL QUALIFICATIONS OF CHANGE. KEEP FIGHTING. KEEP STANDING FOR WHAT IS

RIGHT. TRUTH IS ALWAYS RIGHT EVEN THOUGH IT MAY NOT BE POPULAR OR HAVE THE MAJORITY CONSENSUS. AS YOU ARE BEGINNING TO UNDERSTAND, ONE AND GOD MAKES A MAJORITY. TO GO FORWARD YOU WILL HAVE TO SACRIFICE MORE THAN YOU ALREADY HAVE!

December 4, 2000

Prophecy

I AM HEALING PEOPLE ON THE RIGHT AND ON THE LEFT. I AM HEALING YOUR MOTHER. BE OBEDIENT IN THE THINGS I GIVE YOU TO DO. MAN IS NOT YOUR GUIDE. LOOK NOT TO THE RIGHT AND NEITHER TO THE LEFT. LET MY SPIRIT BE YOUR GUIDE. I STAY THE HAND OF THE WICKED ONE. PRAYERS OF CONSECRATION AND SUBMISSION WILL ENABLE YOU TO MOVE FORWARD FOR THE TASKS THAT I HAVE FOR YOU TO DO. I WILL PROVE YOU AND SUSTAIN YOU. LEAVE DETAILS IN MY HANDS. LET ME BE THE INSTIGATOR OF ALL ACTIONS AND PLANS. MY PRESENCE IS YOUR PEACE AND POTENTATE! YOU HAVE NO LACK AS YOU RELAX IN MY SPIRIT AND MEDITATE UPON MY NEEDS. MY NEEDS ARE INSTRUMENTAL IN INITIATING YOUR COURSE OF ACTION. BE SWIFT TO HEAR AND SLOW TO SPEAK SAITH THE LORD OF HOSTS!!! MY MEANS BY WHICH I INITIATE YOUR COURSE OF ACTION IS THE SPOKEN WORD. LISTEN. BE STILL AND KNOW THAT I AM GOD. WHY SIT YOU HERE GAZING AS IN WONDER AT THE THINGS THAT ARE HAPPENING? ALL THINGS THAT ARE COMING UPON THE WORLD HAVE BEEN SPOKEN BY MY PROPHETS. NOTHING IS HAPPENING THAT HAS NOT BEEN REVEALED TO MY PROPHETS. LET MY PROPHETS FOREWARN YOU OF THINGS TO COME. LET THEM SPEAK FOR ME SO THAT I MAY PREPARE YOU FOR THE THINGS, WHICH ARE YET TO COME UPON THE EARTH. MUCH DESTRUCTION SHALL COME TO THIS NATION IN THE MONTHS AHEAD. I AM GOING TO UNLEASH A PORTION OF MY WRATH FOR THE DIABOLICAL LAWS, WHICH ARE UPON YOUR BOOKS. CAN YOU NOT YET SEE THE CYNICISM AND THE BRUTALITY THAT HAS TAKEN THIS NATION TO THE BARBARISM OF KILLING ITS OWN BABIES???

December 5, 2000

Prophecy

THE NEXT MOVE WILL BE EVEN A BRAVER MOVE THAN THOSE IN TIME PAST. YOU HAVE MOVED MANY TIMES AS IT WAS IMPORTUNED UPON YOU. BUT THIS MOVE WILL BE EVEN BRAVER SAITH THE LORD! I AM STABILIZING GOVERNMENTS. STAY IN MY WILL AT ALL COSTS!!! MY SPIRIT IS MOVING IN A MOST UNUSUAL WAY FOR YOU. BRIDGES OF POWER AND DISCERNMENT ARE BEING BUILT TO TAKE YOU TO THE NEXT LEVEL OF MANIFESTATION! REGARD NOT ANY INADEQUACIES. ALL THINGS ARE TO BRING YOU TO YOUR ULTIMATE POSITION OF PURPOSE. NOTHING HAS BEEN SUFFERED IN VAIN. ALL PAIN PROMOTES GAIN IF IT IS ACKNOWLEDGED FOR MY GLORY! YOU HAVE CONTINUALLY SOUGHT MY FACE FOR GUIDANCE IN ADVERSITY. AS YOU MOVE FORWARD, I WILL INSTILL IN YOU NEW DIMENSIONS OF INSIGHT, INTEGRITY OF SOUL, PERSEVERANCE OF SPIRIT AND IMMEASURABLE COURAGE, STRENGTH AND FORTITUDE! YOU SHALL LEAD MANY THAT ARE IN THE TRENCHES. YOU WILL SEE BEYOND THE VAIL. STAY CONSECRATED. YOUR OBEDIENCE TO ME WILL ENABLE OTHERS TO COME UP IN THE SPIRIT, TO SANCTION ONLY STEADFASTNESS AND PURITY OF THE HEART ... THE MEASURE WHEREBY EACH SOUL WILL BE WEIGHED. AS IT IS WRITTEN, "A MAN'S LIFE DOES NOT CONSIST IN THE ABUNDANCE OF THINGS THAT HE POSSESSES, BUT IN RIGHTEOUSNESS AND PEACE AND JOY IN THE HOLY GHOST!!!" THE KINGDOM OF GOD IS NOT IN MEAT AND DRINK! BETTER IT IS TO BE IN THE UPPER ROOM THAN THE SUPPER ROOM. FASTING REGULARLY IS MANDATORY.

December 6, 2000

Prophecy

MY PEOPLE WHICH ARE CALLED BY MY NAME ARE DELIVERED FROM THE PRIDE OF SELF IN VANITY OF CLOTHING, HAIR STYLE AND TRADITIONS!!! MY PEOPLE TAKE PRIDE ONLY IN HAVING ON THE WHOLE ARMOR OF GOD!!!

THE PEOPLE FOR THE DEMOCRATIC PLATFORM, ABORTION ON DEMAND, ARE GETTING A LITTLE FEELING OF WHAT IT IS LIKE TO HAVE "NO VOICE IN YOUR FUTURE." THE ABORTED BABIES HAVE NO CHOICE!!!

December 12, 2000

MY SPIRIT IS QUICKENING YOU TO FULL OBEDIENCE AT ALL TIMES IN EVERY SITUATION NO MATTER WHO IS AGAINST YOU. I WILL DISPEL THE EVILS OF DARKNESS AND DEGRADATION! I WILL BEGIN TO MANIFEST THROUGH PURITY ONLY! NO ONE WHO CONDONES SIN WILL BE QUICKENED TO WORK MIRACLES! WE KNOW IT IS WRITTEN SATAN HAS LYING WONDERS. BUT THE MIRACLE WORKING POWER OF ALMIGHTY GOD WORKS MIRACLES TO CONFIRM THE WORD OF GOD! WHEN MY WORD IS CONFIRMED, MY COMPLETE WILL IS MANIFESTED THROUGH FORGIVENESS AND HEALING OF THE BODY, MIND, WILL, EMOTIONS, AND SPIRIT!!! NOTHING LEFT BROKEN IN THE FLESH, ONLY BROKENNESS AND HUMILITY UNTO THE LORD!!! I LOVE YOU, MY LITTLE ONE, WITH AN EVERLASTING LOVE!!! YOU HAVE RENDERED UNTO ME ALL THAT YOU HAVE! AFTER WHICH I WAS CAUGHT UP IN THE SPIRIT AND SAW PEOPLE VOMITING UP EVIL SPIRITS! I SAW EVIL SPIRITS COMING OUT PEOPLE: PRIDE! ARROGANCE! PERVERSION! SEX ADDICTION! PORNOGRAPHY! PEDOPHILIA, MANIA, SELF, SUICIDE! MURDER! OBSTRUCTION OF JUSTICE! MALICE! MALIGNITY! EVIL CONCUPISCENCE! GREED! AVARICE! VICE! GAMBLING! UNFAITHFULNESS! UN-HOLINESS! UNGODLINESS! GAINSAYING! BRIBERY! AUTISM! REBELLION! GUILE! GALL! BITTERNESS! SUBSTANCE ABUSE! DRUG TRAFFICKING! SLAVE TRADE! PROSTITUTION! WIFE-SWAPPING!

BABY-KILLING! NAME CALLING! CURSING! SEX MURDERS! RAPE! MUTILATION! STRANGLING! BABY SACRIFICES! HUMANISM! THE OCCULT! SEGREGATION! DECEPTION! UNCLEANNESS! PERJURY! POLYGAMY! BIGAMY! GRAFT! MISUSE OF POWER! PERMISSIVENESS! BIGOTRY! SEX DISCRIMINATION! HATRED! SELFISHNESS! HARASSMENT! LYING! CHEATING! STEALING! INFANTICIDE! GENOCIDE! TREASON! UN-FORGIVENESS! TORTURE! PUTRID-NESS! EMULATION! RESISTANCE! SATANISM! WITCHCRAFT! HATERS OF GOOD! VOODOO! HATERS OF GOD! WHISKEY-MAKING! DRUNKENNESS! FILTH! BRAZENNESS! RAGE! VIOLENCE! WRATH! UN-THANKFULNESS! INCEST! SAME SEX UNIONS! JEALOUSY! ENVY! ADULTERY! FORNICATION! LASCIVIOUSNESS! CAPRICE! STRIFE! CONTENTION! DISCORD! VAIN JANGLING! WHISPERING! BACKBITING! FAULTFINDING! MISERY! LUST! MIND CONTROL! STUPIDITY! CARNALITY! RIDICULE! CRITICISM! BOASTFULNESS! PRESUMPTION! SOUL CONTROL! SEDUCING SPIRITS! STRONGHOLDS OF DEVILS, COME OUT IN THE NAME OF JESUS! LOOSE YOUR HOLD, SERPENTS OF FIRE AND FILTH! TORMENT THESE VESSELS NO LONGER!!! SELF-WILL, BE BROKEN IN JESUS' NAME!!!

December 14, 2000

Deliverance

I SPEAK TO THE TORMENTED NOW AND THE DEMONIZED, RID
YOURSELVES OF YOUR PERVERSE THOUGHTS AND FEELINGS BY
BEING SUBJECT TO THE SPIRIT OF GOD AND TO THE WORD OF
GOD!!!   MANIAC DOMINION, TORMENT THESE PEOPLE NO
LONGER! BE SET FREE FROM YOUR PERVERSE BEHAVIORS! LOOSE
YOURSELVES FROM ASSOCIATION WITH THE FILTHY AND THE
VILE!!! BE TORMENTED NO LONGER! RENDER UNTO TO CAESAR
THE THINGS THAT ARE CAESAR'S AND UNTO GOD THE THINGS
THAT ARE GOD'S!!! POMP AND CEREMONY IS FOR CAESAR.
POWER AND CONFORMING TO HIS IMAGE IS FOR GOD! GAIN IS
ONLY GOOD IF IT IS FOR GOD! IF IT INCORPORATES GODLINESS!
EVIL WITH SINCERITY IS STILL SIN!!! STRAPPING ON ACCEPTABLE
APPAREL DOES NOT MAKE ONE HOLY!!! GOD MAKES US HOLY
WITH HIS PRESENCE!!!

December 14, 2000

Prophecy

I HAVE HEARD YOUR PRAYERS FOR THIS NATION, I HAVE HEARD YOUR CRIES AND SEEN YOUR TEARS. TO THE NATION: PRIDE IS PREJUDICE! IT IS NOT ABOUT YOU AND ANYTHING YOU'VE GOT! IT'S ABOUT ME AND EVERYTHING I'VE GOT! I RELEASE NOW MINISTERING ANGELS THROUGHOUT THIS NATION! I CALL FORTH PEOPLE TO INTERCEDE IN THE SPIRIT FOR THE SOUL OF THIS NATION!!! THAT THIS NATION UNDER GOD, WOULD HAVE A NEW BIRTH OF FREEDOM AND THAT THE GOVERNMENT AND THE PEOPLE WOULD KNOW THAT IT WAS GOD THAT FOUNDED THIS NATION! THAT MEN WERE THE MERE INSTRUMENTS OF HIS PROVISION! AND THAT WITHOUT A CALL TO ARMS, AN ARMY OF PRAYER ... THIS NATION WILL SEE UNPRECEDENTED BLOODSHED FOR WHICH SHE ALONE IS RESPONSIBLE! IN YOUR ROBES ARE FOUND THE BLOOD OF THE SOULS OF THE POOR INNOCENTS! I HAVE NOT FOUND IT BY SECRET SEARCH, BUT UPON ALL! ALL SHALL SUFFER FOR THE SINS OF THIS GOVERNMENT!!! I PLEAD WITH YOU BECAUSE YOU SAY, "I HAVE NOT SINNED!" IT IS WRITTEN ... THAT MEANS I, GOD, HAVE SAID IT: THESE SIX THINGS DO I HATE, YEA, EVEN THESE SEVEN ARE AN ABOMINATION TO ME: A PROUD LOOK, A LYING TONGUE, HANDS THAT SHED INNOCENT BLOOD!!! A HEART THAT DEVISES NATURAL REASONINGS THAT EXALTS ITSELF ABOVE THE KNOWLEDGE OF GOD! FEET THAT ARE SWIFT IN RUNNING TO MISCHIEF. A FALSE WITNESS THAT SPEAKS LIES (LIES ARE ANYTHING CONTRARY TO WHAT I SAY!) AND HE THAT SOWS DISCORD AMONG THE PEOPLE!

IF YOU DO NOT BELIEVE I WILL TAKE VENGEANCE UPON THAT WHICH IS ABOMINATION IN MY SIGHT YOU HAVE A FALSE SENSE OF SECURITY BECAUSE AMERICA WILL BE SHAKEN TO THE ROOTS!!! YOU RUN TO OTHER NATIONS TO STOP THEM FROM KILLING THEIR OWN AND YOU YOURSELF SLAUGHTER AMERICANS DAILY THAT I HAVE CREATED IN THE WOMB!!! AMERICA, JUDGMENT IS AT YOUR DOOR! I GIVE YOU A SHORT SPACE TO REPENT AND TO ABOLISH THE DECREE THAT GIVES

LIBERTY TO SLAUGHTER MY CREATION!!! YOU WILL ALSO SEND MILLIONS TO HELL BECAUSE OF THE SANCTIONING OF THIS ATROCITY OF ABORTION ... BECAUSE ... THERE IS ALWAYS A BECAUSE ... BY STANDING FOR THIS EVIL ISSUE YOU HAVE DECEIVED THE HEARTS OF MANY BY ALLOWING THEM TO BELIEVE A LIE AND DAMNING THEIR OWN SOUL! THE INNOCENTS THAT YOU HAVE KILLED ARE WITH ME! BUT THE MURDERERS OF BABIES, THOSE WHO DO THE ACT AND THOSE WHO ALLOW IT TO BE DONE ARE HEADED FOR HELL EXCEPT THEY REPENT AND DENOUNCE THIS EVIL DESTRUCTION!!!

INNOCENT BLOOD IS NOW ON YOUR HANDS, AMERICA! YOU HAVE POLLUTED YOUR OWN NATION AND YOUR OWN PEOPLE WITH EVIL VICES AND PRACTICES! YOU WILL NOT GO UNPUNISHED, EVEN THOUGH YOU REPENT, NOW AND FORSAKE YOUR WICKEDNESS! BUT YOUR CORRECTIONS WILL BE SWIFT AND GREAT! IF YOU REFUSE TO TURN FROM YOUR WICKEDNESS, I SHALL SEND GREATER DESTRUCTIONS SAITH THE LORD!!! I AM NOT A MAN THAT I SHOULD LIE. THE ONLY REASON THAT I HAVE HELD BACK MY JUDGMENTS IS THAT THE INNOCENT SHALL SUFFER AS WELL AS THE GUILTY!!! AS IT IS WRITTEN: WHEN MY JUDGMENTS ARE IN THE EARTH, THE INHABITANTS WILL LEARN RIGHTEOUSNESS! AMERICA BOASTS ITSELF OF BEING THE GREATEST NATION BECAUSE OF ITS MILITARY MIGHT, BUT AMERICA IS NO LONGER THE GREATEST NATION IN TRUTH AND CHARACTER! AT 10 P.M. THE WORD CAME: GREAT DESTRUCTION IS COMING TO CINCINNATI!

THIS NATION WAS NOT FOUNDED FOR OR BY PEDOPHILES OR CRACK HEADS!!! IT WAS FOUNDED BY GOD THROUGH MEN OF TRUTH ... NOBLE AND FORTHRIGHT! THIS NATION WAS FOUNDED PRIMARILY FOR PEOPLE FLEEING RELIGIOUS OPPRESSION! NOT FOR GANGSTERS, CON MEN AND GOD FIGHTERS! IF YOU THINK THAT THIS NATION, UNDER GOD, IS GOING TO TURN OVER AND PLAY DEAD ANY LONGER, YOU DO NOT KNOW OR HAVE THE REAL SPIRIT OF AMERICA, IT'S PEOPLE AND IT'S HERITAGE!!! YOU ARE GOING TO SEE MAJOR CHANGES

IN THE GOVERNMENT! YOU ARE GOING TO SEE PEOPLE RISE UP TO STAND FOR WHAT GOD STANDS FOR AND TO DENOUNCE WHAT GOD STANDS AGAINST!!!

AMERICA IS HEADED FOR A MAJOR CRASH IN THE STOCK MARKET. GOD IS SAYING "IF YOU THINK THAT I CANNOT HIT YOU WHERE IT HURTS THE MOST YOU ARE GOING TO FIND OUT THAT I WILL DO WHATEVER IT TAKES TO GET YOUR ATTENTION!" SLAUGHTERING BABIES IS STILL MURDER! IT IS MAYHEM! THE LORD HAS SPOKEN ...

December 16, 2000

Note: This Word of the LORD given to this child of God on December 16, 2000 was faxed to the incoming President at his home in Texas, to the incoming Vice-President, to Governor Robert Taft, Apostle John Hagee-Apostle to the Nation, to Senator Trent Lott, Congressman Dick Army, to D. James Kennedy on December 22, 2000. This Word of the Lord of the coming judgments was faxed to Pastor to the Nation-Dr. Creflo Dollar, Teacher to the Nation-Kenneth Copeland, to Apostle Prophet Morris Cerullo, to Apostles Paul Crouch, Benny Hinn, and James Dobson, to Marilyn Hickey, to James Robison on December 21, 2000. Then it was mailed to various government and spiritual leaders who I was unable to reach by fax including Pat Robertson, Rod Parsley, T. D. Jakes, Jerry Falwell, Dennis Hastert, Dick Gephardt and many others. On December 28, 2000 this Word from our Lord was faxed to Apostle Bishop Bill Hamon of Christian International, to Senator Tom Daschle, to Intercessors of America, and to Pentecostal Evangel. It was faxed to Evangelist Billy Graham, the Assembly of God Headquarters and to the Church of God Headquarters on December 29, 2000. It was mailed to the Church of God in Christ Headquarters as well as to various denominational heads, and faxed and mailed to many too numerous to mention! I was thankful that I had been obedient, when the atrocity of 9/11 took place, that no ones blood was on my hands, that I had done all that a human could do! I have asked the Lord, "Why me?" since I am well aware that a prominent figure would seemingly be much more believable and acceptable than a relatively unknown vessel. The Lord only says, I have a purpose in using an unknown. On January 21, 2001 the preceding Prophecy telling of the GREAT DESTRUCTION TO AMERICA WITH UNPRECEDENTED BLOODSHED and of the WARNING to the STOCK MARKET was mailed to each of the NINE SUPREME COURT JUDGES. It was also sent to Robert Mueller, Director of the FBI, to John Ashcroft, Attorney General of the United States, to Thomas J. Ridge, Secretary of the Department of Homeland Security, to Condoleeza Rice, National Security Advisor, to Donald Rumsfeld, Secretary of Defense, and to General Henry H. Shelton, Chairman of the Joint Chiefs of Staff. In January of 2002, while still faxing, still writing, still fasting, still praying, still crying out to God, the thought went through my mind as I was putting the Word of the Lord into the fax machine, I don't even know if the people that the faxes are meant to reach are even receiving them. The Lord spoke immediately to me, That's not your job. It's only your job to send them!

As the result of the terrorist attacks on September 11, 2001 against the United States of America: The Pentagon, The World Trade Center, Our Commercial Airlines, Our Citizens, Five Thousand Three Hundred and Seventy Human Beings were either Killed or Injured, including Three Hundred and Forty Three brave Fire-fighters and Seventy-Five courageous Police Officers, among the Multitude of Unsung Heroes. Those are the physical deaths and injuries. The Holes of Hell and Devastation in the Hearts of Americans continue. To the maimed and to the grief stricken because of that horrid day. Some of the Frontline Emergency Responders at Ground Zero later committed suicide because of the horrendous memories of the decapitated heads and mutilated bodies, some of which were reported to be three and four feet deep at Ground Zero.

World News – March 2, 2002: The United States Government alone has lost $200 Billion in the Stock Market.

Note: ie Destruction in Cincinnati: APRIL 2001, FOUR DAYS OF RIOTING, CONSIDERED THE LARGEST URBAN DISORDER IN THE UNITED STATES SINCE THE LOS ANGELES RIOTS OF 1992. IMMEDIATE DAMAGES $3.6 MILLION. THE RESULTING BOYCOTT CAUSED CINCINNATI TO LOSE MORE THAN $10 MILLION IN CONVENTION AND ENTERTAINMENT REVENUE.

Prophecy

IT'S NOT ABOUT YOUR ISSUES! IT'S ABOUT <u>MY</u> ISSUES! IT'S ABOUT THE <u>FINAL</u> ISSUE! WHERE ARE YOU GOING TO SPEND ETERNITY? DON'T BE TELLING ME YOU WANT ME AND DON'T WANT MY PEOPLE! WHO DO YOU THINK THAT I AM? MY BODY <u>IS</u> MY PEOPLE! THE PEOPLE OF GOD! MY PEOPLE *IS* MY BODY! WHICH PART OF MY BODY DON'T YOU WANT? MY EYES? THE SEER. MY EARS? THE TEACHER. MY MOUTH? THE WORKER OF MIRACLES! WHICH PART OF MY BODY DO YOU NOT WANT TO FUNCTION? I SEE YOU. NOTHING IS HID FROM ME! YOU ARE NOT HIDING FROM ME WHAT I SEE DOWN INSIDE OF YOUR HEART! YOU ARE A QUICK FIX BUT YOU ARE NOT THE REMEDY!!! <u>ALL</u> OF MY BODY PARTS MUST BE IN ACTION FOR THE CHURCH TO BE WHOLE AND HEALTHY! WHEN YOU REJECT, SET ASIDE, AND REFUSE TO ACCEPT WHOM I HAVE SENT, YOU ARE SENDING ME AWAY! YOU WILL NOT REFUSE ME AT MY COMING, BUT IF YOU DENY MY PROPHETS, YOU WILL BE TAKEN OUT BY DEATH BEFORE MY COMING SAITH THE LORD!!!

December 16, 2000

CONSIDER THE END TIME!!! FOR TIME IS OF THE ESSENCE SAITH THE LORD! NO WONDER FOR IT IS JUDGMENT THAT MUST COME TO THE HOUSE OF THE LORD BEFORE THE SAINTS OF THE MOST HIGH, EL ELYON, WILL BE TRANSFORMED INTO HIS LIKENESS AND INTO HIS IMAGE!!! I WILL BRING TO NAUGHT THE NAY-SAYERS SAITH THE LORD! I AM COMING BACK AFTER A PEOPLE THAT IS PURE, UNTAINTED, SET APART IN THE AUTHORITY OF THE WORD AND THE POWER OF THE SPIRIT!!! SOME SET THEMSELVES APART IN OUTWARD APPEARANCES AND DRESS CODES. MY DRESS CODE IS THE WHOLE ARMOR OF GOD!!! SOME HAVE EAR PIERCINGS. I ENDEAVOR TO PIERCE YOUR SPIRITUAL EARS TO PRAY IN TONGUES DAILY UNTIL YOUR HUMAN SPIRIT IS CLEANED OUT OF EVERYTHING THAT IS UNLIKE ME! I PIERCE YOUR HUMAN SPIRIT EVEN NOW TO RID ITSELF OF ALL CLUTTER AND CALAMITY! TO DENOUNCE ALL SPEECH THAT IS NOT

SANCTIFIED WITH WORD AND PRAYER! TO REPENT OF ALL THOUGHTS, FEELINGS, IDEAS, PLANS, ASPIRATIONS AND OPINIONS THAT ARE NOT IN LINE WITH MY WORD AND MY WILL FOR YOUR LIFE!!! ABOMINATIONS ARE GOING TO BE DEALT WITH SECURELY AND SWIFTLY!!! SIN, FROM HENCEFORTH UNTIL I RETURN TO CATCH MY BRIDE AWAY, SHALL BE LABELED SIN. NOT HURTS. NOT SHORTCOMINGS! NOT FAILURES! SIN. SIN!!!!! ALL THAT IS NOT OF FAITH IS SIN! REBUKE DOUBT! REBUKE UNBELIEF! REBUKE FEAR! REBUKE LAZINESS! REBUKE SELF-WILL! REBUKE TURMOIL!!! SIN IS ANYTHING AND EVERYTHING THAT IS NOT SUBMITTED UNTO THE WILL OF GOD! SINS OF OMISSION, AS WELL AS, COMMISSION!!! IF YOU DO NOT OBEY FASTING AND PRAYER, I DO NOT SPEAK! IF I DO NOT SPEAK, YOU FAIL BECAUSE YOU CANNOT FOLLOW MY WILL FOR YOUR LIFE WITHOUT ME SPEAKING INTO YOUR LIFE! YOU CONTINUE TO FAIL, TO FALTER AND FAIL BECAUSE YOU DO NOT FOLLOW SPECIFICALLY, CONTINUOUSLY IN HUMILITY THE PREPROGRAMMED GUIDELINES AND SPECIFICATIONS OF COMMITTED SOLDIERS!!! MY WORD WORKS, BUT YOU HAVE TO WORK IT! SPEAK IT! CONFESS IT! UTTER IT! PROCLAIM IT! DEMAND IT! DECREE IT! PUT IT IN ACTION FOR YOUR PARTICULAR NEED OR PROBLEM BY CONFESSING IT, THE WORD, OVER YOUR PROBLEM!!! TIME IS SHORT. I AM GIVING YOU EVERYTHING I'VE GOT! THE WHOLE THING: SIGNS, WONDERS, MIRACLES!!! I AM GIVING YOU A MIRACLE SOON IN YOUR FINANCES! I AM GIVING YOU STABILITY SAITH THE LORD! GO ONLY WHEN I INSTRUCT YOU TO GO, AS YOU HAVE BEEN DOING. YOU HAVE BEEN REAPING MANY BENEFITS NOW FOR ALL OF YOUR OBEDIENCES. I SEE ALL THE SACRIFICES YOU MAKE, ESPECIALLY THE FASTING. YOU HAVE BEEN VERY FAITHFUL TO ME. I AM GIVING YOU AN ABUNDANCE OF PEACE, JOY, HOPE, LOVE. YOUR SON KNOWS HIS OBLIGATIONS. HE WILL OBEY SOON. GRACE, MY CHILD! GRACE AND PEACE, BE MULTIPLIED UNTO YOU, MY CHILD!

December 18, 2000

Prophecy

GIRD UP YOUR LOINS! THE BATTLE IS ON! IT IS RAGING!!! EACH DAY FOR FOUR STRAIGHT DAYS ~ THE LORD HAS AWAKENED ME WITH: SOULS ARE AT STAKE! SOULS ARE AT STAKE!

December 21, 2000

GRAVE DESTRUCTIONS WILL BEGIN IN THIS NATION ON TUESDAY! THERE WILL BE SEVERAL DEATHS. SOME PEOPLE'S MINDS WILL BEGIN TO SNAP BECAUSE OF THE THINGS COMING UPON THIS LAND. SEVERAL SENATORS ARE GOING TO BE EXPOSED OF THEIR ILLEGAL PRACTICES. SOME GOVERNORS ARE GOING TO PLEAD THE FIFTH AMENDMENT BECAUSE OF THEIR SHADY DEALS. I AM PULLING THE COVERS OFF OF GRAFT AND BRIBERY. SOME JAIL CELLS ARE GOING TO OPEN UP BECAUSE OF BLACKMAIL. I AM RIPPING TO SHREDS THE MAJOR MONUMENTS OF GREED AND MIND CONTROL. MY PEOPLE WILL NO LONGER BE HERDED LIKE CATTLE. THEY ARE SHEEP. I WILL LEAD THEM. MY SAVIORS IN THE FORM OF PASTORS, HELPS, GOVERNMENTS, SHALL TAKE THEIR PLACES. GRAFT WILL NO LONGER BE THE MEANS TO SHUFFLE THIS GOVERNMENT. I WILL SPEAK TO MEN AND WOMEN OF CHARACTER AND DUTY AND THEY SHALL STAND UP FOR THE TRUTHS OF MEN'S NEEDS. MY COUNTRY SHALL HAVE A NEW BIRTH OF JUSTICE IN GOVERNMENT. MIGHT OF MONEY WILL NO LONGER PULL THE STRINGS, THE PUPPETS AND THE PUPPETEERS!!! TRUTH AND JUSTICE SHALL HAVE A NEW BIRTH OF FREEDOM! SOLDIERS WILL STAND GUARD AT THEIR POSTS!!! SOLDIERS OF FAITH AND FREEDOM! AN ARMY OF PRAYER WARRIORS SHALL BEGIN TO DO BATTLE ON CAPITOL HILL! I AM STILL KING AND IT'S MY HILL SAITH THE LORD!!! JUSTICE SHALL PREVAIL UNDER THE SHADOW OF THE ALMIGHTY!!!

December 22, 2000

On Tuesday, December 26, Michael McDermott, wielding a semi-automatic assault rifle and a 12-gauge shotgun at Edgewater Technology, an Internet consulting company in Massachusetts, killed seven co-workers. And so it was, also, of men in government, brought to justice because of their shady deals and under-handed practices. GOD KNOWS EVERYTHING *BEFORE* IT HAPPENS!

Prophecy

SURELY I HEAR YOUR CRIES AND I HAVE SEEN YOUR TEARS! SURELY I AM MOVING ON THE RIGHT AND ON THE LEFT. NOW YOU WILL SEE A GREAT RESURGENCE OF PRAYER AND FASTING SAITH THE LORD! I AM GIVING YOU THE KEY FOR MY PEOPLE! THE KEY TO SPEAK THE WORD!!! WHEN THE WORD IS SPOKEN OVER, TO, AND ABOUT THE OBSTACLES THAT STAND IN THE WAY OF RIGHTEOUSNESS, OBSTACLES ARE MOVED AND RIGHTEOUSNESS PREVAILS! ONCE AGAIN PEOPLE WILL KNOW THAT I AM KING! THAT I AM IS JUDGE! THAT "I AM" IS RIGHT! FOR TRULY AS IT IS WRITTEN, EVERY KNEE SHALL BOW AND EVERY TONGUE SHALL CONFESS! BUT FOR MANY THE GESTURE WILL BE TOO LATE! IT IS NOT EVERYONE THAT WILL MAKE IT INTO ETERNAL LIFE, BUT HE THAT DOES THE WILL OF MY FATHER! NOT EVERYONE THAT SAYS, LORD, LORD, BUT HE THAT LABORS WHILE IT IS YET DAY, FOR THE NIGHT SOON COMES WHEN NO MAN CAN LABOR! WHAT ARE YOU LABORING FOR? LABOR NOT FOR THE MEAT, WHICH PERISHES AND THE TREASURES THAT MOTH AND RUST DOTH CORRUPT! BUT LAY UP TREASURES IN HEAVEN WHERE THIEVES CANNOT STEAL! WHEREVER YOUR TREASURES ARE, THERE WILL YOUR HEART BE ALSO! WHAT CAN A MAN GIVE IN EXCHANGE FOR HIS SOUL? WHAT HAVE YOU GAINED IF YOU GAIN THE WHOLE WORLD AND LOSE YOUR OWN SOUL? TO DIE TRUE IS TO JUST TO BEGIN TO LIVE!!! WONDER-FARE WAGING WAR ON GREED!

December 25, 2000

GIVE ME MORE PRAISE! AS YOU PRAISE ME, I WILL BREAK THE SHACKLES OFF YOUR MINISTRY! I AM MOVING IN A MOST UNUSUAL WAY!!!

December 28, 2000

A BURIAL SOON. A BURIAL SOON. WHEN YOU ARE IN THE ARMY AND YOU KNOW THAT LIVES ARE AT STAKE, YOU FORSAKE FLESH AND BLOOD THAT ARE STUBBORN AND REBELLIOUS! YOU STAND FOR TRUTH AND DISCIPLINE EVEN THOUGH IT MEANS FORSAKING YOUR OWN, BECAUSE YOU REALIZE THAT WITHOUT FOLLOWING YOUR ORDERS, MANY, MANY LIVES WILL BE LOST. THAT IT IS BETTER TO ADHERE TO THE CODE OF HONOR THAN TO COMPROMISE INTEGRITY AND PUT MANY LIVES IN DANGER.

December 29, 2000

Spiritual Warfare

I TEAR DOWN THE CORDS OF DISCORD! I TRAMPLE UNDER THE SERPENTS OF DISUNITY!!! I CALL FORTH THE TRIBES OF JUDAH, ISSACHAR, AND ZEBULUN! COME FORTH MIGHTY MEN OF VALOR!!! COME FORTH DAN! COME FORTH THE SONS OF ZEBEDEE! COME FORTH ISAAC AND JACOB!!! COME FORTH O, ISRAEL! CALL! AND I WILL ANSWER THEE! WHAT GREAT THINGS I SHALL DO FOR THEE, O, GREAT EXPANSE OF MIGHT AND POWER!!! YOUR TIME HAS COME! GENTILES, BE STILL AND SEE THE GLORY OF THE LORD! JEHOVAH ISRAEL!!! JEHOVAH SHALOM! JEHOVAH TSIDKENU! JEHOVAH JIREH! JEHOVAH NISSE! JEHOVAH MEKUDDISHKIM! JEHOVAH ROHI! JEHOVAH SHAMMAH! JEHOVAH ROPHEKA! JEHOVAH ELOHIM! JEHOVAH SABOATH! ADONAI JEHOVAH! EL ELYON!!! EL OLAM!!! EL SHADDAI!!! YAHWEH!!!

December 22, 2000

Discerning of Spirits

THE FACT THAT THEY WOULD AGREE TO KILL GOD'S PROGENY!!!
DENYING THAT IT IS A BABY!   AFTER ALL, IF A WOMAN IS
PREGNANT WITH A BABY…THAT IS A REAL PERSON!!!   WE
CANNOT KILL REAL PEOPLE!   SO LET'S JUST NOT CALL THEM
BABIES! I MEAN, AFTER ALL, IT WILL COST US VOTES, ELECTIONS,
IF WE DON'T AGREE TO KILL THEM!!! HOW ELSE CAN WE WIN THIS
SEAT???   WE MUST GIVE THE PEOPLE SOMETHING THAT THEY
WANT…SOMETHING THAT THE OTHER PARTY REFUSES TO GIVE
THEM!   AFTER ALL, THEY DON'T HAVE A NAME YET, SO THEY
COULDN'T BE A REAL PERSON!   BABIES OR BALLOTS!?!?!?!?   OUR
OWN SUPREME COURT HAS PASSED LEGISLATION THAT HAS
ALLOWED THE BUTCHERING OF 40 MILLION AMERICANS SINCE
1973!!! GOD IS NOT AGAINST BIRTH CONTROL! ABORTION IS NOT
BIRTH CONTROL!!!!!!!   ABORTION IS THE SLAUGHTER OF THE
INNOCENTS!!!!!!!!! IS IT ANY WONDER THAT THE NUMBER 3, THE
NUMBER OF THE FATHER, THE SON AND THE HOLY GHOST – THE
REAL SUPREME COURT, WHO ARE ONE, WAS THE NUMBER BY
WHICH THE ABORTIONIST CANDIDATE LOST THE ELECTORAL
COLLEGE! THE BALLOTS WERE IN THE HANDS OF THE LORD AND
SO ARE THE BABIES!!!!!!!!   THE REFORM CANDIDATE WON THE
ELECTORAL COLLEGE BY ONE VOTE OVER WHAT IS NEEDED!
GOD'S! HE IS THE MAJORITY!!!

December 15, 2000

Wisdom

IT'S NOT ABOUT BEING WHITE! IT'S ABOUT BEING RIGHT! IT'S NOT ABOUT BEING BLACK! IT'S ABOUT FINDING OUT WHAT YOU <u>REALLY</u> LACK! IT'S NOT ABOUT MONEY! MONEY IS NOT THE PROBLEM! THE GOVERNMENT HAS THROWN BILLIONS OF DOLLARS AT THE PROBLEM, YET NOT SOLVING THE PROBLEM!!! THE PROBLEM IS NOT LACK OF MONEY! THE PROBLEM IS FINDING OUT WHO YOU REALLY ARE! WHEN YOU KNOW WHO YOU ARE ... WHO GOD MADE YOU TO BE ... WHAT PURPOSE HE MADE YOU TO FULFILL, MONEY WILL COME TO YOU AS YOU FOLLOW AFTER YOUR GOD-GIVEN PURPOSE! SO WILL WORK, DILIGENCE, EDUCATION AND RESPONSIBILITY!!!

December 16, 2000

IF YOU AREN'T CRYIN' OUT TO GOD! YOU AREN'T DYIN' OUT TO SELF! IF YOU SAY YOU ARE ALREADY DEAD ... CRUCIFIED WITH CHRIST ... AND YOU'RE STILL CRYIN,' . . ABOUT ANYTHING OTHER THAN SOULS ... YOU AIN'T DEAD!!! DEAD FOLKS DON'T CRY! NOT ABOUT THEIR CIRCUMSTANCES. THEY CRY OUT FOR LOST SOULS! THAT IS WHY OUR CIRCUMSTANCES ARE BROKEN, AT TIMES, SO THAT WE WILL SUBMIT TO GOD!!! YOU CRUCIFY YOUR BODY WITH INTERCESSION! PRAYING IN THE HOLY GHOST! YOU RENEW YOUR MIND, WILL AND EMOTIONS WITH THE WORD OF GOD! READING, STUDYING, MEDITATING, MEMORIZING! YOU KEEP YOUR SPIRIT CLEAN THROUGH OBEDIENCE TO GOD'S WILL AND TO HIS WORD! GOD DOES NOT MOVE BECAUSE WE HAVE PROBLEMS! HE MOVES BECAUSE WE TAKE HIM AT HIS WORD AND WE WORK THE WORD INSTEAD OF THE PROBLEM!!! THE WORD ... GOD ... WORKS THE WAY THAT GOD ... THE WORD ... HAS WORKED SINCE THE BEGINNING OF TIME! BY SPEAKING! GOD SPOKE. IT WAS. WE SPEAK AND SO SHALL IT BE!!! SPEAK WORD ONLY! NOT MIXED AND MINGLED! BUT PURE WORD BRINGS A PURE HARVEST BECAUSE THE SEED IS PURE!!! WE DON'T KNOW WHERE WE ARE GOING BECAUSE WE DO NOT FOLLOW THE DIRECTIONS OF OUR LEADER TO GET WHERE WE

ARE SUPPOSED TO GO! IT IS AMAZING HOW ONE CAN KNOW AND REALIZE AND OBTAIN SPECIFIC DIRECTIONS SO THAT THEY MAY ARRIVE AT A SPECIFIC BUILDING IN A CERTAIN CITY. YET, EXPECT TO HAPHAZARDLY, UNRESTRICTEDLY, LOP ALONG, ANY OLD WAY TO GET TO THAT HEAVENLY CITY WHOSE BUILDER AND MAKER IS GOD!!! DECEIVED AND BEING DECEIVED!!! AS THE SONG HAS SAID, "EVERYBODY TALKIN' 'BOUT HEAV'N AIN'T GOIN' THERE!"

December 18, 2000

CONFESSION IS POSSESSION!!! POSSESSION IS 9/10 OF THE LAW. BUT IN GOD, CONFESSION IS POSSESSION <u>AND</u> THE LAW!!!

December 19, 2000

Knowledge

NO MAN KNOWS THE DAY NOR THE HOUR. BUT IT IS NOT UNLAWFUL TO KNOW THE YEAR.

December 20, 2000

MAN CAN GIVE YOU A PAT ON THE BACK, BUT GOD CAN GIVE YOU A NEW BACK. GOD STILL REIGNS SUPREME!!! HIS JUDGMENTS ARE TRUE AND RIGHTEOUS ALTOGETHER!!! HE SETS UP KINGS AND PULLS DOWN AUTHORITIES! HIS WORD IS MIGHT AND POWER! HE WILL HAVE JURISDICTION IN THE HALLS OF JUSTICE! HE WILL NO LONGER BE SET ASIDE FOR PRIDE AND PRIVILEGE! HE IS THE MIGHTY ONE! HIS WORD RULES! THE LAST GOVERNMENT WAS ONLY A TEST. IT FAILED MISERABLY IN HONESTY, INTEGRITY, TRUTH! HIT: H FOR HONESTY, I FOR INTEGRITY, AND T FOR TRUTH! THESE ARE THE BIG THREE IN MY INNER CIRCLE!!! IF YOU ARE NOT ON THE FOUNDATION OF TRUTH ... YOUR HOUSE SHALL FALL ... YOUR GOVERNMENT SHALL FAIL ... WHETHER POLITICAL, DOMESTIC, ECONOMIC OR SOCIAL! THE HIERARCHIES OF THE HEAVENS SHALL HAVE DOMINION. THE LAST LEG OF HONOR SHALL BE TRIED FOR CREDIBILITY. I AM PUTTING IN PLACE MEN AND WOMEN OF HONOR. DO NOT ANSWER THE CALL TO SERVE IF YOU ARE FRAGILE IN FORTHRIGHTNESS! TRUTH IS AN ARMY! IF YOU CANNOT KEEP PACE WITH ITS POWER AND DIGNITY, STEP ASIDE!!! THERE ARE NO FREELOADERS IN THE ARMY OF GOD! GUT-BUSTING GALL WILL TAKE PRECEDENCE OVER LIES AND LAURELS! IF IT AIN'T TRUTH IT AIN'T GOD! IF IT AIN'T GOD IT'S GOING DOWN!!! YOU CHOOSE ... DOWN AND DIRTY IS GOING UNDER. THE WICKED ONE IS LOSING HIS THUNDER. <u>THE NATIONS ARE GETTING IN ALIGNMENT FOR THE BIG BATTLE! WHO IS ON THE LORD'S SIDE ... COME ON DOWN!!! ARMAGEDDON IS THE ARK OF SAFETY!!!</u>

December 22, 2000

Affirmation of Faith

WHENEVER YOU DECLARE THE NAME OF GOD YOU ARE DECLARING HIS WORD! HIS WORD IS HIS NAME! WHAT EVER GOD DECLARES ... I DECLARE! WHATEVER GOD MAKES, I MAKE BECAUSE I SPEAK HIS WORD AND HIS WORD MAKES WHATEVER IS SPOKEN!!! WHATEVER GOD DESIRES, I DESIRE! I HAVE THE FAITH OF GOD!!! FAITH THAT MOVES MOUNTAINS BECAUSE I WALK IN LOVE, I TALK IN LOVE, I THINK IN LOVE, I OBEY IN LOVE, I OVERCOME IN LOVE!!! GOD IS LOVE SO I ALWAYS HAVE VICTORY BECAUSE I ALWAYS HAVE GOD!!! I AM THE RIGHTEOUSNESS OF GOD!! AND I DO HAVE GOOD SUCCESS, BECAUSE I WALK IN GOD! I TALK IN GOD! I THINK IN GOD! I ACT IN GOD! AND ALL MY WAYS ARE PROSPEROUS BECAUSE GOD OBEYS HIS WORD!!! THE WORD WORKS BUT YOU HAVE TO SPEAK IT CONTINUOUSLY IN ORDER FOR IT TO WORK! AND TO KEEP ON WORKING!!!

WHATEVER GOD DOES ... I DO!!! WHATEVER GOD SAYS ... I SAY!!! WHATEVER GOD THINKS ... I THINK!!! WHATEVER GOD WANTS ... I WANT!!! WHATEVER GOD HATES ... I HATE!!! WHATEVER GOD GLORIES IN ... I GLORY IN!!! WHATEVER GOD PURPOSES ... I PURPOSE!!! WHATEVER GOD SPEAKS ... I SPEAK!!! WHATEVER GOD CORRECTS ... I CORRECT!!! WHATEVER GOD SETS IN ORDER ... I SET IN ORDER!!! WHATEVER GOD REWARDS ... I REWARD!!! I AM BEING CONFORMED INTO HIS IMAGE AND INTO HIS LIKENESS!!! HALLELUJAH TO THE LAMB OF GOD WHICH TAKES AWAY OUR CARNAL NATURE!!!

December 27, 2000

January
2001

Babies see the great good force ... Amor.
Filtering every facet of the abundant activity,
Parcels of impregnated ... Odes of Love.

Part III

Thus Saith The Lord
The Redeemer of Israel
and His Holy One

Thus saith the Lord, thy redeemer and He that formed thee in the womb. I am the Lord that makes all things, that stretches forth the heavens alone, that spreads abroad the earth by myself, that frustrates the tokens of the liars, and makes the diviners mad, that turns the wise men backward and makes their knowledge foolish, that confirms the word of his servant and performs the counsel of his messengers.

Isaiah Chapter Forty-Four,
Verses Twenty-Four to Twenty-Six

Prophecy

I FORMED THEM IN THE WOMB! THAT IS WHERE THEY ARE CREATED! THE DECLARATION OF INDEPENDENCE DECLARES THAT: THEY ARE ENDOWED BY THEIR CREATOR WITH THE INALIENABLE RIGHT TO LIFE! THE UNITED STATES GOVERNMENT HAS ABOLISHED THIS RIGHT TO LIFE!!! IF THIS INALIENABLE RIGHT TO LIFE IS NOT REINSTATED IN THE GOVERNMENT OF THE UNITED STATES ... AMERICA WILL SEE UNPRECEDENTED HORROR AND MAYHEM!!! JUDGMENT SAITH THE LORD!!!

THE ADMINISTRATION THAT HAS BEEN REPLACED IN THE WHITE HOUSE HAS BEEN A TOWER OF BABEL! A GOVERNMENT THAT HAS REPEATEDLY ADVOCATED LAWS AND PRECEPTS THAT HAVE ABOLISHED THE LAWS OF GOD! THE NUMBER ONE LAW OF GOD IS: YOU SHALL HAVE NO OTHER GODS BEFORE ME!!! IN AMERICA NOW THERE ARE VERY FEW GODS THAT ARE NOT BEFORE THE ONE TRUE LIVING GOD! IN AMERICA THE GODS OF TV AND COMPUTER, CDS AND VIDEOS, DVDS AND SPORTS AND ENTERTAINMENT TAKE PRIORITY, ABOVE PRAYER, AMENITIES, SOCIAL GRACES. IN AMERICA THE GOVERNMENT AND THE MEDIA HAVE APPROVED AND SANCTIONED, MADE LEGAL, PALATABLE THE KILLING OF AMERICAN BABIES!!! WHICH GOD SAYS IS ABOMINATION IN PROVERBS 6:17, "HANDS THAT SHED INNOCENT BLOOD!" THE AMERICAN GOVERNMENT HAS LEGALIZED AND MADE REPUTABLE ANOTHER LAW THAT GOD'S WORD SAYS IS ABOMINATION. LEVITICUS 18:22 THOU SHALL NOT LIE WITH MANKIND AS WITH WOMANKIND! IT IS ABOMINATION! LEVITICUS 20:13 IF A MAN LIES WITH MANKIND AS HE LIES WITH WOMANKIND BOTH OF THEM HAVE COMMITTED ABOMINATION: THEY SHALL SURELY BE PUT TO DEATH! VERSE 22, YOU SHALL KEEP ALL MY STATUTES AND ALL MY JUDGMENTS AND DO THEM: THAT THE LAND (AMERICA IN OUR CASE) SPEW YOU NOT OUT! BECAUSE UNDER THE NEW COVENANT WE DO NOT LITERALLY KILL THOSE WHO DO COMMIT EVIL DOES NOT MAKE THEIR EVILS LESS EVIL. IT ONLY MEANS THAT A BETTER COVENANT IS IN FORCE! A COVENANT OF FORGIVENESS! NOT A

COVENANT OF DEBAUCHERY ... THAT ANYTHING GOES ... IS ALLOWED AND PERMITTED UNDER THE AUSPICES OF FREEDOM AND FREE RIGHTS! FREEDOM AND FREE RIGHTS DO NOT ABOLISH THE LAWS OF GOD!!! THE NEW COVENANT ALLOWS FOR COMPLETE FORGIVENESS! FORGIVENESS, WHEN SIN IS REPENTED OF AND FORSAKEN! SIN IS STILL SIN NO MATTER HOW MANY LAWS WASHINGTON, DC MAKES LEGAL! JUDGMENT IS AT THE DOOR! HAS ALREADY BEGUN IN SMALL MEASURE! BUT WILL INCREASE SOON IF MEASURES ARE NOT PUT IN PLACE TO ERADICATE THE KILLING OF AMERICAN BABIES!!!

January 3, 2001

Note: The destructions foretold came to pass. But the worst is not yet over. On April 1, 2004, Special Agent from the Capitol Building in Washington, D.C. phoned me to inform me that he is sending a recommendation to the Assistant Attorney General's Office that I be arrested and prosecuted because of the warnings of more and greater destructions that I continue to send to the officials in the government.

Prophecy

THE MINISTRIES SHALL SEE YOU AGAIN AND AGAIN FOR YOU ARE MINE ANOINTED SAITH THE LORD. REBUKE WHEN I SAY TO REBUKE. REFRAIN WHEN I SAY TO REFRAIN. REGARD NO MAN'S IMAGE. YOU ARE MADE IN MY LIKENESS. TAKE HEED ONLY UNTO ME AND TO MY WORD. I QUICKEN WHOM I WILL QUICKEN AND RAISE WHOM I WILL RAISE, BUT I WILL NOT BE CONTAMINATED WITH DROSS SAITH THE LORD. REMOVE FROM MY HOUSE ALL THAT POLLUTES AND DEFILES. DENY WHOM I DENY AND REWARD WHOM I REWARD. CHASTISE WHOM I CHASTISE AND COUNSEL WHOM I COUNSEL, SAITH THE LORD GOD ALMIGHTY!!! JEHOVAH IS MY NAME!!!

January 5, 2001

THE MYSTERY OF MIRACLES IS IN YOU SAITH THE LORD. I AM GIVING YOU A NEW BEGINNING! DO NOT BE ALARMED WHEN I BEGIN TO MOVE IN SIGNS AND WONDERS! I WILL SHOW YOU THINGS TO COME. I WILL GIVE YOU FAVOR AND REQUIRE FULL OBEDIENCE FROM YOU. I HAVE TESTED YOUR SURVIVAL SKILLS BECAUSE OF THE TASK THAT IS SET BEFORE YOU. YOU WILL HAVE DISCERNMENT IN THE MIDST OF CHAOS AND YOU WILL SEE THE BIG PICTURE AND NOT BE MOVED BY SITUATIONAL ETHICS BUT BY THE SPIRIT, SAITH THE LORD OF HOSTS!!! VICTORY IS A BY-PRODUCT OF PERSISTENCE. I AM GIVING YOU THE KEYS TO JUSTICE AND RIGHTEOUSNESS!!! GUARD YOUR HEART!!! LET NOT AMBIGUITY AND HYPOCRISY ENTER YOUR KNOWLEDGE OF WISDOM. BUT LET BIBLICAL CONSERVATISM BE THE GUIDELINE FOR ACTION AND STRENGTH. IF IT ISN'T RIGHT...IT ISN'T GOD! AND IF IT ISN'T GODLY, IT ISN'T RIGHT! NOT RIGHT-WING POLITICS!!! BUT ULTIMATE POWER OF TRUTH, SANITY, PRINCIPLE, JUSTICE, FORTHRIGHTNESS, AND MORAL INTEGRITY!!!

January 7, 2001

I AM SUPPLYING <u>ALL</u> OF YOUR NEEDS, YOUR DESIRES ALSO! I AM GIVING YOU THE DESIRES OF YOUR HEART AND ALL THE THINGS THAT DELIGHT YOU BECAUSE YOU DO THE THINGS THAT DELIGHT ME ... HEAL OTHERS, WIN SOULS AND MEET THEIR NEEDS!!!

January 10, 2001

Prophecy

ABORTION IS COMING DOWN! ABORTION IS COMING DOWN!

January 12, 2001

GO ON MY CHILD! FULFILL YOUR DESTINY. PURITY OF POWER. LOVE UNTAINTED. MEEK, YET BOLD. WALK ON IN MY SPIRIT AS YOU ARE DOING. DO NOT LOOK BACK. DO NOT LET YOUR CHILDREN'S FAILURE TO WALK IN MY WILL DIMINISH YOUR ULTIMATE GOALS AND CALLING. I AM JUDGING MY PEOPLE ON THEIR OWN INDIVIDUAL OBEDIENCES. YOU TAUGHT. YOU TRAINED. WHEN CHILDREN ARE OF AGE, THEY ARE HELD ACCOUNTABLE FOR THEIR OWN CHOICES. I AM COMING SOON AND MY REWARD IS WITH ME TO GIVE EVERY MAN ACCORDING TO HIS OWN WORKS, WHETHER THEY BE GOOD OR EVIL. I LOVE YOU, MY CHILD. REST IN ME AND CONTINUE TO OBEY ME. I AM OPENING DOORS FOR YOU TO FULFILL YOUR DESTINY AND CALLING. STAY CONSECRATED AND CONTENT. GODLINESS WITH CONTENTMENT IS GREAT GAIN. HEALING IS THE CHILDREN'S BREAD! CONTINUE TO SERVE IT TO THE MASSES. LOVE IS ETERNAL. THE ONLY THING THAT WILL LAST. BESTOW MY GOODNESS.

January 15, 2001

I SEE YOU. I SEE INSIDE YOUR HEART. I KNOW YOUR HEART'S CRY. I SEE THE PAIN YOU BEAR. I KNOW YOUR INNERMOST THOUGHTS AND FEELINGS. I AM GIVING YOU POWER TO COMMIT ALL THINGS UNTO ME. I AM GIVING YOU FORTITUDE. YOUR FAITH IS IN ME. I WILL NOT DISAPPOINT. I WILL GIVE YOU THE THINGS THAT YOU ASK OF ME. I WILL KEEP YOUR FAMILY SAFE FROM HARM AND DANGER. I WILL BRING THEM INTO OBEDIENCE. I WILL GIVE YOU NEW INSIGHT INTO REACHING THE LOST, THE DYING, THE SICK AND THE SUFFERING. I AM TELLING YOUR LOVED ONES TO PREPARE FOR MY COMING FOR IT IS VERY SOON, SAITH THE LORD!

TIME IS OF THE ESSENCE, MY CHILD! BE ABOUT THY FATHER'S BUSINESS. I KNOW YOUR HEART'S DESIRE. I KNOW YOU WANT TO BE ALL THINGS TO ALL PEOPLE. I KNOW YOU WANT TO HELP EVERYONE YOU SEE AND EVEN THOSE YOU DO NOT SEE! I KNOW FIRST AND FOREMOST, YOU WANT YOUR LOVED ONES SAVED, SANCTIFIED, AND FILLED WITH THE HOLY GHOST, WALKING IN THE WILL AND THE WAYS OF THIS MINISTRY. I KNOW THAT YOU CANNOT ALWAYS SEE THE GOOD THAT YOU ARE DOING AND YOU WONDER WHY IT IS TAKING SUCH A LONG TIME TO GET YOUR PRAYERS ANSWERED FOR YOUR FAMILY. YOUR PRAYERS ARE ANSWERED. FUNCTION IN FAITH. BE NOT MOVED BY CIRCUMSTANCES. BY WHAT YOU SEE OR WHAT YOU DO NOT SEE. IF I SAID...IF I PROMISED IT...IT IS FINISHED!!!

January 16, 2001

Prophecy

FIGHT ON FOR THE TRUTHS OF MY WILL BEING DONE IN THE SANCTUARY! IT IS NOT BY MIGHT, NOR BY POWER, BUT BY THE SPIRIT, SAITH THE LORD OF HOSTS!!! I PROCLAIM YOUR DESTINY. I SPOKE IT INTO EXISTENCE. YOU WILL FULFILL ALL THAT I HAVE FOR YOU TO DO. BE NOT WEARY. BE STRONG AND OF GOOD COURAGE! GOOD COURAGE ALWAYS SAYS EXACTLY WHAT I SAY...WHAT IS WRITTEN!!! STRENGTH IS ME! BE FILLED WITH ME AT ALL TIMES...IN EVERY SITUATION! I AM MORE THAN ENOUGH! I AM ALL THINGS TO ALL PEOPLE! DISPLAY MY GIFTS! GIVE MY PEOPLE WHATEVER THEY NEED!!! GIVE THEM MY GLORY! GIVE THEM MY POWER TO CONQUER ALL SIN AND ALL DOMINION THAT RISES TO BE ABOVE MY AUTHORITY! MY WORD IS FINAL AUTHORITY!!! USE WORD TO CONQUER. USE WORD TO LIVE! USE WORD TO BREATH! USE WORD TO THINK! USE WORD TO UNDERSTAND! USE WORD TO SOLVE EVERY PROBLEM! USE WORD TO DIMINISH THE DARKNESS! USE WORD TO BE VICTORIOUS! USE WORD TO BE SUBMISSIVE TO MY WILL AND TO MY PURPOSE! USE WORD IN EVERY CIRCUMSTANCE! USE WORD IN YOUR SITTING DOWN AND IN YOUR RISING UP! USE WORD IN YOUR GOING OUT AND IN YOUR COMING IN! USE WORD TO SAY, TO DO, AND TO MOVE! USE MY WORD! WITHOUT MY WORD YOU ARE NOTHING! MY WORD *IS* ME! I AM LOVE! LOVE CONQUERS!!!

January 16, 2001

YOU HAVE STOOD BEFORE ME IN HONESTY AND INTEGRITY. YOU HAVE BEEN COUNTED AMONG THE MIGHTY IN THIS NATION. YOUR CRIES AND PETITIONS WILL BE ANSWERED. YOUR PRAISES ARE WHAT MOVES MY ANGELS TO PERFORM!!! GREATER GRACE IS UPON YOU THAN EVER BEFORE. THE GRACE OF GOD AND THE COUNSEL OF GLORY. I AM GIVING YOU MANY PEOPLE TO WORK WITH YOU, SAITH THE LORD!!!!! COUNSELS OF GREATNESS ARE EMANATING FROM MY THRONE. I AM MOVING IN HIGH PLACES THROUGHOUT THIS NATION. I AM GIVING GLORY BACK TO THE GOVERNMENT. I AM STABILIZING THE MONUMENTS OF

GREATNESS THAT HAVE BEEN ABOUT TO TOPPLE. THE FOUNDATION THAT THIS NATION WAS BUILT UPON SHALL BE SHORED UP AND MAINTAINED! I WILL BE RIDICULED NO LONGER FOR MY TRUTH, FOR IT IS I THAT ESTABLISHED THIS NATION! AND I WILL BE THE ONE WHO BRINGS BACK THE GLORY! LIBERALISM IS COMING DOWN. SIN IS STILL SIN NO MATTER WHAT NAME YOU LABEL IT. CALLING EVIL GOOD AND GOOD EVIL IS STILL ABOMINATION!!!!!!! ABOMINATIONS ARE COMING DOWN SAITH THE LORD GOD ALMIGHTY!!! AMERICA IS A MIGHTY NATION BECAUSE SHE WAS BUILT UPON GODLY PRINCIPLES. WHEN SHE BEGAN TO INCORPORATE UNGODLY PRINCIPLES SHE BEGAN TO DETERIORATE. I AM RESTORING HER GREATNESS BECAUSE I AM RESTORING HER GOODNESS. I AM RESTORING AMERICA BACK TO ME SAITH THE LORD OF HOSTS! WHAT CAN MAN DO WHEN THE LORD HAS SPOKEN!!! THE MIGHTIEST SHALL PREVAIL! THERE IS BUT ONE GOD AND MY POWER SHALL HAVE DOMINION!!! BONDAGES, BE BROKEN AND SET ASIDE NOW IN THESE UNITED STATES OF AMERICA! BE LOOSED, AMERICA, INTO YOUR DESTINY! A DESTINY OF PRIDE AND LOVE FOR INTEGRITY AND DECENCY AND HONOR! YOU ARE DELIVERED FROM FILTH, DEBAUCHERY, AND DEGRADATION! YOU ARE RESTORED TO RIGHTEOUSNESS AND WHOLENESS SAITH THE LORD OF THE UNIVERSE!!!

January 18, 2001

Prophecy

MY GLORY OR YOURS?

January 19, 2001

I AM CALLING MINISTRIES OF MIRACLES INTO THE PRISON MINISTRY. I AM REESTABLISHING HEALTH, WEALTH AND POWER TO THE REALM OF THE FAITHFUL!!!! WHAT IS MINE BELONGS TO YOU! WHAT I HAVE, I GIVE TO YOU. YOU ARE FAITHFUL AND I AM RESTORING WEALTH TO MY PEOPLE. FINANCES ARE NOT TO HEAP UP!!!!! FINANCES ARE TO SPREAD THE GOSPEL! I GIVE TO MY PEOPLE SO THAT MY GLORY WILL BE MADE KNOWN TO THE EARTH. I AM THE "I AM." SPREAD MY WORD. DELIVER MY PEOPLE. SET THEM FREE FROM BONDAGES, PERVERSION, AND ADDICTIONS. HEAL THE SICK! RAISE THE DEAD! CAST OUT DEVILS! FREELY YOU HAVE RECEIVED!!! FREELY GIVE! HEAP NOT UP TO YOURSELVES TREASURES ON EARTH, BUT LAY UP TREASURES IN HEAVEN AS YOU WIN THE LOST AT ANY COST!!! I AM GRACING MY DESTINY – LOCK – STOCK – AND BARREL!!! BONDAGES ARE BROKEN THUS SAITH THE LORD! THE ALMIGHTY! THE HOLY ONE OF ISRAEL! I AM THAT I AM! I HAVE SPOKEN! I AM LOOSING MINISTERING SPIRITS NOW!!! IT IS DONE!!!

January 23, 2001

YES, MY CHILD! OBEY ME! GIVE ME PRAISE ABUNDANTLY! DO NOT FRET AND DO NOT DOUBT! I WILL SAFELY BRING YOU OUT. I HAVE CALLED YOU, MY CHILD. OBEY MY VOICE AT ALL TIMES! YES, MY CHILD ... I SEE THE THINGS THAT HINDER YOU ... BUT SOON A GREAT AWAKENING IN THIS LAND! I WILL OVERSEE. I WILL MAKE THE CROOKED PLACES COME IN LINE WITH MY WORD!!! I WILL BRING DOWN HIGH PLACES ... AND MAKE YOU TO RIDE THE WINGS OF THE WIND! YOU ARE MINE ANOINTED ... STAY IN MY WILL AT ALL COSTS SAITH THE HOLY RIGHTEOUS

ONE!!! I AM SEVERING THE UMBILICAL CORD OF RITUAL AND TRADITION! MY POWER WILL NOT BE RESTRAINED!!!

January 27, 2001

A DEARTH IS COMING UPON THIS LAND!

January 28, 2001

Note: September 30, 2002 World News: Worst drought in recorded history in the United States. The Colorado River is the lowest in one hundred and fifty years. Cost to tourism in Colorado alone is $700 million.

THE BRIDGE IS THE BLESSING! PURITY IS THE POWER!!!

January 29, 2001

Wisdom

READY-MADE RITUALS WHEN YOU JOIN A CHURCH THAT IS NOT BUILT UPON THE STATUTES OF THE FAITH!

January 1, 2001

POWER IS THE MOST IMPORTANT THING! THERE IS PLENTY OF PREACHING AND TEACHING IN THE CHURCHES, BUT THE POWER TO HEAL THE SICK AND TO CAST DEVILS IS MISSING IN AN ONGOING CONSISTENT MANNER AS THE LORD COMMANDED! THE WORD OF GOD IS POWER, BUT FOR IT TO BE MANIFESTED CONSISTENTLY AND IN FULL MEASURE, PEOPLE MUST BE RELEASED TO OBEY THE GIFTS AND THE CALLINGS OF GOD UPON THEIR LIVES!!! WHEN PASTORS RESTRICT THE MOVING OF THE SPIRIT OF GOD IN THEIR CHURCHES THEY ARE RESPONSIBLE FOR HOLDING BACK HEALINGS, MIRACLES AND DELIVERANCES BECAUSE GOD UTILIZES THE WHOLE BODY OF CHRIST, NOT JUST ONE PERSON TO FULFILL ALL MINISTRY!!! THIS IS TRUE, ALSO, FOR THE SPOKEN GIFTS OF PROPHECY, TONGUES AND INTERPRETATION WHICH ARE NEEDED TO EDIFY, EXHORT AND COMFORT!!!!!

January 11, 2001

THE FEAR OF DEATH HAS CAUSED MANY TO SUCCUMB AND FALTER AT THEIR BURDENS AND THEIR TRIALS. THE FEAR OF DEATH TO ONESELF. THE FEAR OF BEING COMPLETELY SOLD OUT TO GOD SO AS TO BE OSTRACIZED FROM FRIENDS AND FAMILY AND EVEN OTHER SPIRITUAL PEOPLE. THE FEAR OF NOT BEING UNDERSTOOD. THE FEAR OF NOT BEING SEEN IN THE PROPER MANNER. THE FEAR OF NOT BEING ESTEEMED AS PART OF THE GROUP. THE FEAR OF BEING EXCLUDED FROM ONE'S OWN PEER GROUP. BUT WHAT IS THIS COMPARED TO THE LORD SAYING "NOT EVERYONE THAT SAYS, LORD, LORD, BUT," THAT IS A BIG WORD, "BUT HE THAT DOES THE WILL OF MY FATHER WHICH IS IN HEAVEN SHALL ENTER INTO THE KINGDOM OF HEAVEN!"

THIS CERTAINLY DOES AWAY WITH THE FALSE TEACHING, A LITTLE DAB WILL DO YOU! OR EVEN MORE PERVERSE, YOU CAN KEEP ON SINNING AND STILL MAKE IT INTO HEAVEN!

January 17, 2001

Wisdom

GOD IS LOOKING FOR SOMEONE LITTLE ENOUGH SO THAT HE CAN BE BIG!!! HE IS LOOKING FOR SOMEONE QUIET ENOUGH SO THAT THEY CAN HEAR HIS VOICE! HE IS LOOKING FOR SOMEONE WHO NO LONGER NEEDS PATS ON THE BACK, APPROVAL OF THE MASSES, ACCOLADES AND HONORS! HE IS LOOKING FOR SOMEONE WHO WILL HONOR HIM AT <u>ALL</u> TIMES AND IN <u>EVERY</u> SITUATION! IN HARD TIMES. IN HELLS AND HIGH WATERS. HE IS LOOKING FOR SOMEONE HE CAN PROMOTE AND EXALT WITH HIS PRESENCE AND HIS POWER! SOMEONE WHO IS NOT MOVED BY ANYTHING BUT HIM! WHO IS COMPLETELY SOLD OUT TO HIS FORTITUDE AND TO HIS FAITHFULNESS! WHO SAYS, YES, LORD, YES, TO YOUR WILL AND TO YOUR WAY! WHO SAYS YES, LORD, YES, I WILL TRUST YOU AND OBEY! WHEN THE SPIRIT SPEAKS TO ME (YOU HAVE TO SHUT UP SO THAT HE CAN!) WITH MY WHOLE HEART I'LL AGREE AND MY ANSWER WILL BE YES, LORD, YES!!!

HE IS LOOKING FOR SOMEONE WHO THRILLS TO HIS TOUCH! AND IS NOT AFRAID TO GO ALL THE WAY!!! TO BE PREGNANT WITH SOULS...YOU HAVE TO GO ALL THE WAY! YOU HAVE TO BE INTIMATE WITH THE GROOM IN ORDER TO BEAR CHILDREN! A LITTLE KISS AND A LITTLE HAND CLAPPING DOES NOT GET THE JOB DONE! BUT WHEN HE GETS DOWN INSIDE OF YOU ... YOU DO GET PREGNANT AND BRING FORTH CHILDREN!!! WHEN ZION TRAVAILS SHE WILL BRING FORTH SONS AND DAUGHTERS! WHEN YOU BECOME INTIMATE WITH THE CHRIST YOU WILL BIRTH CHRISTIANS!!!

January 19, 2001

LITTLE FOXES SPOIL THE VINE! Song of Solomon 2:16 LITTLE SINS SPOIL THE FRUIT! FRUIT WORKS THE GIFTS! GIFTS CONFIRM THE WORD! LITTLE SINS PREVENT THE WORD FROM BEING CONFIRMED! WHEN THE WORD IS NOT CONFIRMED, DOUBT AND FEAR PREVENT SOULS FROM COMING TO JESUS! THUS, SOULS ARE LOST BECAUSE OF YOUR LITTLE SINS! FOXES THAT SPOIL THE

VINE! A LITTLE LEAVEN LEAVENS THE WHOLE LUMP! I Corinthians 5:6 WHAT KILLS THE WORD? WORDS THAT ARE SPOKEN OUT OF THE WILL OF GOD DIMINISH POWER! POWER OF THE WORD IS DIMINISHED BY THE BELITTLING OF SPIRITUAL AUTHORITY!!! THE NAME OF GOD IS BLASPHEMED THROUGH THE EVIL INFLUENCE OF THE DISOBEDIENT!!! IF ANY MAN SPEAK, LET HIM SPEAK AS THE ORACLES OF GOD THAT GOD IN ALL THINGS MAY BE GLORIFIED!!! I Peter 4:11 THE WORDS OF OUR MOUTH ARE THE SWORD OF THE SPIRIT! MAKE SURE IT'S THE RIGHT SPIRIT!

IN THE SPIRIT REALM OF FAITH THERE DOES NOT ALWAYS NEED TO BE CONVERSATION AND FILLER. SOME QUIETNESS CAN BE HOLY QUIETNESS IF GIVEN TO THE LORD. ALL PRAYER DOES NOT EVEN NEED TO BE IN WORDS. SOME PRAYER NEEDS TO BE QUIETNESS. SOME PRAYER NEEDS TO BE SUBMITTED LISTENING, HEARING, EARNESTLY DESIRING THE LORD'S VOICE TO SPEAK DIRECTION, WISDOM, INSTRUCTION, COUNSEL. IF WE ARE ALWAYS SPEAKING, THE LORD WILL RARELY INTERRUPT TO SAY, "MY TURN!" HE SPEAKS READILY WHEN THERE IS A HEARING EAR!!! IS IT NOT A SAD COMMENTARY, ADDENDUM, THAT THE WORKS OF THE FLESH ARE MANIFESTED MORE OFTEN EVEN AMONG PROPONENTS OF CHRISTIANITY THAN THE WORKS OF GOD???

January 23, 2001

Prophetic Teaching

PRAYER IS NOT TO GET GOD TO DO WHAT HE SAID HE WOULD DO! IT IS TO GET US INTO HIS PRESENCE! BECAUSE WHEN WE GET INTO HIS PRESENCE ENOUGH WE WILL BELIEVE WHAT HE SAID! AND WHEN WE BELIEVE WHAT HE SAID HE WOULD DO ... HE DOES IT! I AM NOT TALKING ABOUT THINGS THAT ARE ON A CERTAIN TIMEFRAME OR SEASON. I AM TALKING ABOUT WHAT WE ARE SUPPOSED TO HAVE AND TO BE ENJOYING NOW! IT IS HIGH TIME FOR THE WEALTH OF THE WICKED TO BE TRANSFERRED OVER TO THE JUST! IT IS PAST TIME FOR THE RIGHTEOUS TO RECEIVE THEIR HEALINGS AND HEALTH! WHEN YOU ARE WILLING TO WORSHIP YOU DO RECEIVE! WHEN YOU DO NOT WORSHIP THAT IS DOUBT ... YOU DO NOT RECEIVE. BELIEVERS WORSHIP. DOUBTERS DO NOT. BELIEVERS ANTICIPATE PROVISION AND BLESSING. DOUBTERS ANTICIPATE LACK AND UNANSWERED PRAYER. WORSHIPPERS WIN. NON-WORSHIPPERS LOSE. WORSHIP IS SUBMISSION TO WORD! NOT A FEELING OF EUPHORIA. WORSHIP IS A WORK OF OBEDIENCE. IT IS WRITTEN, "BY WORKS WAS FAITH MADE PERFECT!" JAMES SAID IN CHAPTER 2, "SHOW ME YOUR FAITH WITHOUT YOUR WORKS, AND I WILL SHOW YOU MY FAITH BY MY WORKS!" WORSHIP IS WORK, THOUGH SEEMINGLY NOT SO WHEN SUBMITTED TO THE "I AM"! IT BECOMES AN ACT OF LOVE AND SURRENDER TO YOUR BELOVED!!! WHEN YOU ARE SUBMITTED TO WORD YOU ARE SURRENDERED!!! IT IS AN ACT OF LOVE! WHEN OFFERED UP IN OBEDIENCE IT BECOMES A BLISSFUL EXPERIENCE. THE FIRST STEP IS TO DO IT. TO OBEY. SOME SAY, I DON'T FEEL IT ... THE POWER BURNING AND SURGING. JESUS DIDN'T FEEL LIKE HAVING HIS HANDS AND FEET NAILED TO A TREE!!! BUT THAT WAS THE ORDER OF OPERATION FOR THE END RESULT THAT WAS DESIRED!

DESIRE WITHOUT SUBMISSION LEAVES A VERY FRUSTRATED PERSON! ASK ANYONE WHO HAS EXPERIENCED THIS BREACH IN A RELATIONSHIP. WE ARE NOT RECEIVING THE THINGS WE NEED FROM OUR BRIDEGROOM BECAUSE WE HAVE REFUSED TO LAY OUR LIFE DOWN FOR THE MANIFESTATION OF HIS GLORY. WHEN

WE LAY OUR LIFE DOWN TO THE ABANDONMENT OF WORSHIP WE MANIFEST THE GLORY OF THE LORD AND SUBMIT OUR LIFE TO DIVINE AUTHORITY, THUS RELEASING THE PROVISION AND DESIRE THAT WE LONG FOR! OBEDIENCE TO WORSHIP BRINGS PEACE, JOY, AND LOVE, ENABLING FAITH TO RISE TO ACCEPT THE PROMISES DESIRED!!! IF ANYTHING IS NOT RECEIVED, THE HEART OF THE WORSHIPPER IS SO FULL OF HIM THAT DELAY IS ENDURED WITH PEACE AND SUBMISSION. YOU MAY NEED TO GET A PICTURE OF HOW YOU WILLINGLY DESIRED TO PLEASE YOUR HUSBAND OR YOUR WIFE WHEN YOU FIRST MARRIED!!! YOU WANTED TO PLEASE! WITH THIS SAME MINDSET AND ABANDONMENT, EVEN NOW, SURRENDER YOUR HANG-UPS AND FOIBLES AND GIVE YOURSELF TO YOUR BRIDEGROOM SO THAT HE CAN THRILL YOU AND FILL YOU WITH SUCH JOY THAT EVERYTHING ELSE PALES IN COMPARISON TO THE PEACE AND POWER OF ALMIGHTY GOD!!! WE RECEIVE WHEN WE BELIEVE. WHEN WE <u>TRULY</u> BELIEVE HIS WORD WE OBEY IT, ACT UPON IT AND WORSHIP HIM FOR HIS GOODNESS AND HIS MIGHTY ACTS! WHEN WE OBEY HIM...NOTHING IS MISSING! JUST AS WHEN EVERYTHING WAS JUST RIGHT IN OUR EARTHLY RELATIONSHIP ... HOW SWEET IT WAS! GIVE THAT BODY OF YOURS TO THE MAN CHRIST JESUS! LET <u>HIM</u> WHIP (NO HE'S NOT A MASOCHIST) YOU INTO SHAPE WITH HIS PRESENCE AND HIS POWER!!! GO THE EXTRA MILE! DIE A LITTLE MORE ... THE THRILL IS WELL WORTH THE CHILL OR WHATEVER ELSE CRITICS GIVE YOU. THE INTIMACY WITH THE MAN JESUS IS MORE THAN ENOUGH TO OVERCOME <u>ALL</u> OBSTACLES! LET HIM MAKE YOU AND BREAK YOU AND LOVE YOU!!! COME INTO HIS <u>PRESENCE</u> WITH SURRENDER! YOU WILL DELIGHT HIM. AND HE WILL MEET YOUR EVERY NEED! AS IT IS WRITTEN, <u>DELIGHT YOURSELF IN THE LORD AND HE SHALL GIVE YOU THE DESIRES OF YOUR HEART</u>! WHY? BECAUSE HE KNOWS HE IS <u>FIRST</u> IN YOUR LIFE AND HIS LOVE FOR YOU GIVES HIM PLEASURE WHEN HE GIVES YOU YOUR HEART'S DESIRE! O, HALLELUJAH!!! WHAT A LOVER HE IS! YOU CAN READ ABOUT HIM IN THE HOLY SCRIPTURES IN THE SONG OF SOLOMON. HE DELIGHTS US! HIS LOVE FOR US IS PAST FINDING OUT! WHY SHOULD WE NOT LOSE OURSELVES IN SO GREAT A

LOVE AND GIVE TO HIM PLEASURE AS WE DANCE BEFORE HIM ENRAPTURED IN HIS PRESENCE?!? HIS PRESENCE IS WHAT FILLS ALL OF OUR NEEDS TO OVERFLOWING. AS WE SPILL OUT HIS LOVE AND PROVISION OTHERS RECEIVE HIS GLORY! WHAT A DEMONSTRATION OF THE ABUNDANCE OF GOD! WE WORSHIP HIM IN LOVE AND HIS LOVE RADIATES TO THE WORLD. WORSHIP IS THE WORK OF GOD! MANIFEST HIS GLORY! SATURATE THE EARTH! LET THE WORLD DRINK OF HIS GOODNESS AND TASTE OF HIS PLEASURE! IN THY PRESENCE IS FULLNESS OF JOY! THE JOY OF THE LORD IS MY STRENGTH!!! Psalms 29:2, 37:4, 149:3, John 4:24, Nehemiah 8:10

January 25, 2001

Fasting

FASTING IS MORE THAN DOING WITHOUT FOOD! FASTING IS TO PRODUCE BROKENNESS! GOD SPOKE THE THREE PURPOSES OF FASTING:

1)   TO BREAK THE BONDAGES OFF OF YOUR <u>OWN</u> MIND, YOUR WILL, AND YOUR EMOTIONS!!!

2)   TO LEAD YOU INTO A LIFE OF HUMILITY WHICH IS WALKING IN THE SPIRIT, TALKING IN THE SPIRIT, THINKING IN THE SPIRIT, ACTING IN THE SPIRIT, REACTING IN THE SPIRIT!

3)   TO SET THE CAPTIVES FREE!!! WITHOUT BEING FREE FROM HANG-UPS YOURSELF YOU CANNOT FULLY SET OTHERS FREE! FREEDOM COMES FROM FAITH! FAITH ... FULL BIBLE BELIEVING FAITH ... COMES FROM FASTING AND PRAYER! DOING WITHOUT FOOD IS NOT BIBLE FASTING! BIBLE FASTING IS DOING WITHOUT FOOD <u>AND</u> CRYING OUT TO GOD! WITHOUT CRYING OUT TO GOD ONE IS NOT ON A BIBLE FAST!!!

SOME SAY I AM GOING TO FAST AND DO A WORK FOR GOD! THE GREATEST THING THAT YOU CAN DO FOR GOD IS TO GET YOUR OWN MIND, YOUR OWN WILL, AND YOUR OWN EMOTIONS CLEANED OUT AND FULLY SUBMITTED TO THE WILL AND WORK OF ALMIGHTY GOD!!! THE MOST FRUITFUL FAST YOU CAN HAVE IS BY SHUTTING YOUR MOUTH! NOT JUST SHUTTING YOUR MOUTH TO FOOD, BUT SHUTTING YOUR MOUTH TO THE FRUIT OF YOUR OWN LIPS! SURRENDERING YOUR WORDS SO THAT THE MAN...THE MAIN ONE, CAN GIVE YOU HIS WORDS! SOME NEED TO FAST FROM TALKING!!! WHEN WE HUSH...GOD CAN SPEAK! WHEN GOD CAN SPEAK HE RELEASES POWER!!! WHEN POWER IS RELEASED...BONDAGES ARE BROKEN!!!   WHEN WE ARE BROKEN...FULLY SUBMITTED TO HIS PERFECT WILL AND WAYS...HIS MIGHTY ACTS CAN COME FORTH!!!   WHEN THAT TAKES PLACE...SIGNS, HEALINGS, MIRACLES, WONDERS...THE WORD OF GOD IS CONFIRMED!!! WHEN THE WORD OF GOD IS

CONFIRMED...REPENTANCE AMONG THE UNSAVED TAKES PLACE!!! IT'S CALLED REVIVAL!!!

FIVE STEPS TO REVIVAL:

1. SHUT UP!
2. FAST AND PRAY UP!
3. LISTEN UP! (TO GOD)
4. TALK UP! (EVANGELIZE)
5. ACT UPON WORD ONLY!!!

January 27, 2001

BED AT 2:30 AM. IN LOUISIANA FOR THREE-DAY REVIVAL IN FEDERAL PRISON, ALSO TEN DAY CITY-WIDE TENT REVIVAL. THE LORD AWAKENED ME AT 5 AM GIVING ME THIS WORD OF WISDOM. HOW AWESOME IS OUR GOD!

February 2001

To die true
Is to just begin to live.
Wonder fare
Waging War
on Greed.
Starlight humanity.
   Embracing the embryo.
   World-System seed.
Bubble bath
   Of bestial blood-letting
Severing our progeny.
   Where is destiny?
   Triumphant seed
Of provocative shrouds
   Negating man's
Eternal treasures.
   Speak forth – O Truth.
   The World is in Need!

Part IV

Behold
the
Fear
of
the
Lord

Lo, children are an heritage of the Lord!
And the fruit of the womb is His reward! As arrows in
the hand of a mighty man, so are children of the youth!

**Psalms One Hundred Twenty-Seven
Verses Three to Four**

Prophecy

YOU MUST TAKE HEED TO MY SPIRIT!!! I AM NOT A GOD THAT I SHOULD LIE! WHAT I HAVE SPOKEN SHALL SURELY COME TO PASS! I AM GETTING READY TO POUR OUT MY SPIRIT UPON ALL FLESH, BUT JUDGMENT MUST COME FIRST TO PURIFY THE CHURCH IN ORDER THAT THE SOULS SAVED WILL BE CHILDREN OF THE MOST HIGH AND NOT TWO-FOLD MORE THE CHILDREN OF HELL!!! INDEED, MANY APPEAR BEAUTIFUL OUTWARDLY, BUT WITHIN ARE FULL OF DEAD MEN'S BONES AND OF ALL UNCLEANNESS, LAWLESS, SAME SEX FORNICATION, DESPISING THE AUTHORITY OF THE WORD, ENVIOUS, PRESUMPTUOUS, PERNICIOUS, COVETOUS. EVEN SOME, ALSO, OUTWARDLY, APPEAR RIGHTEOUS UNTO MEN, BUT WITHIN ARE FULL OF HYPOCRISY AND INIQUITY, SELF-WILLED, NOT AFRAID TO SPEAK EVIL OF THOSE GOD IS USING, DESPISING THE AUTHORITY OF THE WORD, AND BLASPHEMING HIS GLORY! REJECTING THE GIFTS OF THE SPIRIT AND THE MOVING OF THE POWER OF GOD! I COUNSEL YOU TO BUY OF ME GOLD TRIED IN THE FIRE! THE FIRE OF FAITH THROUGH FASTING AND INTERCESSION! PRAYING IN THE HOLY GHOST OUTFITS THE VESSEL FOR SERVICE! SANCTIFYING THE INNER MAN WITH GRACE AND GLORY! PREPARING THE WAY OF THE LORD! READYING THE CHURCH FOR END TIME MINISTRY! CLEANSING IT FROM ALL FILTHINESS OF THE FLESH AND SPIRIT!!! GIVING UNCTION, INSTRUCTION, PREPARING FOR THE COMING OF THE MESSIAH!!! THE HOLY ONE OF ISRAEL!!!

I AM CONFUSING THE MINDS OF PEOPLE RIGHT NOW BECAUSE I AM BRINGING DOWN KINGDOMS AND SETTING UP AUTHORITIES! I WILL HAVE THE LAST SAY SAITH THE LORD! I WILL READY MY ARMIES TO FIGHT AT THE GREAT BATTLE. I WILL ROUND UP MY MEN OF MIGHT AND MY WOMEN OF POWER. I WILL ACCUSE THE ACCUSER OF MY BRETHREN! I WILL TAKE DOMINION OVER THE POWERS OF <u>ALL</u> LIVING AND THEN WILL I THRUST IN MY SICKLE AND I WILL REAP MY HARVEST!!! JUDGMENT IS AT THE DOOR!!! RIDICULE MINE ANOINTED NO

LONGER! FOR YOU SHALL SEE THE REAPER THRUST IN THE HARVEST! THE COMMUNION OF POWER SHALL BRING DOWN THE FORCES OF EVIL! I WILL STAY THE HAND OF THE WICKED ONE! HIS AUTHORITY AND MIGHT SHALL BE CONSUMED WITH THE BRIGHTNESS OF MY COMING!!! DELAY MY POWER NO LONGER BY HOLDING BACK MY SPIRIT FROM PERFORMING MIGHTY ACTS AND DEMONSTRATIONS OF POWER!!! BEFORE MY COMING TO CATCH MY BRIDE AWAY I SHALL USURP AUTHORITY IN HIGH PLACES!!! RIDICULE AND RUIN SHALL BEFALL KINGDOMS OF FRAUD! I AM CANCELING DEBTS AND BRINGING OUT OF PRISON MANY THAT WILL PREACH MY GOSPEL TO THE NATIONS! RELEASE MY POWER TO BRING IN MY HARVEST! DEMONSTRATIONS OF MIGHT AND MIRACLE HEALINGS AND DELIVERANCES FROM DRUGS AND ADDICTIONS! STOP THE FLOW OF MY GLORY NO LONGER LEST I REMOVE YOUR CANDLESTICK AND THE POWER OF YOUR DOMINION! MY SPIRIT SHALL PREVAIL UPON THIS NATION FOR THE LAST DAY END TIME HARVEST! PERJURE NOT YOURSELF AND BE NOT SO FOOLISH AS TO THINK YOU ARE AND THERE IS NO OTHER! I HAVE MANY THAT HAVE NOT BOWED TO THE GODS OF THIS WORLD WHO ARE WILLING TO DIE FOR TRUTH, JUSTICE AND HONOR!!! MY SPIRIT WILL PREVAIL IN THIS NATION AND I WILL TAKE BACK THE GLORY OF MY DOMINION!!!

STOP THE KILLING FIELDS OF ABORTION!!! STOP THE MUTILATION OF MY CREATION! CEASE THIS MADNESS SAITH THE LORD OF THE UNIVERSE! PLUNDER NO LONGER THE CREATION OF THE ALMIGHTY! THE CURSE CAUSELESS DOES NOT COME!!! BRING NOT THE DEVOURER UPON YOUR LAND! IT IS FUTILE FOR YOU TO FIGHT YOUR OWN CREATOR! DEATH WILL SHOW NO MERCY EVEN AS YOU HAVE SHOWN NO MERCY TO THE INNOCENT! THEIR BLOOD IS UPON YOUR HANDS AND UPON YOUR HEADS OF STATE! EXCEPT THE DECREE TO KILL THE UNBORN IS REMOVED FROM YOUR LAWS I WILL TAKE VENGEANCE SOON UPON THIS NATION! NOT JUST THE SAMPLING THAT HAS BEEN UNLEASHED THESE PAST MONTHS OF MURDER, MAYHEM, DEATH, FINANCIAL AND WEATHER

DISTRESSES, BUT BLOOD SHED IN THE STREETS!!! DO YOU THINK THAT IT CANNOT HAPPEN AGAIN ON THIS SOIL? CIVIL WAR? EVEN DEARTH? A FAMINE? NOT IN THIS NATION YOU SAY? WATCH AND WAIT. YOU CAN PRAY AND YOU CAN OBEY. OR THIS EVIL DAY OF DEATH WILL TAKE DOMINION UPON THIS LAND! YOU HAVE KILLED NEARLY 40 MILLION OF YOUR OWN FLESH AND BLOOD IN TAKING THE LIVES OF THE PRE-BORN BABIES SINCE JANUARY 1973! I WILL NO LONGER TOLERATE DEATH BY DECISION!!!!! LIFE IS MY DECISION AND SO IS DEATH. IT IS NOT YOUR POWER THAT BEGINS LIFE AND IT SHALL NOT BE YOUR POWER THAT TAKES LIFE SAYS THE GOD OF ALL FORCES, AND ALL POWERS AND ALL DOMINIONS!!! YOU CANNOT GAINSAY JUDGMENT!!! IT DOES NOT COME FROM YOUR LAWS. IT COMES FROM MINE.

February 2, 2001

The February 2 Prophecies telling of bloodshed in the streets and the vengeance of the Lord against Abortion was faxed to George W. Bush, President of the United States and to Trinity Broadcasting Network President Paul Crouch on April 4, 2001.

Prophecy

THERE WAS A TIME AT THE FOREFRONT OF THIS NATION'S GOVERNMENT THAT OUR LAWS WERE ONE. IT IS NO LONGER TRUE, FOR THIS NATION ERRS IN ITS JUDGMENTS AND DECISIONS OF LIFE! LIFE BELONGS TO ME. IT IS MY AUTHORITY TO KILL OR TO STAY THE HAND OF DEATH. MAN IS NOT GOD. AND MAN SHALL SOON SUFFER THE CONSEQUENCES OF THIS GREAT ERROR IN TAKING THE LIFE OF THE PRE-BORN!!! THE PRE-BORN HAVE SOULS! THE SOULS OF THE PRE-BORN THAT YOU HAVE MURDERED ARE WITH ME!!! YOU WILL SEE MUCH DESTRUCTION IN THIS LAND OF MIGHT AND POWER! IF YOU CONTINUE TO KILL THE PRE-BORN I WILL SET AT NAUGHT BROTHER AGAINST BROTHER AND CITY AGAINST CITY!!! YOU WILL SEE THE KILLING OF LOVED ONES AND FRIENDS! STOP THE MURDER OF THE INNOCENTS BEFORE I SEND GREATER DESTRUCTIONS UPON THIS NATION! <u>DO YOU BELIEVE THE ECONOMIC DECLINE IS THE POLITICS OF MEN? I HAVE INSTIGATED SANCTIONS UPON THESE UNITED STATES IN ORDER TO GET YOUR ATTENTION FOR THE CIVIL RIGHTS OF THE PRE-BORN!!!</u> YOU DO NOT WANT TO SEE HOW TIGHTLY I CAN MAKE THESE SANCTIONS!!! FAMINE DOES NOT COME UNLESS I ALLOW IT TO COME. DEATH BY STARVATION IS A HORRIBLE DEATH BUT NOT NEARLY AS HORRIBLE AS INTENTIONALLY KILLING THE FRUIT OF YOUR OWN WOMB!!!

February 2, 2001

Prophecy

I TEAR DOWN THE CANKERED DOMINIONS OF DOUBT AND UNBELIEF!!! I BREAK THE DOMINIONS OF DEATH AND DESTRUCTION! I OBLITERATE THE GREEDS OF THE GODS OF THIS WORLD! I ANNIHILATE THE OBESITIES OF HELLISH POWER STRUGGLES AND THE HATRED OF SO-CALLED CHRISTIANS AGAINST MY ANOINTED VESSELS! MY CALLED-OUT ONES! I CURSE TO THE ROOTS THE GLORY SEEKERS AND GAINSAYERS! YOU WILL NO LONGER TAINT MY SANCTUARY! YOU WILL BE DELIVERED OR YOU WILL GO OUT BY DEATH! YOU CAN NO LONGER STAND IN THE HOLY PLACE AND DISREGARD MY VESSELS OF HONOR AND AUTHORITY! I PURGE YOU EVEN NOW OF YOUR FILTHY DISREGARD OF THAT WHICH IS HOLY BEFORE ME ... HONORABLE AND FORTHRIGHT!!! YOU CAN NO LONGER SET ASIDE THE TRUTH OF MY WORD AND HOLD BACK MY GLORY AND MY GIFTS!!! I PURGE THESE VESSELS THAT REFUSE TO ACCEPT THE MOVING OF MY SPIRIT AND MY POWER TO WORK THE SIGNS AND THE WONDERS! MIRACLES, COME FORTH IN MY SANCTUARY!!! HEALINGS AND DELIVERANCES, BE DEMONSTRATED WITH MIGHT AND WITH POWER!!! I SURGICALLY REMOVE THE WHORE-MONGERING, DIABOLICAL DECREES THAT CALL MY PROGENY DESPICABLE AND MY SERVANTS UNWORTHY! REMOVE YOUR BLINDERS, LEADERS! I AM THE JUDGE! RIDICULE NO LONGER THE CALLED-OUT ONES! SAVE YOUR JUDGMENTS FOR THE END TIME LIARS! WHATEVER IS NOT ACCORDING TO MY WORD IS FALSEHOOD! DENY ME NO LONGER! MY WORD IS ALIVE!!! LET IT BE DEMONSTRATED IN ITS FULLNESS AND POWER SAITH THE MIGHTY ONE OF ISRAEL! THE FIRST AND THE LAST! I AM ALPHA AND OMEGA! THE BEGINNING AND THE END! BESIDES ME THERE IS NONE OTHER! LET THE MIRACLES BEGIN IN SPLENDOR AND IN RADIANCE!!! LET MY CHOSEN ONES COME FORTH IN DIGNITY AND IN FAVOR!!! I AM HAS SPOKEN!!!

February 7, 2001

Prophecy

I AM GIVING YOUR MANTLE TO YOUR SON. I AM GIVING IT TO HIM NOW WHILE YOU ARE ALIVE TO SEE IT.

February 25, 2001

MY PEOPLE WHICH ARE CALLED BY NAME SHALL DO EXPLOITS!!
 MY PEOPLE WHICH ARE CALLED BY NAME SHALL DO EXPLOITS!!
  MY PEOPLE WHICH ARE CALLED BY NAME SHALL DO EXPLOITS!!

February 26, 2001

Prophecy

THIS IS A NEW ERA! NO ONE THAT CALLS UPON MY NAME WILL BE LEFT BEHIND! I AM HEALING THE ONES THAT CALL IN SINCERITY AND TRUTH. THE OTHERS WILL NO LONGER BE ABLE TO STAND IN THE HOLY PLACE. I AM REMOVING THE TARES FROM THE WHEAT. THE DROSS FROM THE SILVER. THE IMITATORS FROM THE GOLD. THE GOATS FROM THE SHEEP. WHAT I SAY IS PURE. THE OTHERS WILL NO LONGER BE ABLE TO MIX AND MINGLE AND CONTAMINATE MY SANCTUARY. I AM CLEANING HOUSE! I AM DRESSING MY BRIDE FOR HER BRIDEGROOM! KEEP AWAY FROM THE WAYWARD AND THE LUKEWARM LEST THEY CONTAMINATE YOU WITH THEIR PRESENCE! BE NOT PARTAKER OF ANOTHER MAN'S SINS! HAVE NO COMPANY WITH A FORNICATOR, OR A RAILER, OR ONE WHO SPEAKS REPROACHFULLY OR BITTERLY. DO NOT ASSOCIATE WITH MALICE OR WICKEDNESS IN ANY FORM!!! DO NOT BID THE COVETOUS AND THE IDOLATER GODSPEED! KEEP YOURSELVES PURE FROM ALL UNGODLINESS! WITHOUT HOLINESS NO MAN SHALL SEE ME AT MY COMING!

February 27, 2001

Word of Exhortation

HOLINESS, WITHOUT WHICH NO MAN SHALL SEE THE LORD, COMES FROM BEING ... CONFORMED TO HIS IMAGE BY OBEDIENCE TO HIS WORD AND TO HIS WILL!   BY BEING TRANSFORMED BY THE RENEWING OF YOUR MIND AND BEING MADE PARTAKER OF HIS HOLINESS!!! NOW ... TODAY IS THE DAY OF SALVATION ... DELIVERANCE FOR BODY, MIND, SOUL, AND SPIRIT! NOW THE GOD OF PEACE MAKE YOU PERFECT, MATURE, THOROUGHLY FURNISHED IN THE GIFTS AND CALLINGS OF HIS HOLINESS!!! IN EVERY GOOD WORK TO DO HIS WILL, WORKING IN YOU THAT WHICH IS WELL-PLEASING IN HIS SIGHT, THROUGH JESUS CHRIST TO WHOM BE GLORY FOREVER AND EVER! SUFFER, ALLOW THE WORD OF EXHORTATION AND DELIVERANCE!!! LET THE PROPHETS SPEAK! LET US HAVE GRACE WHEREBY WE MAY SERVE GOD ACCEPTABLY WITH REVERENCE AND GODLY FEAR!!! FOR OUR GOD IS A CONSUMING FIRE!!! SEE THAT YOU REFUSE NOT HIM THAT SPEAKS! FOR IF THEY ESCAPED NOT WHO REFUSED HIM THAT SPOKE ON EARTH, MOSES AND THE PROPHETS, MUCH MORE SHALL NOT WE ESCAPE, IF WE TURN AWAY FROM HIM THAT SPEAKS FROM HEAVEN!!!

February 2, 2001

EVERY MIRACLE HAS A PRICE TAG! SOMEONE PAYS WITH SUBMISSION AND OBEDIENCE! THE LORD SUFFERED STRIPES FOR THE HEALING, BUT YOUR OWN OBEDIENCE HELPS OR YOUR OWN DISOBEDIENCE HINDERS THE DELIVERANCE AND MANIFESTATION OF MIRACLES!!!

February 14, 2001

THE COMMANDMENT ~ THOU SHALT NOT KILL ~ IS NOT ONLY FOR THE PHYSICAL MURDERING OF A PERSON'S BODY, BUT IT MEANS, ALSO THOU SHALT NOT KILL A PERSON'S REPUTATION, NAME, STANDING, CHARACTER, OR POSITION!!! WHEN YOU SPEAK DEROGATORILY ABOUT SOMEONE YOU ARE KILLING

THEIR INFLUENCE! IF YOU HAVE SOMETHING AGAINST ANOTHER YOU ARE TO GO TO THEM PERSONALLY WITHOUT TALKING ABOUT THE MATTER TO ANYONE ELSE. YOU ARE TO BE RECONCILED TO THE PERSON THAT YOU HAVE AN OUGHT AGAINST. YOU MAY NOT AGREE WITH THE PERSON ABOUT EVERYTHING, BUT YOU ARE TO PRAY AND TO BE LED BY THE SPIRIT AND NOT YOUR OWN MIND, WILL, THOUGHTS, IDEAS, OPINIONS, AND EMOTIONS! GET OFF THE THRONE! YOU ARE NOT KING! NO MAN LIVES TO HIMSELF AND NO MAN IS TO BE ANOTHER'S JUDGE AND JURY! THERE IS ONE LAWGIVER WHO IS ABLE TO SAVE AND TO DESTROY: WHO ART THOU THAT JUDGES ANOTHER???

Deliverance

YOU DON'T HAVE ANY PROBLEMS!!! NO, YOU CAN'T LIVE IT! BUT YOU DON'T HAVE TO! ALL YOU HAVE TO DO IS <u>LET</u> HIM LIVE IN YOU! LET <u>HIM</u> BE GOD! LET HIM BE HIMSELF! IN YOU! CHRIST IN YOU! THE HOPE OF GLORY!!! WELL, LET'S SEE ... CAN I LET GOD BE HIMSELF? HMMM, FOR SOME OF YOU IT'S RATHER DIFFICULT! YOU ARE INTO SO MUCH MIND CONTROL! YOU WANT CONTROL!!! WELL, IF THAT IS YOUR PRIORITY, NO YOU CANNOT LET GOD LIVE THROUGH YOU BECAUSE YOU WANT TO BE IN CHARGE!!! THE ONLY BOSS IN CHRISTIANITY IS GOD HIMSELF! THE REST OF THOSE, EVEN IN AUTHORITY ARE JUST SUPPOSED TO TAKE ORDERS AND DO WHAT THEY ARE TOLD!!! NO DIFFICULTY HERE UNLESS YOU CAN'T TAKE ORDERS! UNLESS YOU CAN'T GET YOUR MOUTH OFF OF SOMEBODY ELSE. OBEYING GOD IS EASY IF YOU KNOW HOW TO SHUT YOUR MOUTH! THAT IS THE ONLY PROBLEM!!! SHUT YOUR MOUTH! OPEN YOUR SPIRITUAL EARS!!! LISTEN FOR HIS VOICE! SAY WHAT HE SAYS OR DON'T SAY! FOR IT IS WRITTEN, <u>IF</u> ANY MAN SPEAK LET HIM SPEAK AS THE ORACLE OF GOD! AND IF HE'S SPEAKING AS THE ORACLE OF GOD YOU BETTER SHUT UP AND LISTEN!!! HE IS SPEAKING FOR GOD ~ THE MOST HIGH!!! YOU WANT A QUICK FIX? DRINK HIM! EAT HIM! BREATHE HIM! WALK HIM! TALK HIM!!! SPEAK HIM!!! THERE IS NO HIGH LIKE THE MOST HIGH!!! SPIRIT TO SPIRIT IS THE ETERNAL ... ONGOING HIGH-ROLLING DRUG DEAL OF THE MILLENNIUM!!! NO HANGOVERS! NO SHAKES EXCEPT UNDER THE POWER OF GOD!!! NO D.T.'S ... JUST LET THE RUST AND FILTH OF SIN AND DEGRADATION FLOW OUT OF YOU AND BE FILLED WITH THE SPIRIT OF THE ALMIGHTY!!! NO HIGH LIKE THE MOST HIGH!!! NO JOY LIKE HIS JOY JUICE!!! THE OIL OF THE HOLY GHOST!!! NO DELIGHT LIKE THE THRILL OF HIS TOUCH!!! NO FOUNTAIN LIKE HIM CONTINUOUSLY FLOWING INSIDE OF YOU!!! NO PEACE LIKE THIS PRINCE WHO HAS COME TO FILL YOU UP WITH HIMSELF!!! THE JOY IN JESUS IS THE CONTINUOUS FLOW OF HIS OIL IN YOUR OPEN VESSEL!!! THE MANIFESTED GLORY OF GOD IS MORE THAN PREACHING... EVEN MORE THAN REPENTING OF YOUR SINS! COMPLETE DELIVERANCE BY THE

GLORY OF GOD!!! DELIVERANCE OF ADDICTIONS! HEALINGS AND MIRACLES! RESTORATIONS! NOT JUST NOT DRINKING ANY MORE! NOT JUST NOT SHOOTING UP OR SNORTING ANYMORE! BUT THE DESIRE TO IS GONE! NO SLIPPIN' DIPPIN' OR SIPPIN'! AND NO-SWEAT IN THE PROCESS! IT'S YOURS NOW!!! WHATEVER YOU NEED, TAKE IT!!! LET GOD FILL YOU WITH HIS GLORY!!! HEAL! DELIVER! SET FREE! IN THAT NAME THAT IS ABOVE EVERY NAME, BE MADE EVERY WHIT WHOLE, BODY, MIND, SOUL AND SPIRIT!!! CRY HOLY UNTO THE LORD AND LET HIM COVER YOU WITH HIMSELF! JESUS! CALL ON HIS NAME! HE WILL HEAR AND ANSWER! O, HALLELUJAH TO THE GLORY OF GOD!!!

February 26, 2001

Spiritual Warfare

I AM THE KING OF GLORY! I ADMINISTER MY GLORY AND DOMINION UNTO YOU! CAST DOWN THESE PRODIGAL SPIRITS OVER NATIONS!!! SPIRITS OF SPIRITUALISM! SPIRITS OF VOODOO! SPIRITS OF PANDERING! SPIRITS OF INCEST!!! SPIRITS OF BESTIALITY! SPIRITS OF SECTARIANISM! SPIRITS OF BIGOTRY AND RACISM! SPIRITS OF MENTAL ILLNESS! SPIRITS OF SUICIDE! SPIRITS OF LIES! SPIRITS OF DECEPTION! SPIRITS OF MELANCHOLY! SPIRITS OF POVERTY! SPIRITS OF GENERATIONAL CURSES!!! SPIRITS OF CRIME AND MURDER! SPIRITS OF RAPE AND MUTILATION! SPIRITS OF MANY GODS! SPIRITS OF BRAZEN ALTARS THAT DEFAME THE ALTAR OF GOD!!! SPIRITS OF MAJESTY AND MIGHT THAT TAKE AWAY FROM THE ONE TRUE LIVING GOD! BE DISMANTLED, YOU RUTHLESS PARASITES!!! BE SET FREE FROM YOUR MALIGNITIES AND SORCERIES!!! WITCHCRAFT, BE THOU CURSED TO THE ROOTS!!! THE CORE OF HUMANITY! COME OUT OF MY COUNTRIES, SAITH THE LORD OF HOSTS! THE BRIDE OF CHRIST CONQUERS YOU IN THE NAME OF JESUS!!! COME OUT, PARASITES OF POMP AND CEREMONY! CHURCH OF THE ONE TRUE LIVING GOD, ARISE AND TAKE UP YOUR ARMOR AND CONQUER THE DEMONS OF PRIDE AND PRIVILEGE! I AM THAT I AM! AND THERE IS NO OTHER! MOTHER OF HARLOTS, LOOSE YOUR HOLD ON MY TRUE CHURCH! THE CHURCH OF THE LIVING GOD! MY CHURCH SHALL PREVAIL! WITHOUT SPOT OR BLEMISH OR WRINKLE OR ANY SUCH THING! I SPEW OUT NOW ALL THE EVILS OF PEDOPHILIA, HOMOSEXUALITY, LESBIANISM, IMMORALITY, FORNICATION, ADULTERY, WORSHIP OF ANGELS!!! COME OUT OF HER!!! BE RELEASED FROM THE CURSES OF YOUR PAST! THERE IS ONE TRUE LIVING GOD!!! SERVE HIM!!! ALL SIN WILL BE DESTROYED! AND THOSE WHO CONTINUE IN SIN WILL BE DESTROYED! CHOOSE YOU THIS DAY WHOM YOU WILL SERVE! THE LIVING GOD OR MAN-MADE RITUAL!

I AM THE I AM! I MIX NOT AND I TAINT NOT! THE MIXED ... MIXED WITH SIN. THE TAINTED ... TAINTED WITH PERVERSION

WILL NOT SEE MY HOLY HEAVEN!!! NOTHING DEFILED OR PERVERTED WILL ENTER IN! SAME SEX UNIONS WILL NOT ENTER MY HOLY HEAVEN! NEITHER SORCERIES! NOR ABDICATORS ... THOSE WHO REFUSE THE TRUTH OF MY WRITTEN WORD! NONE OF THESE SHALL ENTER MY HOLY DOMINION! KEEP OUT PERVERSIONS AND THE DEFILED!!! LET THEM NOT MINISTER MY SACRAMENTS AND MY STATUTES!!! I WILL SOON SHOW MY POWER EVEN IN THE HOLY SANCTUARIES! FOR I WILL MAKE KNOWN MY JUDGMENTS! MY CHURCHES ARE DEFILED WITH GRAFT, BRIBERY, PERVERSION, SAME SEX UNIONS, HYPOCRITES, BACKBITERS, FAULTFINDERS, LIARS, LOVERS OF THEMSELVES MORE THAN LOVERS OF GOD, UNTHANKFUL. UNHOLY, DEFILERS OF THE TRUTH, DESIROUS OF PRIVILEGE AND PREEMINENCE MORE THAN MY POWER AND GLORY! I SHALL TAKE VENGEANCE IN THE SANCTUARY! CHURCHES WILL BE CLEANSED AND MADE HOLY! MY POWER IS IN MY JUDGMENTS! JUDGMENTS SHALL BE ADMINISTERED AT MY ALTARS! MY PULPITS WILL BE CLEANSED! FOR JUDGMENT SHALL BEGIN AT THE HOUSE OF GOD! THE LORD HAS SPOKEN IT!!! TRY NO LONGER TO MIX AND MINGLE MY SPIRIT, MY SPIRITUAL THINGS WITH YOUR OPINIONS AND SURMISINGS! YOU WILL BE CORRECTED! EVEN SOME TO THE POINT OF DEATH! THOSE WHO WILL HEED MY VOICE I WILL SPARE. OTHERS SHALL GIVE UP THE GHOST THUS SAITH THE LORD.

February 22, 2001

March
2001

Nations move to the ... Beat of Now.
What is ... Programmed in Youth
Will be the future ... How.

Part V

Behold
the
Word
of
God

And unto man the Lord says, Behold the fear of the Lord!
That is Wisdom! And to depart from evil is Understanding!

Job Chapter Twenty-Eight,
Verse Twenty-Eight

Prophecy

I BRING THE SUNSHINE! AND I SEND THE RAIN! NO ONE CAN DEPLETE MY STOREHOUSE! I AM ON THE CUTTING EDGE OF ALL THAT IS HAPPENING. NOTHING ESCAPES MY KNOWLEDGE. HEALING PORTRAYS MY LOVE. WHOLENESS IS MY FAITHFULNESS. WHAT IS MAN THAT I AM MINDFUL OF HIM? THE CREATION OF MY HANDS! THE MOLDING OF MY INTEGRITY! I SEND PEACE TO THOSE IN PAIN! I GIVE ORDER TO CHAOS! I AM GOING TO PROVE WHO I AM TO THIS GROPING WORLD! LOVE IS NOT A CURE ALL! LOVE IS ALL! PERIOD! WITHOUT LOVE THERE IS NO LASTING JOY! WITHOUT LOVE THERE IS NO POWER TO CONFIRM MY WORD!!! WITHOUT CONFIRMING MY WORD THERE IS NO DEMONSTRATION OF MY POWER! WITHOUT THE DEMONSTRATION OF MY WORD THE MASSES WILL NOT KNOW MY POWER TO FORGIVE SIN AND TO TRANSFORM LIVES!!! DEMONSTRATE THE POWER OF MY WORD WITH SIGNS AND WONDERS! MIRACLES COME FORTH! HEALINGS BE SET IN MOTION BY THE AUTHORITY OF THE ALMIGHTY!

March 2, 2001

Prophecy

PEOPLE HAVE TRIED TO STOP YOU! BUT NO MAN STOPS ME! AND I AM IN YOU, SO YOU WILL NOT BE HELD BACK ANY LONGER! FOR THE MOST PART I AM ABLE TO HAVE AUTHORITY IN THE CHURCHES, BUT SOON THERE WILL BE SOME DEATHS SO THAT COMPLETE POWER AND DEMONSTRATION MAY BE ABLE TO COME FORTH WITHOUT OPPOSITION. COUNSEL TO BE SURE, MY GIFTS AND MY CALLINGS WILL NO LONGER BE BARRED FROM MY PLACE OF BUSINESS ... THE CHURCHES OF THE MOST HIGH GOD!!! BAR MY PROPHETS NO LONGER FROM THEIR RIGHTFUL PLACES! STEP ASIDE. LET THE POWER MANIFEST IN DELIVERANCE AND CASTING OUT OF DEVILS! WORD OF WISDOM AND KNOWLEDGE, COME FORTH!!! SET THE CAPTIVES FREE!!!!! POWER STRUGGLES CEASE! I HAVE SET IN MY CHAIN OF COMMAND BY THE AUTHORITY OF MY WORD!!! STOP THE CHARACTER KILLING OF MY PROPHETS! I AM REESTABLISHING, REINFORCING THE FOUNDATIONS OF MY CHURCH! MY GLORIOUS CHURCH! WHICH IS BUILT UPON THE FOUNDATION OF THE APOSTLES AND PROPHETS WHICH STILL ARE SET IN MY BODY AS IT PLEASES ME IN ORDER THAT MY WORD IS MANIFESTED IN IT'S FULLNESS AND NOT JUST PREACHED ABOUT BUT IS FULLY DEMONSTRATED IN HEALINGS AND MIRACLES! POWER GIFTS, BE FREE TO DEMONSTRATE! APOSTLES, BE LOOSED TO SPEAK DOMINION! PROPHECY, COME FORTH! DISCERNING OF SPIRITS, MANIFEST AND DISPEL RITUAL AND DECEIT! I HAVE NO RESPECT OF PERSONS!!! WHEN YOU DO, YOU ARE UNGODLY! I HAVE RESPECT ONLY UNTO THE LOWLY!!! WHEN YOU DO NOT, YOU ARE MARKED AS A TRANSGRESSOR AND YOU ARE COMMITTING SIN! YOU ARE TOUCHING MINE ANOINTED!!! YOU ARE DOING HARM TO MY PROPHETS!!! I WILL JUDGE YOU SOON SAYS THE LORD! I HAVE BEEN SLOW TO ANGER IN ORDER TO GIVE YOU SPACE TO REPENT, BUT YOU REFUSE TO RECOGNIZE WHOM I RECOGNIZE! YOU REFUSE TO HONOR WHOM I HONOR!!! SO NOW I WILL MAKE IT PLAIN TO YOU SO THAT THERE WILL BE NO DOUBT. STOP THE SETTING ASIDE OF MY PROPHETS! WITHOUT THEIR OBEDIENCE AND PROCLAMATION THE CHURCH WILL NOT PROCEED INTO

THE FULLNESS OF ITS GLORY! THEY ARE MY SPOKESPERSONS!!! WHEN YOU REFUSE THEIR OFFICE YOU ARE LIMITING THE MIGHT OF THE MINISTRY WHICH CAN ONLY COME FORTH IN MAGNIFICENCE BY BEING SPOKEN FORTH BY MY PROPHETS! STEP ASIDE AND STAY IN YOUR PROPER PLACES. DO NOT USURP AUTHORITY OVER PROPHETS LEST YOU BRING JUDGMENT UPON YOUR HEAD! JUDGMENT IS IMMINENT IF I DO NOT HAVE AUTHORITY IN RELEASING MY PROPHETS IN MY SANCTUARY. YOU DID NOT SET THE CHURCH IN ORDER! IT WAS BY <u>MY</u> DECREE! IT IS ESTABLISHED: APOSTLES, PROPHETS, AS WELL AS, EVANGELISTS (YOU HAVE SET SOME OF THEM ASIDE AS WELL) PASTORS AND TEACHERS!!! STOP THE CHARACTER KILLING, LEST I KILL IN THE SANCTUARY! ANANIAS AND SAPPHIRA WERE KILLED IN CHURCH BECAUSE OF GREED OF MONEY. SOME WILL SOON GIVE UP THE GHOST BECAUSE OF GREED OF POSITION AND POWER! YOU HAVE BEEN FOREWARNED! POWER OF POSITION IS MY CALL!!! NOT MAN'S! STEP ASIDE SAITH THE LORD!!!

March 5, 2001

Prophecy

YOU HAVE GIVEN ME EVERYTHING! NOW I AM GOING TO OPEN DOORS THAT NO MAN CAN CLOSE! I HAVE ALREADY CLOSED DOORS THAT NO MAN CAN OPEN. SPIRALING DISCORD HAS CAUSED MINISTRIES TO FOLD! WITHOUT FASTING AND PRAYER THE MINISTRIES WILL NOT FUNCTION TO FULL CAPACITY AND HEADSHIP WILL NOT BE IN PROPER ALIGNMENT. I AM SETTING MY APOSTLES AND PROPHETS IN THEIR ASSIGNED PLACES IN THE BODY! I AM THE CHRIST! I POSITIONED THEM BEFORE THE FOUNDATION OF THE WORLD AND IF MAN THINKS HE HAS A BETTER IDEA HE NEEDS TO THINK AGAIN! A BODY WITH TWO HEADS IS A MONSTROSITY! A BODY WITH POSITIONS NOT IN ORDER DOES NOT FUNCTION PROPERLY! AS IT IS WRITTEN, GOD HAS SET IN THE CHURCH, <u>FIRST</u> APOSTLES, <u>SECONDARILY</u> PROPHETS, THIRDLY TEACHERS AND AFTER THAT MIRACLES, THEN GIFTS OF HEALINGS, HELPS, GOVERNMENTS, DIVERSITIES OF TONGUES!!! I Corinthians 12:28

I GAVE SOME APOSTLES AND SOME PROPHETS AND SOME EVANGELISTS AND SOME PASTORS AND TEACHERS FOR THE PERFECTING OF THE SAINTS, FOR THE WORK OF THE MINISTRY, FOR THE EDIFYING OF THE BODY OF CHRIST, THE CHURCH, TILL YOU ALL COME INTO THE UNITY OF THE FAITH, THE FAITH OF GOD, AND OF THE KNOWLEDGE OF THE SON OF GOD (TO REALLY <u>KNOW</u> ME IS TO <u>FULLY</u> OBEY ME!) UNTO A PERFECT MAN (MATURE AND OPERATING IN ALL FACETS OF MINISTRY!) UNTO THE MEASURE OF THE STATURE OF THE FULLNESS OF CHRIST!!! TO GREATER WORKS THAN THOSE DONE BY ME, GREATER IN NUMBER, YOU MUST FIRST GET IN PROPER ALIGNMENT CONCERNING HEADSHIP! FOR OTHER FOUNDATION CAN NO MAN LAY THAN THAT IS LAID WHICH IS JESUS CHRIST! I Corinthians 3:11 PASTORS MUST RECEIVE, HEAR AND ACCEPT THE OTHER OFFICES I HAVE PLACED IN MY BODY, THE CHURCH! IT TAKES ALL <u>FIVE</u> MINISTRY OFFICES TO BRING MY BODY TO PERFECTION!!! EACH ONE MUST BE ABLE TO FUNCTION IN THEIR OWN GIVEN CAPACITY! EACH ONE LABORS TOGETHER

WITH ME!!! DENY MY MINISTRY OFFICERS NO LONGER!!! I HAVE SET IN ORDER A CHAIN OF COMMAND!!! PLAY THE CAPTAIN NO LONGER!!!

March 8, 2001

Prophecy

REGARD NOT MAN. LOOK ONLY TO ME. THOUGH SOME HAVE SET YOU ASIDE, I WILL ESTABLISH YOU AND SEND YOU FORTH SAITH THE LORD. YOU WILL DETERMINE DESTINIES OF NATIONS. GIVE MY PEOPLE HEALING. I AM HEALING AND YOU ARE FULL OF ME SO YOU ARE FULL OF HEALING! GIVE IT TO MY PEOPLE. ESTABLISH MY PEOPLE IN THE DOCTRINE OF FAITH. I HAVE HIDDEN THE HIDDEN MANNA FROM THE MASSES BECAUSE THEY DO NOT SEEK ME AS FOR HIDDEN RICHES ... WITH <u>ALL</u> THEIR HEART AND WITH <u>ALL</u> THEIR MIND AND WITH <u>ALL</u> THEIR STRENGTH! I ESTABLISH DOCTRINES OF MIRACLES NOW! MISUSE OF POWER SHALL BE REMOVED FROM MY SANCTUARY! I AM GIVING YOU THE BREASTPLATE OF RIGHTEOUSNESS FOR THIS PEOPLE. I AM ESTABLISHING YOUR MINISTRY. BE NOT DISMAYED BY ANYTHING THAT TAKES PLACE OUTSIDE THE REALM OF MY AUTHORITY! I AM THE HEAD. NOT MAN. OR WOMAN. I AM JUST AND I AM HOLY. ESTABLISH MY WILL AT ALL COSTS!!! MY WILL IS TO BE OF PRIME PRIORITY! NOT MAN'S PREFERENCES AND PASSIONS, BUT MY AUTHORITY AND MY DOMINION! TAKE HEED! PROPHETS DIE BEFORE THEIR TIME AS WELL AS OTHERS WHO REFUSE TO DO MY BIDDING AND MY ORDERS. ESTABLISH MY WORD SAITH THE LORD OF HOSTS! JEHOVAH IS MY NAME. ABOVE ME THERE IS NONE OTHER. I AM NEVER ENDING. I AM THE FIRST AND I AM THE LAST. TAKE COUNSEL ONLY WITH ME, AS I WILL SHOW YOU MY PURPOSE. MAN SHALL TRY TO DISSUADE AND TO TAKE DOWN, BUT MY WORD IS CLEAR. IT IS WRITTEN. THAT ALONE IS MY <u>PURE</u> AUTHORITY.

March 10, 2001

THE REASON FOR SO MUCH FASTING IS I WANT YOU TO RAISE THE DEAD AGAIN.

March 12, 2001

Prophecy

GIVE ME MORE PRAISE! GIVE ME MORE PRAISE! YOUR GPA IS 90. GLORY AND PRAISE AND ADORATION! I WANT IT TO BE 100! I WANT YOU TO RAISE THE DEAD!!!

March 13, 2001

I'LL TAKE YOU THERE! SOME RECEIVE YOU AND SOME DON'T RECEIVE YOU. YOU'RE JUST LIKE ME. O, HALLELUJAH TO THE GLORY OF GOD! MINISTRIES OF MIRACLES ARE IN YOUR HANDS. YOU ARE PERFECT BEFORE ME. YOU ARE PERFECT BEFORE ME. SEEK MY FACE FOR AS YOU GO HIGHER, I WILL REQUIRE MORE PRAYER FROM YOU.

March 17, 2001

DON'T BE TELLING ME YOU NEED ME, AND YOUR BROTHER OR YOUR SISTER HAS A NEED AND YOU'RE TOO BUSY TO MEET IT! OR YOU JUST DON'T WANT TO MEET THEIR NEED.

March 18, 2001

Prophecy

I AM PLEASED AT YOUR OBEDIENCES. YOU DO EXACTLY WHAT I SAY IN SPITE OF EVERYTHING. IN SPITE OF EVERYBODY. I AM SENDING YOU FORTH IN VICTORY AND POWER TO THE NATION.

March 20, 2001

I'M SO PROUD OF YOU. YOU DID EVERYTHING I BID YOU TO DO. YOU STAYED UNTIL I WAS FINISHED. TODAY IS A NEW DAY FOR YOU. YOU WILL GO MANY PLACES. I WILL GO BEFORE YOU. I WILL RAISE THE DEAD THROUGH YOU. I WILL HEAL CRIPPLED LIMBS AND UNSTOP DEAF EARS. I WILL CAUSE THE BLIND TO SEE. I WILL STRENGTHEN YOUR BODY SAITH THE LORD. BE NOT WEARY. I WILL UPHOLD YOU WITH THE RIGHT HAND OF MY RIGHTEOUSNESS.

March 21, 2001

GRAVE CHANGES. GRAVE CHANGES. GRAVE CHANGES SAITH THE LORD. GRAVE CHANGES IN THE CULTURE!!!

March 22, 2001

COME DOWN, SAITH THE LORD! BOW AT MY FEET! GIVE ME REVERENCE AND GLORY! HUSH YOUR WRANGLINGS! SILENCE YOUR THREATENINGS! GIVE ME OBEISANCE AND HONOR! THRUST YOURSELF ON MY MERCY AND GIVE ME YOUR INNERMOST BEING, FOR UNTIL YOU GIVE ME ALL OF YOU, I CANNOT DO THE THINGS THAT YOU ARE DESIRING OF ME! I CAN ONLY WORK WITH WHAT YOU GIVE ME. IF YOU DO NOT GIVE ME ALL: YOUR POWER, YOUR DESIRE, YOUR STRUGGLE, YOUR ASPIRATION, YOUR PAIN, YOUR HATRED, YOUR ANGER, YOUR HURT, YOUR DISAPPOINTMENT, YOUR FAILURES, YOUR UN-FORGIVENESS, YOUR PAST, THE HOLES IN YOUR HEART ... I CANNOT MAKE THE CROOKED PLACES STRAIGHT. I CANNOT BRING DOWN THE HIGH PLACES. I CANNOT BRING UP THE LOW PLACES. I CAN ONLY WORK WITH WHAT YOU GIVE TO ME!!! I AM

NOT A DICTATOR. I AM THE CREATOR!!! I CHANGE WHATEVER NEEDS TO BE CHANGED WHEN IT IS SURRENDERED COMPLETELY UNTO ME WITH NO RESERVATION! WITH NO RESTRICTIONS ATTACHED!!! YOU HAVE AS MUCH JOY AND PEACE AS YOU HAVE SURRENDERED OF YOUR PASSION AND PAIN! YOU HAVE AS MUCH GRACE AS YOU HAVE SURRENDERED SIN! WHATEVER IS MISSING OR BROKEN IN YOUR LIFE HAS NOT BEEN FULLY SURRENDERED UNTO ME!!!

March 28, 2001

Prayer and Submission

I AM ROLLING ALL OF MY CARE OF MY SON OVER ON YOU, LORD! I RELEASE HIM FULLY UNTO YOU, LORD!!! DEVIL, I AM NOT IMPRESSED BY YOUR MOVE AGAINST MY SON! BECAUSE MY GOD HAS <u>ALL</u> POWER OVER YOU AND I RELEASE MY SON UNTO THE POWER OF ALMIGHTY GOD!!! I TAKE MY HANDS OFF OF YOUR SERVANT, MY SON. I GIVE HIM TO YOU, LORD. I PLACE HIM UPON YOUR ALTAR OF LOVE!!!

March 26, 2001

AS AN ACT OF MY WILL, BECAUSE I HATE HELL, AND I HAVE HAD SO MUCH HELL HERE ON EARTH, I REFUSE TO ALLOW THE DEVIL TO DELEGATE MY FUTURE TO SPEND ETERNITY WITH HIM. I, THEREFORE, NOW SURRENDER MY THOUGHTS, MY FEELINGS, ALL MY HELLISH POWER STRUGGLES, ALL THE HOLES IN MY HEART, IN MY MIND, ALL OF THE AGONIES AND THE TORMENTS OF NOT HAVING MY NEEDS MET! I SURRENDER MY BROKEN AND BLEEDING HEART TO YOU, JESUS! IF YOU CAN FIX ME, GIVE ME SOME HOPE! SOMETHING TO LATCH ON TO! PLEASE JESUS, I CANNOT GO ON ANY LONGER IN THIS HOLE OF HELL! GIVE ME A REASON TO LIVE! I SURRENDER TO YOU NOW AND I RECEIVE <u>ALL</u> THE BENEFITS OF A CHILD OF GOD! I RECEIVE YOUR PEACE! I ACCEPT YOUR LORDSHIP! I WILL OBEY YOUR VOICE! ! ! ! !

March 28, 2001

Exhortation

GRACE IS A PLACE IN THE SPIRIT! IT IS A POSITION THAT YOU PUT YOURSELF IN BY DECISION! IT IS NOT A ZAP FROM HEAVEN! YOU'VE BEEN ZAPPED SO MANY TIMES YOU WOULD BE IN THE THIRD HEAVEN BY NOW! GRACE COMES WHEN WE SURRENDER!!! SOME SURRENDER FOR A MOMENT ... FOR A MOMENT OF RELIEF AND THEN IT'S THE SAME OLD ... SAME OLD HABIT OF WORKING OUT EVERYTHING YOURSELF INSTEAD OF BEING LED BY THE SPIRIT OF THE LORD!!! YOU CAN BE LED BY THE SPIRIT OF THE LORD WHEN YOU SURRENDER YOUR SELF-WILL, HURT, EGO, PRIDE, POSITION. SOME ARE PARTIALLY LED BY THE SPIRIT OF THE LORD. SOME ARE LED BY THE SPIRIT OF THE LORD AT TIMES AND THEIR OWN SPIRIT AT OTHER TIMES! IF YOU WANT GOD'S RESULTS YOU HAVE TO GO GOD'S WAYS <u>ALL</u> THE TIME! OTHERWISE YOU HAVE SPORADIC TIMES OF UP AND DOWN AND IN AND OUT. GOD IS THE SAME EACH DAY.

JESUS THE CHRIST, THE SAME YESTERDAY, TODAY AND FOREVER!!! IF YOU WANT JESUS' RESULTS YOU HAVE TO DO WHAT HE DID! EACH DAY! A TIME OF SUBMISSION, A TIME OF QUIETNESS, A TIME OF INTERCESSION, PRAYING IN THE HOLY GHOST! NOT JUST WHEN YOU GET IN TROUBLE, BUT DAILY TO KEEP YOU OUT OF TROUBLE! IF YOU WANT TO HEAR WHAT SOMEONE IS SAYING TO YOU, YOU HAVE TO BE QUIET AND LISTEN. SAME PRINCIPLE WITH THE LORD GOD ALMIGHTY! IF YOU WANT TO KNOW WHAT HE WANTS TO SAY TO YOU ... SHUT UP! YOU WAIT IN SILENCE! YOU LISTEN! SOME PEOPLE TRY TO HEAR FROM GOD ... TO BE INTIMATE WITH LORDSHIP ... THE SAME WAY THEY ENDEAVOR TO HAVE RELATIONSHIP WITH OTHERS ... ON THEIR OWN TIME FRAME, ACCORDING TO WHAT THEY DESIRE AND NEED AND WHEN THEY GET GOOD AND READY. IT DOESN'T WORK FOR INTIMACY IN MARRIAGE OR ANY OTHER CLOSE RELATIONSHIP AND IF YOU THINK YOU ARE GOING TO GIVE GOD LESS THAN YOU DO EARTHLY RELATIONSHIPS AND HAVE IT GOING ON, YOU ARE STUPID!

March 28, 2001

Discerning of Spirits

WHAT DO YOU EXPECT? DO YOU ACTUALLY THINK A CONTINUOUS BARRAGE IN OUR YOUNG PEOPLE'S MINDS, WILLS AND EMOTIONS OF VIOLENCE, KILLING, SLAUGHTER IN MOVIES AND MUSIC ... THE SAME VIDEO GAMES THAT WERE USED BY THE GREEN BERETS TO DESENSITIZE MEN TO HUMANITY SO THAT THEY CAN KILL WITHOUT RESERVATION ... THAT THIS WOULD NOT BRING ABOUT KILLING AND SLAUGHTER IN OUR OWN STREETS AND SCHOOLS??? DUMB, DUMBER, DUMBEST!

WAKE UP, AMERICA! THE WORLD IS ALREADY ON FIRE! THE FIRES OF FILTH AND RAGE ARE RAMPANT AND WE WRING OUR LITTLE HANDS SAYING, OH, WHAT ARE WE TO DO??? VIOLENCE AND MURDER AND MAYHEM FLOOD OUR NATION IN TELEVISION, MUSIC, VIDEO AND COMPUTER VICES. AND IF YOU HAVEN'T FIGURED IT OUT YET ... IT'S AN OLD, OLD TRUTH ... WHAT YOU SEE IS WHAT YOU GET!!! ANOTHER ONE, TOO ... WHATEVER GOES IN, COMES OUT! WE HAVE NOT ONLY SLAUGHTERED OUR OWN BABIES MERCILESSLY IN AMERICA ... KILLING OUR OWN PROGENY! BUT WE CONTINUE TO DISEMBOWEL THE BRAIN AND PSYCHE OF OUR OWN OFFSPRING BY MURDERING THEIR MINDS WITH WHOLESALE SLAUGHTER, THE BRUTISH KILLING OF HUMANITY IN GRUESOME DIABOLICAL MOVIES, MUSIC AND VIDEO GAMES! WEEPING WILL NOT CHANGE THE DOWNWARD SPIRAL OF DESTITUTE HUMANITY! GREED IS A SPIRIT! IT MUST BE DEALT WITH IN THE SPIRIT REALM! MURDER SELLS TAPES, MOVIES, VIDEOS, CDS! IT, ALSO, IS A SPIRIT! AND MUST BE DEALT WITH AS SUCH! UNTIL AMERICA REALLY DESIRES CHANGE, MURDER AND MAYHEM WILL CONTINUE! GREED WILL PREVAIL. IT IS A CHOICE!!!

March 6, 2001

SPEAK UP, PSYCHOLOGISTS! SPEAK OUT, COUNSELORS! VIOLENCE BREEDS VIOLENCE! WE HAVE KNOWN THIS TRUTH FOR MANY YEARS. YET, WE HAVE THE MEDIA ... MOVIES, TV,

VIDEO GAMES, MUSIC, TO FEED OUR CHILDREN A CONTINUOUS DIET OF DEATH, DESTRUCTION, DOOM. YES, EVEN THE GAME "DOOM" IS CHARACTERIZING OUR CHILDREN'S CHARACTER. WHEN WILL THE KILLING CEASE? WHEN WE PARENT OUR PROGENY INSTEAD OF PROVOKING THEM TO WRATH! THE CONSTANT INFILTRATION OF VIOLENCE INTO THEIR EYE-GATES AND EAR-GATES PROVOKES THEM TO WRATH!!! PROVOKE THEM TO SERVICE! PROVOKE THEM TO VOLUNTEER! PROVOKE THEM TO READ!!! GIVE THEM GUTS! COURAGE! STRENGTH! POWER TO SAY 'NO' TO GREED! TO SAY 'NO' TO EVIL! GIVE THEM "<u>YOU</u>!!!" EXERCISE TOGETHER! PRAY TOGETHER!!! MOVIES AND VIOLENCE ARE NOT "<u>THEIR</u> RIGHT," THEIR "RIGHT" IS WHAT IS RIGHT!!! VIEWING THE SLAUGHTER OF HUMANS, THE VIOLENT MAIMING OF LIFE AND LIMB IS NOT A CHILD'S RIGHT!!! PERSONALLY KILLING AND DESTROYING THE HUMAN RACE WHILE PLAYING VIDEO GAMES SHOULD NOT BE A CHILD'S CHARACTER BUILDER! DISCIPLINE, RELATIONSHIP, LOVE, BUILD CHARACTER! "DOOM" BREEDS DEATH! PARENTS, BUILD CHARACTER IN YOUR CHILDREN WITH WORK, STUDY, PLAY, EXERCISE AND TIME TOGETHER! DO NOT LET EVIL GAMES AND MUSIC, VIOLENCE IN MOVIES AND COMPUTERS MOLD YOUR OFFSPRING! YOU ARE RESPONSIBLE FOR WHAT IS BUILDING YOUR CHILDREN'S CHARACTER! BUILD A LIFE! NOT A MONSTER!

March 7, 2001

Wisdom

FASTING BIRTHS PURPOSE!

March 7, 2001

WHEN YOU HEAR THE HEARTBEATS OF HELL YOU CAN PREVENT OTHERS FROM GOING THERE. HELL IS TORMENT. HOURLY. MINUTE BY MINUTE. HELL IS EXCRUCIATING PAIN THAT NEVER ENDS. HELL IS ALL THE THINGS YOU KNOW ABOUT PAIN MAGNIFIED MANY TIMES. IN HELL THERE IS NEVER ANY HOPE OF LESSENING THE AGONY AND TORMENT. IN HELL THERE IS NEVER A RESPITE! IN HELL THERE IS NEVER A BREATHER! IN HELL THERE IS NEVER A GRACE PERIOD! THERE IS NO PEACE DAY NOR NIGHT! IN HELL THERE IS ONLY DARKNESS! THERE IS NO LOVE! THERE IS NO JOY! THERE IS NO HOPE! THERE IS NO FORGIVENESS! THERE IS NOTHING EVER TO LOOK FORWARD TO EXCEPT MORE PAIN, MORE HELL, MORE TORMENT, MORE DIABOLICAL DEVILMENT! NO KINDNESS! NO CONSIDERATION! NO HELP! ONLY COMPLETE AND UTTER FUTILITY FOREVER AND FOREVER AND FOREVER! DEVOURING AND BEING DEVOURED! ONLY IT NEVER STOPS! KILLING AND BEING KILLED. ONLY IT NEVER STOPS! THE HUSTLE IS THE HATE!!! THE HATE IS FOREVER. FOREVER IS NONSTOP. YOUR NERVE ENDINGS ARE NEVER DEADENED WITH DRUGS. YOU ARE IN TOTAL PAIN ... BUT YOU NEVER GO INSANE! YOU FEEL EACH BLOW. YOU SEE BLOOD FLOW. BUT NEVER DIE. DAY AFTER DAY. MONTH AFTER MONTH. YEAR AFTER YEAR. DECADE AFTER DECADE. CENTURY AFTER CENTURY. MILLENNIUM AFTER MILLENNIUM! NO, OUR GOD IS NOT DEMENTED!!! HE GIVES US EVIDENT CHOICE. CHOOSE LIFE OR CHOOSE DEATH!

March 13, 2001

Wisdom

WE MAKE THE CHOICE TO GO TO HEAVEN OR TO GO TO HELL! WE ARE FREE AGENTS. MORAL? THAT IS THE QUESTION! <u>MORAL AGENTS MAKE MORAL CHOICES</u>. WITHOUT MORALS THE DEVIL MAKES OUR CHOICES FOR US. CHOOSE YOU THIS DAY WHOM YOU WILL SERVE! IF GOD BE THE GOD OF THE UNIVERSE, TIME AND ETERNITY ... SERVE HIM! BUT YOU WILL SERVE SOMEBODY! THE SUM OF YOUR BODY ... ALL THAT YOU ARE MADE UP OF WILL SERVE SOMEBODY! IF GOD BE GOD ... SERVE HIM! CHOOSE YOU THIS DAY!!! THE DEVIL IS NOT THE GOD OF THE UNIVERSE ... HE ONLY HAS TRESPASSING RIGHTS AT THIS TIME. HE WILL SOON BE THROWN INTO THE BOTTOMLESS PIT! AFTER THE 1000 YEARS HE WILL BE CAST INTO THE LAKE OF FIRE WHICH IS THE SECOND DEATH. IF THAT IS WHAT YOU WANT FOR YOUR FUTURE ... HAVE AT IT. SIN WILL SERVE THIS SENTENCE! NO IFS! NO ANDS! AND NO BUTS! ALL GOATS GO TO HELL! THERE IS NO IN-BETWEEN. NO PURGATORY! NO LIMBO! IT'S HEAVEN OR HELL! WHEN YOU KNOWINGLY CONTINUE IN SIN, SIN MAKES YOUR CHOICES FOR YOU! SIN TAKES AWAY YOUR RIGHT TO CHOOSE! SIN IS AN ADDICTION! THE POWER OF THE ALMIGHTY ONE CAN RELEASE YOU AND SET YOU FREE! BUT YOU HAVE TO RENOUNCE THE EVIL IN YOUR LIFE AND ACCEPT THE LORD JESUS CHRIST AS YOUR SAVIOR AND LORD!!! HE'S NO PIMP! HE'S THE SAVIOR OF THE WORLD TO WHOEVER WILL LET HIM BE!!! HE WON'T BE SECOND IN YOUR LIFE AND HE PLAYS NO FAVORITES! HE HAS NO RESPECT OF PERSONS ... EXCEPT TO THE LOWLY!!! THE MEEK ARE HIS MINISTERS. HIS RESERVOIRS OF POWER! LET THE MAN TAKE YOU! BREAK YOU! AND MAKE YOU! HE HAS A REPUTATION OF MAKING SPIRITUAL SUPERSTARS. ONES WHO KNOW WHO THE STAR REALLY IS! JESUS! THAT BRIGHT AND MORNING STAR! THE STAR OF DAVID! THE STONE WHICH THE BUILDERS ... REJECTED! THE ONE THAT HAS BECOME THE CHIEF CORNERSTONE! EXCEPT YOU BUILD UPON THIS ROCK YOU LABOR IN VAIN! THE FOUNDATION IS SURE!!! CHOOSE LIFE!!! THE COMMANDMENTS ARE COMMANDMENTS! NOT MULTIPLE CHOICES! WHEN YOU DISOBEY, YOU SUFFER CONSEQUENCES. WHEN YOU CONTINUE

TO DISOBEY YOU SUFFER DEATH! DESTRUCTION COMES UPON THE CHILDREN OF DISOBEDIENCE.

March 13, 2001

THE WORD "POWER" IS GOING TO BE CHANGED INTO "PRESENCE."

March 18, 2001

PERFECTION "COSTS" SOMETHING! IT TAKES WORK! BUT SOME PEOPLE WANT IT RIGHT NOW! THE SAME WAY THEY DO PATIENCE! PERFECTION IS <u>ALL</u> THE FRUIT OF THE SPIRIT: LOVE, JOY, PEACE, LONG-SUFFERING, GENTLENESS, GOODNESS, FAITH, MEEKNESS, TEMPERANCE, MATURED THROUGH THE POWER OF USE! FRUIT DOESN'T GROW OVER NIGHT. JUST AS NATURAL FRUIT TAKES MUCH WATER, AIR, GOOD SOIL AND SUN LIGHT. SO PERFECTION COMES ... THROUGH CONTINUED OBEDIENCE TO THE PRECEPTS, STATUTES, COMMANDMENTS AND SUBMISSION TO THE WORD OF GOD, WITH THE BREATH OF THE SPIRIT, THE GOOD COUNSEL, DISCIPLINE, AND SELF-DENIAL ... SPIRITUAL NUTRIENTS AND THE SON HIMSELF SPEAKING INTO OUR HEART'S CRY! BALANCE AND NURTURING COME THROUGH COMPLETE SURRENDER TO PRAYER, POWER AND PURITY! THIS IS PERFECTION.

March 20, 2001

Wisdom

GRACE IS THE GAUGE.

March 22, 2001

GROUP THERAPY. TIME IS SHORT. THERE IS NOT MUCH TIME TO GET THE PEOPLE DELIVERED!!! PEOPLE THAT ARE CHRISTIANS AND ARE NOT DELIVERED OF ANGER, STRIFE, UN-FORGIVENESS, FEAR AND WHO ARE EASILY HURT NEED TO BE IN A SETTING WHERE THEY CAN TALK OF ALL THESE THINGS WITHOUT BEING JUDGED OR CRITICIZED. WE HAVE BEEN DEALING WITH SURFACE ISSUES AND WE NEED TO BE DEALING WITH DEEPER MATTERS THAT CAUSE THE BEHAVIOR TO COME TO THE SURFACE! WOUNDED SPIRITS ARE BEHAVIOR ISSUES. THERE'S HEALING BALM! BUT THE HURTS MUST BE HEALED BY BEING BROUGHT TO THE SURFACE AND DEALT WITH! NOT LEFT INSIDE TO FESTER AND FOMENT!

GOD IS ONLY LORD OF THE THINGS WE GIVE COMPLETELY UNTO HIM! THIS IS WHY THERE ARE FEW SOULS COMPLETELY SAVED, WHOLE AND DELIVERED ... BECAUSE SO FEW SOULS COMPLETELY AND WHOLEHEARTEDLY GIVE THEIR ENTIRE BEINGS OVER TO THE ... CREATOR WHO THEN IS ABLE (WE HAVE TO GIVE PERMISSION. HE DOES NOT VIOLATE OUR FREE WILL!) TO RECREATE WHOLENESS, COMPLETENESS... NOTHING MISSING, NOTHING BROKEN!!! "THE TIME IS SHORT. I WILL DELIVER WHOEVER WILL CALL UPON MY NAME! I WILL SHOW THEM MY PLAN FOR THEIR LIFE!"

A GOOD DAY IS NOT ACCOMPLISHING EVERYTHING NATURALLY THAT WE WOULD LIKE TO ACCOMPLISH. A GOOD DAY IS DOING WHAT GOD IS DIRECTING US TO DO.

A PROPHET IS NOT CALLED TO THE UNBELIEVER. A PROPHET IS CALLED TO THE HOUSE OF GOD.

March 27, 2001

Prophetic Teaching

I AM ALPHA AND OMEGA, THE BEGINNING AND THE END! I WILL GIVE UNTO HIM THAT IS ATHIRST OF THE FOUNTAIN OF THE WATER OF LIFE FREELY! HE THAT OVERCOMES SHALL INHERIT ALL THINGS! AND I WILL BE HIS GOD! AND HE SHALL BE MY SON! BUT THE FEARFUL AND THE UNBELIEVING, AND THE ABOMINABLE (HOMOSEXUALS, LESBIANS, AND ABORTIONISTS LEVITICUS 18:22; 20:13 PROVERBS 6:16-19) AND MURDERERS (WHOSOEVER DOES NOT LOVE HIS BROTHER OR SISTER IS A MURDERER. I JOHN 3:15) AND WHOREMONGERS (WHOSOEVER LOOKS ON ANOTHER TO LUST AFTER THEM HAS COMMITTED ADULTERY WITH THEM ALREADY IN THEIR HEART! MATTHEW 5:28) AND SORCERERS (DRUG DEALERS) AND IDOLATERS (ALL WHO DO NOT GIVE GOD FIRST PLACE IN THEIR LIVES) AND ALL LIARS (WHITE AND BLACK AND RED AND YELLOW AND BROWN, LITTLE AND BIG OR IN BETWEEN!) SHALL HAVE THEIR PART IN THE LAKE WHICH BURNS WITH FIRE AND BRIMSTONE: WHICH IS THE SECOND DEATH!!! REVELATION 21:6-8

FASTING DRIVES OUT FEAR! OR ANYTHING ELSE THAT IS IN YOUR HEART THAT SHOULD NOT BE THERE! PRAYING IN THE SPIRIT CONSTRICTS UNBELIEF! JUDE 20. FEAR OF MAN HOLDS BACK THE GLORIES OF THE LORD! UNBELIEF ... TOWARDS YOUR BROTHER OR YOUR SISTER ... NOT ACCEPTING THEIR CALLING AND GIFTS, HINDERS THE MOVE OF GOD! YOU MOVE OR GOD IS GOING TO ... WITH YOU OR WITHOUT YOU! MOVE WITH WHOMEVER GOD IS MOVING THROUGH! IT ISN'T ABOUT YOUR PROGRAM OR YOUR PREFERENCE! IT'S ABOUT GOD CALLING THE SHOTS! IT'S ABOUT REMEMBERING WE ARE HERE TO SHOOT THE DEVIL, NOT ONE ANOTHER! TO SHOOT THE SERPENT AND NOT OUR BROTHER! TO GIVE OUT LIFE AND NOT STRIFE! TO LOVE AND TO BE LOVED AS HE HAS LOVED US! AMEN!

GOING TO CHURCH IS NOT YOUR MOST IMPORTANT PREROGATIVE! SPENDING TIME ALONE WITH THE GOD OF THE CHURCH IS YOUR TOP PRIORITY! THE CHURCH ... THE BUILDING,

THE PEOPLE ... IMPORTANT, YES, BUT NOT NEARLY AS IMPORTANT AS YOUR PERSONAL RELATIONS WITH THE HEAD OF THE CHURCH, GOD HIMSELF!!! IF THIS RELATIONSHIP WITH THE HEAD OF THE CHURCH HAS ITS PROPER POSITIONING ... THROUGH FASTING, PRAYER, MEDITATION, STUDY OF THE WORD, AND OBEDIENCE, YOU ARE BETTER PREPARED TO FILL YOUR POSITION IN CHURCH DUTIES, STRUCTURE AND RELATIONSHIPS! CHURCH ATTENDANCE THOUGH OBLIGATORY AND NECESSARY, IS NOT THE TOP PRIORITY! NUMBER ONE DUTY IN ALL CHRISTIAN LIVES: PRAY, HEAR AND THEN DO! S Y F ... SEEK YE FIRST! IF HE ... THE MAIN MAN... SAID SEEK FIRST THE KINGDOM OF GOD AND HIS RIGHTEOUSNESS, THAT IS PRECISELY WHAT HE MEANT THAT WAS TO BE THE MOST IMPORTANT DUTY KNOWN TO MAN!!! COMMUNICATION WITH GOD! OBEDIENCE TO GOD!!!

DON'T BE LOOKING TO GO FULL TIME FOR GOD IF YOU ARE NOT PRAYING AN HOUR IN THE HOLY GHOST EACH DAY! THAT IS MINIMUM FOR HIS POWER AND HIS ANOINTING! DON'T BE LOOKING TO BE ON A MINISTRY PAYROLL IF YOU ARE NOT FASTING AT LEAST ONE FULL DAY EACH WEEK! IF YOU ARE NOT FAITHFUL IN FASTING AND PRAYER GOD DOESN'T NEED YOU! IT'S NOT ABOUT HOW MANY CARS YOU'VE GOT! IT'S ABOUT HOW MANY STARS YOU'VE GOT! LOST SOULS WON TO JESUS IS THE MEASURING STICK OF MINISTRY! IT'S NOT ABOUT HOW GOOD YOU SING! IT'S ABOUT HOW MANY DISCIPLES YOU BRING! IT'S NOT ABOUT HOW GREAT YOU CAN PREACH! IT'S ABOUT YOUR LIFE ... WHAT DOES IT TEACH? IT'S NOT ABOUT HOW BEAUTIFUL YOU LOOK! IT'S ABOUT WHAT YOU DO WHEN THERE'S A DRY BROOK! IT'S NOT ABOUT THE CROP OF WHICH YOU THINK YOU'RE THE CREAM! IT'S ABOUT HIS BLOOD ...THAT HEAVENLY STREAM!!! IT AIN'T ABOUT NO DREAM TEAM, BUT IT'S ABOUT THAT HOLY BEAM THAT FLOWS DOWN FROM HEAVEN! THE SON OF GOD! THE CHASTENING ROD! THE POWER TO PROD! THE LIFE OF LOVE! SENT FROM ABOVE! THAT HOLY DOVE! WHAT APOSTLES ARE MADE OF! HOLY HALLELUJAH! GLORY TO YA! JEHOVAH RAPHA!

YOU CAN HAVE YOUR WAY OR YOU CAN HAVE GOD'S WAY! YOU
CAN BE IN CHARGE OR YOU CAN LEAD THE CHARGE! BUT GOD <u>IS</u>
THE ONLY WONDER! AND IF YOU LEAD HIS CHARGE YOU HAVE
THE FAITH OF GOD! IF YOU HAVE THE FAITH OF GOD YOU
ACCOMPLISH THE WORKS OF GOD WHICH ARE THESE: SIGNS,
WONDERS, MIRACLES!!! IT IS A CHOICE. IF YOU WANT HIS
WORKS, YOU HAVE TO DO IT HIS WAY! THERE IS AN ORDER! GOD
SET THE CHURCH IN ORDER AS IT PLEASED HIM! FIRST APOSTLES,
SECONDARILY PROPHETS. THIS IS HIS ORDER! NOT MAN'S! THIS
IS THE EDICT OF THE HOLY WRIT! NOT OPINIONS! IT IS
ESTABLISHED FOREVER! NOT WISHES, PREFERENCES OR IDEAS!
BUT THE HOLY MAN JESUS SET THE CHURCH IN ORDER!
ESTABLISHED ORDER! LET THE GOD OF ALL FORCES AND ALL
DOMINION AND ALL AUTHORITY RULE WITH POWER! NOT POMP,
NOT TRADITION. BUT POWER!!! APOSTLES AND PROPHETS ARE
TO ESTABLISH THE CHURCH ON GOD'S WORD OF POWER WITH
MIGHTY DEEDS!!!

THE FIRST CENTURY CHURCH WITH APOSTLES AND PROPHETS
HAD DISCERNING OF SPIRITS AND POWER OVER ANYTHING
THAT MIGHT GET OUT OF HAND. THEY WERE NOT NON-PROPHET
CHURCHES!!! NOTICE I DID NOT SAY ORGANIZATIONS. THE
CHURCH IS SET UP BY GOD AS A BODY WITH ALL MEMBERS
ACTIVELY PARTICIPATING. CONTINUING TO REITERATE AS DO
THE HOLY SCRIPTURES ON EDIFICATION: FOLLOW AFTER
CHARITY, AND DESIRE SPIRITUAL GIFTS (COMMANDMENT, NOT
SUGGESTION), BUT <u>RATHER</u> THAT YOU MAY PROPHESY! I
CORINTHIANS 14:1 BUT RATHER MEANS MORE PROPERLY OR
JUSTLY, WITH BETTER REASON, FOR PREFERENCE, CORRECTLY
SPEAKING. SOON THE CHURCH OF THE LORD JESUS CHRIST WILL
KNOW AND UNDERSTAND THAT PROPHECY IS THE LORD GOD
ALMIGHTY SPEAKING TO HIS BELOVED! BRIDEGROOMS DO
SPEAK TO THEIR BRIDES! O, HALLELUJAH, TO THE LAMB OF GOD!
THANK YOU FOR YOUR GLORIOUS PRESENCE AND YOUR SURE
WORD OF PROPHECY! EVEN SO YOU, FORASMUCH AS YOU ARE
ZEALOUS OF SPIRITUAL GIFTS, SEEK THAT YOU MAY EXCEL TO
THE EDIFYING OF THE CHURCH! WHEREFORE, LET HIM THAT

SPEAKS IN AN UNKNOWN TONGUE PRAY THAT HE MAY INTERPRET! I CORINTHIANS 14:12-13 IT STILL AMAZES ME THAT PEOPLE WOULD RATHER HEAR PEOPLE, INSTEAD OF GOD! THEY ACTUALLY PREFER WHAT MAN HAS TO SAY ABOUT GOD, RATHER THAN HEARING WHAT GOD IS SAYING TO THE CHURCH NOW ABOUT ITS OWN PARTICULAR NEEDS AND ASPIRATIONS!

LET THE PROPHETS SPEAK TWO OR THREE, AND LET THE OTHER JUDGE! IF ANYTHING IS REVEALED TO ANOTHER THAT IS SITTING BY, LET THE FIRST HOLD HIS PEACE! FOR YOU MAY ALL PROPHESY ONE BY ONE, THAT ALL MAY LEARN AND ALL MAY BE COMFORTED! I CORINTHIANS 14:29-31 MY, MY, MY, MY, MY, MY! GOD IS SAYING, THAT'S MY WORD!!! AND DON'T YOU COME AGAINST IT!!! WHY WOULD YOU WANT TO BRING DESTRUCTION UPON YOURSELF? IS THE PRAISES OF MAN AND THE OPINIONS OF MAN MORE IMPORTANT THAN OBEDIENCE TO THE WORD OF GOD??? WHEREFORE, BRETHREN, COVET TO PROPHESY, AND FORBID NOT TO SPEAK WITH TONGUES!!! BOTH ARE REQUIRED TO BE IN FULL SUBMISSION TO THE WILL AND TO THE WORD OF GOD! AND DOES NOT DESIGNATE MULTIPLE CHOICE! AND MEANS BOTH TONGUES AND PROPHECY! IF YOU ALLOW TONGUES AND DO NOT ALLOW PROPHECY YOU ARE STILL IN ERROR! MY WORD IS MY WORD! WHY DO YOU WANT TO TAKE AWAY FROM THE BOOK OF THIS PROPHECY? LET ALL THINGS BE DONE DECENTLY AND IN ORDER! I Corinthians 14:39-40 COVET: TO DESIRE UNRESTRAINED WITHOUT DUE REGARD TO THE RIGHTS OF OTHERS. TECHNICALLY, WHEN YOU ARE A BOND-SLAVE TO THE LORD YOU HAVE NO RIGHTS EXCEPT TO BE OBEDIENT TO HIM AND TO HIS WORD IN HIS SPIRIT! IN ACTUALITY, SUBMISSION TO PROPHECY IS SUBMITTING TO CORRECTION, TO EXHORTATION, TO WARNING, TO REPROOF. IMAGINE, ONE REALLY DOES NOT HAVE TO IMAGINE THIS SCENARIO, FOR IT IS IN FULL VIEW, ONE OF YOUR CHILDREN NOT ADHERING TO THE WORDS OF THOSE IN AUTHORITY. NOW THE OUTCOME OF THAT REBELLION IS EVIDENT IN CHURCH LEADERSHIP. DOING WHAT ONE WANTS TO DO OR WHAT ONE FEELS IS BEST, RATHER THAN WHAT THUS SAYS THE LORD! THE WORD IS MY ORDER, SAITH THE LORD! WHEN YOU

DO NOT ALLOW THE GIFTS OF THE SPIRIT TO HAVE FREEDOM IN YOUR ASSEMBLIES, YOU ARE OUT OF ORDER!!! WILL YOU BRAZENLY DO AWAY WITH THIS PART OF HOLY SCRIPTURES? AS IT IS WRITTEN, IN UNDERSTANDING, "BE MEN!" TRUE MEN. MEN OF COURAGE AND OBEDIENCE FEAR GOD! AND KEEP HIS COMMANDMENTS! THUS THEY ALLOW GOD ALMIGHTY TO MOVE BY HIS SPIRIT ACCORDING TO HIS WORD!!! TO EDIFY: TO BUILD OR INCREASE THE FAITH OF, TO INSTRUCT MORALLY!

THUS SAITH THE LORD, THE HEAVEN IS MY THRONE AND THE EARTH IS MY FOOTSTOOL! WHERE IS THE HOUSE THAT YOU BUILD UNTO ME? AND WHERE IS THE PLACE OF MY REST??? FOR ALL THESE THINGS HAS MY HAND MADE AND ALL THESE THINGS HAVE BEEN, SAITH THE LORD: BUT TO THIS MAN WILL I LOOK, EVEN TO HIM THAT IS POOR AND OF A CONTRITE SPIRIT AND (THERE'S THAT WORD, AGAIN ... AND) <u>AND</u> TREMBLES AT MY WORD!!! Isaiah 66. DEVILS BELIEVE AND TREMBLE! THAT'S MORE THAN MOST CHRISTIANS DO! THEY SAY THEY BELIEVE, BUT THEY DON'T TREMBLE! <u>AND</u> IS A LITTLE WORD, BUT IT REALLY MEANS SOMETHING, SOMETHING VERY IMPORTANT! YOU MAY BE OF A POOR AND A CONTRITE SPIRIT, BUT IF YOU DON'T TREMBLE AT THE WORD OF GOD, FORGET YOU! AND THEN YOU WONDER WHY HE DOES! WHY HE DOES NOT FULFILL <u>ALL</u> OF YOUR PETITIONS! ARE YOU FULFILLING <u>ALL</u> OF HIS? IT WORKS BOTH WAYS. IT IS A RELATIONSHIP! NOT A RIGHT! REMEMBER, YOU DON'T HAVE ANY! YOU ARE A BONDSERVANT OF JESUS CHRIST! HIS WORD <u>IS</u> YOUR COMMAND! SO LET'S JUST DO IT! AND SO FULFILL THE LAW OF CHRIST! AND BRING BACK THE KING!!! THE GLORY AS OF THE ONLY BEGOTTEN OF THE FATHER! FULL OF GRACE AND TRUTH! WE BEHOLD THY GLORY AND THY DOMINION AND THY POWER! THE REASON MOST PEOPLE ARE NOT WORKING THE WORKS OF GOD AND OBEYING THE GIFTS OF THE SPIRIT IS MOST PEOPLE DO NOT <u>TREMBLE</u> AT GOD'S WORD!!! SOME MAN'S, BUT NOT GOD'S!!!

March 5, 2001

April 2001

Prayers are people ...
turned prostrate.
Laying down their lives ...
giving time to eternity.

Part VI

Cry Aloud
and
Spare Not

Cry aloud, spare not, lift up thy voice like a trumpet and show my people their transgression and the house of Jacob their sins! Yet they seek me daily, as a Nation that did righteousness and that forsook not the ordinance of their God! They ask of me the ordinances of justice, taking delight in approaching to God! Yet there is strife and debate! But what I have chosen is to loose the bands of wickedness, to undo the heavy burdens, and to let the oppressed go free, and that you break <u>every</u> yoke!!! If thou turn away thy foot from the Sabbath, from doing thy pleasure on my holy day and call the Sabbath a delight, the holy of the Lord, honorable, and shalt honor him, not doing thine own ways, nor finding thine own pleasure, nor speaking thine own words: <u>then</u> shalt thou delight thyself in the Lord and I will cause thee to ride upon the high places of the earth and feed thee with the heritage of Jacob thy father for the mouth of the Lord hast spoken it!!!

Isaiah Fifty-Eight

Prophecy

TODAY IS A MIRACLE DAY! I AM RESTORING MARRIAGES TODAY! I AM SOLIDIFYING THE MARRIAGES THAT I HAVE PUT TOGETHER. NO WEAPON SHALL DESTROY MY SIGN TO THE UNBELIEVER. MARRIAGE IS A SIGN TO THE UNBELIEVER OF MY GLORY WHICH IS TO COME! STABILIZE YOUR THINKING AND TAKE MY <u>WORD</u> AS <u>FINAL</u> AUTHORITY! MY WORD RESTORES AND MAKES EVERYTHING NEW! SO RECEIVE THE GOODNESS OF THE LORD WHICH IS ABLE TO CHANGE ALL SITUATIONS, CIRCUMSTANCES AND FAILURES! WHICH CAN MAKE CROOKED PLACES STRAIGHT! HIGH PLACES LOW! LOW PLACES COME UP TO GOD'S STANDARD! WHY BE DENIED ANY LONGER WHEN THE LORD IS SAYING, BE HEALED! BE WHOLE! BE SECURE! BE FREE! BE OBEDIENT! BE SOUND IN YOUR BODY AND IN YOUR MIND AND IN YOUR WILL AND IN YOUR EMOTIONS! I STAY THE HAND OF DEATH!!! I CURTAIL ALL DREAD AND GLOOM! AND I MAKE GLORIOUS ALL DECISIONS AND SETTLEMENTS. I AM THE I AM! AND I HAVE FINAL SAY! IT IS ME! AND THERE IS NONE OTHER! REST! RECUPERATE! RENOUNCE ALL LEGALISTIC MINDSETS, IDEAS AND OPINIONS! JUMP INTO THE RIVER OF LIFE WHERE IT IS JOY UNSPEAKABLE AND FULL OF GLORY AND THE HALF HAS NOT BEEN TOLD!!! JOY IS IN JESUS! I RENEW STRENGTH AND SET IN ORDER KINGS AND KINGDOMS ... SECULAR AND SPIRITUAL! DENY MY GLORY NO LONGER. IT IS TIME FOR FULLNESS OF POWER AND DEMONSTRATION! RESIST MAN'S INSISTENCE OF ORDER THAT IS NOT OF MY ORDER! MY ORDER IS BY DIVINE INTERVENTION! LET MY SPIRIT GO FREE AND MAKE GLORIOUS MY DOMINION AND MY AUTHORITY! WHO IS THE HEAD OF THIS CHURCH ANYWAY? NOT YOU! WERE YOU THE ONE WHO HUNG THE STARS IN SPACE? WERE YOU THE ONE THAT MADE THE MIGHT AND THE WAY? THE NIGHT AND THE DAY? WAS IT YOU THAT MEASURED THE WATERS IN THE HOLLOW OF YOUR HAND? AND METED OUT THE HEAVENS WITH A SPAN? WHY DO YET WANT TO DOMINATE THE CHURCH??? SOME CHURCHES ARE COMING DOWN BECAUSE THEY ARE MAN'S CREATION, DOMINION AND POWER! MY CHURCH, THE GLORIOUS CHURCH

TRIUMPHANT, SHALL STAND UNMOVED IN THIS LAST DAY
MANIFESTATION OF POWER, DOMINION AND GLORY!!! MOVE
WITH MY SPIRIT OR DO NOT MOVE! SPEAK IN MY SPIRIT OR
DO NOT SPEAK! FORETELL IN MY SPIRIT OR HOLD YOUR
PEACE! SAYS THE HIGH AND LOFTY ONE! THE DOMINATOR
AND THE EXTERMINATOR! (TO PUT MY POWER INTO EARTHLY
VERNACULAR!) 'I AM' AND THERE IS NO OTHER! I SET UP KINGS
AND I OVERTHROW KINGDOMS! MY MIGHT AND MY DOMINION
AND MY POWER SHALL RULE IN THIS LAST AND EVIL DAY! I WILL
BE SET ASIDE NO LONGER! JUDGMENT HAS COME!!!

April 6, 2001

A MONUMENTAL CHANGE IN THE GOVERNMENT!
A MONUMENTAL CHANGE IN THE GOVERNMENT.
A MONUMENTAL CHANGE IN THE GOVERNMENT.
A DEFECTION SAYS THE LORD!

April 9, 2001

Note: Senator James Jeffords from Vermont switched from the Republican
Party to Independent on May 24, 2001. The above Word from the Lord was
faxed to Washington on May 21, 2001. But that was not the only defection,
even as the Lord spoke to me of one who was not doing what was needful
and necessary to help halt abortion.

Prophecy

I HAVE CHOSEN YOU FOR A SPECIFIC PURPOSE. TO INFILTRATE AND TO BRING FORTH DOMINION OF MIGHT! PREPARE TO GO. I WANT FULL AUTHORITY TO BE DEMONSTRATED. THE BLIND WILL SEE SAYS THE LORD! I WILL HEAL CANCER AND SICKLE CELL ANEMIA! I AM GOING TO SHOW YOU A MULTITUDE OF PEOPLE. PEOPLE WITH CANCER AND PEOPLE WITH DEMONIC INFILTRATION IN THEIR PSYCHES. DO NOT BE INTIMIDATED! IF I CANNOT BREAK A PERSON, I CANNOT MAKE A PERSON! I MUST BE IN ABSOLUTE AUTHORITY OR I DO NOT RECEIVE ULTIMATE GLORY! MAN CANNOT GIVE FULLNESS OF GLORY WITHOUT FULLNESS OF SPIRIT! IF MY SPIRIT IS NOT IN <u>FULL</u> AUTHORITY I DO NOT RECEIVE MY RIGHTFUL PLACE AND GLORY IS GIVEN TO MAN! I WILL NO LONGER TOLERATE THE HIERARCHY OF MAN WORSHIP! I AM THE ONLY TRUE LIVING GOD! WORSHIP ME IN SPIRIT AND IN TRUTH! TRUTH IS ... ULTIMATE! TRUTH IS FULL HEADSHIP UNDER MY AUTHORITY ... APOSTLES, PROPHETS, EVANGELISTS, PASTORS, AND TEACHERS. APOSTLES, PROPHETS, EVANGELISTS, PASTORS AND TEACHERS IS THE EPITOME OF TRUTH! IN PROPER ALIGNMENT! WITHOUT FULL HEADSHIP IN PROPER ALIGNMENT, FULL MANIFESTATION OF MY GLORY IN SIGNS, WONDERS AND MIRACLES IS DIMINISHED AND SPORADIC. I PERFORM MY GLORY THROUGH MY ANOINTED WHEN THEY HAVE THEIR PROPER PLACES AND ARE NOT SET ASIDE BY MAN MADE RITUAL, FEAR AND JEALOUSY. I WILL PREVAIL WITH THOSE WHO OBEY ME AND WITHOUT THOSE WHO FAIL TO GET IN AND STAY IN THEIR PROPER PLACES!!!

MY HOUSE SHALL BE CALLED A HOUSE OF PRAYER. PRAYER WITHOUT SUBMISSION IS FUTILE. WHY GO THROUGH THE DISCIPLINE AND SACRIFICE OF PRAYER IF YOU DO NOT OBEY MY DIRECTIVES? I AM HOLY. THAT MEANS YOU DO NOT MIX YOUR IDEAS AND OPINIONS WITH MY SPIRIT TO ENHANCE YOUR PREROGATIVES. I AM IN CONTROL. I AM HEADSHIP. POWER AND MIGHT COME THROUGH COMPLETE SURRENDER TO MY

AUTHORITY. ALL GLORY IS TO GO TO ME. ALL DOMINION IS TO BRING YOU INTO FULL AUTHORITY. MINE. NOT YOURS.

April 9, 2001

Prophecy

A GREAT DEARTH IS COMING UPON THIS LAND. A GREAT DEARTH IS COMING UPON THIS LAND EXCEPT THE ABORTION LAW IS EXPUNGED. DELIVER MY PEOPLE! SET THEM FREE!

April 10, 2001

May 2, 2002 U.S. News and World Report: Great Drying Drought: Fourteen states across the east coast and fourteen more states down the Rockies and into the plains and desert southwest. August 1, 2002: Extreme and increasing drought affects the regions wildlife. Animals are suffering because of the worst drought in a century. Hungry and thirsty animals are straying across highways and into yards ravaging for food and water.

I SEE EVERYTHING. NOTHING IS HID FROM ME. I SEE EVERY TIME THAT THE ENEMY HAS TRIED TO STOP THE FLOW OF MY SPIRIT. I KNOW WHO HE WAS USING AND I KNOW THEIR THOUGHTS BEHIND IT. I RECORDED THE DISCORD. I GIVE PEOPLE AMPLE TIME TO REPENT FOR THEIR DISUNITY AND THEN IF THEY DO NOT REPENT I SEND CHASTISEMENT. IF THEY DO NOT TAKE CORRECTION I SEND GREATER DISCIPLINES. INTEGRITY IS AT STAKE! TRUTH IS ON THE LINE! BRIDLING MY BRIDE RESTRAINS MY TESTIMONY! SERIOUS REPERCUSSIONS ARE ABOUT TO BE UNLEASHED UPON THOSE WHO RESTRAIN MINE ANOINTED! GLIB CLICHÉS WILL NOT BE ADMINISTERED TO APPEASE ME. I HAVE <u>PERFECT</u> ORDER SET IN ORDER! <u>FIRSTLY</u> APOSTLES! <u>SECONDARILY</u> PROPHETS! ! ! ! ! AS IT IS WRITTEN, THIS IS MY ORDER!!! WHEN WILL MAN STOP SETTING HIS OWN AGENDA??? WHEN I TAKE SOME OUT BY DEATH? PERHAPS, SOME ARE SET IN THEIR OWN STONE. BUT I KNOW HOW TO REMOVE THE STUMBLING BLOCKS! ! !

April 12, 2001

Prophecy

IN THREE DAYS AN OUTBREAK OF THE ANOINTING AND POWER WILL COME UPON THIS NATION GREATER THAN SINCE IT WAS FOUNDED!

April 14, 2001

THERE IS GOING TO BE MARTIAL LAW IN THIS LAND.

April 15, 2001

MIRACLES ARE COMING FORTH!!! MIRACLES ARE COMING FORTH! I AM RELEASING TONGUES OF FIRE UPON THIS NATION!

April 16, 2001

Prophecy

TODAY IS A VERY SPECIAL DAY. I HAVE REVIEWED YOUR SACRIFICES AND THEY ARE HOLY BEFORE ME. I COUNSEL WITH YOU NOW AND ASCRIBE POWER AND AUTHORITY AND DOMINION TO YOU. NO ONE STOPS ME AND NO ONE WILL STOP YOU. I HAVE PLACED YOU HERE FOR A SEASON AND THEN I AM SENDING YOU FORTH TO NATIONS SAITH THE LORD. DOORS WILL OPEN TO YOU, MY CHILD. YOU HAVE FERVENCY AND POWER, THE GIFTS OF THE SPIRIT TO WORK THE WORKS OF THE ALMIGHTY. I WILL HOLD YOU BACK NO LONGER FROM GOING FORTH IN DOMINION. THE SAME ANOINTING THAT I PLACED IN YOU OVER THIRTY YEARS AGO IS IN YOU FOR THE END TIME MANIFESTATION OF MY GLORY! YOU ALWAYS HONOR AND GIVE ME ALL THE GLORY. I CAN USE YOU TO HEAL ALL MANNER OF SICKNESS AND DISEASE, RAISE THE DEAD AND OPEN THE BLINDED EYES WITHOUT YOU GETTING EXALTED BECAUSE YOU ACKNOWLEDGE ME AS THE ALL-POWERFUL ONE! I CAN USE YOU IN THE ORIENT TO BREAK BONDAGES OF OTHER GODS AND TO RELEASE MY GLORY! TODAY I RELEASE YOU INTO YOUR DESTINY. I PREPARE THE WAY FOR THE FULFILLMENT OF ALL THINGS! I GIVE YOU ALL AUTHORITY AND ALL POWER AND ALL DOMINION TO PROCLAIM THE DAY OF THE LORD! SUBJECT ALL SIN TO CORRECTION! ALL EVIL TO JUDGMENT!

TRADITION, BE BROKEN! OBLIGATE THE POWERS THAT BE TO HEAR THE VOICE OF THE ALMIGHTY! FULFILL YOUR DESTINY! REVIVE DEAD CHURCHES! CAST OUT DEVILS! HEAL THE SICK! MAKE WHOLE THE LAME! THE CRIPPLED AND THE DISEASED! TAKE AUTHORITY OVER THE WICKED ONE! SET IN ORDER THE THINGS THAT ARE OUT OF ALIGNMENT! SPEAK MY WORD! IT IS FINISHED! THE MINISTRY OF MIRACLES IS IN YOU, MY CHILD. OPEN YOUR MOUTH AND TAKE DOMINION OVER ALL MANNER OF SICKNESS AND DISEASE! ! ! I HAVE HEALED YOUR DAUGHTER AND SET HER FREE! SHE IS IN POSITION. I WILL USE HER MIGHTILY IN THESE LAST DAYS AS SHE CONTINUES TO SEEK MY FACE AND TO STAY HUMBLE BEFORE ME. I WILL REQUIRE MORE

AND MORE CONSECRATION FROM HER AS I USE HER AND TAKE HER HIGHER. SHE WILL INSTRUCT MANY IN THE GIFTS OF THE SPIRIT. I LOOSE HER EVEN NOW FOR MIRACLES AND DELIVERANCES. SPEAK THE WORD ONLY! ENACT POWER THROUGH THE AUTHORITY OF MY WORD! JUSTIFY NO MAN BY PERSON. ENABLE NO MAN TO CONTINUE IN SELF. I TEAR DOWN AND STRIP AWAY THE BONDAGES OF PRIDE, MALICE, UN-FORGIVENESS, RESENTMENT, ANGER, DISCORD, MALIGNITY, WRATH, SEDITION AND HERESY! MY WORD IS MY WAY! MY WAY OR NO WAY! SOME WILL YET GO OUT BY DEATH BECAUSE THEY CHOOSE TO STAND AGAINST ME AND MY AUTHORITY! WHEN YOU STAND AGAINST MINE ANOINTED YOU STAND AGAINST ME! WHEN YOU STAND AGAINST ME YOU ARE CONDEMNED TO DIE! SOME EVEN NOW ARE DEAD WHILE THEY LIVE. DEAD IN TRESPASSES AND SIN! TIME IS ALMOST UP TO REPENT OF YOUR WICKEDNESS AND DISOBEDIENCE! DEATH IS AT THE DOOR.

I HEAL MY PEOPLE OF THEIR WICKEDNESS AND THEIR CANKERDNESS. I RIP FROM THEIR SOULS THEIR DISCORD AND DISMAY! I REVIVE TRUTH INTO THEIR SPIRIT AND SET THEM FREE FROM THEIR WAYWARDNESS. BE STRONG IN THE LORD AND IN THE POWER OF HIS MIGHT! HIS WORD IS POWER! HIS WORD IS MIGHT! LET NO CORRUPT COMMUNICATION PROCEED OUT OF YOUR MOUTH! EXCEPT THAT WHICH WILL EDIFY! BUILD OR BE SILENT! SPEAK MY WORD OR DON'T SPEAK! STAY IN TUNE TO MY SPIRIT SO THAT I CAN MANIFEST MY GLORY! MY GLORY REPUDIATES PAIN! MY GLORY SETS CAPTIVES FREE! MY GLORY BRINGS UNITY! LET IT STRIP AWAY ALL DROSS AND UNITE MY CHURCH IN TRIUMPH! VICTORY IS ME!!! ALL MY OFFICERS! REFUSE NOT ANY OF MY OFFICERS LEST JUDGMENTS COME UPON YOU AND YOUR FAMILY! I HAVE HELD BACK MANY JUDGMENTS, BUT I WILL NO LONGER RESTRAIN THEM, FOR WHEN JUDGMENTS ARE IN THE LAND THE INHABITANTS LEARN RIGHTEOUSNESS!!!

April 17, 2001

Prophecy

DON'T HOLD BACK ANYTHING I BID YOU TO DO. THIS IS THE END. THE CULMINATION OF <u>ALL</u> THINGS. STAY CONSECRATED. YEA, YEA, MY CHILD, NO MORE BEING HELD BACK. EVEN AS IT WAS THIS DAY, WITH GREAT REVERENCE AND AWE YOU WILL BE RECEIVED IN YOUR GOING OUT AND IN YOUR COMING IN. TWO-FOLD ... THE POWER <u>AND</u> THE AUTHORITY! ! ! ALL RESISTANCE IS BROKEN. I SHALL OPEN DOORS AS NEVER BEFORE. YOU ARE AN END TIME MESSENGER! BE PREPARED TO TRAVEL. I AM OPENING BIG DOORS. STAY VERY CONSECRATED BECAUSE I WANT TO ESTABLISH YOUR MINISTRY IN HEALING AND MIRACLES. SOME NOTABLE MIRACLES WILL TAKE PLACE IN YOUR MINISTRY SOON. THEY WILL BE MADE KNOWN AMONG THE PEOPLE. STAY VERY HUMBLE. LET OTHERS PRAISE YOU. YOU WILL NOT HAVE TO MAKE MENTION OF IT. YOU ARE CELEBRATED IN THE HEAVENLIES! THE BARRIERS THAT HAVE HELD BACK MY GLORY HAVE BEEN BROKEN. I WILL SHOW YOU A VISION SOON. KEEP OBEYING ME AT <u>ALL</u> COSTS. SUBSTANTIAL MONEY IS COMING TO YOU VERY SOON.

April 21, 2001

I DON'T NEED NO JOCKEY! I RIDE MY OWN HORSE! MY TESTIMONY IS THE SPIRIT OF PROPHECY! MY NAME IS CALLED THE WORD OF GOD!!! I AM FAITHFUL AND TRUE! AND IN RIGHTEOUSNESS I WILL JUDGE AND MAKE WAR! ! !

April 28, 2001

Wisdom

<u>THE IMPORTANCE OF HEALING IS THAT WE ARE HIS BODY. WE
ARE HIS BODY!!! A SICK BODY DOES NOT PORTRAY THE
INTEGRITY OF JESUS!!!!!</u>

April 22, 2001

THERE ARE PEOPLE THAT WILL STEAL YOUR VERY LIFE FROM YOU.
THAT WILL TAKE YOUR TIME FROM YOU ... BECAUSE THEY
REFUSE TO FULLY SUBMIT TO GOD ... SO THEY ALWAYS NEED YOU
TO POUR INTO THEM YOUR OIL INSTEAD OF THEM SEEKING
GOD'S FACE TO GET THEIR OWN OIL! THEY TAKE YOURS AND
ROB YOU OF THE THINGS THAT GOD HAD INTENDED FOR YOU
TO ACCOMPLISH!

WHEN YOU GET WILLING TO FORGIVE, YOU CAN FORGIVE!
FEELINGS DO NOT BRING FORGIVENESS. WILLINGNESS TO OBEY
GOD'S WORD BRINGS FORGIVENESS!

April 23, 2001

Prophetic Teaching

CHURCH AIN'T ABOUT A PROGRAM! TEAR IT UP! CHURCH IS A PERSON! WHEN YOU KNOW HOW TO DO IT, HE'S GONE! HE AIN'T A PROGRAM! AND HE SURE AIN'T GONNA BE A PART OF YOURS. IF IT WERE NOT FOR *LOST SOULS* HE WOULD NOT EVEN SHOW UP THE LITTLE BIT HE DOES IN SOME CHURCHES! HE IS SICK OF THE LITTLE BIT OF SPACE YOU METE OUT TO HIM ... WHEN YOU GET ALL YOUR THANG DONE!!! IT IS SO FAR ABOVE AND BEYOND YOUR LITTLE SHOW ... IT IS SICKENING TO THINK HOW GOD WOULD LIKE TO SHOW UP AND SHOW OUT, BUT YOU HARNESS HIM IN WITH YOUR REINS! YOU ARE PATHETIC ... THINKING YOU KNOW SO MUCH! DO YOU LAY IN HIS PRESENCE UNDER THE ANOINTING EACH DAY??? THEN HOW ARE YOU GOING TO OVERSEE? OR USHER IN THE SPIRIT OF THE LORD???

PEOPLE ARE DYING AND ON THEIR WAY TO A DEVIL'S HELL AND YOU ARE AFRAID THE DEVIL WILL GET TURNED LOOSE ... SO YOU DON'T EVEN LET <u>GOD</u> PERFORM! HE DOES MIGHTY SIGNS AND WONDERS WHEN GIVEN THE FREEDOM TO MOVE! WOULDN'T IT BE SOMETHING TO FULLY GIVE THE LORD FREE REIN TO LET HIM <u>BE</u> GOD!!! MAJESTY AND POWER TAKE DOMINION WHEN HE IS IN CONTROL ... SIGNS AND WONDERS AND MIRACLES OCCUR!!! IF THEY DO NOT ... HE HAS NOT BEEN GIVEN *FULL* HEADSHIP!!! I HAVE SAID AT OTHER TIMES, THERE IS ONLY ONE WONDER AND THAT IS JESUS THE CHRIST! BUT THE LORD IS SAYING, YOU CAN BE A WONDER OR YOU CAN BE A BLUNDER! IT'S UP TO YOU!!! YOU CHOOSE!!! CHOOSE TO OBEY <u>WORD</u> ... CONTINUOUSLY ... CONSCIENTIOUSLY ... COURTEOUSLY ... CORDIALLY! WITH <u>ALL</u> YOUR HEART, WITH <u>ALL</u> YOUR SOUL, WITH <u>ALL</u> YOUR MIND! AS THE LORD SAYS, IN MATTHEW 22:35-39.

THOU SHALT LOVE THE LORD THY GOD WITH *ALL* THY HEART, AND WITH *ALL* THY SOUL, AND WITH *ALL* THY MIND! THIS IS THE FIRST AND GREAT COMMANDMENT! AND THE SECOND IS LIKE UNTO IT, THOU SHALT LOVE THY NEIGHBOR AS THYSELF! I LIKE THE WAY MOSES SAYS IT IN DEUTERONOMY 6:4. HEAR, O ISRAEL:

THE LORD OUR GOD IS <u>ONE</u> LORD: AND THOU SHALT LOVE THE LORD THY GOD WITH <u>ALL</u> THINE HEART, AND WITH ... AND WITH <u>ALL</u> THY MIGHT! AS IT IS WRITTEN IN MARK 12:30, JESUS INCLUDES WITH *ALL* WITH <u>ALL</u> THY STRENGTH! IN VERSE 40 OF MATTHEW 22, JESUS WENT ON TO SAY, <u>*ON THESE TWO COMMANDMENTS*</u> HANG <u>*ALL*</u> THE LAW <u>*AND*</u> THE PROPHETS! AND YOU WONDER WHY PROPHETS ARE <u>ALL</u> ABOUT EXHORTING YOU TO <u>LOVE</u> ONE ANOTHER AND TO <u>FULLY</u> OBEY GOD??? 'CAUSE JESUS SAID TO!!! HE SAID ON THESE TWO COMMANDMENTS <u>ALONE</u> HANG <u>*ALL*</u> THE LAW <u>*AND*</u> THE PROPHETS! A B C ... 1 2 3. LIKE THE SAYING GOES, EVERYTHING I NEEDED TO KNOW, THE BASE OF ALL KNOWLEDGE, I LEARNED IN KINDERGARTEN ... OBEY THE RULES AND BE NICE! OBEY THE RULES AND BE NICE! BUT SOME OF YOU ARE FINDING OUT YOU CAN'T! AND I AM HERE TO TELL YOU WHY!

PEOPLE KEEP TALKING ABOUT THE COVENANT! THE COVENANT! THE COVENANT! YES, THE LAW IS THE SCHOOLMASTER OF THE NEW COVENANT! YES, UNDER THE LAW YOU CIRCUMCISE THAT CHILD. BUT CIRCUMCISION IS NOT DONE AWAY WITH UNDER THE CHRIST OF THE NEW COVENANT! THE CIRCUMCISION NOW INCLUDES THE CIRCUMCISION OF THE HEART! BECAUSE THE HEART IS THE WOMB OF THE SOUL!!! THE HEART IS WHERE CHILDREN ARE BIRTHED INTO THE NEW COVENANT! THE HEART MUST BE ... CIRCUMCISED FOR IT TO LOVE THE LORD YOUR GOD WITH <u>*ALL*</u> YOUR INNERMOST BEING AND WITH <u>*ALL*</u> YOUR SOUL AND WITH <u>*ALL*</u> YOUR STRENGTH! THE LORD THY GOD WILL CIRCUMCISE THINE HEART AND THE HEART OF THY SEED, TO LOVE THE LORD THY GOD WITH ALL THINE HEART AND WITH ALL THY SOUL THAT THOU MAYEST LIVE! AND THOU SHALT RETURN AND OBEY THE VOICE OF THE LORD, AND DO <u>ALL</u> HIS COMMANDMENTS! AND THE LORD WILL MAKE THEE PLENTEOUS IN EVERY WORK OF THINE HAND, <u>*IF*</u> THOU SHALT HEARKEN TO THE VOICE OF THE LORD THY GOD, TO KEEP HIS COMMANDMENTS AND HIS STATUTES WHICH ARE WRITTEN IN THE BOOK! Deuteronomy 30:6-10

YOU NEED TO HAVE SOME THINGS CUT AWAY ... CUT OUT OF YOUR HEART!!! THAT IS CALLED CIRCUMCISION! THE CIRCUMCISION OF THE HEART IS NOT DONE WITH A KNIFE OR A SURGICAL TOOL! IT IS DONE WITH A SWORD! IT IS CALLED THE WORD OF GOD! IT IS QUICK! THAT MEANS IT MOVES! AND POWERFUL! THAT MEANS IT HAS AUTHORITY! ITS AUTHORITY IS ALMIGHTY GOD!!! IT IS SHARPER THAN ANY TWO-EDGED SWORD! IT DIVIDES THE SOUL AND THE SPIRIT SO THAT YOU CAN MAKE A CHOICE WHICH ONE YOU AIM TO PLEASE!!! YOUR MIND ... OR THE MAN??? THE MAN CHRIST JESUS!!! IT CAN GET DOWN INTO THE JOINTS AND THE VERY MARROW OF YOUR BONES WHEN YOU READ ... STUDY AND LISTEN TO THE WORDS OF THE ALMIGHTY!!! *IF* ... *IF* ANY MAN HAS A ... BROKEN ... SURRENDERED ... SUBMITTED ... SOULED OUT HEART ... NOT JUST SOLD LIKE MONEY! SOME OF YOU PAY THE TENTH OF THE MONEY YOU MAKE, BUT YOU AIN'T SOULED OUT! YOU AIN'T DUG OUT! YOU AIN'T CLEANED OUT! THAT IS SOULED OUT! S-O-U-L-E-D OUT! THAT IS YOUR MIND ... YOUR THOUGHTS, YOUR UNDERSTANDING, YOUR INTELLIGENCE *AND* YOUR WILL! THAT IS YOUR DREAMS, YOUR PLANS AND YOUR EMOTIONS! THAT IS EVERYTHING ELSE THAT IS IN THERE ... FEELINGS, GOOD AND BAD. YOU CAN EITHER BE DEMOTED OR PROMOTED BY JUST WHAT YOU *EMOTED!* SOME OF YOU SAYING ... WELL, I'M BROWN, SO I'M DOWN! OR I'M BLACK SO I LACK! YOU NEED TO SHUT UP SO YOU CAN GO UP! UP IN THE SPIRIT REALM ... SO GOD CAN DO HIS THANG! AND YOU ARE JUST WATCHING HIM BUILD BY THE WORDS YOU PROMOTED! BY HEARING, RETAINING AND SAYING GOD'S WORDS THAT MAKE THE CROOKED PLACES STRAIGHT AND THE HIGH PLACES TO COME DOWN AND LOW PLACES TO BE BUILT UP ... SO GOD CAN DO HIS THANG! AND YOU ARE JUST WATCHING HIM BUILD ... BY THE WORDS YOU ARE UTTERING! YEA! YEA! GO AHEAD ON LORD! I SAID IT ... NOW YOU ARE PERFORMING IT! NOW AIN'T THAT HIP! NOW I KNOW THEY DON'T USE THAT TERM ANYMORE, BUT I DID, 'CAUSE I LIKE THAT ERA! I MEAN WHEN YOU SAID GOOD, IT MEANT GOOD! IT WAS LIKE THIS WORD ... IT MEANS WHAT IT SAYS AND SAYS WHAT IT MEANS! WHEN IT SAYS, DEATH AND LIFE ARE IN THE POWER OF

THE TONGUE, IT STILL MEANS, WHAT YOU SAY IS WHAT YOU GET!!! Proverbs 18:21 THE WORLDS WERE FORMED AT THE ONSET BY WORDS AND OUR WORLD ... THE LITTLE COSMOS OF OUR EXISTENCE ... THE GOOD, THE BAD AND THE UGLY IS IN THE SHOW ROOM OF OUR MOUTH BECAUSE WE ARE THE ARCHITECT OF WHAT TAKES PLACE IN OUR FUTURE BY THE WORDS WE BEEN SAYIN'! SAYIN' HAS MORE POWER THAN PRAYIN'! PRAYIN' IS TO GET YOU INTO HIS PRESENCE SO YOU WILL STOP SAYIN' THE THINGS THAT YOU DON'T WANT! IF YOU KEEP TALKIN' THE DOOM AND THE GLOOM ... YOU ARE JUST MAKIN' ROOM FOR MORE OF THE SAME! SAYIN' IS PRAYIN' IN A HIGHER FORM. WHEN YOU ARE IN THE SPIRIT ... YOU SAY WHAT GOD SAYS! THAT'S THE MAIN REASON WE ARE SUPPOSED TO WALK IN THE SPIRIT ... SO THAT WE CAN TALK LIKE GOD! IN THE SPIRIT! IF WE TALK IN THE SPIRIT ON A CONTINUAL BASIS ... NOT UP AND DOWN AND IN AND OUT ... BUT STEADFASTLY ... WE WILL BEGIN TO SEE IN THE NATURAL REALM WHAT WE HAVE BEEN DECLARING IN THE SPIRITUAL REALM! WORDS MAKE THINGS HAPPEN!!! WORDS ARE SUBSTANCE! THEY MAKE THINGS HAPPEN! THEY ARE POWER TO BRING ABOUT GOOD OR TO RELEASE EVIL!!! YOU CHOOSE! THIS DAY! WHOM YOU WILL SERVE WITH THE WORDS THAT COME OUT OF YOUR MOUTH! THE WORDS THAT YOU CHOOSE TO SPEAK EITHER TO AFFIRM THE WORDS THAT GOD HAS SPOKEN OR TO IGNORE AND TO LOSE THE BLESSINGS THAT GOD HAD INTENDED FOR YOU TO HAVE! WORDS ARE THE BENEFACTORS OF WHAT YOU TRULY BELIEVE! YOU GET WHAT YOU SPEAK AND AFFIRM. CONFESS ON A CONTINUING AND ONGOING DAY TO DAY BASIS! Proverbs 13:2-3, 12:14, 4:20-27, 22:17-21, Ecclesiastes 12:11, Isaiah 51:16, John 6:63, Job 6:24-25, Jeremiah 15:19, Hosea 14:2, Proverbs 7:24. HE THAT LOVETH ME NOT DOETH NOT MY SAYINGS! John 14:23 IF ANY MAN TEACH OTHERWISE AND CONSENT NOT TO WHOLESOME WORDS, EVEN THE WORDS OF THE LORD JESUS CHRIST, AND TO THE DOCTRINE WHICH IS ACCORDING TO GODLINESS, HE IS PROUD, KNOWING NOTHING, BUT DOTING ABOUT QUESTIONS AND STRIFES OF WORDS, WHEREOF COMETH ENVY, STRIFE, RAILINGS, EVIL SURMISINGS, PERVERSE DISPUTINGS OF MEN OF CORRUPT

MINDS AND DESTITUTE OF THE TRUTH, SUPPOSING THAT GAIN IS GODLINESS, FROM SUCH WITHDRAW THYSELF. BUT GODLINESS WITH CONTENTMENT IS GREAT GAIN! FOR WE BROUGHT NOTHING INTO THIS WORLD, AND IT IS CERTAIN WE CAN CARRY NOTHING OUT! AND HAVING FOOD AND RAIMENT LET US BE THEREWITH CONTENT! I Timothy 6

DECLARE RIGHTEOUSNESS!!! DECLARE DOMINION! DECLARE THE AUTHORITY OF THE WORD OF POWER OVER THE DEMONIC FORCES THAT HOLD BACK YOUR BLESSING! DECREE A THING AND IT SHALL BE ESTABLISHED UNTO YOU! Job 22:28 PUT GOD IN REMEMBRANCE! AS IT IS WRITTEN, PUT ME IN REMEMBRANCE! DECLARE THOU THAT YOU MAY BE JUSTIFIED!!! I, EVEN I, AM HE THAT BLOTS OUT YOUR TRANSGRESSIONS FOR MINE OWN SAKE AND WILL NOT REMEMBER YOUR SINS! Isaiah 43:25-26 AS IT IS WRITTEN, LET THE PEOPLE RENEW THEIR STRENGTH! THE WORD IS YOUR STRENGTH!!! LET THEM COME NEAR! WHEN YOU GET IN THE WORD YOU ARE DRAWING NEAR TO GOD! THEN LET THEM SPEAK!!! SHUT UP UNTIL YOU DRAW NEAR TO GOD'S WORD AND HIS WORD GETS IN YOU. THEN SPEAK! I John 5:7 IF YOU ABIDE ... THAT'S LIVING ... IF YOU ARE LIVING IN ME (ME IS HIS WORD BECAUSE HE IS THE WORD!) AND MY WORDS ARE LIVING IN YOU ... DAILY, HOURLY, MINUTE BY MINUTE YOU SHALL ASK WHAT YOU WILL AND IT SHALL BE DONE UNTO YOU! YOU WANT TO BRING GLORY TO GOD? FOR REAL? THE NEXT VERSE SAYS ... HEREIN IS MY FATHER GLORIFIED!!! WHEN IS HE GLORIFIED??? WHEN YOU BEAR MUCH FRUIT! THEN HE SAYS, SO SHALL YOU BE MY DISCIPLES. IF YOU AIN'T BEARING FRUIT YOU AIN'T HIS DISCIPLINE! CHRISTIANS ARE CHRIST-LIKE! THEY BEAR FRUIT! Romans 8:14

FOR AS MANY AS ARE LED BY THE SPIRIT OF GOD, THEY ARE THE SONS OF GOD! WHO ARE THE SONS OF GOD? IT IS WRITTEN, AS MANY AS ARE LED BY THE SPIRIT OF GOD! AS IT IS WRITTEN, I JOHN 3:6 WHOEVER ABIDES IN HIM DOES NOT KEEP SINNING! WHOEVER KEEPS ON SINNING HAS NOT SEEN HIM, NEITHER KNOWN HIM! THE SCRIPTURE SAYS, IF ANY MAN BE IN CHRIST,

HE IS A NEW CREATURE, OLD THINGS ARE PASSED AWAY AND ALL THINGS BECOME NEW!!! WHAT THINGS? WHAT THINGS BECOME NEW? ALL THE THINGS THAT YOU GIVE HIM! IF YOU DON'T TAKE YOUR SUITS TO THE CLEANERS THEY DON'T CLEAN THEM! IF YOU DON'T GIVE GOD ALL YOUR FILTH HE CAN'T MAKE IT NEW! EVERYONE WHO SAYS A SINNER'S PRAYER IS *NOT IN* CHRIST! IF THEY WERE, OLD THINGS WOULD BE PASSING AWAY! THE REASON OLD THINGS DO NOT PASS AWAY AND DIE IS THE PERSON IS NOT *IN* CHRIST! TO BE IN CHRIST MEANS TO BE IN THE WORD! IF YOU ARE IN THE WORD ... READING, CONFESSING, STUDYING, SURRENDERING OLD THINGS, OLD THINGS ARE PASSING AWAY! IF YOU ARE NOT READING, CONFESSING, STUDYING, SURRENDERING OLD THINGS, OLD THINGS DO NOT DIE! YOU ARE NOT IN CHRIST! IT IS WRITTEN, I JOHN 3:9 WHOSOEVER IS BORN OF GOD DOES NOT KEEP COMMITTING SIN FOR HIS SEED REMAINS IN HIM AND HE CANNOT SIN BECAUSE HE IS BORN OF GOD!

WHEN YOU ARE BORN OF GOD, YOU EAT THE WORD!!!!! THE WORD OF GOD KEEPS YOU FROM CONTINUING IN SIN! THAT SEED THAT REMAINS IN YOU IS THE WORD OF GOD! WHEN YOU ARE TRULY BORN OF GOD YOU EAT WHAT GOD HAS SAID TO EAT WHICH IS HIS WORD! IF YOU ARE NOT EATING HIS WORD DAILY, TRIBULATION OR PERSECUTION, OR THE CARES OF THIS WORLD, OR THE DECEITFULNESS OF RICHES WILL CHOKE THE WORD AND YOU WILL BECOME UNFRUITFUL! IF YOU ARE UNFRUITFUL YOU ARE NOT A DISCIPLE OF CHRIST. DISCIPLE MEANS TO DISCIPLINE YOURSELF. CHRISTIANS ARE FRUITFUL. OTHERWISE, IF A MAN ABIDE NOT IN ME (THE WORD) HE IS CAST FORTH AS A BRANCH AND IS WITHERED AND MEN GATHER THEM AND CAST THEM INTO THE FIRE AND THEY ARE BURNED! John 15:6 JESUS SAID, IF YOU CONTINUE IN MY WORD, THEN ARE YOU MY DISCIPLES INDEED! AND YOU SHALL KNOW THE TRUTH AND THE TRUTH SHALL MAKE YOU FREE! John 8:31-32 JESUS SAID IN VERSE 34, VERILY, VERILY, MEANING THE TRUTH! THE TRUTH!

I SAY UNTO YOU, <u>WHOSOEVER COMMITS SIN IS THE SERVANT OF SIN</u>! Romans 6:16 <u>KNOW YOU NOT THAT TO WHOM YOU YIELD YOURSELVES SERVANTS TO OBEY, HIS SERVANTS YOU ARE TO WHOM YOU OBEY! WHOEVER YOU OBEY, THAT IS WHOSE SERVANT YOU ARE! WHETHER OF SIN UNTO DEATH OR OF OBEDIENCE UNTO RIGHTEOUSNESS</u>!!!

BE A JEW WHICH IS ONE INWARDLY, BY THE CIRCUMCISION OF THE HEART, IN THE SPIRIT, WHOSE PRAISE IS NOT OF MEN, BUT OF GOD! Romans 2:29 IN WHOM ALSO YOU ARE CIRCUMCISED WITH THE CIRCUMCISION MADE WITHOUT HANDS IN PUTTING OFF THE BODY OF SINS OF THE FLESH BY CIRCUMCISION OF CHRIST! Colossians 2:11 PUT ON THE NEW MAN WHICH IS RENEWED IN KNOWLEDGE AFTER THE IMAGE OF HIM THAT CREATED HIM IN RIGHTEOUSNESS AND <u>TRUE</u> HOLINESS! Colossians 3:10 Ephesians 4:24 BE RENEWED DAILY BY THE WASHING OF THE WORD! Ephesians 5:26-27 BE RENEWED DAILY IN THE SPIRIT BY PRAYING IN THE HOLY GHOST! Ephesians 4:23 Jude 20 BE NOT CONFORMED TO THIS WORLD BUT BE TRANSFORMED BY THE RENEWING OF YOUR MIND, PRAYING IN THE HOLY GHOST SO THAT YOU MAY KNOW WHAT IS THE PERFECT WILL OF GOD!!! I BESEECH YOU, THEREFORE BRETHREN, BY THE MERCIES OF GOD THAT YOU PRESENT YOUR BODIES, A LIVING SACRIFICE, HOLY AND ACCEPTABLE UNTO GOD WHICH IS YOUR INTELLIGENT WORSHIP!!! Romans 12:1-2

WORK OUT YOUR OWN SALVATION WITH FEAR AND TREMBLING FOR IT IS GOD WHICH WORKS IN YOU BOTH TO WILL <u>AND</u> TO DO OF HIS GOOD PLEASURE! DO ALL THINGS WITHOUT MURMURINGS AND DISPUTINGS: THAT YOU MAY BE BLAMELESS, THE SONS OF GOD, WITHOUT REBUKE, IN THE MIDST OF A CROOKED AND PERVERSE NATION, AMONG WHOM YOU SHINE AS LIGHTS IN THE WORLD: HOLDING FORTH THE WORD OF LIFE!!! Philippians 2:12-16

CHRIST LOVED THE CHURCH AND GAVE HIMSELF FOR IT!!! Ephesians 5:26-27 THERE IS THE RUB ... THE LACK ... THE FAULT

... THE REASON ... FOR THE LACK OF BEING MADE EVERY WHIT WHOLE AND EVERY WHIT CLEAN!!! HE GAVE HIMSELF! HIS ALL!!! HIS LIFE'S BLOOD! WHEN YOU GIVE YOUR BLOOD ... YOUR LIFE ... THERE IS NOTHING ELSE LEFT! THE WORK WAS DONE ... WAS ACCOMPLISHED ... BECAUSE HE GAVE ALL! TO BE A RECIPIENT OF HIS ALL WE MUST GIVE OUR SELF ... OUR ALL ... UNTO HIM!!! THE REASON WE GET HALF-SAVED, HALF DELIVERED, HALF SET FREE, IS: WE ONLY GIVE HIM PART OF US! WE DO NOT FULLY SURRENDER EVERY PART OF OUR BEING! HE CAN ONLY WORK ON ... DELIVER, ... SET FREE, WHAT WE GIVE TO HIM! HE CANNOT WASH WHAT WE DON'T GIVE HIM! IT WOULD BE LIKE GOING TO THE CLEANERS TO PICK UP OUR TWO SUITS THAT WE DROPPED OFF TO BE CLEANED, AND EXPECTING OUR WHOLE WARDROBE ... EVERYTHING WE GOT TO BE CLEANED, SEWN AND PRESSED, WHEN ALL WE HAD GIVEN THEM IS TWO SUITS! YES, WE GIVE GOD OUR TWO SUITS. THE ONE WE WEAR TO CHURCH AND THE ONE WE WEAR TO WORK. GOD CLEANS WHAT WE GIVE HIM! WHAT WE SURRENDER UNTO HIM AND WHAT WE KEEP BEFORE HIM CONTINUALLY! SURRENDERING DAILY OUR THOUGHTS, OUR FEELINGS, OUR HURTS, OUR HEARTACHES, OUR HELLS, THE HOLES IN OUR HEART, THE WEEPING, THE TORMENT!!! GIVE UP! YOU CAN'T!!! BUT HE CAN!!! SURRENDER THE STRIFE, THE BITTERNESS, THE ANGER, THE SELF-WILL, THE STUBBORNNESS, THE REBELLION, THE ABUSE, THE HATE, THE LIVING DEATHS, THE BRUTALITY, THE HUNGER AND THE LACK! GIVE HIM YOUR NEEDLE, YOUR BOTTLE, YOUR JOINT!!! GIVE HIM YOUR PORNOGRAPHY, YOUR WEB SITES, YOUR ADULT VIDEOS!!! GIVE HIM YOU!!! YOURSELF!!! HE CLEANS <u>ALL</u> OF IT WHEN WE GIVE HIM <u>ALL</u> OF US! WHATEVER YOU GIVE TO HIM HE TAKES AND MAKES YOU HIS OWN. HE IS THEN ABLE TO LIVE IN YOU ... WALK IN YOU ... TALK IN YOU! YOU BECOME HIS LIVING EPISTLE!!! WRITTEN NOT WITH INK, BUT WITH THE SPIRIT OF THE LIVING GOD!!!!! YOUR SUFFICIENCY IS OF GOD!!! ALL YOU HAVE TO DO IS TO GIVE HIM YOU! CHRIST LOVED THE CHURCH AND GAVE HIMSELF FOR IT WITH THE WASHING OF WATER BY THE WORD!!! CHRIST LOVED THE CHURCH AND GAVE HIMSELF FOR IT THAT HE MIGHT SANCTIFY AND CLEANSE IT! Ephesians 5:25-26 TO

SANCTIFY IS TO BE FREE FROM SIN! TO SANCTIFY IS TO MAKE PRODUCTIVE AND CONDUCIVE TO SPIRITUAL BLESSING! TO SANCTIFY IS TO MAKE HOLY! TO SET APART AS SACRED! TO CONSECRATE! TO SANCTIFY IS TO IMPART RELIGIOUS SANCTION, TO RENDER LEGITIMATE AND BINDING!!! TO SANCTIFY MEANS TO ENTITLE TO REVERENCE AND RESPECT!!! AND CLEANSE IT WITH THE WASHING OF WATER BY THE WORD! THE WORD WORKS, DEAR ONES, <u>IF WE LET IT</u>!!!

HEARKEN UNTO ME, O JACOB AND ISRAEL, MY CALLED! I AM HE! I AM THE FIRST! I ALSO AM THE LAST! MINE HAND ALSO HAS LAID THE FOUNDATION OF THE EARTH AND MY RIGHT HAND HAS SPANNED THE HEAVENS! WHEN I CALL UNTO THEM, THEY STAND UP TOGETHER! ALL YE, ASSEMBLE YOURSELVES AND HEAR! I, EVEN I HAVE SPOKEN! I HAVE CALLED MY PROPHETS. I HAVE BROUGHT THEM FORTH AND SHALL MAKE THEIR WAY PROSPEROUS. COME NEAR UNTO ME IN PRAYER AND CONSECRATION! THUS SAITH THE LORD, THY REDEEMER, THE HOLY ONE OF ISRAEL!!! I AM THE LORD THY GOD WHICH TEACHES THEE TO PROFIT, WHICH LEADS THEE BY THE WAY THAT THOU SHOULD GO!!! Isaiah 48 YEA, BEFORE THE DAY WAS I AM HE! AND THERE IS NONE THAT CAN DELIVER OUT OF MY HAND!!! I WILL WORK AND WHO SHALL LET ME??? Isaiah 43 WHO HAS AMENED THE FAITH OF THE LORD??? AND TO WHOM IS THE ARM OF THE LORD REVEALED?

<u>SURELY HE HAS BORNE OUR GRIEFS AND CARRIED OUR SORROWS! HE WAS WOUNDED FOR OUR TRANSGRESSIONS! HE WAS BRUISED AND BEATEN FOR OUR INIQUITIES! THE CHASTISEMENT OUR PEACE WAS UPON HIM AND WITH HIS STRIPES WE ARE HEALED!</u> Isaiah 53 BUT ABOVE ALL HE GAVE HIMSELF FOR US THAT HE MIGHT REDEEM US FROM <u>ALL</u> INIQUITY AND PURIFY UNTO HIMSELF A PECULIAR PEOPLE, ZEALOUS OF GOOD WORKS! Hebrews 8:10-13 Titus 2:11-15 *HONEY, IF YOU AIN'T ZEALOUS OF GOOD WORKS YOU HAVEN'T LET HIM PURIFY AND CLEAN YOU UP YET! 'CAUSE WHEN YOU'RE CLEAN ... YOU ARE ZEALOUS! HAH! HOLY GHOST! SPEAK! THE WORD CAN'T*

WASH YOU AND CLEAN YOU UP IF YOU DON'T GET IN IT OR UNDER IT!!! GET UNDER THE SPOUT WHERE THE GLORY COMES OUT!!! WASH YOU, MAKE YOU CLEAN!!! PUT AWAY THE EVIL OF YOUR DOINGS! CEASE TO DO EVIL!!! LEARN TO DO WELL! SEEK TRUTH! COME NOW AND LET US REASON TOGETHER, SAITH LORD!!! THOUGH YOUR SINS BE AS SCARLET THEY SHALL BE AS WHITE AS SNOW!!! IF YOU BE WILLING AND OBEDIENT YOU SHALL EAT THE GOOD OF THE LAND! BUT IF YOU REFUSE AND REBEL YOU SHALL BE DEVOURED WITH THE SWORD! THE MOUTH OF THE LORD HAS SPOKEN IT! Isaiah 1

April 2, 2001

May
2001

Power is Word Strategy!
  Making Mountains Bow!
  Words!
True Wonders of the World!
  Epitome of Creation!
Power in Progression!
Capability of the Gods.
  Monarchy of Magical
Movement of Matter.
  Missions of Creativity
Crying out to you and me!
Speak Forth, O Truth!
Our Leasehold of Legacy!

Part VII

Lift Up Your Voice Like A Trumpet

I have set watchmen upon thy walls, O Jerusalem,
which shall never hold their peace day nor night!
Ye that are the Lord's remembrancers, keep not silence!

Isaiah Sixty-Two Verse Six

Prophecy

TODAY IS THE BEGINNING OF THE END TIME MINISTRY! I HAVE HELD BACK APOSTLES AND PROPHETS UNTIL THIS DAY FOR MANY WOULD HAVE BEEN KILLED BEFORE THEIR TIME! TODAY I AM RELEASING FULL MANTLES UPON EVEN THE UNSKILLED THAT I HAVE RAISED UP FOR THIS DAY. THEY WILL LEARN QUICKLY TO BREAK DOWN BARRIERS OF GREED, LUST FOR POSITION AND POWER SEEKERS. MY GLORY WILL I NOT GIVE TO ANOTHER. THOSE WHO USE MY AUTHORITY FOR GREED AND FOR PROMOTING THEIR OWN PURPOSES WILL BE BROUGHT DOWN SUDDENLY. I AM STILL THE HEAD OF THE CHURCH. I AM STILL THE ONE WHO DOES THE PROMOTING. I AM STILL THE ONE WHO SETS PEOPLE INTO THEIR PROPER PLACES AND POSITIONS. I AM NOT TO BE MANIPULATED OR GAINSAYED. STEP ASIDE AND LET THE HOLY GHOST HAVE HIS PROPER PLACE! WHEN THE HOLY GHOST HAS HIS PROPER PLACE I STILL BESTOW MANTLES AND PUT PEOPLE INTO POSITIONS OF AUTHORITY AND CALLING! MAN DID NOT ORDAIN MY PROPHETS. NOR DOES HE YET SANCTION MY APOSTLES. BUT I HAVE STRATEGICALLY PLACED THEM IN GHETTOES AND GOVERNMENTS. KINGS WILL NO LONGER MAKE DECISIONS WITHOUT MY DOMINION. FOR EVEN THE LAST DAY HARVEST MUST BE BROUGHT IN BEFORE THE BATTLE OF ARMAGEDDON! RELEASE PRAYER WARRIORS TO DO SPIRITUAL WARFARE! ! !

MY PEOPLE ARE MANDATED BY ME. NO LONGER WILL MAN HOLD BACK THE PROPHETIC ANOINTING. IT IS RELEASED TO CALL FORTH THE RESTORATION OF ALL THINGS! PRIMARILY THE FOUNDATION OF THE CHURCH WHICH IS APOSTLES AND PROPHETS! MANY DEATHS WILL OCCUR SOON BECAUSE OF THE MUFFLING OF THE PROPHETS! STAND STILL AND SEE THE SALVATION OF THE LORD! DEATH BRINGS FORTH LIFE! EVEN AS SEED CANNOT BRING FORTH FRUIT AND HERB UNTIL IT DIES, I AM GOING TO USE THE DEATHS OF THE DISOBEDIENT FOR THE FURTHERANCE OF MY KINGDOM! FOR EVEN AS THEY DIE, OTHERS SHALL BE RAISED UP IN THE NEWNESS OF LIFE AND

CONSECRATED UNTO ME FOR THEIR DOMINION! EVEN IN DEATH I SHALL BE PRAISED FOR I SHALL USE ALL THINGS FOR MY GLORY! I SHALL SHOW PEOPLE THAT I AM MAJESTY AND I AM DOMINION!!!

May 6, 2001

Prophecy

MY HOUSE SHALL BE CALLED A HOUSE OF PRAYER. PRAYER WITHOUT SUBMISSION IS FUTILE. WHY GO THROUGH THE DISCIPLINE AND SACRIFICE OF PRAYER IF YOU DO NOT OBEY MY DIRECTIVES? I AM HOLY. THAT MEANS YOU DO NOT MIX YOUR IDEAS AND OPINIONS WITH MY SPIRIT TO ENHANCE YOUR PREROGATIVES. I AM IN CONTROL. I AM HEADSHIP. POWER AND MIGHT COME THROUGH COMPLETE SURRENDER TO MY AUTHORITY. ALL GLORY IS TO GO TO ME. ALL DOMINION IS TO BRING YOU INTO FULL AUTHORITY. MINE. NOT YOURS.

DELIVER MY PEOPLE SAITH THE LORD. DELIVER MY PEOPLE FROM BONDAGES OF WRATH! GET THE CELL GROUPS TOGETHER SAITH THE LORD!!! TAINTED CELL GROUPS WILL NOT PREVAIL. I AM HOLDING BACK MANY WHO ARE NOT FULLY SOLD OUT TO ME. I GIVE ONLY APPROVAL TO THOSE WHO ARE FASTING AND PRAYING REGULARLY. WHO DEDICATE ALL THEIR POTENTIAL UNTO MY WILL AND TO MY WORD!!! SINCERITY WITHOUT OBEDIENCE IS NOT JUSTIFICATION BY FAITH! OBEDIENCE IS THE ONLY PREREQUISITE TO FULFILL THE OBLIGATION OF PROTOCOL. STAY ROOTED IN ME AT <u>ALL</u> TIMES AND AT <u>ALL</u> COSTS. BELIEVERS WILL SEE MY MIGHTY HAND AND STRETCHED OUT ARM. I AM CALLING <u>ALL</u> TROOPS TO MARCH IN UNISON AND TO CRY HOLY UNTO ME WITHOUT RESERVATION OR HESITANCE! I CANNOT USE THE LUKEWARM FOR MY GLORY AND MY DOMINION! I CANCEL EVEN NOW SOME PROMOTIONS THAT DO NOT FOLLOW THE GUIDELINES OF FULL MATURITY AND DEDICATION! I AM RECALLING SOME TROOPS FROM THE FIELD TO BRING UNITY TO THE HOUSE!

May 9, 2001

POWER, DOMINION AND MIGHT!
   POWER, DOMINION AND MIGHT!
      POWER, AUTHORITY, DOMINION AND MIGHT!
         POWER, AUTHORITY, DOMINION AND MIGHT!

POWER, AUTHORITY, DOMINION AND MIGHT!
POWER, AUTHORITY, DOMINION AND MIGHT!!!

May 10, 2001

Prophecy

ARE YOU DEAD YET? IF NOT, FAST MORE OFTEN. PRAY MORE OFTEN. DO AS MY SERVANT ... GROAN IN THE SPIRIT AS YOU GO. I RECEIVE ALL PRAYER. EVEN THE SHALLOW GROANING THAT DOES NOT TAKE ALL ONE'S STRENGTH, BUT STILL BUFFERS AND BATTLES AS YOU GO. IN SECLUSION I REQUIRE MORE DEDICATED SUBMISSION AND WARFARE. GROAN DEEPLY OUT OF THE DEPTHS OF YOUR BEING. CRY ALOUD. WEEP. TEAR DOWN THE STRONGHOLDS OF GREED! <u>ALL</u> SIN IS A FORM OF GREED! SUBMIT YOUR INNERMOST BEING UNTO ME FOR WITHOUT TOTAL SUBMISSION UNTO MY RIGHTEOUSNESS THERE IS NO SANCTIFICATION! WITHOUT SANCTIFICATION, THERE IS NO FULLNESS OF GLORY AND DOMINION!

MY POWER REIGNS WHEN YOU GET <u>OFF</u> THE THRONE. LET ME HAVE THE THROTTLE! LET ME BE IN FULL CONTROL!!! PASTORS AND PRIESTS. PRIESTS OFFER UP SACRIFICES. WHEN THE SACRIFICE OF A BROKEN AND CONTRITE HEART IS RENDERED UNTO ME, I RELEASE THE FIRE OF MY GLORY TO BURN OUT <u>ALL</u> DROSS AND SELF-WILL SO THAT POWER AND DOMINION AND MIGHT IS DEMONSTRATED SO MEN WILL KNOW THAT I HAVE POWER TO FORGIVE SIN AND TO BREAK BONDAGES, TO RESTORE MINDS, TO SETTLE NERVES, TO CURE DISEASES. TO SET THE ADDICTED FREE, TO RESTORE MARRIAGES, TO GIVE BEAUTY FOR ASHES, STRENGTH FOR FEAR. JOY FOR MOURNING AND PEACE FOR DESPAIR. I AM HOLY. BE YE HOLY. WITHOUT HOLINESS YOU ARE NOT DELIVERED FROM YOUR SINS. REPENT AND OBEY.

May 11, 2001

ABIDE NOT IN THAT HOUSE FOR THEY ARE A SPLINTERED HOUSE!

May 14, 2001

<u>SIGNS IN THE HEAVENS!</u> <u>THERE WILL BE SIGNS IN THE HEAVENS!</u>

May 16, 2001

Prophecy

SEVERAL PEOPLE KNOW YOU IN THE SPIRIT THAT DON'T EVEN KNOW YOUR NAME. THEY HAVE FELT YOUR SPIRITUAL WARFARE! I AM CALLING YOU TO WORK WARFARE OVER THE COLUMBIAN DRUG CARTEL. ARE YOU UP TO IT?

May 18, 2001

TODAY IS THE BEGINNING OF TRIBULATION. SOME HAVE ERRED IN THEIR TEACHING THAT THE CHURCH WOULD NOT BE HERE DURING THIS TIME. BUT I HAVE CALLED THE CHURCH TO PURIFICATION AS BY FIRE. THE CHURCH WILL BE PURIFIED DURING THIS TIME. CANCEL ALL DEBTS THAT YOU ARE HOLDING AGAINST ONE ANOTHER! NO BITTERNESS OR RESENTMENT WILL BE ABLE TO ENTER INTO THE KINGDOM OF HEAVEN! NO CROSS-FIRES! NO RESPECT OF PERSONS! NO BELITTLING OF ONE ANOTHER! NO HOLDING OF GRUDGES! NO SMALL TALKS OF THE FLESH! NO JURISDICTIONS OF DOMINATING THE SPIRIT AND THE POWER OF ME! I AM CANCELING ASSIGNMENTS AND PROMOTIONS OF THOSE WHO STILL CONTINUE TO FIGHT AND TO STAND AGAINST MY ANOINTED VESSELS. WITHOUT MY ANOINTING YOUR PROGRAMS WILL FALTER. YOUR LOOPHOLES WILL ENSNARE. YOUR PRIDE OF POSITION WILL CAUSE YOU TO FAIL. ONLY MY ANOINTING WILL PREVAIL IN THIS LAST AND EVIL DAY.

DO NOT SAY "I AM" UNLESS THE REAL "I AM" IS TELLING YOU TO SAY. UNLESS THE REAL "I AM" IS GIVING YOU HIS PROGRAM. GOD IS NOT SECOND IN COMMAND. GOD IS THE COMMAND!!! GET OFF THE THRONE! THERE IS ONLY ONE KING AND HIS NAME IS STILL JESUS! NOT PASTOR. YOU AIN'T THE HEAD! I AM! I AM THAT I AM! WHY ARE YOU SO OBSTINATE? WHY DO YOU NOT ACCEPT MY WORD, MY WRITTEN WORD? IN BLACK AND WHITE IT IS WRITTEN BY MY HOLY SPIRIT, "FIRSTLY APOSTLES, SECONDARILY PROPHETS." WHY DO YOU DISCARD THIS TRUTH? WHY DO YOU WANT TO BRING JUDGMENT UPON YOUR HEADS?

CAN YOU NOT DISCERN TRUTH? WILL YOU CONTINUE IN YOUR OWN SELF-WILL TO THE DESTRUCTION OF YOUR FLESH?

I AM NOT A GOD THAT I SHOULD LIE! IF YOU CONTINUE TO REFUSE TO HEAR MY VOICE THROUGH MY PROPHETS YOU ARE THE ONE WHO IS BRINGING WRATH UPON YOURSELF. YOU HAVE NO ONE TO BLAME EXCEPT YOUR OWN PRIDEFUL HEART. IF ANY MAN HAS AN EAR, LET HIM HEAR WHAT THE SPIRIT SPEAKS TO THE CHURCH. IF YOU CUT OFF MY SPOKESPERSONS I WILL UTTERLY CUT YOU OFF FROM THE LAND OF THE LIVING THUS SAITH THE LORD GOD JEHOVAH! THE FIRST AND THE LAST. THE BEGINNING AND THE END. I AM AND THERE IS NO OTHER! WHY PROFANE MY NAME BY DENYING MY TESTIMONY THROUGH MY PROPHETS?

May 21, 2001

THERE ARE FIVE DISEASES OF THE MIND THAT I AM GIVING YOU POWER OVER: SCHIZOPHRENIA, NERVOUS DISORDERS, BIPOLAR, DEMENTIA, AND BRAIN MALFUNCTION, INCLUDING MANY DISORDERS, PHOBIAS AND FEARS!

May 22, 2001

Spiritual Warfare

I BREAK THE BONDAGES OF RITUAL, TRADITION, SUFFERING, SADNESS, UN-FORGIVENESS, TO SELF AND TO OTHERS! I CURSE TO THE ROOTS ALL FORNICATION, SELF-WILL, SELF-MUTILATION, WITCHCRAFT, NECROMANCY, INCEST!!! BONDAGES OF RACIAL PROFILING, I CURSE YOU TO THE ROOTS! YOU NO LONGER HOLD IN BONDAGE MEN OF COLOR!!! BE LOOSED! SET FREE IN JESUS NAME!!! BE LOOSED INTO YOUR DESTINY!!! SPANISH BROTHERS, BE SET FREE INTO YOUR DESTINY! MONEY, YOU ARE LOOSED TO MINISTER THE GOSPEL OF JESUS CHRIST! RICHES, FLOW TO THE BOSOM OF MINISTERS EVERYWHERE! BE SUBJECT TO THE POWER OF THE ANOINTING OF ALMIGHTY GOD!!! RESCUE THE SUFFERING! MAKE GLAD THE HEART OF THE BEREAVED AND THE HEART OF THE DESPONDENT! I CAPTURE EVEN NOW THE FOOTHOLDS THAT HAVE HELD BACK THE ANOINTING, THE ANOINTED!!! HOLY GHOST, SLAY THE DRAGON OF BONDAGE TO FORM AND CEREMONY!

CATHOLIC CHURCH, BE ENLIGHTENED TO THE PURITY OF THE FLOW OF THE SPIRIT AND TO THE INFILLING OF THE HOLY GHOST WITH SPEAKING IN TONGUES AND INTERCESSORY PRAYER! DENOMINATIONAL BARRIERS BE SMASHED!!! I BREAK DOWN EVEN NOW <u>ALL</u> CANKERED THRUSTS OF AUTHORITY THAT ARE NOT BUILT UPON THE WORD OF GOD!!! SANCTIMONY AND PRIDE, BE DISPERSED AND BROKEN! HOLY GHOST, LEAD THE CHURCH INTO ALL AUTHORITY AND RIGHTEOUSNESS! BUT BE THOU LOOSED TO PERFORM THE MAGNIFICENT WORK OF THE ALMIGHTY GOD! LET GOD BE TRUE AND EVERY MAN THAT DOES NOT SPEAK BY THE AUTHORITY OF THE WORD TO BE A LIAR AND A FALSE TEACHER! CEASE AND BE SET FREE! THE WORD IS NOT TO BE ADDED TO AND TAKEN AWAY FROM!!! CURSED BE THE MAN OR WOMAN WHO DOES SUCH THINGS! THE AMEN HAS SPOKEN!

May 22, 2001

Healing and Deliverance

SOME ON THE VERGE OF DEATH I AM GIVING THEM BACK THEIR LIFE! I AM RESTORING EYES! CATARACTS ARE GOING TO DISSOLVE. BURDENS ARE LIFTING OFF OF THE BEREAVED. JOHN ...I AM GIVING HIM A NEW LEASE ON LIFE. I AM RESTORING MARRIAGES. I AM GIVING A MAN A NEW LUNG. I'M GIVING A WOMAN A BETTER JOB. A WOMAN WHO LIVES ALONE IS GOING TO FIND A ROOMMATE, NOT TO JUST HELP WITH EXPENSES BUT TO HELP HER SPIRITUALLY. AN ELDERLY MAN IS LOSING HIS EYESIGHT. GOD IS RESTORING THAT. A MAN WHO SEES DOUBLE IS HEALED. A JOB MARKET PROGRAMMER IS BEING PROMOTED. AN INGROWN TOE IS HEALED.

May 12, 2001

Wisdom

ENLIGHTENMENT IS POWER. WHEN POWER IS NOT TRANSFERRED OR TRANSMITTED, DARKNESS PRECEDES BEING DECEIVED ... ONE GETS DECEIVED BY REASONING CONTRARY TO TRUTH, THE WORD OF GOD. THERE IS PROTOCOL AND THEN THERE IS THE HIGHER CALL! RELEASE PRAYER WARRIORS NOW TO BATTLE EVIL FORCES!!!

May 10, 2001

THE THINGS OF THE SPIRIT ARE SPIRITUALLY DISCERNED! NO MAN KNOWS THE THINGS OF GOD, BUT BY THE SPIRIT OF GOD! AND WE HAVE RECEIVED NOT THE SPIRIT OF THE WORLD, BUT THE SPIRIT OF GOD THAT WE MAY KNOW THE THINGS THAT ARE FREELY GIVEN TO US BY GOD! THE NATURAL MAN DOES NOT RECEIVE THE THINGS OF THE SPIRIT OF GOD, FOR THEY ARE FOOLISHNESS UNTO HIM, NEITHER CAN HE KNOW THEM! BUT HE THAT IS SPIRITUAL JUDGES ALL THINGS, FOR THE HOLY SPIRIT SEARCHES ALL THINGS, YEA, THE DEEP THINGS OF GOD. WHICH THINGS ALSO WE SPEAK! NOT IN THE WORDS WHICH MAN'S WISDOM TEACHES, BUT WHICH THE HOLY GHOST TEACHES, COMPARING SPIRITUAL THINGS WITH SPIRITUAL! WE HAVE THE MIND OF CHRIST! I CORINTHIANS TWO. IF YOU DO NOT RECEIVE THE INFILLING OF THE HOLY SPIRIT, HOW CAN YOU KNOW THE THINGS OF GOD? IF YOU DO NOT RECEIVE THE HOLY SPIRIT, ARE YOU REALLY HIS? FULLY? IT IS WRITTEN, AS MANY AS ARE LED BY THE SPIRIT OF GOD, THEY ARE THE SONS OF GOD! Romans 8:14 THEY THAT ARE IN THE FLESH CANNOT PLEASE GOD. Romans 8:8

<u>THE CARNAL MIND IS THE ENEMY OF GOD, FOR IT IS NOT SUBJECT TO THE LAWS OF GOD, NEITHER INDEED CAN BE</u>! Romans 8:7 THAT IS WHY IT IS WRITTEN, <u>WALK IN THE SPIRIT</u>! Galatians 5:16 IF YOU ARE NOT LED BY THE SPIRIT OF GOD, YOU ARE A SON IN NAME ONLY. YOUR NAME. NOT HIS! IF YOU ARE TRULY HIS SON, YOU WALK IN THE SPIRIT! HIS SPIRIT! THEY THAT ARE OF THE FLESH DO MIND THE THINGS OF THE FLESH! Romans 8:5

POSITION. POPULARITY. OPINIONS OF MEN. TO BE CARNALLY
MINDED IS DEATH! DEATH TO THE THINGS OF GOD! AGAIN, NOT
EVERYONE THAT SAYS LORD, LORD, BUT HE THAT DOES THE
WILL OF MY DADDY! YOU CAN'T DO HIS WILL IF YOU DO NOT
STUDY HIS WILL AND SUBMIT YOUR KINGDOM TO THE WILL OF
SPIRITUAL AUTHORITY! BE CONFORMED TO HIS IMAGE!
MAKING A PROFESSION OF FAITH DOES NOT SAVE YOU!
REPENTING OF YOUR SINS AND RECEIVING A REGENERATED
SPIRIT QUALIFIES YOU TO WALK IN THE SPIRIT, THUS RECEIVING
THE ENGRAFTED WORD WHICH IS ABLE TO SAVE YOUR SOUL!
James 1:21 YOUR SPIRIT IS RESTORED, RENEWED, MADE WHOLE
WHEN YOU RECEIVE THE REMISSION OF SINS. YOUR SOUL, MADE
UP OF YOUR MIND, INTELLECT, WILL AND EMOTIONS MUST BE
MADE CONFORMABLE TO THE LORD JESUS CHRIST BY BEING
RENEWED IN THE SPIRIT DAY BY DAY, RECEIVING THE
ENGRAFTED WORD AND READILY OBEYING IT!

May 14, 2001

Brokenhearted

PROCLAIMING LIBERTY TO SOMEONE WHO HAS A BROKEN HEART IS LIKE TELLING SOMEONE WHO IS IN THE MIDDLE OF A HEART ATTACK TO DANCE!!! <u>BIND</u> UP THE BROKEN HEARTED AND <u>THEN</u> PROCLAIM LIBERTY! THE SPIRIT OF THE LORD GOD IS UPON ME! THE LORD HAS ANOINTED ME TO PREACH GOOD TIDINGS UNTO THE MEEK! HE HAS SENT ME TO BIND UP THE BROKENHEARTED! TO PROCLAIM LIBERTY TO THE CAPTIVES AND OPENING OF THE PRISON TO THEM THAT ARE BOUND!!! Isaiah 61 WHY DO YOU THINK THE LORD JESUS CHRIST HEALED PEOPLE <u>BEFORE</u> HE TOLD THEM TO GO AND SIN NO MORE??? YEA, YOU OVERWHELM THE FATHERLESS AND YOU DIG A PIT FOR YOUR FRIEND!!! DO YOU IMAGINE TO REPROVE WORDS AND THE SPEECHES OF ONE THAT IS DESPERATE??? THE FATHERLESS ARE BROKENHEARTED!!! YOU DON'T REBUKE A BROKEN HEART! YOU DON'T REPROVE WORDS AND THE VAIN SPEECHES OF ONE WHO HAS A BROKEN HEART! YOU BIND UP A BROKEN HEART! THE SPIRIT OF THE LORD IS UPON ME BECAUSE HE HAS ANOINTED ME TO PREACH THE GOSPEL TO THE POOR! HE HAS SENT ME TO HEAL THE BROKEN! THE BROKENHEARTED! TO PREACH DELIVERANCE TO THE CAPTIVES! AND RECOVERING OF SIGHT TO THE BLIND! TO SET AT LIBERTY THEM THAT ARE BRUISED!!! Luke 4:18

PROCLAIMING LIBERTY BEFORE BINDING UP THE WOUNDS WOULD BE LIKE THE GOOD SAMARITAN PAYING THE HOTEL BILL WITHOUT DOING ANYTHING ABOUT THE WOUNDS! Luke 10:30 BUT THAT IS BASICALLY WHAT IS TAKING PLACE, NOT JUST IN CHURCHES, BUT THE GOVERNMENT AND THE WORLD! THROW SOME MONEY AT IT, BUT NEVER GETTING TO THE REAL ... THE <u>HEART</u> PROBLEM! EVERY PROBLEM IS A <u>HEART</u> PROBLEM! WHEN YOU ARE BROKENHEARTED, WHEN YOU HAVE BEEN INJURED, YOU NEED OIL AND WINE POURED INTO THE WOUNDS! THE OIL OF THE HOLY GHOST! THE WINE OF THE NEW TESTAMENT! JUST AS WINE POURED INTO THE WOUND, CLEANSED IT AND PREPARED IT FOR THE OIL TO SOOTHE AND TO HEAL. TRULY THE BLOOD AND STRIPES OF JESUS CAN MAKE WHOLE INSTANTLY!

BUT HEALING IS A PROCESS SOMETIMES. JUST AS THE NATURAL BODY NEEDS TO HAVE GROWTHS, CYSTS, TUMORS REMOVED. SOMETIMES THINGS NEED TO BE EXTRICATED FROM ONE'S SPIRIT, YOUR MIND, YOUR WILL AND EMOTIONS BEFORE THE OIL IS POURED IN! SOMETIMES WE ARE TRYING TO POUR SPIRIT INTO WOUNDS THAT NEED TO BE CLEANED OUT AND PURGED RATHER THAN COVERED! SOMETIMES SPIRITS NEED TO BE CAST OUT BEFORE HEALING CAN TAKE PLACE!!!

WORDS ARE POWER! GRIEF, SORROW FOR SIN IN ACCORD WITH GOD, WORKS REPENTANCE TO SALVATION, BUT THE GRIEF OF THE WORLD WORKS DEATH! II Corinthians 7:10 SOMETIMES WE NEED TO LET PATIENCE HAVE HER PERFECT WORK BECAUSE IN PATIENCE, YOU POSSESS YOUR SOUL ... MIND, INTELLECT, WILL AND EMOTIONS. James 1:4 Luke 21:19 WHEN PATIENCE IS NOT WORKED OUT OR INTO A PERSON, THEY DO NOT REALLY HAVE CONTROL OVER THEIR OWN SPIRIT. AS IT IS WRITTEN, NOT BY WORKS OF RIGHTEOUSNESS WHICH WE HAVE DONE, BUT ACCORDING TO HIS MERCY HE SAVED US! (GREEK LITERALLY SAYS, IS SAVING US, A PROCESS) BY THE WASHING OF REGENERATION AND RENEWING OF THE HOLY GHOST! WHICH HE SHED ON US ABUNDANTLY THROUGH JESUS CHRIST OUR SAVIOR!!! THAT BEING JUSTIFIED BY HIS GRACE, WE SHOULD BE MADE HEIRS ACCORDING TO THE HOPE OF ETERNAL LIFE! THIS IS A FAITHFUL SAYING AND THESE THINGS I WILL THAT YOU AFFIRM CONSTANTLY, THAT THEY WHICH HAVE BELIEVED IN GOD MIGHT BE CAREFUL TO MAINTAIN GOOD WORKS! THESE THINGS ARE GOOD AND PROFITABLE UNTO MEN, BUT AVOID FOOLISH QUESTIONS AND CONTENTIONS AND STRIVINGS FOR THEY ARE UNPROFITABLE AND VAIN! Titus 3

BITTERNESS IS NOT OF GOD! TO BE EASILY ANGERED AND UPSET IS UNGODLY! TO BE FREE FROM SPIRITS OF RAGE, PRIDE, ARROGANCE, BOASTING, INDIFFERENCE, DISOBEDIENCE, REBELLION, SELF-WILL, SELF-INDULGENCE, ADDICTIONS, UNDER CONTROL OF ANY OTHER EVIL SPIRIT OR TENDENCY, YOU MUST SURRENDER TO THE ONE WHO HAS ALL POWER TO FREE, TO

HEAL, TO BIND UP!!! WHEN ONE IS CONVERTED, <u>THEIR SPIRIT IS REFORMED, REGENERATED, RENEWED AND RESTORED!</u> YOU ARE SPIRIT! <u>YOU HAVE A SOUL,</u> MADE UP OF YOUR MIND, INTELLECT, WILL AND EMOTIONS. YOU LIVE IN A BODY.

<u>AS MUCH OF YOURSELF AS YOU SURRENDER TO THE LORD, THAT IS HOW MUCH HE IS SAVING!!! HE CANNOT SAVE, SANCTIFY AND FILL WITH HIMSELF THAT WHICH IS NOT SURRENDERED TO HIM!</u> HE GAVE HIMSELF FOR US THAT HE MIGHT REDEEM US FROM <u>ALL</u> INIQUITY! AND PURIFY UNTO HIMSELF A PECULIAR PEOPLE ZEALOUS OF GOOD WORKS! Titus 2:1 HE CAN ONLY PURIFY WHAT WE GIVE TO HIM!!! IF WE DO NOT SURRENDER <u>ALL</u>, HE CANNOT PURIFY <u>ALL</u>!!! SURRENDER NOW YOUR HURTS, HEARTACHES, YOUR BROKEN HEART, YOUR DISGUST, YOUR HATRED, SELF-HATRED, YOUR PRIDE, YOUR INCEST, YOUR VIOLENCE, YOUR CIGARETTES, DRUGS, ALCOHOL. SURRENDER THE HOLE IN YOUR HEART! THE CESSPOOL OF YOUR PASSIONS. THE GORE. THE CRUELTY. THE MURDER. THE SPITE. THAT UNQUENCHABLE THIRST. THE PASSION AND THE PAIN!

<u>LOVE, POUR INTO THESE BROKEN VESSELS! FILL THEM WITH YOUR SELF</u>!!! TAKE AWAY THE PAIN! PEACE! PEACE! SWEEP OVER THESE SOULS! MANIFEST YOURSELF! THE LORD OF <u>ALL</u> LIFE! THE BEGINNING AND THE ENDING! THESE THINGS SPEAK AND EXHORT AND REBUKE WITH <u>ALL</u> AUTHORITY! BELOVED, REMEMBER THE WORDS WHICH WERE SPOKEN BEFORE OF THE APOSTLES OF OUR LORD JESUS CHRIST: HOW THAT THEY TOLD YOU THERE WOULD BE MOCKERS IN THE LAST DAYS, WHO WOULD WALK AFTER THEIR OWN UNGODLY LUSTS, MURMURERS, COMPLAINERS, BOASTERS, RESPECTER OF PERSONS, WELLS WITHOUT WATER, WANDERING STARS, SPOTS IN YOUR FEASTS OF CHARITY, TURNING THE GRACE OF GOD INTO LASCIVIOUSNESS, UNGODLY MEN, DENYING THE LORD GOD BY THEIR UNGODLY DEEDS WHICH THEY HAVE UNGODLY COMMITTED! FEEDING THEMSELVES WITHOUT FEAR, TREES WHOSE FRUIT WITHERS. WITHOUT FRUIT, TWICE DEAD, PLUCKED UP BY THE ROOTS, RAGING WAVES OF THE SEA, FOAMING OUT

THEIR OWN SHAME TO WHOM IS RESERVED THE BLACKNESS OF THE DARKNESS FOREVER! THESE ARE THEY, WHO SEPARATE THEMSELVES, WHO ARE SENSUAL, HAVING NOT THE SPIRIT OF GOD! BUT YOU, BELOVED, BUILDING UP YOURSELVES ON YOUR MOST HOLY FAITH, PRAYING IN THE HOLY SPIRIT. <u>KEEP YOURSELVES IN THE LOVE OF GOD!</u> LOOKING FOR THE MERCY OF OUR LORD JESUS UNTO ETERNAL LIFE! AND OF SOME HAVE COMPASSION, MAKING A DIFFERENCE!!! AND OTHERS SAVE WITH FEAR, PULLING OUT OF THE FIRE!!! HATING EVEN THE GARMENT SPOTTED BY THE FLESH! TO THE ONLY WISE GOD OUR SAVIOR, BE GLORY AND MAJESTY, DOMINION AND POWER, BOTH NOW AND EVERMORE UNTO HIM THAT IS ABLE TO KEEP YOU FROM FALLING AND TO PRESENT YOU FAULTLESS BEFORE THE PRESENCE OF HIS GLORY!

May 8, 2001

Submission and Declaration

ONE THING ABOUT IT WHEN YOU HAVE MESSED UP BIG TIME AND NO ONE WANTS TO HEAR WHAT YOU'VE GOT TO SAY AND NO ONE REALLY RECEIVES YOU BECAUSE OF YOUR PAST AND YOU ACTUALLY WOULD RATHER JUST BE TAKEN OUT OF THIS LIFE, BUT AFTER A WHILE YOU REALIZE GOD AIN'T GONNA KILL YOU AND HE AIN'T GONNA LET YOU KILL YOURSELF AND HE AINT GONNA LET ANYBODY ELSE KILL YOU ... AT LEAST NOT UNTIL IT'S TIME TO GO.

THERE ARE GOING TO BE END TIME MARTYRS. (SOME HAVE BEEN MARTYRED EVEN IN THIS COUNTRY SINCE THIS WRITING) YOU COME TO THE REALIZATION THAT SINCE YOU'RE GOING TO KEEP ON LIVING... YOUR BODY IS GOING TO KEEP ON BREATHING, EVEN THOUGH YOUR WILL TO LIVE IS GONE ... THAT YOU JUST GIVE THAT WILL OVER TO JESUS AND HE LIVES HIS WILL AND HIS TESTAMENT THROUGH YOU. YOU ARE DEAD NOW AND THE LIFE OF CHRIST CAN LIVE THROUGH YOU 'CAUSE IT'S NO MORE I BUT THE LORD THAT DWELLS WITHIN! IT BECOMES SO MUCH EASIER, FOR THE LORD TO LIVE THROUGH YOU ... YOUR SURRENDERED SOUL (MADE UP OF YOUR WILL, MIND, THOUGHTS AND EMOTIONS) THAN YOU TRYING TO TRIUMPH IN A DEFEATED WORLD.

AS IT IS WRITTEN, <u>IN THE WORLD YOU WILL HAVE TRIBULATION, BUT IN ME YOU WILL HAVE PEACE! NOT AS THE WORLD GIVES, GIVE I UNTO YOU. LET NOT YOUR HEART BE TROUBLED! NEITHER LET IT BE AFRAID! BE OF GOOD CHEER! I HAVE OVERCOME THE WORLD!!!</u> John 16:33, 14:27 WELL, WHAT DOES THAT MEAN? IT MEANS THE OVERCOMING POWER OF ALMIGHTY GOD IS LIVING ON THE INSIDE OF YOU! SO WHAT'S YOUR PROBLEM? IT AIN'T GOD, 'CAUSE HE DOESN'T HAVE ANY! IF WE COULD NOT, NOT LET OUR HEARTS BE TROUBLED, HE WOULD NOT HAVE SAID, LET NOT YOUR HEART BE TROUBLED!!! WE LET NOT OUR HEARTS BE TROUBLED BY REPLACING THE THOUGHTS THAT TROUBLE OUR HEARTS BY GOD. THROWING OUT THE TROUBLED THOUGHTS

AND REPLACING THEM WITH GOD'S WORDS! THAT IS "LETTING NOT YOUR HEART BE TROUBLED!" THROW OUT THE BAD THOUGHTS AND REPLACE THEM WITH GOD'S THOUGHTS! GOD'S THOUGHTS ARE HIS WRITTEN WORD! IT IS QUICK AND SHARPER AND MORE POWERFUL THAN ANY TWO-EDGED SWORD!!!

YOUR ONLY PROBLEM IS YOU. WHEN YOU SURRENDER YOU, THE MAN DOES THE REST THROUGH YOU!!! GIVE IT UP! CONFESS: I SURRENDER MYSELF UNTO YOU, LORD. I GIVE YOU MY WILL, MY PURPOSE, MY MIND, MY THOUGHTS, MY HOPES, MY DREAMS, MY ASPIRATIONS, MY ABILITIES, MY TALENTS, MY TRUTH, MY LIES, MY FAULTS, MY FAILURES, MY HANG-UPS, ALL THE GOOD AND THE BAD AND THE UGLY, I GIVE IT UP TO YOU, LORD! I AM GOING TO WALK IN YOUR SPIRIT BECAUSE I KNOW YOU DO ALL THINGS WELL AND I WANT TO BE SUCCESSFUL! SO I RELINQUISH ALL MY RIGHTS AND IN EXCHANGE I RECEIVE ALL YOUR MERCIES AND YOUR POWERS!!! YOUR MERCIES OF FORGIVENESS. YOUR MERCIES OF HOPE. YOUR MERCIES OF DIVINE INTERVENTION. YOUR MERCIES OF PROBLEM SOLVING. YOUR MERCIES OF DEVIL DEFEATING. YOUR MERCIES OF CHANNEL SURFING IN THE SPIRIT OF THE HOLY GHOST OF GOD! YOUR POWERS OF ... RECEIVING LIFE FOR DEATH! YOUR POWERS OF GAINING FINANCIAL SECURITY. YOUR POWERS OF RATIONAL RELATIONSHIPS AND FAMILY FOCUS. I GIVE YOU ME AND IN EXCHANGE I RECEIVE YOU AND EVERYTHING YOU'VE GOT! WHAT A SWAP! HOW CAN I NOT BE BLESSED WHEN THE BLESSOR RESIDES INSIDE OF ME, TAKING UP HIS ABODE? I GIVE YOU MY INTELLECT! I GIVE YOU MY ALL! I WANT TO SUCCEED TO THE GLORY OF GOD AND NOT FOR MY OWN WILL AND PURPOSE! I WANT TO FULFILL GOD'S PURPOSE FOR MY LIFE! I WANT MY FAMILY, MY CHILDREN AND EVERYONE THAT I HAVE INFLUENCE IN THEIR LIVES TO KNOW AND TO REALIZE THAT WALKING WITH GOD IS THE EPITOME OF A SUCCESSFUL LIFE. SOME SUCCEED IN FINANCES, BUT THAT IS NOT THE BOTTOM LINE MEASURE OF SUCCESS IN LIFE. A SUCCESSFUL LIFE IS ONE THAT IS SUBMITTED TO THE LORD WHETHER THERE IS A PREPONDERANCE OF MATERIAL BLESSINGS OR NOT.

MOTHER TERESA WAS SUCCESSFUL, BUT SHE WAS NOT INTO COMFORTS AND TRAPPINGS. WHEN YOU ARE SUBMITTED TO THE LORD AND HE LIVES THROUGH YOU, YOU LIVE TO <u>HIS</u> GLORY AND NOT YOUR OWN. YOU ACTUALLY RECEIVE GLORY IN THE LIGHT OF HIS! BUT YOUR OBJECTIVE IS TO DO <u>HIS</u> WILL AT <u>ALL</u> TIMES, THUS YOU RECEIVE BENEFITS, THOUGH NOT OBEYING JUST FOR THE FISHES AND THE LOAVES. GOD STILL IS THE JUDGE OF YOUR SOUL. HE KNOWS YOUR INNERMOST THOUGHTS AND FEELINGS. ONLY BY SUBMISSION, COME TOTAL PEACE AND FULFILLMENT. IT IS WORTH EVERY PAIN, SACRIFICE AND DISAPPOINTMENT TO LIVE IN THE GLOW OF GOD'S GLORY!

YOU ARE FULFILLED BY ALL THE ATTRIBUTES THAT CO-EXIST IN YOU BY HAVING THE MAN JESUS TAKE UP HIS ABODE INSIDE OF YOU! WHAT A POWER STRUGGLE! WHAT AN EXCHANGE! YOU GIVE EVERYTHING YOU'VE GOT AND RECEIVE EVERYTHING HE'S GOT! NO COMPARISON! YOU DEFINITELY RECEIVE THE BETTER DEAL! NOT A ROBOT BY SURRENDERING, BUT AN EMPOWERING, BY FORSAKING THE NATURAL FOR THE SUPERNATURAL! BY FORSAKING NATURAL REASONING FOR GODLY WISDOM! BY FORSAKING EARTHLY RICHES FOR HIDDEN TREASURES! BY FORSAKING MAN MADE SUCCESS FOR THE GLORY OF THE KINGDOM! BY FORSAKING THE APPROVAL OF MAN FOR THE PROMOTION OF GOD! BY SURRENDERING YOUR KNOWLEDGE TO THE 'ALL KNOWING' ONE, YOU TAP INTO RESOURCES THAT ARE ONLY ACCESSED BY THE ONE WHO MADE EVERYTHING! THE ONE WHO NOT ONLY KNOWS EVERYTHING ABOUT YOUR PARTICULAR NEED AND DESIRE, BUT KNOWS EXACTLY WHAT NEEDS TO TRANSPIRE IN THE SPIRIT REALM FOR <u>ALL</u> OF YOUR DREAMS TO BE FULFILLED! WHATEVER IS TO TAKE PLACE HAS TO FIRST BE RESOLVED IN THE SPIRIT REALM! WHO BETTER TO HELP YOU FULFILL YOUR DESTINY THAN THE FATHER OF SPIRITS HIMSELF!!!
Hebrews Twelve

May 22, 2001

Exhortation

DO YOU WANT TO BE FILLED OR THRILLED? EVERYTHING GOD PUTS IN YOU DOES NOT THRILL YOU! AT LEAST NOT AT THE TIME ANYWAY. WHEN HE IS WORKING THE PEACEABLE FRUIT OF RIGHTEOUSNESS IN YOU, IT DOESN'T THRILL MOST PEOPLE. BUT IT DOES DISCIPLINE YOU AND MAKE YOU INTO THE IMAGE OF GOD! AND WHEN HIS MIGHTY DEEDS ARE ACCOMPLISHED IN YOU AND THROUGH YOU, OTHERS WILL RECEIVE THE RIGHTEOUSNESS OF GOD! THRILLING? YES. WORK? YES. THE WORD WORKS, BUT WE HAVE TO WORK IT! SPEAK IT! PROCLAIM IT! STAND ON IT! PRACTICE IT! VERBALIZE IT! SING IT! MUTTER IT! MEDITATE IT! SAY IT! DECLARE IT! DECREE IT! ENVISION IT! FIGHT WITH IT BY REFUTING THE DEVIL'S LIES! AFFIRM IT! CONFESS IT! PROFESS IT! RADIATE IT! BACKFIRE IT! RETORT IT! DWELL ON IT! DWELL IN IT! ABIDE IN IT! AND EAT IT!!!!!

May 9, 2001

Reflection

I AM GLAD THAT I DID NOT SEE ALL THE PAIN MY SON WOULD
SUFFER. IF I WOULD HAVE KNOWN THE HORROR, THE HELL, THE
DISAPPOINTMENT, THE ABANDONMENT AND THE REJECTION, I
WOULD HAVE SAID, NO WAY AM I GOING TO GIVE LIFE TO
SOMEONE WHO IS GOING TO SUFFER LIKE THAT!

May 10, 2001

Breaking Racial and Denominational Barriers

IN 1977, I WAS PREACHING NIGHTLY IN REVIVAL IN SANTA ANA, CALIFORNIA IN AN ALL SPANISH CHURCH. SOME SAY, WELL, HOW DID YOU GET IN THERE? BY THE SPIRIT OF GOD. WELL, WHY WOULD AN ALL SPANISH CHURCH WANT A GRINGO? A WOMAN AT THAT! 'CAUSE GOD SAID! AND I AIN'T A GRINGO IN THE SPIRIT! 'CAUSE IN THE SPIRIT THERE IS NEITHER MALE NOR FEMALE! BOND OR FREE! GRINGO NOR CHICANO! REDNECK OR HOMEBOY! IN THE SPIRIT WE ARE ONE! MAYBE IT WAS NOT WHAT SOME OF THEM WANTED, BUT IT WAS WHAT GOD WANTED! WHATEVER BREAKS DOWN BARRIERS IS WHAT GOD SENDS! AFTER THE SERVICE ON THE FIRST NIGHT I VISITED, THE PASTOR SPOKE TO ME AND SAID, "TWO WEEKS AGO I SAW YOU IN A DREAM AND THE LORD TOLD ME THAT HE WAS SENDING YOU FOR REVIVAL!" I TOLD HIM THAT I WAS SCHEDULED THE FOLLOWING WEEK FOR REVIVAL IN LOS ANGELES NEW JERUSALEM CHURCH OF GOD IN CHRIST. HE ASKED ME TO COME WHEN THAT REVIVAL WAS OVER. I ASKED HIM FOR HOW LONG. HE SAID FOR AS LONG AS YOU WILL STAY. THE SPIRIT OF THE LORD SAID, "A MONTH". THEY ADVERTISED IT, "MAY ~ A MONTH OF MIRACLES" AND SO IT WAS! A MAN WHO WAS FIFTY-THREE YEARS OF AGE CAME OUT OF HIS WHEELCHAIR AND WALKED! AS I WAS PRAISING GOD AND REJOICING, HE SAID TO ME, YOU DON'T UNDERSTAND! I HAVE NEVER WALKED IN MY ENTIRE LIFE! NOT ONLY THAT BUT I HAVE NEVER HAD ANY FEELING FROM MY HIPS DOWN! I CAN FEEL MY LEGS FOR THE FIRST TIME IN MY LIFE! AND SO IT WAS! A MOVE OF GOD EVERY SINGLE NIGHT! WHAT A WONDER YOU ARE JESUS! ON ONE NIGHT OF THE REVIVAL, A YOUNG JEWISH MAN CAME IN, RECEIVED JESUS AND THE INFILLING OF THE HOLY GHOST WITH THE EVIDENCE OF SPEAKING IN TONGUES! DEMONS WERE CAST OUT AND PEOPLE DELIVERED NIGHTLY OF ALL MANNER OF SICKNESS AND DISEASE!!! DO YOU REALLY WANT TO KNOW WHAT THE GREATEST MIRACLE OF ALL REALLY WAS??? THE CHURCH FILLED TO CAPACITY AND <u>ALL IN ONE MIND AND IN ONE ACCORD</u>!!! THAT IS WHAT MAKES MIRACLES!!! UNITY IN THE SPIRIT!!! A

COMPLETE STRANGER FROM ANOTHER RACE FROM ANOTHER PART OF THE COUNTRY. BUT GOD! NOW WHAT IS IT THAT YOU WANT? AND HOW MUCH IS IT THAT YOU ARE WILLING TO DIE OUT TO??? AND DO YOU REALLY NOT CARE AT ALL WHO GETS THE CREDIT??? THEN PERHAPS YOU ARE READYING YOURSELF FOR A MIGHTY MIRACLE MOVE OF GOD!!! PERHAPS. IT IS UP TO YOU ... AS INDIVIDUALS, YOU KNOW. GOD IS NOT WILLINGLY RESTRAINING MIRACLES, SIGNS AND WONDERS! HE RELEASES THEM READILY WHEN THE PREREQUISITE OF THE UNITY OF THE SPIRIT IS MET!

SEE WITH GOD, THERE IS GOOD AND THERE IS BAD. SOME PEOPLE DON'T WANT GOD, OR HIS MOVE, HIS WAY, BECAUSE THEY HAVE TO TAKE THE BAD, WHATEVER OR WHOEVER THEY DON'T LIKE WITH THE GOD! I KEEP TELLING PEOPLE, THIS ISN'T IT! THIS IS NOT HEAVEN DOWN HERE. THAT IS WHY WE ARE WORKING OUT THE SALVATION OF THE LORD WITH FEAR AND TREMBLING SO THAT WE CAN GET THERE! THE BIBLE STILL SAYS, IT RAINS ON THE JUST AND THE UNJUST AND THE LORD SENDS HIS SUNSHINE ON THE EVIL AND THE GOOD. Matthew 5:45 BUT SOON THERE WILL BE A SEPARATION. THE WICKED WILL BE CAST INTO HELL. RESPECT OF PERSONS IS EVIL WICKEDNESS! THERE IS SOON COMING A DAY OF RECKONING! WHO IS ON THE LORD'S SIDE? DON'T BE TELLING GOD YOU LOVE HIM AND DON'T WANT TO DO HIS WILL! DO NOT WANT TO RECEIVE WHOM GOD HAS SENT!

THE FIRST TIME I WENT TO CALIFORNIA, I HAD TO LEAVE MY YOUNGEST WITH A SITTER. TAMAH WAS ONLY THREE AND A HALF YEARS OLD. I HAD WORN MY CAR OUT RUNNING FOR JESUS. I RODE A GREYHOUND BUS FOR THREE DAYS FROM OHIO TO CALIFORNIA TO PREACH THE GOSPEL! SOME PEOPLE WON'T GO AROUND THE CORNER TO BACK A MAN OR WOMAN OF GOD, BUT WE ARE GOING TO BE JUDGED BY THE DEEDS DONE IN THIS BODY! AND SOME OF YOU, IF YOU DO NOT GET IN A HURRY ARE GOING TO HAVE BLOOD ON YOUR HANDS WHEN YOU STAND BEFORE GOD! THE BLOOD OF THOSE YOU WERE SUPPOSED TO

WARN OF THE COMING JUDGMENT! OR WITHHOLDING SUPPORT AND OPPORTUNITY TO THOSE WHO WERE CALLED TO DO SO! THE BLOOD OF THOSE THAT YOU WERE SUPPOSED TO PULL OUT OF THE FIRE! THE BLOOD OF THOSE WHO ARE LOST AND DYING WITHOUT A SAVIOR BECAUSE YOU WON'T OPEN YOUR MOUTH AND WARN THEM TO FLEE THE WRATH WHICH IS TO COME! YOU WILL NOT BE HELD ACCOUNTABLE FOR THOSE WHO DO NOT OBEY. YOU <u>WILL</u> BE HELD ACCOUNTABLE TO WARN THEM OF THE CONSEQUENCES OF THEIR DISOBEDIENCE! WHY DID IT TAKE A LITTLE WHITE WOMAN TO LEAVE HER CHILDREN AND TRAVEL TWO THOUSAND MILES? YOU BETTER STOP ASKING SO MANY QUESTIONS AND START TO OBEY THE ANSWERS YOU ALREADY KNOW! YOU ARE NOT YOUR OWN! YOU ARE BOUGHT WITH A PRICE! THE PRECIOUS BLOOD OF JESUS! THE VERY SON OF GOD! THE ONLY BEGOTTEN OF THE FATHER! AND YOU THINK YOU WON'T SUFFER THE CONSEQUENCES OF REJECTING GOD'S ONLY SON? OF HAVING RESPECT OF PERSONS FOR WHOM YOU WANT TO MINISTER AND TO PREACH?

<u>WAKE UP, MEN! WAKE UP, WOMEN! WAKE UP, TEENAGERS! WAKE UP, CHILDREN! IF YOU KNOW THE DIFFERENCE BETWEEN RIGHT AND WRONG, YOU ARE HELD ACCOUNTABLE FOR YOUR ACTIONS! NO MATTER HOW DIFFICULT IT IS TO DO THE RIGHT THING!</u> GOD'S POWER, HIS QUICKENING POWER, IS AVAILABLE TO YOU TO GIVE YOU POWER OVER <u>ALL</u> THE POWER OF THE ENEMY! RESPECT OF PERSONS! PREJUDICE! PARTIALITY! Luke Ten YOU WON'T GET BY! THERE WILL BE NO EXCUSES FOR DISOBEYING THE WORD! GOD'S WILL AND HIS PURPOSE FOR YOUR LIFE! I FOUND OUT A LONG TIME AGO THAT ONE AND GOD ARE A MAJORITY! IT DON'T MATTER WHO IS AGAINST YOU OR HOW MANY! GOD IS MORE THAN THE WHOLE WORLD AGAINST YOU! LET HIM <u>BE</u> GOD! GET OFF THE THRONE! YOU AIN'T THE BOSS! YOU WANT GOD'S GOODS? YOU HAVE TO GET THEM GOD'S WAY! YOU WANT GOD'S POWER? SURRENDER YOURS! TWO BOSSES IN THE SAME BODY WON'T WORK! THAT IS WHY IT IS WRITTEN, I BESEECH YOU THEREFORE BY THE MERCIES OF GOD, THAT YOU PRESENT YOUR BODY A LIVING SACRIFICE UNTO

THE LORD! Romans 12:1 YOU DO IT BY HIS MERCIES! YOU PRESENT YOUR BODY A LIVING SACRIFICE UNTO THE LORD BECAUSE IT IS YOUR INTELLIGENT SERVICE! THE GREEK WORD TRANSLATED SERVICE BY THE KING JAMES SCHOLARS IS ACTUALLY THE WORD FOR WORSHIP! YOU WORSHIP THE LORD WITH YOUR WHOLE BEING, BODY, SOUL, MIND AND SPIRIT BECAUSE HE PAID THE PRICE FOR YOU TO LIVE ETERNALLY! FOREVER AND FOREVER IN THE MAJESTY OF HIS KINGDOM!

BE NOT DRUNK WITH WINE BUT BE FILLED WITH THE SPIRIT! Ephesians 5:18 HONEY, GOD'S GOT BETTER STUFF FOR HIGHS THAN THIS WORLD DOES! WHY DO YOU THINK IT IS WRITTEN, BE NOT DRUNK WITH EARTHLY SPIRITS BUT BE FILLED WITH THE SPIRIT? THE SUPREME SPIRIT! THE SPIRIT OF THE LIVING GOD! I CAN TELL YOU! BECAUSE THERE IS NO HIGH LIKE THE MOST HIGH! ONE CONTINUOUS HIGH WITH NEVER A HANGOVER AT ANY TIME! YOU CAN STAY FILLED ALL THE TIME AND NEVER O D!!! COME ON! COME ON! COME ON! YOU WOULD HAVE TO BE CRAZY NOT TO WANT A HIGH LIKE THAT! ALL IT COSTS IS EVERYTHING YOU'VE GOT AND EVERYTHING YOU ARE! WE KNOW IN THE STREET IT WAS WORTH IT! TO FEEL NO MORE PAIN! THE REASON THIS HIGH COSTS SO MUCH IS BECAUSE IT LASTS FOR ETERNITY! NEVER ENDING! NEVER SUBSIDING! ALL A GOOD FIX! NO BAD STUFF! NO MIXTURE! THE REAL DEAL! IN THE STREET YOU DON'T WANT TO ADMIT IT ... BUT YOU SURRENDERED EVERYTHING ANYWAY! IT WASN'T ALWAYS WITH YOUR APPROVAL OR SUBMISSION. BUT THE HIGH WAS YOUR MASTER! AND ALL GOD IS SAYING, COME ON HOME TO THE REAL MASTER! NOT THE EARTHLY MASTER THAT CAN KILL YOUR BODY, BUT THE HEAVENLY MASTER THAT HAS POWER NOT ONLY TO KILL YOUR BODY, BUT HAS POWER TO DESTROY YOUR SOUL AND BODY AND CAST IT INTO THE LAKE OF FIRE! IF YOU CALL THAT A CHOICE ... HEAVEN OR HELL? HELL AIN'T NO CHOICE! HELL IS TORMENT ... FOREVER AND FOREVER AND FOREVER! EVEN A FOOL CAN SEE THAT! WHOSE FOOL ARE YOU? THE TORMENTOR'S OR THE TESTATOR'S? EVERLASTING PEACE, JOY AND LOVE OR ETERNAL DAMNATION WHERE THE FIRE IS NEVER QUENCHED AND THE

BODY NEVER DIES, BUT CONTINUES TO SUFFER PAIN AND AGONY
FOREVER AND FOREVER AND FOREVER!!!

IT IS WRITTEN THAT GOD HAS SPOKEN BY HIS PROPHETS, RISING
UP EARLY TO WARN YOU OF THE THINGS TO COME! SERVING THE
LORD WITH ALL HUMILITY OF MIND AND WITH MANY TEARS
AND PERSECUTIONS, KEEPING BACK NOTHING THAT WAS
PROFITABLE, BUT SHOWING YOU AND TEACHING YOU PUBLICLY
AND FROM HOUSE TO HOUSE. TESTIFYING BOTH TO THE JEWS
AND TO ALL MEN REPENTANCE TOWARD GOD AND FAITH
TOWARD OUR LORD JESUS CHRIST! YES, EVEN AS THE LORD
GAVE ME GRACE TO WITNESS TO ONE OF MY PROFESSORS IN
SOUTHERN CALIFORNIA IN 1978. AFTER WHICH HE CRIED, I
BELIEVE! I BELIEVE! EVEN AS THE LORD CONSTRAINED ME TO
BEGIN AN INTERFAITH FELLOWSHIP THERE, INCLUDING JEWS,
BLACKS, HISPANICS, ALL DENOMINATIONS OF FAITH IN GOD, SO
I DID IN OBEDIENCE TO THE LORD MY GOD AND MY SAVIOR! IF
YOU ARE GOING TO MAKE IT THROUGH TO THE END (HE THAT
ENDURES TO THE END, THE SAME <u>SHALL</u> BE SAVED!) IN THIS
LAST AND EVIL DAY YOU MUST RELINQUISH YOUR RIGHTS AND
MAKE HIM <u>LORD</u>! AS WELL AS SAVIOR! THE BOSS MAN! EVEN AS
THE LORD SPOKE THROUGH A PROPHET IN 1970, THAT I WOULD
BE AN END TIME MARTYR. BUT NONE OF THESE THINGS MOVE
ME! NEITHER COUNT I MY LIFE DEAR UNTO MYSELF SO THAT I
MIGHT FINISH MY COURSE WITH JOY AND THE MINISTRY WHICH
I HAVE RECEIVED OF THE LORD JESUS TO TESTIFY OF THE GOSPEL
OF THE GRACE OF GOD! O HALLELUJAH TO THE GLORY OF GOD!
TO THE GLORY OF HIS DOMINION! TO THE GLORY OF HIS POWER!
I SUBMIT <u>ALL</u> THINGS TO YOU! TO THE WORD OF YOUR GRACE!
WHICH IS NEVER DISGRACE! SOME PERCHANCE CHOOSE TO
REMEMBER FAULTS AND FAILURES OF THOSE WHO HAVE BEEN
REDEEMED. BUT THE BLOOD OF JESUS CLEANSES US FROM <u>ALL</u>
SIN!!! AND IT IS REMEMBERED NO MORE BY THE LORD! JESUS
DIED FOR ALL SIN EVEN THE SIN THAT IS COMMITTED AFTER
BECOMING A CHRISTIAN! THERE IS ONLY ONE SIN THAT IS NOT
PARDONABLE! THE SIN AGAINST THE HOLY GHOST! MURDER IS
NOT THE UNPARDONABLE SIN! DIVORCE AND REMARRIAGE IS

NOT THE UNPARDONABLE SIN! FAITH IN GOD, THE BLOOD OF JESUS AND GODLY SORROW WHICH WORKS REPENTANCE BRINGS FORGIVENESS OF ALL ERRORS, MISTAKES, SHORTCOMINGS, EVILS, SNARES, <u>ALL</u> MANNER OF SIN! REPENT AND ACCEPT DELIVERANCE! FROM PRIDE, PREJUDICE, RESPECT OF PERSONS!

TAKE HEED THEREFORE UNTO YOURSELVES AND TO ALL THE FLOCK OVER WHICH THE HOLY GHOST HAS MADE YOU OVERSEERS TO FEED THE CHURCH OF GOD WHICH HE PURCHASED WITH HIS OWN BLOOD! FOR I KNOW THIS, THAT GRIEVOUS WOLVES SHALL ENTER IN AMONG THE CHURCHES NOT SPARING THE FLOCK. ALSO OF YOUR OWN SELVES SHALL MEN ARISE, SPEAKING PERVERSE THINGS TO DRAW AWAY DISCIPLES AFTER THEMSELVES. THEREFORE, WATCH AND PRAY. REPROVE AND REBUKE OPENLY THEM THAT CONTINUE TO DEFY THE WILL AND WORD OF GOD SO THAT OTHERS WILL FEAR! AGAINST AN ELDER RECEIVE NOT AN ACCUSATION BUT BEFORE TWO OR THREE WITNESSES! I CHARGE YOU BEFORE GOD AND THE LORD JESUS CHRIST AND THE ELECT ANGELS THAT YOU OBSERVE THESE THINGS WITHOUT PREFERRING ONE BEFORE ANOTHER! EVEN YOUR BIG TITHE PAYERS, DOING NOTHING BY PARTIALITY! AND NOW BRETHREN, I COMMEND YOU TO GOD AND TO THE WORD OF HIS GRACE WHICH IS ABLE TO BUILD YOU UP AND TO GIVE AN INHERITANCE AMONG ALL THEM WHICH ARE SANCTIFIED! Acts Twenty

May 22, 2001

June
2001

Play the part,
  Little Unknown
  Though the Script ...
  Be Incomplete!
Let a Moment of Magic ...
Fill thy Spirit to Overflow,
  Coursing the pages
  Of the Greatest Age!

Part VIII

Shew My People Their Transgressions

Son of man, I have made thee a watchman unto this house, therefore hear the word of the Lord at my mouth and give them warning from me. When I say unto the wicked, Thou shalt surely die; and thou givest him not warning, nor speakest to warn the wicked from his errant ways, to save his life, the same wicked man shall die in his iniquity, but his blood will I require at thine hand! Yet if thou warn the wicked and he turn not from his wickedness, nor from his wicked way, he shall die in his iniquity, but thou hast delivered thy soul.

Ezekiel Three Seventeen Through Nineteen

Prophecy

I AM GIVING MANY OF MY PEOPLE SECOND CHANCES. THEY HAVE REJECTED MY PROPHETS AND MY APOSTLES. THEY HAVE MISJUDGED THEM AND FALSELY ACCUSED THEM! WHAT I HAVE CLEANSED, CALL NOT THOU COMMON OR UNCLEAN! WHAT I HAVE CLEANSED IS WORTHY TO HOUSE MY ANOINTING AND MY WORD! JUSTIFICATION BY FAITH IS STILL BIBLE DOCTRINE! TEAR IT NOT FROM THE PAGES, LEST I TEAR YOU AND RIP YOU TO SHREDS!!! YOU HAVE MISGUIDED OTHERS BY YOUR REJECTION OF MY ANOINTED. YOU WILL SUFFER LOSS BUT I TRAIN YOUR EARS TO HEAR AND YOUR EYES TO SEE AS YOU ALLOW ME TO REMAIN THE HEAD OF THE CHURCH. IF YOU REFUSE OTHERS THAT ARE SENT IN MY NAME, I WILL REJECT YOUR SOLEMN ASSEMBLIES AND YOUR HOLY CONVOCATIONS. I WILL DIMINISH YOUR ANOINTINGS AND SET YOU ASIDE FOR CORRECTIONS. STAY NOT MY HAND SAITH THE HIGH AND LOFTY ONE! I AM JUDGE AND THERE IS NONE OTHER! THERE IS ONE LAWGIVER WHO IS ABLE TO SAVE AND TO DESTROY! WHO ART THOU THAT JUDGES MY PROPHETS???

June 1, 2001

THERE WILL BE A DEATH SOON IN THE GOVERNMENT. I WILL NO LONGER HOLD BACK THE JUDGMENT THAT HAS COME TO THE WHITE HOUSE. I AM SHIFTING THINGS EVEN NOW! WHEN I SAY TO STOP THE KILLING, STOP THE KILLING! ABORTION IS MURDER!!!

June 2, 2001

GIVE PEOPLE REALITY! REALITY IS LIFE! LIFE IS ME!

June 8, 2001

Prophecy

TEACH MY PEOPLE TO WORK ON PERCEPTION, ATTITUDE, AND RESPONSE. P A R

June 10, 2001

I AM IMPARTING MIRACLE-WORKING POWER UNTO YOU! TODAY IS THE BEGINNING OF END TIME MIRACLES! YOU WILL IMPART THE MIRACLES IN AFRICA.

June 13, 2001

Prophecy

HEAL MY PEOPLE! HEAL MY PEOPLE SAITH THE LORD! KNOW YOU NOT THAT THE HEALING POWER OF GOD SANCTIFIES, CLEANSES AND SETS FREE FROM <u>ALL</u> BONDAGES OF PAST PAINS AND HEARTACHE!!! I DELIVER FROM GRIEF! I DELIVER FROM POWER STRUGGLES! I DELIVER FROM MISUNDERSTANDING! I GIVE UNDERSTANDING, WISDOM, DISCRETION TO THOSE WHO WILL SEEK MY FACE AND NOT THEIR OWN PROGRAM! I CANNOT USE VESSELS THAT ARE NOT SOLD OUT TO MY SPIRIT, TO <u>MY</u> PROGRAM! MY PROGRAM IS WRITTEN: I GAVE SOME APOSTLES AND SOME PROPHETS AND SOME EVANGELISTS AND SOME PASTORS AND SOME TEACHERS FOR THE PERFECTING OF THE SAINTS! WHEN I AM PERMITTED TO SPEAK TO MY CHURCH AND TO MY PEOPLE INDIVIDUALLY I STATE EXACTLY WHAT IS TO BE DONE AND WHAT IS NEEDED TO ATTAIN TO PERFECTION, FULL MATURITY!!!!

THE OFFICERS OF THE CHURCH: APOSTLES, PROPHETS, EVANGELISTS, PASTORS, TEACHERS, ALL, ARE TO WORK THE MINISTRY FOR THE EDIFYING OF THE BODY OF CHRIST, UNTIL YOU <u>ALL</u> COME TO THE UNITY OF THE FAITH, AND OF THE KNOWLEDGE OF THE SON OF GOD, UNTO A PERFECT MAN, UNTO THE MEASURE OF THE STATURE OF THE FULLNESS OF CHRIST!!! AS IT IS WRITTEN BY APOSTLE PAUL UNDER THE DIRECTION OF THE HOLY GHOST OF GOD IN HOLY SCRIPTURE. Ephesians 4: 11-13.

YOU ARE NOT PURIFIED AND SANCTIFIED BY MUCH CHURCH GOING AND HEARING OF THE WORD ONLY. YOU ARE PERFECTED UNTO THE MEASURE OF THE STATURE OF THE FULLNESS OF CHRIST WHEN YOU FULLY <u>OBEY</u> THE DOCTRINE OF JESUS CHRIST AS IT IS WRITTEN IN FULL MEASURE AND NOT IN BITS AND PIECES OF ONE'S OWN CHOOSING! AS IT IS WRITTEN, QUENCH NOT THE SPIRIT AND DESPISE NOT PROPHESYINGS! DO NOT SET ASIDE PROPHECY! WHEN YOU DO NOT ACKNOWLEDGE <u>ALL</u> OF MY BODY PARTS, INCLUDING APOSTLES AND PROPHETS AND <u>ALL</u>

NINE SPIRITUAL GIFTS WORKING IN WHOMEVER I CHOOSE TO USE, YOU ARE DOING DESPITE TO THE HOLY GHOST OF GOD!

June 16, 2001

GRACE IS COMING TO YOU TODAY. GREAT GRACE, MY CHILD. TIME HAS COME FOR YOU TO GO. I AM OPENING A BIG DOOR TO YOU. ONE OF PROMINENCE.

June 20, 2001

Prophecy

I WILL CALL MAGISTRATES FORWARD NOW TO BRING DOWN ABORTION. I HAVE THE ATTENTION OF SOME NOW THAT HAVE WITHSTOOD THE REMOVAL OF THIS DECREE FROM THE LAW OF THIS LAND. I WILL NO LONGER TOLERATE THE REFUSAL TO TERMINATE THE ABORTION LAW. SOME LAWMAKERS ARE BEGINNING TO SEE THE HANDWRITING ON THE WALL. BUT I CAN MAKE THE SANCTIONS AGAINST AMERICA TIGHTER IF I NEED TO.

A DEATH WILL TAKE PLACE IN WASHINGTON SOON. I AM NOT PLAYING GOD. I <u>AM</u> GOD. AND NO ONE GETS TOO BIG FOR ME TO RULE AGAINST. MY VOTE ALONE OUTNUMBERS THE LOBBYIST AND THE SPECIAL INTEREST GROUPS. WHO DO YOU THINK YOU ARE??? GOVERNMENT HAS GOTTEN OUT OF HAND. GOVERNMENT THINKS THEY RULE THIS NATION. THERE IS ONE RULER AND IT'S NOT THE GOVERNMENT. THE GOVERNMENT HAS FORSAKEN LAWS THAT ARE BRINGING JUDGMENTS TO THIS NATION!!! THERE IS ONE LAWGIVER! Isaiah 33:32 James 4:12

June 22, 2001

I AM GOING TO GIVE YOU A MIRACLE OF FINANCE SOON. I AM GOING TO SHOW YOU EXACTLY WHAT I WANT YOU TO DO WITH THE MONEY. I, YEA, AM THE GREAT "I AM!!!" BESIDES ME THERE IS NONE OTHER. I WILL WASH AWAY <u>ALL</u> THE STRIFE THAT HAS BEEN IN YOUR FAMILY. DO NOT DISREGARD ANYTHING THAT I SPEAK TO YOU, BUT BE STEADFAST IN CARRYING OUT EACH INSTRUCTION THAT I GIVE TO YOU. YOUR PASTOR KNOWS YOU ARE OF ME. PASTORS, BEGIN TO SEEK ME ABOUT WHERE I WOULD HAVE YOU TO PLACE MY PEOPLE IN THE MINISTRY! SOME ARE CALLED TO TRAVEL, NOT TO SIT AND TO GET FAT, BUT TO MEET OTHERS NEEDS! TO DELIVER AND TO SET FREE!!!

BE NOT WEARY, BUT FAITHFUL IN ALL THAT I GIVE YOU TO DO. YESTERDAY WAS A SUBMISSION TEST. TODAY AN OBEDIENCE

TEST. TOMORROW WILL BE A PRAYER TEST. EVERY DAY I WILL CONTINUE TO TEST YOU AND TO PERFECT THAT IN YOU THAT I DESIRE TO BE MADE MANIFEST UNTO MY PEOPLE. REGARD NOTHING EXCEPT PURE AND UNADULTERATED OBEDIENCE! OBEDIENCE WITH POWER! OBEDIENCE WITH AUTHORITY! OBEDIENCE WITH PURITY! OBEDIENCE WITHOUT COMPROMISE! OBEDIENCE WITHOUT FAILURE! OBEDIENCE WITHOUT HESITATION! I AM COMING BACK AFTER A PEOPLE THAT ARE PERFECTED IN ME! ONE THAT HAS COME TO THE FULLNESS OF THE STATURE OF ME! ONE THAT IS NOT MOVED BY WIND OF DOCTRINE AND CUNNING CRAFTINESS. ONE THAT IS STEADFAST, UNMOVABLE!!!

June 24, 2001

Prophecy

ALL THINGS ARE IN ALIGNMENT! YOUR MANTLE IS COVERING THE CHURCH. THERE HAS BEEN A TRANSFERENCE OF POWER! YOU ARE TO TRAVEL NOW. I WANT YOU TO PRAY OVER YOUR PASTOR.

June 25, 2001

I RELEASE THE HEALING ANOINTING!!!
POWERS!!! AUTHORITIES!!! DOMINIONS!!! AND MIGHTS!!!
POWERS!!! AUTHORITIES!!! DOMINIONS!!! AND MIGHTS!!!
POWERS! AUTHORITIES! DOMINIONS!!! AND MIGHTS!
POWERS!!! AUTHORITIES!!! DOMINIONS!!! AND MIGHTS!!!
POWERS!!! AUTHORITIES!!! DOMINIONS!!! AND MIGHTS!

O, HALLELUJAH TO THE GLORY OF GOD! <u>ALL</u> PRAISE AND <u>ALL</u> HONOR AND <u>ALL</u> GLORY TO YOU!!!

June 27, 2001

I AM POSITIONING IN THE HEAVENLIES! I AM GIVING DOMINION AND MIGHT, AUTHORITY AND POWER. I AM GOING TO SHOW SIGNS IN THE HEAVENS. THERE IS GOING TO BE A GREAT DESTRUCTION! GREAT DESTRUCTION IN GOVERNMENT! I AM TEARING DOWN STRONGHOLDS OF GREED, OF VICE, OF CULTURAL AND SOCIAL DIFFERENCES! I AM GIVING BACK GOVERNMENT TO THE PEOPLE FOR WHICH IT WAS ESTABLISHED! NO AUTHORITY WILL PREVAIL EXCEPT MINE! THE END TIME GOVERNMENTS ARE BEING POSITIONED. I WILL GIVE THEM THEIR POWER TO BRING TO FULFILLMENT THE DESTRUCTION OF POLITICS. EVEN THE ONE WORLD GOVERNMENT IS BEING PUT INTO PLACE FOR IT'S PURPOSE, WHICH IS TO THWART ALL PREJUDICE! BUT IT SHALL NOT STAND THE SCRUTINY OF MY AUTHORITY! BUT I SHALL USE EVEN THIS TO PLAY THE DEVIL'S ADVOCATE! THERE IS ALWAYS A PURPOSE! I NEVER DO ANYTHING EXCEPT BY DESIGN TO FULFILL MY WILL AND MY DOMINION! END TIME PROPHECY SHALL BE FULFILLED BEFORE YOUR VERY EYES!

SEE THAT YOU STAY IN ONE MIND AND ONE ACCORD TO BRING TO PASS MY PLAN OF ACCOUNTABILITY!!!

June 29, 2001

Prophecy

ALL THINGS ARE WORKING TOGETHER FOR YOUR GOOD AND FOR MY GLORY, EVEN THE THINGS THAT DO NOT SEEM TO BE IN THEIR PROPER PLACE. DO NOT TRY TO JUDGE THE EVENTS THAT ARE BEFORE YOU. FOR I AM BRINGING DOWN THE POWERS OF MAN AND I AM GIVING MY ORDERS FOR THE FULFILLMENT OF MY OBJECTIVES. STAY VERY CONSECRATED, PRAYERFUL, ASTUTE IN HEARING MY VOICE. DO NOT LOOK TO THE LEFT, NOR TO THE RIGHT. KEEP YOUR EYES FIXED UPON ME AS YOUR FINAL AUTHORITY IN ALL DECISIONS, BOTH GREAT AND SMALL! WALK HAND IN HAND WITH ME! KEEP YOUR CONVERSATIONS FREE FROM DISCORD AND DISMAY. STAY PURE IN YOUR THOUGHT LIFE BY MEDITATING AND CONFESSING MY WORD IN EVERY SITUATION! I AM BRINGING CHILDREN AND CHILDREN'S CHILDREN INTO THEIR PROPER PLACES. <u>LET</u> ME HAVE DOMINION. DO NOT DISREGARD MY DIRECTIVES. POWER OF MIGHT COMES FROM EXPLICITLY OBEYING MY VOICE, MY WORD OF POWER, MY PURPOSE OF INTENT. STAY, DO NOT SAY WORDS OF CONFLICT OR DENIAL OF MY AUTHORITY, POWER AND DOMINION. GRACE IS <u>ALWAYS</u> AVAILABLE WHEN STRENGTH IS WANING. I DO MY BEST WORK WHEN YOU SUBMIT TO PURPOSE AND TO MY AUTHORITY. RESIST <u>ALL</u> OBLIGATION THAT PULLS YOU OUT OF MY WILL? YOU HAVE ONE ULTIMATE COMMAND, <u>HEAR</u> MY VOICE! MY SHEEP <u>HEAR</u> MY VOICE AND DO NOT OBEY OTHER VOICES! STILL THE STRUGGLE, BY INTIMACY WITH ME DAILY, HOURLY. I AM INSIDE OF YOU. <u>LET</u> ME SPEAK TO YOU.

TO MY PEOPLE, HUSH! SILENCE, LISTEN, MUSIC IS GOOD, BUT THERE ARE TIMES SILENCE IS BETTER. I SPEAK MORE OFTEN AND MORE CLEARLY WHEN YOU ARE IN SILENCE. I POSITIONED AND I DISPOSITION! SUBMIT YOUR ATTITUDES AND FORTITUDES UNTO ME. I WILL BREAK DISCORDS AND DYSFUNCTIONS. I WILL STABILIZE WEAKNESSES INTO STRENGTHS OF CHARACTER. I WILL MAKE THE CROOKED PLACES STRAIGHT. I WILL GIVE JURISDICTIONS OF LOVE. I BREAK THE BONDAGES NOW OFF OF YOUR MINDSETS OF PAIN OF THE PAST, OFF OF THOUGHT

PATTERNS THAT JEOPARDIZE YOUR FUTURE. I BREAK THE INITIATIVES THAT HAVE SET IN MOTION BONDAGES AND FAILURES. YOU ARE SET FREE OF MODES OF WEAKNESS, OF FAILURE TO PLAN YOUR DAYS, OF FAILURE TO SET GOALS. I BREAK THE SINS OF LAZINESS, THE BONDAGES OF FEAR, OF PROCRASTINATION, YOU ARE SET FREE NOW! READ! STUDY! LISTEN TO TAPES! LET ME GIVE YOU A MINDSET OF SUCCESS, OF DIRECTION OF PURPOSE. FREE YOURSELF NOW OF DISCORD, REJECTION AND FAILURE. RESTORE THE WORD! SPEAK IT FAITHFULLY OVER EVERY NEED, SITUATION, CIRCUMSTANCE. <u>WORK MY WORD</u>. IT IS AUTHORITY. IT IS THE POWER OF DOMINION THAT BREAKS THE YOKES OF DESPAIR. BRIDLE YOUR TONGUE FROM SAYING ANYTHING THAT IS NEGATIVE OR DESPAIRING! I LOOSE MINISTERING SPIRITS NOW TO UNDER-GIRD YOU INTO YOUR DESTINY. SLEEP MY WORD! EAT MY WORD! WALK MY WORD! TALK MY WORD! MY WORD WORKS WHEN IT IS PROCLAIMED, DECLARED, DECREED, AND UNDENIABLY BELIEVED, STOOD ON AT <u>ALL</u> TIMES AND NOT FORSAKEN EVEN IN THE DARKEST HOURS! GROAN CONTINUOUSLY IN MY SPIRIT. THIS CAN BE DONE EVEN ON THE INSIDE. ONLY MY SPIRIT WILL BE ABLE TO TAKE YOU TO THE NEXT LEVEL OF DOMINION. AS YOU DO THE ABOVE AND RELEASE YOURSELF <u>FULLY</u> UNTO ME!

June 29, 2001

Deliverance

I BREAK THE BONDAGE OF REBELLION EVEN NOW BY THE POWER INVESTED IN ME BY ALMIGHTY GOD! SATAN, RELEASE THESE THAT ARE HARBORING RESENTMENT, UN-FORGIVENESS, BITTERNESS, HOPELESSNESS, DESPAIR! I TAKE AUTHORITY OVER THE DECEPTION ... IF ONLY! HE ALREADY DID! IT IS DONE! IT IS FINISHED! HE PAID THE PRICE FOR <u>ALL</u> ... FOR <u>EVERYTHING</u> THAT HOLDS BACK THE ABUNDANT LIFE!!! I BREAK THE YOKES OF TORMENT IN THE MIND! IN THE WILL AND IN THE EMOTIONS! I RELEASE POWER ... THE ANOINTING OF THE ANOINTED ONE TO FREE YOU NOW FROM <u>ALL</u> DESTRUCTIONS! I RELEASE NOW POWER TO FORGIVE! POWER TO RETURN GOOD FOR EVIL! POWER TO SPEAK THE WORD OF GOD IN <u>EVERY</u> SITUATION AND CIRCUMSTANCE! POWER TO SUBMIT FULLY TO HIS POWER AND ANOINTING! LET HIS ANOINTING FLOW THROUGH YOU NOW! LET HIM BURN OUT THE DROSS, THE DREGS OF <u>ALL</u> THE REPROACHES, SHAME, LOSSES, HELLS, BATTLES, POVERTY, DEBAUCHERY, LACK, DISAPPOINTMENTS! JUST THIS ONCE IF YOU HAVE NEVER SURRENDERED <u>TOTALLY</u> TO THE BISHOP OF YOUR SOUL, JUST THIS ONCE, OPEN UP THE TOTALITY OF YOUR BEING TO THE ONE WHO CREATED YOU! EXPECT WHAT YOU THINK THAT IS IMPOSSIBLE! YOU SAY, WELL, IF I THINK IT IS IMPOSSIBLE, HOW CAN I REALLY EXPECT A CHANGE? YOU RECEIVE WITH YOUR SPIRIT! <u>NOT</u> YOUR INTELLECT OR REASONING FACULTIES! <u>SUBMIT</u> <u>YOUR</u> <u>SPIRIT</u>! YOUR INNERMOST BEING! YOUR VERY HEART'S CRY!!! TAKE IT! TAKE IT! IT'S YOURS! TAKE IT!

June 25, 2001

Wisdom and Discernment

IT AIN'T ABOUT BEING 'CUTE'. IT'S ABOUT BEING CUT! DROP THE 'E' FROM CUTE AND YOU'LL HAVE WHAT GOD WANTS YOU TO BE. TO BE CIRCUMCISED. TO HAVE A HEART THAT IS CLEANSED FROM <u>ALL</u> THAT DOES NOT PERTAIN TO HIM! YOU CAN BE 'CUTE' BUT IF THAT'S ALL YOU'VE GOT, STEP ASIDE AND LET SOMEBODY THAT IS BLOODY PASS THROUGH! BECAUSE IT'S THE BRUISED AND BROKEN ... THE BLOODY THAT ARE GOING TO BE USED BY GOD! SOME PEOPLE ARE BEING USED, BUT NOT BY GOD! BUT BY THEIR OWN SELF-WILL AND SELF-AGGRANDIZEMENT! WHAT ARE YOU DOING WHAT YOU ARE DOING FOR??? DOES GOD REALLY RECEIVE <u>ALL</u> THE GLORY???

June 10, 2001

ALL PROBLEMS ARE <u>HEART</u> PROBLEMS! THE HEART IS YOUR INNERMOST BEING ... YOUR SPIRIT. WHEN YOU ALLOW THE HOLY SPIRIT TO REGENERATE YOUR SPIRIT MAN (WE OFTEN ERRINGLY CALL IT SAVING THE SOUL) ALL OTHER PROBLEMS CAN BE DEALT WITH. YOU DON'T HAVE A WEIGHT PROBLEM. YOU HAVE A HEART PROBLEM. A SPIRIT PROBLEM. YOU DON'T HAVE AN EATING PROBLEM. IT IS A SPIRITUAL PROBLEM. THE PROBLEM IS NOT GAMBLING, ALCOHOLISM, DRUGS, MARITAL, SEXUAL, PARENTING, LAZINESS, LACK OF MOTIVATION, HOPELESSNESS, HELPLESSNESS. THOSE ARE NOT PROBLEMS. THEY ARE SYMPTOMS. THERE IS ONLY <u>ONE</u> PROBLEM. A HEART PROBLEM. A SPIRIT PROBLEM WHICH IS IN ESSENCE A <u>SUBMISSION</u> PROBLEM! IF YOU WILL SUBMIT, HE WILL ACQUIT! HE WILL ADHERE TO HIS WORD! HE WILL BREAK <u>ALL</u> BONDAGES OF PAIN, AGONY, LETHARGY, DISEASE, ADDICTIONS AND TORMENTS!!! GOD WILL RELEASE YOU TO FRUITFULNESS!

THE MIRACLE OF RESTORATION, BE MANIFESTED IN THESE THAT ARE BROKEN HEARTED!!! THANK YOU, MY FATHER, FOR CONFIRMING YOUR WORD! THANK YOU, SWEET JESUS, FOR THE ANOINTING THAT BREAKS THE YOKE! SPIRIT OF THE LIVING

GOD, FLOW THROUGH THESE THAT ARE BEING DELIVERED, SET FREE AND RELEASED INTO THEIR DESTINY!!!

June 25, 2001

WHATEVER IS OUT OF ORDER HAS NOT BEEN <u>FULLY</u> SUBMITTED UNTO THE LORD! LACK OF OBEDIENCE IS <u>LACK</u> OF SUBMISSION! WHATEVER IS <u>FULLY</u> SUBMITTED UNTO THE LORD <u>IS</u> IN ORDER.

June 29, 2001

Prophecy

GROSS NEGLECT IS GIVING POWER TO THE ENEMY TO BLASPHEME THE WORK AND THE WORD OF GOD BY YOU BEING NEGLIGENT IN SOME AREAS OF YOUR LIFE THAT YOU HAVE NOT FULLY SURRENDERED YOUR WILL TO WORK IN THOSE AREAS. AFFIRM: I SUBMIT MY SELF TO THE ORDER OF THE LORD ... TO HIS WILL AND TO HIS PURPOSE! THERE ARE SOME WHO TRULY DESIRE TO CHANGE, TO FORGIVE, TO TRULY REPENT, BUT ARE GROPING. THEY HAVE NOT ACKNOWLEDGED "THE TRUTH!" THEY ACKNOWLEDGE EVERYTHING ELSE ... THEIR PAIN, THEIR DISAPPOINTMENTS, THEIR HEARTACHES, THEIR HEARTBREAKS, TORMENTS AND TORTURES ... BUT THEY REFUSE TO ACKNOWLEDGE "THE TRUTH!"

YOU SHALL KNOW THE TRUTH AND THE TRUTH IS WHAT MAKES YOU FREE!!! ACKNOWLEDGE!!! ACKNOWLEDGE: TO ADMIT TO BE REAL, TRUE! RECOGNIZE THE EXISTENCE, TRUTH AND FACT! TO EXPRESS RECOGNITION OR REALIZATION OF! TO RECOGNIZE THE AUTHORITY OR CLAIMS OF! TO INDICATE APPRECIATION OR GRATITUDE FOR! TO ADMIT OR CERTIFY THE RECEIPT OF! TO OWN AS BINDING OR OF LEGAL FORCE! ADMIT: TO ALLOW TO ENTER, GRANT, OR AFFORD ENTRANCE TO! TO GIVE RIGHT OR MEANS OF ENTRANCE TO! ALLOW, CONCEDE, AVOW, OWN! ALLOW: PERMIT! TO GRANT PERMISSION! TO LET HAVE! CONCEDE: TO ADMIT AS TRUE, JUST, PROPER! TO GRANT AS A RIGHT OR PRIVILEGE! YIELD: TO SUBMIT! TO SURRENDER! TO COMPLY! TO GIVE WAY TO! PRODUCE! BEAR! SURRENDER: TO YIELD OR HAND OVER POWER TO ANOTHER. TO CEASE RESISTANCE. SUBMIT: TO YIELD ONESELF TO ANOTHER, IN HUMILITY, MEEKNESS, OBEDIENCE. AVOW: TO DECLARE OPENLY. TO CONFESS FREELY. OPEN DECLARATION OR ADMISSION. TESTIMONY. TO OWN: TO POSSESS. ADMIT. CONFESS. WHEN YOU WILL ADMIT, HE WILL ACQUIT! CLEAR OF ALL CHARGES. HELP YOU IN ALL YOUR STRUGGLES!!!

June 29, 2001

July
2001

Can God? Where is the Lord, right now?
Does He really know how to bind and loose?
Make sane the gristled minds ...
Shrapnel riddled with dope, divorce, death and demons?
Can He recreate the pieces that have been ripped out?
Scraps of ... Who am I? Broken Bits of ...
It doesn't really matter anymore.
Gnarled proclivity ... of my life ain't much.
Who cares? ... Can this Jesus Really ... ???

Part IX

My Salvation is Near

And he that sat upon the throne said, behold I make all things new! And he said unto me Write: for these words are true and faithful. And he said unto me, it is done. I am Alpha and Omega, the beginning and the end. I will give unto him that is athirst of the fountain of the water of life freely. He that overcometh shall inherit all things, and I will be his God and he shall be my son. But the fearful and unbelieving and the abominable (abortion and homosexual) and murderers (pro-abortionists) and sorcerers (drug trafficking) and idolaters (anything that removes God from being First place in your life) and all liars (little, big, red, black, white) shall have their part in the lake which burns with fire and brimstone.

Revelation Twenty-One: Six Through Eight

Prophecy

TURBULENCE IN THE LAND WILL CONTINUE!!!!!
                    TURBULENCE IN THE LAND WILL CONTINUE!!!!!

July 15, 2001

GRAVE BONDAGES ARE BEING BROKEN OFF THE CITY!!!

July 18, 2001

ALL I HAVE IS HERE! IN MY CHURCH!!! HEALING! DELIVERANCE! SALVATION!!! WEALTH! RICHES! PROSPERITY! I WILL MOVE THOSE OUT OF THE WAY THAT WILL NOT LET IT FLOW! I HAVE CALLED MANY TO REPENTANCE OVER DEAD WORKS, BUT THEY GO ON IN THEIR OWN SELF-WILL! SOON MANY WILL GO OUT BY DEATH! MANY WILL BE LOST FOREVER! OTHERS WILL ONLY BE SAVED AT THE LAST HOUR BECAUSE OF THE CRIES OF THEIR LOVED ONES! BUT O, MY CHILDREN, HOW GLORIOUS TO WALK IN OBEDIENCE IN THESE LAST DAYS! HOW WONDERFUL TO BE DOING THE WILL OF YOUR FATHER AT THE RETURN OF YOUR MESSIAH! HOW PRECIOUS, HOW GRAND TO BE DOING THE WORKS OF THE RIGHTEOUS ONE AS HE SPLITS THE EASTERN SKY! THERE WILL BE NO TIME TO MAKE YOURSELF READY ONCE I APPEAR!!! IT IS SETTLED! FINISHED!

WHATEVER YOU'RE DOING AT MY RETURN WILL DETERMINE YOUR DESTINY! I CANNOT SAVE THOSE FROM THE TYRANNY OF ETERNAL DAMNATION THAT WILL NOT SURRENDER UNTO ME!!! MY YOKE IS SO EASY AND MY BURDEN IS SO LIGHT! TO WALK IN MY POWER IS SUCH A DELIGHT!!! TO BE IN THE SPIRIT 24/7 IS THE FORETASTE OF GLORIES OF HEAVEN! WAITING ON THE LORD IS THE REREWARD! HE IS OUR REARGUARD! SPECIAL ASSIGNMENTS IN THESE LAST DAYS WILL STRIP AWAY THE DISCORD AND THE DISMAY! STOP THE CLAMOR! STAY THE TWO-FACEDNESS!!! I SPECIALIZE IN PURITY OF PURPOSE AND STEADFASTNESS OF HOPE! I UNDER-GIRD THE WAITING WITH

THE POWER TO COPE!!! TANGLE NOT WITH FRACAS THAT DOES NOT BELONG TO YOU! TAKE CARE OF YOUR OWN HOME! YOUR OWN BUSINESS! AND WHAT I GIVE YOU TO DO! GIVE NOT THAT WHICH IS HOLY TO THE DOGS! NEITHER MY PEARLS OF WISDOM TO THE HOGS! I CANNOT USE THAT ANY LONGER WHICH IS NOT FULLY COMPLETELY DEDICATED UNTO ME! THIS IS THE SEVERANCE TIME! NOT ONLY IN THE ECONOMY OF LOSING JOBS, BUT OF BEING CUT OFF FROM THE VINE BECAUSE YOU REFUSE TO BRING FORTH THE PEACEABLE FRUIT OF RIGHTEOUSNESS!!! TARNISHED, REPROBATE SILVER WILL NO LONGER BE ABLE TO REMAIN IN MY PRESENCE!!! I BREAK DOWN THE DARKNESS! I REPUDIATE <u>ALL</u> SELF-WILL AND PRIDE! YOU WILL NOT CONTAMINATE MY TRUE VINE! BUT I CUT OFF EVEN NOW THE EVIL SEED OF REPROBATE SILVER!!!

July 31, 2001

Prophetic Teaching

IF YOU ARE HOLDING ON TO BITTERNESS AND PAIN THERE IS A PAY-OFF! THERE IS A REASON FOR HOLDING ON TO PAIN. YOU ARE ALLOWING THE DEVIL TO KEEP YOU FROM YOUR PROVISION! ANGER IS NOT THE PROBLEM. ANGER IS A SYMPTOM OF THE REAL PROBLEM. IF YOU REFUSE TO GIVE GOD YOUR PAIN WHOLEHEARTEDLY AND UNRESERVEDLY YOU ARE DENYING THE WORD OF GOD! IT IS WRITTEN, CAST ALL YOUR CARE UPON THE LORD FOR HE WILL TAKE CARE OF YOU! I Peter 5:7 GOD CANNOT HELP YOU WHEN YOU DENY HIM, BY REFUSING TO SUBMIT TO THE HOLY WRIT!!! HE IS THE WORD OF GOD! DENYING SCRIPTURE IS CALLING GOD A LIAR! BY LIVING IN DENIAL OF THE TRUTH OF GOD'S WORD YOU ARE THE LIAR!!! ALL LIARS ARE LIVING IN HELL RIGHT NOW ON EARTH! HELL IS ABSENCE OF PEACE, HARMONY, JOY! LIARS LIVE HELL ON EARTH. WITHOUT REPENTING, A CHANGE OF LIFESTYLE AND SUBMISSION TO THE GOD OF THE WORD, THE WORD OF GOD STATES, ALL LIARS WILL LIVE IN ETERNAL TORMENT! Revelation 21:8

HAPPINESS IS NOT THE ABSENCE OF AGONY, TYRANNY, SCARRING AND BLUDGEONING. HAPPINESS IS GIVING THE PIT OF THE PAST HELLS, THE PRESENT TORTURES AND THE MANIPULATIVE MIND GAMES TO THE CREATOR OF THE MIND HIMSELF! AND LETTING HIM REMAKE OUR MIND!!! TAKING OUT ALL THE SCARS, THE DAMAGED TISSUE, THE BRUISED AND BLOODY MEMORIES OF DEATHS AND HELLS AND TORMENTS! HAPPINESS IS GOD GIVING US THE MIND OF CHRIST IN EXCHANGE FOR OUR OLD MAGGOT-RIDDEN, ROTTEN, BLEEDING, UNFORGIVING SOB OF A SOUL!!!

YOU AIN'T LIVED UNTIL YOU GIVE IT UP!!! WHAT HAVE YOU GOT TO LOSE??? YOU'RE IN MISERY NOW. GIVE THAT FILTHY TORMENT TO THE GOD OF ALL CREATION! LET HIM TAKE IT! HE'S BIG ENOUGH! LET HIM GIVE YOU HIS GLORY! THE GLORY AS OF THE ONLY BEGOTTEN OF THE FATHER! THE CHRIST INVALIDATES GRIEF, GROTESQUE GROVELLINGS, FRUSTRATIONS,

FEARS, AGONIES, SORROWS, BLEEDING BROKEN HEARTS, CRUSHED SPIRITS AND BLUDGEONED MINDS AND WILLS!!! HE TAKES THE BROKEN, THE BATTERED AND THE CRUSTED AND CREATES MIRACLES!!!

July 8, 2001

Deliverance

I BREAK THE TORMENT OF YOUR PAST!!! I CURSE TO THE ROOTS THE EVIL CORRUPTION OF YOUR AGONY! I CALL FORTH AND CAST OUT OF YOU <u>ALL</u> BITTERNESS, STRIFE, ANGER, MALICE, MALIGNITY, BLAME GAME, UN-FORGIVENESS! BE FREE TO EXPERIENCE GRACE, PEACE, HARMONY, HOPE, LOVE, JOY!!! TELL EACH ONE OF THE SPIRITS THAT IS BINDING YOU TO LOOSE IT'S HOLD!!! CALL EACH ONE BY NAME!!! <u>COME</u> <u>OUT</u>!!!

FORGIVE, AS AN ACT OF YOUR WILL, THOSE WHO HAVE ABUSED YOU AND FALSELY ACCUSED! GOOD FEELINGS COME WITH SUBMISSION TO THE GOD OF <u>ALL</u> FORCES!!! WE FORGIVE OTHERS BECAUSE GOD 'SAYS SO', NOT BECAUSE IT IS EASY AND WE FEEL WARM FUZZIES ABOUT IT!!! WE FORGIVE BECAUSE UN-FORGIVENESS IS FILTH!!! FILTH WILL TAKE YOU TO HELL AND ETERNAL TORMENT!!! WHERE IT NEVER ENDS!!! TO BE FREE OF FILTH ... WE CAST THE FILTH OVER ON THE LORD JESUS CHRIST!!! HE TAKES IT BECAUSE HE ALREADY SUFFERED THE SINS OF THE WHOLE WORLD WHEN HE DIED ON THE CROSS! IN EXCHANGE FOR THE FILTH HE GIVES YOU A <u>NEW</u> HEART ... FREE AND CLEAR OF PAIN!!! WHEN YOU GIVE IT <u>ALL</u> ... HE TAKES IT <u>ALL</u>!!! KEEP GIVING IT TO HIM UNTIL YOU ARE EMPTIED OF <u>ALL</u> YOUR PAIN!!! EVERY THOUGHT AND FEELING THAT COMES TO YOU TO ROB YOU OF YOUR PEACE AND JOY, GIVE TO JESUS! CONTINUE TO CAST <u>ALL</u> OF IT UPON HIM UNTIL YOU ARE EMPTIED OF IT <u>ALL</u>! LET HIM MAKE YOU INTO <u>HIS</u> IMAGE! SURRENDER YOURSELF ENTIRELY INTO <u>HIS</u> DEITY! HE DOES GOOD WORK! THE FEAR OF THE LORD (HE WILL PUT YOU IN HELL IF YOU DO NOT FORGIVE OTHERS!) IS REVERENCING AND RESPECTING THE LORD ENOUGH TO DO WHAT HE TELLS YOU TO DO!!! HIS WORD SAYS <u>IF</u> YOU DO NOT FORGIVE OTHERS THEIR TRESPASSES AND SINS THAT GOD WILL NOT FORGIVE YOU OF YOUR TRESPASSES AND SINS!!!

THE FEAR OF THE LORD WILL ALSO CAUSE YOU TO OBEY YOUR PARENTS AND OTHERS WHO ARE IN AUTHORITY! IF YOU DO NOT ACCEPT WHAT GOD IS DOING NOW YOU WILL NOT BE PREPARED

FOR WHAT HE IS GOING TO DO NEXT! MANY TIMES GOD DOES NOT CHANGE YOUR CIRCUMSTANCES. HE CHANGES YOUR PERCEPTION OF THE CIRCUMSTANCES!

FORGIVENESS IS A DECISION, NOT A FEELING! THE DECISION TO FORGIVE MEANS, I AM NOT GOING TO HOLD ON TO HATRED AND BITTERNESS ANYMORE! I AM NOT GOING TO LET WHAT WAS DONE TO ME OR DENIED ME DETERMINE MY DESTINY! MY DESTINY IS STILL IN GOD AND I REFUSE TO LET ANYONE BUT GOD FORMULATE MY FUTURE! I AM NOT GOING TO BE HELD IN THIS PRISON OF PAIN ANY LONGER! I AM SURRENDERING ALL OF IT UNTO THE GOD THAT IS MORE THAN ENOUGH ... EL SHADDAI ... THE ALL-SUFFICIENT ONE!!!

TO HELP CLOSE THE BOOK ON THIS TRAGEDY AND TO NOT READ FROM ITS PAGES ANYMORE, YOU MAY NEED TO CONFRONT YOUR PERPETRATOR FACE TO FACE! TO TELL THE OFFENDER HOW THEIR ACTIONS, WORDS, BEHAVIORS DEVALUED YOU AND DEVASTATED YOU! EXPRESS IN DETAIL WHAT YOU EXPERIENCED BY WHAT THEY DID TO YOU! LET THE PAIN COME OUT! LET IT ALL OUT! SO THAT THE RELEASE OF IT ALL CAN ALLOW RELIEF AND PEACE TO FLOW INTO YOUR SPIRIT!

IF CONFRONTING THE ONE WHO HAS HURT YOU IS NOT POSSIBLE OR WOULD BE DANGEROUS, YOU MAY NEED TO WRITE TO THEM OR PUT IT ON TAPE! BUT YOU HAVE TO LET IT OUT AND TURN LOOSE OF THE PAIN BEFORE YOU CAN BE FREE TO EXPERIENCE HAPPINESS AND FULLNESS OF JOY! FOR THOSE WHO ARE DECEASED, IT MAY BE BENEFICIAL TO EVEN WRITE A LETTER TO THEM, THUS RELEASING YOURSELF OF ALL THE BITTERNESS AND RESENTMENT! EVEN THOUGH THEY ARE DEAD YOU WILL STILL BENEFIT FROM EXTRICATING ALL OF THIS PUTRID-NESS FROM YOUR SPIRIT AND PSYCHE! EACH DAY CONTINUE TO CAST ALL OF YOUR CARES, WORRIES, DISAPPOINTMENTS, MISERY AND PAIN OVER UPON THE LORD JESUS! LET HIM FILL YOU WITH HIS PATIENCE, PURITY, PEACEFULNESS AND POWER!!! BE FILLED WITH THE AUTHORITY OF THE WORD OF GOD!!! BE FILLED WITH

THE GLORY OF HIS DOMINION! BE FILLED WITH THE HOLY SPIRIT
OF THE OMNIPOTENT POTENTATE! BE BLESSED WITH THE POWER
OF THE LORD JESUS CHRIST! LET HIS PRESENCE QUICKEN YOUR
BODY AND IMPREGNATE YOUR SPIRIT WITH LIFE, FORTITUDE,
GRACIOUSNESS AND GLORY!!! LET THE <u>LIGHT</u> OF THE WORLD
LIGHTEN YOUR LOAD! LET <u>JESUS</u> HIMSELF BE YOUR BURDEN
BEARER! THE HOLY GHOST, WITH SPEAKING IN AN UNKNOWN
TONGUE, TAKES YOUR PRAYERS DIRECTLY TO THE THRONE OF
GOD! AS YOU PRAY IN TONGUES YOU ARE AUTOMATICALLY
PRAYING ACCORDING TO THE WILL OF YOUR HEAVENLY FATHER!
LET <u>GO AND LET GOD</u>!!! IT IS JOY UNSPEAKABLE AND FULL OF
GLORY!!! Ephesians 3

SIN IS DEFIANCE AND REJECTION OF GOD'S WORDS! IF YOU DO
NOT CHANGE THE SETTING OF YOUR MIND, YOUR MIND-SET,
YOU WILL NOT CHANGE. IF YOU DO NOT CHANGE YOUR MIND,
YOUR DESTINY WILL BE DETERMINED BY AN UN-RENEWED MIND,
INSTEAD OF THE PURPOSE OF GOD! DO YOU WANT TO KNOW
WHY PEOPLE CANNOT LIVE SAVED? WHY THEY CANNOT LIVE
WITHOUT SINNING DAILY? YOU HAVE TO BE IN THE SPIRIT TO
LIVE SAVED! Romans 8 HOW WE RESPOND TO SITUATIONS IS
BASED ON WHAT IS INSIDE OF US! THAT IS THE REASON IT IS SO
IMPORTANT TO BE DUG OUT DEEPLY ... DOWN INTO THE VERY
DEPTH OF OUR HEART AND SOUL! SO THAT THE PAST AGONIES
AND ATROCITIES DO NOT TAINT OUR PRESENT RELATIONSHIPS!
WE GIVE GOD OUR PAIN, AGONY, GRIEF AND GUILT AND HE FILLS
US WITH PEACE, SOLACE, GRACE AND GLORY! THE FAILED
RELATIONSHIPS OF THE PAST NEED TO BE SURRENDERED TO THE
GOD OF <u>ALL</u> GLORY! WE NEED TO BE CLEANSED OF WRONG
ATTITUDES, RESPONSES AND PERCEPTIONS! WE NEED TO STAY
FULL OF THE HOLY GHOST SO THAT JESUS LIVING THROUGH US
IS OUR ATTITUDE, RESPONSE AND PERCEPTION!!! WE NEED TO
STAY <u>FULL</u> OF THE HOLY GHOST SO THAT JESUS LIVING
THROUGH US IS OUR ATTITUDE, RESPONSE AND PERCEPTION!!!!!
WE HAVE STOPPED TALKING ABOUT CHARACTER. INSTEAD WE
TALK ABOUT ACCOMPLISHMENTS. WE NEED TO REPAIR THE
BRIDGES THAT CONNECT US WITH OTHERS. WE NEED TO SPEAK

OF WHAT BEING SUCCESSFUL <u>REALLY</u> MEANS. IT MEANS TO BE ABLE TO INTERACT WELL WITH OTHERS, TO GET ALONG WITH PEOPLE. DON'T TELL ME CHRIST IS IN YOU AND YOU KEEP ADDING SIN TO SIN! YOU'RE A LIAR! DON'T TELL ME THAT <u>LOVE</u> HIMSELF IS IN YOU AND YOU WALK IN STRIFE AND CONFUSION! James 3 I John 3

GIVE UP YOUR VICTIM IDENTITY, MENTALITY! ONCE SOMETHING HAS HAPPENED TO YOU, THAT SEEMS TO ALWAYS DEFINE YOUR REALITY! BUT TRUE REALITY IS FOUND ONLY IN THE PERSON OF JESUS CHRIST! HIS NAME <u>IS</u> LIFE! HIS WAY <u>IS</u> LIFE! HIS WORD <u>IS</u> LIFE! <u>FORGIVING OTHERS DOES NOT MEAN THEY ARE RIGHT, BUT IT DOES MAKE YOU FREE!!!</u> IF YOU DO NOT STOP PUNISHING, HOLDING RESENTMENT AGAINST OTHERS OR YOURSELF, YOU ARE NOT LEARNING FROM WHAT HAS HAPPENED TO YOU! CHOOSE TO FORGIVE RATHER THAN TO HOLD ONTO THE PUTRID PAIN, THE REJECTION, THE ABANDONMENT, THE HOLES IN YOUR SOUL FROM NOT HAVING YOUR NEEDS MET! CAST THIS BURDEN OVER ON THE LORD! OFFENSES COME TO BRING OUT WHAT IS IN YOUR HEART! BY OFFENSES GOD WILL ROOT OUT AND EXPOSE HIDDEN FAULTS AND FEELINGS OR WEAKNESSES! JESUS WILL TAKE THESE THINGS OUT OF YOU OR HE WILL TAKE YOU OUT! THE OFFENDING TIMES ARE REALLY WHAT PROVES WHAT IS IN YOUR HEART, YOUR CHARACTER. WHAT YOU <u>REALLY</u> ARE INSIDE. GOD WANTS TO TAKE THE HATEFUL HURTS AND GIVE YOU PEACE IN EXCHANGE FOR YOUR PAIN, JOY IN PLACE OF JUDGMENT, LOVE FOR THE LIES TOLD BY OTHERS OR THE DEVIL'S LIES, POWER FOR <u>ALL</u> THE PRESSURES, STRENGTH IN EXCHANGE FOR THE STRESSES, GRACE FOR <u>ALL</u> THE GARBAGE, HAPPINESS FOR THE HATE, CARING FOR THE CRITICISM, SAFETY FOR THE CYNICISM! FEAR IS DESIGNED TO STOP THE EXCHANGE! GRIEF IS DESIGNED TO STOP THE EXCHANGE! FRIENDS, SPOUSES, MONEY, ACCOMPLISHMENTS, EDUCATION, SUCCESS, CANNOT FILL THE VOID OF CHILDHOOD HURTS, ABANDONMENTS, FAILURES, LOSSES. <u>ONLY GOD'S SPIRIT AND GRACE CAN FILL UP THE HOLES IN YOUR HEART!</u> BY HUMILITY AND THE FEAR OF THE LORD

COME RICHES AND HONOR AND LIFE! Proverbs 22:4 EVER HOW MUCH WE AGREE WITH GOD, HIS WORD, IN OBEDIENCE TO HIS WILL AND TO HIS WORD IS HOW MUCH WE HAVE THE BLESSING OF GOD IN OUR LIFE. NOT CIRCUMSTANCES. THEY DO NOT DETERMINE HOW BLESSED WE ARE!!! OUR WORDS AND OBEDIENCES DETERMINE HOW BLESSED WE ARE! THE BLESSING OF THE LORD MAKES RICH AND ADDS NO SORROW! Proverbs 10:22 SORROW IS NOT THE ABSENCE OF PAIN.

BLESSING IS THE ABSENCE OF DWELLING ON PAIN! OUR OWN WORDS COMING INTO AGREEMENT WITH AND CONFESSING GOD'S WORDS CAN CHANGE THE CIRCUMSTANCES AND/OR CHANGE US ENOUGH TO GO THROUGH AND GROW THROUGH SOME ADVERSITY. GIVE YOUR SORROWS TO THE SAVIOR! LET HIM GIVE YOU JOY UNSPEAKABLE AND FULLNESS OF GLORY!!! WHEN GOD'S GLORY IS PRESENT, DISCOMFORTS AND PAIN ARE DIMINISHED OR ABSOLVED!!! YOU HAVE TO BE WILLING TO OPEN YOUR HEART, YOUR MIND, YOUR SPIRIT! YOU HAVE TO REOPEN TO THE EXPERIENCING OF THE PAIN! TO VALIDATE IT AND THEN TO CONFRONT IT! YOU ARE AFRAID TO LET IT GO, THINKING THAT TO RELEASE IT AND TO LET IT GO, YOU WOULD BE DENYING THE DEVASTATION OF THE GRIEF! YOU HAVE TO GO PAST THE PAIN AND TO GIVE YOURSELF PERMISSION TO HEAL, TO BE WHOLE, TO BE HAPPY! DECLARE YOUR RIGHT TO HEAL! WHAT YOU ARE RESPONSIBLE FOR IS WHAT YOU ARE DOING WITH THE CARDS THAT YOU HAVE BEEN DEALT!!! <u>JESUS IS THE ACE IN THE HOLE</u>! HIS SPREAD WINS HANDS DOWN EVERY TIME!!! EXPERIENCE HIS WHOLENESS AND HIS GLORY! TOUCH NOW. THE HEART OF GOD! RELEASE THE PAIN!

July 8, 2001

Release of Pain

I DON'T WANT TO BE HARD AND CYNICAL. I DON'T WANT TO BE MEAN AND NASTY. I DON'T WANT TO BE HURT ANY MORE!!! THAT IS WHY I PRESENT THIS FAÇADE OF EVERYTHING IS COOL. I'M BLEEDING INSIDE. I AM SO EMPTY. I GO THROUGH THE MOTIONS, BUT DOWN INSIDE I WANT REALITY!!! I WANT THE PEACE AND THE JOY! I WANT TO BE FREE OF THE PAIN, OF THE MALICE, OF THE UN-FORGIVENESS! LORD JESUS, HAVE MERCY ON ME! I GIVE YOU <u>ALL</u> OF MY SORROW! MY DISGUST! MY UNHAPPINESS! MY STENCH! MY SELF-RIGHTEOUSNESS! I FORGIVE THOSE WHO HAVE USED ME AND ABUSED ME. I FORGIVE THOSE WHO HAVE ABANDONED ME, MISLED ME AND HAVE LEFT ME DESOLATE! I GIVE MYSELF TO YOU! I THANK YOU FOR YOUR DEATH AND SUFFERING ON THE CROSS! I AM A <u>NEW</u> CREATION! OLD THINGS ARE PASSING AWAY! MY PAIN WAS NAILED TO THE CROSS! AND NOW I ACKNOWLEDGE MY RIGHTEOUSNESS IN YOU!!! I GIVE THOSE THAT I HELD IN BONDAGE BY UN-FORGIVENESS TO YOU, LORD!!! WITH <u>ALL</u> THE RIDICULES AND THE TORMENTS! WITH <u>ALL</u> THE BADGERINGS AND BLAMINGS!!! I AM FREE FROM TURMOIL!!! I AM DELIVERED TO BE MADE INTO THE IMAGE AND THE GLORY OF GOD!!! BY FAITH, NOT FEELINGS, I RESOLVE TO WALK IN LOVE AND TO BE SET FREE FROM THE PAIN OF THE PAST!!! HERE IT IS, LORD!!! TAKE <u>ALL</u> MY PAIN! I DON'T NEED IT!!! I DON'T WANT IT! I REFUSE TO LET IT DESTROY MY PRESENT AND MY FUTURE!!!!! ANGER IS AN AUTOMATIC INDICATION THAT HURT HAS OCCURRED. ANGER IS ALWAYS A SECONDARY EMOTION. IF YOU ADMIT THE HURT, YOU WILL WEAKEN THE WALLS THAT SEPARATE YOU FROM THE PEOPLE THAT LOVE YOU, EVEN THOUGH SOME OF THEM MAY BE THE VERY ONES WHO HAVE HURT YOU DEEPLY. IT IS A LOW LEVEL OF MORALITY NOT TO LOOK AT THE INTENT OF THE ONE YOU FEEL HAS DEVASTATED YOU. YOU HAD NO CONTROL. NO WAY TO AVERT IT. YOU WERE A VICTIM! BUT NOW CHOOSE TO LOVE YOURSELF! WHEN YOU REALLY LOVE YOURSELF, YOU WILL DO WHAT IS RIGHT FOR YOU EVEN IF IT GIVES PLEASURE OR COMFORT TO WHO SEEMINGLY IS YOUR ENEMY AND THE

SOURCE OF ALL YOUR PAIN! CHOOSE TO LOVE YOURSELF BY FREEING YOURSELF FROM THE BITTERNESS OF THIS PAIN!!! CAST IT FROM YOUR INNERMOST BEING! CAST IT UPON THE LORD! BE FREE NOW FROM THE VICE THAT HAS HELD YOU A PRISONER IN IT'S CLUTCHES!!! <u>PAIN, I CAST YOU OUT OF MY SPIRIT!!!</u> <u>GO!!!</u> <u>UN-FORGIVENESS, I THROW YOU OUT!</u> <u>THE FILTH OF BLAMING AND GRUDGING, I CAST YOU FORTH!!!</u> <u>TORMENT ME NO LONGER!!!</u> <u>I AM VICTORIOUS IN CHRIST JESUS!!!</u> HE IS SETTING ME FREE FROM THE PAST!!! THE AGONY OF DESOLATION AND ABANDONMENT, I HURL YOU OUT AND I RECEIVE GOODNESS AND FAVOR AND POWER AND LOVE!!! I EXPOSE THE TORMENTOR OF MY SOUL TO THE LIGHT OF THE GLORIOUS GOSPEL OF MY LORD AND SAVIOR JESUS CHRIST!!!!! I REFUSE TO ALLOW THE PAIN OF THE PAST TO HOLD ME IN BONDAGE!!! I BREAK THE CHAINS OF DISCORD AND STRIFE!!! I LOOSE MINISTERING SPIRITS, ANGELS OF RIGHTEOUSNESS TO BIND UP THE BROKEN-HEARTED AND TO RESTORE DIGNITY AND HONOR AND DOMINION!!! WHOM THE SON, THE LORD OF GLORY, SETS FREE IS FREE INDEED!!! I FREE YOUR WHOLE SPIRIT, SOUL AND BODY NOW TO RECEIVE WHOLEHEARTEDLY THE GRACE OF GOD, THE POWER TO OVERCOME, THE FORTITUDE TO SPEAK THE WORD OF GOD, THE ABILITY TO GROW UP INTO THE FULL MEASURE OF THE RIGHTEOUSNESS OF THE ONLY BEGOTTEN OF THE FATHER!!!

July 8, 2001

Declaration of Deliverance

I RENOUNCE VARIANCE, WHICH IS BEING A SELF-CENTERED PERSON WHO ALWAYS HAS TO BE RIGHT!!! I RENOUNCE THIS OPPOSITIONAL SPIRIT OF CONTROL AND STRIFE!!! I RENOUNCE AND EJECT THE SPIRIT OF HOMOSEXUALITY!!! (NAME THE SPIRIT OR SPIRITS OR ADDICTIONS OR SHORTCOMINGS OR FAILURES THAT HAVE YOU BOUND!) RENOUNCE THEM BY THE POWER OF GOD AND THE BLOOD OF JESUS, IN THE NAME OF JESUS!!!!! I RENOUNCE THE SPIRIT OF LESBIANISM!!! I RENOUNCE THE SPIRIT OF ADULTERY!!! I RENOUNCE THE SPIRIT OF FORNICATION!!! I RENOUNCE THE SPIRIT OF PORNOGRAPHY!!! I RENOUNCE THE SPIRIT OF DISCORD!!! I RENOUNCE THE SPIRIT OF FAULTFINDING!!! GO!!! I RENOUNCE THE SPIRIT OF POINTING THE FINGER AND THE PLACING OF BLAME!!! GO!!! I RENOUNCE THE SPIRIT OF ARROGANCE!!! GO!!! I RENOUNCE THE SPIRIT OF BOASTING!!! GO!!! I RENOUNCE THE SPIRIT OF PRIDE!!! GO!!! I RENOUNCE THE SPIRIT OF SANCTIMONY!!! GO!!! I RENOUNCE THE PUTRID-NESS OF PREJUDICE! GO!!! I RENOUNCE THE PUTRID-NESS OF RACISM!!! GO!!! I RENOUNCE THE PUTRID-NESS OF BIGOTRY!!! GO!!! YOU FOUL SPIRITS OF LYING!!! GO!!! I WILL NO LONGER LIE AGAINST THE TRUTH!!! I WILL NO LONGER HARBOR SPIRITS OF RESPECT OF PERSONS!!! GO!!! OUT!!! I WILL SPEAK TRUTH AT <u>ALL</u> TIMES!!! IN DIFFICULT TIMES. IN TIMES OF SORROW! IN TIMES OF DEFEAT I WILL SPEAK THE WORD OF GOD!!!

I REFUSE TO LIE AGAINST THE HOLY GHOST!!! I RENOUNCE THE SPIRIT OF ALCOHOL, THE SPIRIT OF DRUGS!!! GO!!! I RENOUNCE THE SPIRIT OF DRUG TRAFFICKING, THE SPIRIT OF GAMBLING! GO! I SETTLE <u>ALL</u> DISPUTES BY PRAYER AND WAITING ON THE VOICE OF THE LORD FOR DIRECTION AND GUIDANCE! I ONLY DO WHAT MY FATHER SPEAKS. I WALK IN VICTORY AND SUBMISSION TO BIBLICAL AND FAMILY AUTHORITY! I DO NOTHING WITHIN MYSELF, BUT I LET THE SPIRIT OF THE LORD BE MY SOURCE OF POWER AND APPROVAL!!!

I DENY <u>ALL</u> ASSOCIATION WITH THE THINGS THAT ARE DETRIMENTAL TO MY SPIRITUAL GROWTH! I SUBMIT MY WILL TO THE AUTHORITY OF THE WORD OF GOD!!! FEELINGS, LINE UP!!! MY HEALTH AND MY WELL-BEING ARE SUBMITTED TO: <u>WITH HIS STRIPES I AM BEING HEALED</u>!!! BODY, SOUL AND SPIRIT!!! I SANCTIFY MYSELF BY THE WORD OF GOD! I DO NOTHING THAT GRIEVES THE HOLY GHOST OF GOD!!! I SURRENDER <u>ALL</u> MY SORCERIES, TIMIDITIES, ANGERS, BACK-BITINGS, GRUMBLINGS, MURMURINGS AND COMPLAININGS TO THE AUTHORITY OF GOD'S WORD!!!

I HOLD MY PEACE! I <u>LET</u> THE LORD LEAD ME AS TO WHAT TO SAY! <u>DEVIL, BACK OFF</u>! YOU ARE NO LONGER WELCOME IN THIS PLACE!!! I RENDER YOUR INFLUENCE NULL AND VOID!!! JESUS CHRIST RULES THIS TEMPLE! NO VACANCY! I AM FILLED WITH THE HOLY GHOST OF GOD! PEACE IS MINE!!! JOY IS MINE!!! LOVE IS MINE!!! ALL POWER OVER POWER OF THE ENEMY IS MINE!!! I BURY MY PAST SO THAT MY PAST WON'T BURY ME!!! HALLELUJAH TO THE HOLY LAMB OF GOD!!! HALLELUJAH TO THE RIGHTEOUSNESS OF THE HOLY ONE!!! I BREAK EVERY FETTER!!! NOTHING IS HOLDING ME BACK FROM COMPLETE VICTORY IN <u>ALL</u> AREAS OF LIFE, LOVE AND RELATIONSHIP!!!

GLORY TO GOD IN THE HIGHEST!!! AND ON EARTH, PEACE AND GOODWILL TO ALL MEN!!! I HAVE BEEN CONVERTED FROM THE PAIN OF THE PAST!!! I AM A <u>NEW</u> CREATURE IN CHRIST JESUS!!! I NO LONGER HARBOR RESENTMENT AND BITTERNESS!!! I AM CLEAN THROUGH AND THROUGH!!! O, HALLELUJAH!!! GLORY, GLORY, GLORY TO THE NAME THAT IS ABOVE EVERY NAME!!! JESUS, HOW GREAT THOU ART!!! LIVING IN ME!!! BREATHE IN ME!!! SHOW LOVE THROUGH ME!!! STABILIZE ME FROM DAY TO DAY FROM THIS DAY FORWARD AND FOREVERMORE!!! AMEN AND AMEN!!! AS THE LORD SPOKE TO ME LAST DECEMBER, "ALL PAIN PROMOTES GAIN IF IT IS ACKNOWLEDGED FOR MY GLORY! NOTHING HAS BEEN SUFFERED IN VAIN!!! ALL THINGS ARE TO BRING YOU TO YOUR ULTIMATE POSITION OF PURPOSE! AS THE PAIN IS GIVEN UNTO ME, I WILL INSTILL IN YOU NEW

DIMENSIONS OF INSIGHT, INTEGRITY OF SOUL AND PERSEVERANCE OF SPIRIT AND IMMEASURABLE COURAGE, STRENGTH AND FORTITUDE!!!!!" II Corinthians One, I Corinthians One And Three, Philippians Three, Luke 11:17, I Timothy Four, II Peter Three, Romans 4:17.

July 8, 2001

Discerning of Spirits

GOD SPOKE TO ME I HAVE A CORRECTION FOR YOU TO GIVE TO THE TEAM. GOD SAID EVERYONE WAS NOT WITH YOU AS YOU MINISTERED YESTERDAY. HE SAID TO TELL THEM NOT TO SAY ANYTHING BUT TO PRAY ABOUT THE MATTER. WHEN I TOLD THEM, INSTANTLY THEY ALL SPOKE UP, NOT DOING AS THE LORD HAD SAID. THE LEADER SPOKE UP AND SAID THAT CORRECTION WAS FOR YOU! I SAID THAT GOD SAID, PEOPLE WEREN'T WITH ME. SHE SAID, SHE PRAYED AND WE WERE PRAYING. I SAID, PEOPLE WERE WANTING ME TO DO WHAT THEY WANTED ME TO DO, NOT WHAT GOD WANTED ME TO DO. SHE SAID, SOMETIMES GOD TELLS SISTER GLORIA WHAT TO DO AND SISTER GLORIA DOES WHAT SHE WANTS TO DO. ANOTHER SPOKE UP AND SAID A CORRECTION, TOO, TO ME ABOUT THE WAY ONE IS SUPPOSED TO PREACH. IT ALL HAS TO HAVE THE SAME FORMAT. I SHARED HOW THAT GOD TOLD ME TO GIVE SOME TESTIMONY AND SOME WORD. SHE SAID YOU ALWAYS HAVE TO GIVE THE SCRIPTURE FIRST! (LIKE THAT IS WRITTEN IN STONE IN THE WORD!) PAUL'S TESTIMONY WAS HIS TESTIMONY! I SHARED HOW MANY PEOPLE YESTERDAY AND TODAY CAME AND TOLD ME HOW MUCH THE MESSAGE BLESSED THEM. THEY DOUBTED THAT. NOTWITHSTANDING, I DIDN'T EVEN MENTION THAT BEFORE THE ALTAR CALL WAS MADE, THE CONGREGATION CLAPPED BECAUSE THEY ENJOYED THE MESSAGE. TRUE THE MESSAGE WAS DIFFERENT, BUT GOD WAS DOING SOME TEACHING THAT WAS NEEDED. I SAID, ALSO I WAS TEACHING PATIENCE AND YOU DON'T TEACH PATIENCE FAST, IT'S A SLOWER MESSAGE. THE LORD HAD ME BRING OUT SOME TRUTHS THAT YOU CANNOT RELATE WHILE YOU ARE PREACHING AND RUNNING THE AISLES. EVEN THOUGH THEY WERE DOUBTING WHAT I SAID, FINALLY THE LORD HAD ME TO TELL THEM WHAT HE HAD SAID TO ME. GOD SAID, THAT I HAD OBEYED HIM AND THAT HE WAS PLEASED WITH ME. IMMEDIATELY, THE LEADER SAID (I GUESS THE FEAR OF GOD CAME UPON THEM) I'M SORRY, SISTER GLORIA, FORGIVE ME. THEN ANOTHER SAID, IF I DID ANYTHING TO OFFEND YOU, SISTER GLORIA, I ASK YOU TO FORGIVE ME. IMMEDIATELY IT

WAS BROKEN! THE SPIRIT OF DIVISION, DISSENSION. WE
PRAYED TOGETHER. BEFORE THE BREAKTHROUGH, ONE, WHO
HAD NOT TRAVELED WITH US BEFORE, SAID, YOU'RE JUST HURT.
YOU'RE FEELINGS WERE HURT. I SAID I KNOW THE DIFFERENCE
IN MY FEELINGS BEING HURT AND HOLY GHOST BEING GRIEVED.
I SAID YOU REALLY DON'T KNOW ME BECAUSE I DON'T GET HURT
OR DON'T LET GETTING HURT <u>HINDER</u> ME FROM OBEYING GOD.
SHE SAID, WELL, IF YOU'VE BEEN OBEYING GOD AS LONG AS YOU
HAVE NOTHING SHOULD BE ABLE TO HINDER YOU. I SAID, JESUS
HIMSELF WAS HINDERED. TEAM LEADER SPOKE UP AND SAID,
YES, IN HIS OWN TOWN. I SAID I DID OBEY GOD, BUT MY
ANOINTING WAS TOUCHED. AND THAT YOU TOUCH SOMEONE'S
ANOINTING WHEN YOU ARE NOT WITH THEM IN THE SPIRIT.

I AM RELATING THIS FOR THE PURPOSE FOR PEOPLE TO CHECK
THEIR OWN SPIRITS. GOD DOESN'T USE EVERYONE IN THE SAME
WAY! EVEN AS IT IS WRITTEN, THERE ARE DIVERSITIES OF GIFTS,
BUT THE <u>SAME</u> SPIRIT! AND THERE ARE DIFFERENCES OF
ADMINISTRATIONS, BUT THE <u>SAME</u> LORD! AND THERE ARE
DIVERSITIES OF OPERATIONS, BUT IT IS THE <u>SAME GOD</u> WHICH
WORKS ALL IN ALL! I Corinthians 12:4-6 MANY ARE IN ERROR IN
JUDGING AND MISJUDGING OTHERS WHO DO NOT OPERATE OR
DEMONSTRATE EXACTLY LIKE THEM! ALSO, A SPIRIT OF
JEALOUSY OR EMULATION CAN SURFACE WHEN MINISTERS FEEL
THREATENED BY SOMEONE ELSE'S ANOINTING OR POPULARITY.

July 29, 2001

August
2001

Speak Boldly ... Servants of Power!
   Just Ahead ... Our Finest Hour.
   Let not Fear of Pain ... Thrust thee Sore.
For Justice ... Prevailing ...Will open the Door
   To Expose the Evil Report ... To Be The Right!
   Giving Grace ... and Credence to the Light!

Part X

My Righteousness to Be Revealed

Again, When a righteous man doth turn from his righteousness and commit iniquity, and I lay a stumbling block before him, he shall die: because thou has not given him warning, he shall die in his sin, and his righteousness which he hath done shall not be remembered; but his blood will I require at thine hand. Nevertheless if thou warn the righteous, that the righteous sin not, and he doth not sin, he shall surely live, because he is warned; also thou hast delivered thy soul.

Ezekiel Three Twenty Through Twenty-One

Prophecy

I ORDAINED YOU BEFORE THE FOUNDATION OF THE WORLD FOR THIS END TIME POSITION!!! AND SO SHALL IT BE!!!

August 5, 2001

THE LORD SPOKE THAT OUR FAMILY SHOULD PRAY OFTEN TOGETHER ON CONFERENCE CALLS. AND EVEN WHEN WE COME TOGETHER, WE SHOULD <u>FIRST</u> PRAY IN THE SPIRIT TOGETHER <u>BEFORE</u> WE CONVERSE. PRAY IN THE SPIRIT BEFORE TALKING!

August 6, 2001

BELIEVE, MY CHILD, BELIEVE! TODAY IS A MIRACLE DAY! MY PEOPLE ARE CALLING ME TO SAVE AND TO HEAL! I AM CALLING MY PEOPLE TO SAVE AND TO HEAL!!! TO REACH OUT AND TO RESCUE! TO TOUCH PEOPLE AT THEIR POINT OF NEED! TO SHOW GENUINE CONCERN FOR PEOPLE'S NEEDS! TO SHARE WHAT THEY HAVE SO THAT I CAN REPLENISH AND GIVE THEM MORE! GO THE SECOND MILE! THAT IS WHAT BREAKS THE YOKES OF BONDAGE! SHOWING TRUE SINCERE LOVE FOR ANOTHER, BREAKS DOWN THE BARRIERS OF REJECTION AND PAIN! YES, I HEAL AND I SAVE THOSE WHO YOU WILL RESCUE FROM THE WATERS THAT ARE RUSHING OVER THEM! SPEAK ENCOURAGEMENT TO THOSE THAT ARE HURTING! GET CLOSE TO THEM SO THAT I CAN USE YOUR LOVE FOR THEM TO DRAW THEM UNTO ME! YES, I SAVE, I HEAL, BUT I AM HINDERED IN FULFILLING THIS TASK IF YOU DO NOT DO YOUR PART! MY HANDS ARE YOUR HANDS ON THE EARTH! MY LIPS ARE YOUR LIPS! MY EARS ARE YOUR EARS! MY HEART IS YOUR HEART! THAT IS WHY I LIVE IN YOU SO THAT YOU CAN DO THE WORK THAT I HAVE INSTRUCTED YOU TO ACCOMPLISH! THE MORE SURRENDERED YOU ARE TO ME, THE MORE I CAN SAVE AND I CAN HEAL! WE ARE LABORERS TOGETHER! HAND IN HAND! AND HEART TO HEART! HEARTBEAT TO HEARTBEAT! MOUTH TO MOUTH! LISTEN!!! AS I SPEAK, YOU OBEY!!! I SAVE AND I HEAL AS YOU ALLOW ME TO

GUIDE YOU TO SUCCOR OTHERS! TO BLESS AND CURSE NOT! TO BE SALT AND LIGHT! TO BE A SWEET SAVOR! TO MAKE MANIFEST THE SAVOR OF MY KNOWLEDGE! OF LIFE UNTO LIFE! IN SINCERITY! AND TRUTH! AS IT IS WRITTEN, O TASTE AND SEE THAT THE LORD IS GOOD! LET OTHERS TASTE ME THROUGH YOUR GOOD WORKS AND I WILL SURELY HEAR, SAVE AND DELIVER THEM SAITH THE LORD!

August 7, 2001

Prophecy

THUS SAITH THE LORD, GRAVE CONSEQUENCES ARE COMING TO MEN OF PROMINENCE! GRAVE CONSEQUENCES ARE COMING TO MEN OF PROMINENCE! GREAT GRACE IS COMING TO THIS NATION!!! GREAT GRACE IS COMING TO THIS NATION!!! I AM GIVING AMERICA A NEW BEGINNING!!! SHE IS GOING TO RECUPERATE FROM SETBACKS AND ATTACKS FROM THE WRONG ELEMENT!

SHE HAS BEEN INFLUENCED BY THE SECULAR MEDIA AND THE PRO-ABORTIONISTS! I AM BRINGING CORRECTION AND UNDERSTANDING TO MAKE CHANGES! I CANNOT TOLERATE THE PRO-ABORTION PLATFORM! I WILL REMOVE PEOPLE IN POLITICS WHO CONTINUE TO THWART THE REMOVAL OF THE ABORTION LAW! PANDERING IS NOT LOBBYING! THERE IS A DIFFERENCE! I WILL CURTAIL THIS PRACTICE OF BUYING VOTES IN ORDER TO PROMOTE ONE'S OWN AGENDA! POWER STRUGGLES ARE GOING TO CEASE! MY PROGRAM IS GOING TO BE MANDATED! JUDGMENTS ARE COMING TO THE CHURCH AND TO THE GOVERNMENT! THE CHURCH HAS THE SAME TYPE OF DISUNITY AS THE POLITICAL PROTOTYPES! I AM SETTING ASIDE MANY THAT REFUSE TO MOVE WITH MY SCHEDULE. MAN IS AN INSTRUMENT. WHEN HE NO LONGER FULFILLS HIS DUTIES, I WILL REMOVE HIM FROM OFFICE IN THE CHURCH AND IN THE GOVERNMENT. JUDGMENTS ARE COMING EXPEDIENTLY. THEY ARE COMING FROM MY THRONE! REGARD NOT HUMAN CONTEMPORARIES, LEST YOU BE FOUND TO BE IN COLLABORATION WITH EVIL FORCES! I MAKE NO APOLOGY FOR TAKING SOME OUT BY DEATH, AS WELL AS, REMOVING SOME FROM OFFICE. OBEDIENCE IS REQUIRED TO REMAIN WHERE I PLACE PEOPLE. I WILL NOT STAY THE HAND OF DEATH ANY LONGER! JOBS ARE UP FOR GRABS, BUT IT IS I WHO SETS IN AUTHORITIES AND POWERS!!! I SEE THE DARKNESS IN THE HEARTS OF MEN AND WOMEN! I SEE THEIR

POTENTIAL AND THEIR MISGUIDED LOYALTIES! WHO IS ON THE LORDS SIDE???

August 10, 2001

This August 10 Prophecy, stating that there would be attacks, grave consequences to men of prominence, judgments coming expediently, that God would no longer stop the hand of death was the last warning I sent to Washington (four pages including June 1 and June 29) on August 16 before 9/11. It was sent to President Bush, to Attorney General John Ashcroft and to Secretary of Health and Human Services Tommy Thompson. It was also sent to Trinity Broadcasting Network President Paul Crouch.

Prophecy

TO THE PRAISE OF HIS GLORY!
TO THE PRAISE OF HIS GLORY!
TO THE PRAISE OF HIS GLORY!
TO THE PRAISE OF HIS GLORY!
TO THE PRAISE OF HIS GLORY!
TO HIM BE ALL GLORY, MIGHT AND POWER!
TO HIM BE ALL GLORY, MIGHT AND POWER!
TO HIM BE ALL GLORY, MIGHT AND POWER!

TRY HARD! TRY HARD! STAY STABILIZED IN SPITE OF <u>ALL</u> THOUGHTS, FEELINGS AND WORDS THAT COME AGAINST YOU! BE QUICK TO HEAR MY VOICE AND SLOW TO ANSWER OTHERS. ANSWER NOT AGAIN EXCEPT I BID YOU TO SPEAK. I TAKE COUNSEL WITH YOU EVEN NOW. DO NOT JEOPARDIZE YOUR FUTURE STANDING BY RESPONDING TO CRITICISM! I WILL FIGHT YOUR BATTLES! DO NOT ANSWER QUESTIONS THAT ARE ASKED IN STRIFE!

STAY CONSECRATED FOR MY DOMINION AND AUTHORITY AND POWER!!! I COUNSEL YOU EVEN NOW TO REMAIN CALM IN THE FACE OF <u>ALL</u> OPPOSITION! I WILL REMAIN YOUR REARGUARD! I AM CALLING PEOPLE INTO CHECK! I AM COUNSELING SOME EVEN NOW CONCERNING YOU. YOU HAVE PROVEN ME AND MANY ARE JEALOUS OF YOU. YOU HAVE CONSECRATED YOURSELF UNTO ME FOR MY GLORY AND NOT YOUR OWN. THAT IS THE REASON I SHALL USE YOU EXPLICITLY AND PROFOUNDLY. YOU ALWAYS GIVE ME <u>ALL</u> THE GLORY! I THANK YOU, MY CHILD, FOR YOUR DEDICATION TO MY WILL AND TO MY WORD. I AM OPENING BIG DOORS, INFLUENTIAL DOORS TO YOUR GIFTS AND CALLINGS. YOU WILL STAND BEFORE GREAT MEN AND WOMEN AND PRONOUNCE THE WORD OF THE LORD. I HAVE GIVEN YOU A PLACE FOR PEOPLE TO COME TO SEE ME PERFORM AND DO MY MIGHTY ACTS, MY SIGNS AND WONDERS!!!

I AM CALLING OUT TO PEOPLE THAT HAVE NEVER HEARD MY NAME! SOME IN AMERICA HAVE NEVER HEARD MY NAME!!! I AM CALLING YOUR RELATIVES TO COME ASIDE AND TO SEEK MY FACE TOGETHER FOR MY GUIDANCE FOR THEIR FUTURE. REGARD NOT MAN'S DISPOSITION! I AM POSITIONING AND REPOSITIONING! MY DISPOSITION IS YOUR DISPOSITION! BE AN EXAMPLE TO OTHERS! BREAK THE CHAINS OF FILTHY DISPOSITION!!! DISPOSITION OF FILTH IS WHEN YOUR POSITION, STAND, ATTITUDE, DEMEANOR, DEPORTMENT, COMMUNICATION, MINDSET IS NOT LIKE MINE!!!

August 15, 2001

On August 15 while in prayer with the Solid Rock Prison Ministry I spoke, THERE IS GOING TO BE A HUGE BLAST AND EVERYONE IS GOING TO SEE IT! ON 9/11 IT WAS SEEN BY ALL OF AMERICA AND THE WORLD ON TV.

Prophecy

YEA, TODAY IS MIRACLE DAY, MY CHILD! TODAY IS MIRACLE DAY! PROPONENTS OF ALL FACETS OF FAITH MATERIAL ARE COMING INTO ALIGNMENT! I AM SETTING MY AUTHORITY IN THE HEAVENLIES AND I AM PUTTING INTO PLACE MY ARSENALS OF DOMINION AND MIGHT! I RESIGN THOSE EVEN NOW WHO WILL NOT FULLY OBEY ME! MY PRECEPTS, MY DOCTRINES AND MY STATUTES! WHO REFUSE TO ALLOW <u>ALL</u> OF MY BODY PARTS, MY OFFICES AND FUNCTIONS TO DEMONSTRATE MY GLORY AND MY DOMINION! I ANTICIPATE STRUGGLES OF POWER! STOP THEM! THEY ARE TO NO AVAIL. I AM GOD! YOU'RE NOT. WHO ARE YOU TO PUT DOWN ONE AND SET UP ANOTHER!!! STOP THE KILLING OF MY PROPHETS! DEATH IN THE SANCTUARY WILL BE DEMONSTRATED VERY SOON! I AM SETTING MY CHURCH IN ORDER! BY DIVINE ORDER!!! NOT POPULAR CONSENSUS! BUT BY PURITY OF PURPOSE! AND DEATH TO PROGRAMS! I ANNIHILATE MEN'S THEORIES, PRACTICES, PINIONS, AS WELL AS OPINIONS! MY COMING IS FOR A GLORIOUS PEOPLE! TO BE GLORIOUS IS TO BE <u>FULL</u> OF MY GLORY!!! NOT MAN'S! DETERMINE YOUR OPTIONS BY REFOCUSING YOUR THOUGHTS, FEELINGS, FAITH AND ATTITUDES!!! I AM! IS THAT YOUR FINAL ANSWER? IT'S MINE!!!

August 16, 2001

HEAL MY PEOPLE WITH YOUR LOVE AND YOUR GOODNESS. <u>LOVE AND GOODNESS IS THE HARD DRIVE OF THE SPIRIT</u>! I AM DIVIDING AND EVEN MAKING SEPARATIONS IN MY MINISTRIES THROUGHOUT THE EARTH BECAUSE I MUST PREPARE THEM FOR THE FINAL TEST. ONE OF COMPLETE SURRENDER! SOME WILL SUFFER DEATH. PREPARE YOUR HEART TO SUFFER! I SUBJECT YOU EVEN NOW TO MORE AUTHORITY. MY AUTHORITY IS PRIMING YOU FOR <u>FULL</u> POTENTIAL OF FAITH AND FULFILLMENT! I AM SPEAKING MY DOMINION INTO YOUR HEART AND MIND! YOU ALWAYS OBEY ME. THUS I TRUST YOU TO OBEY IN THE FUTURE WITHOUT COMPROMISE! STABILIZE THE INCONSISTENCIES OF MANAGEMENT POSITIONS! TELL

THEM TO <u>ALWAYS</u> PRAY BEFORE ANY DECISIONS ARE MADE! TO NOT AUTOMATICALLY THINK THEY KNOW THE ANSWER WITHOUT CONSULTING ME! EVEN THOUGH THEY WALK IN THE SPIRIT, I AM STILL THE HEAD OF THE CHURCH AND I WANT THE FINAL SAY IN <u>ALL</u> DECISIONS BECAUSE MANY WHO PURPORT TO KNOW ME AND TO WALK IN MY SPIRIT ... WALK VERY SHALLOWLY AND NOT <u>FULLY</u> WITH <u>ALL</u> THEIR HEART AND WITH <u>ALL</u> THEIR MIND AND <u>WITH ALL</u> THEIR STRENGTH!!! THUS THE NEED TO CONSULT WITH ME IN <u>ALL</u> DECISIONS.

August 17, 2001

THE LORD SAID, SHE IS TO FULLY OBEY ME NOW AND TO STAY CONSECRATED AT <u>ALL</u> TIMES! I WANT TO USE HER, BUT SHE MUST BE FULLY <u>UP</u> IN THE SPIRIT, PURE, WITH <u>NO SHORT CIRCUITS</u>!!! HE SAID, WHATEVER IT TAKES TO MAKE YOU ANGRY WILL CONTINUE TO HAPPEN UNTIL YOU NO LONGER GET ANGRY!!!

August 20, 2001

To a Prominent Leader

TELL HIM HE IS COMING TO A CROSSROADS. I AM LEADING HIM IN A DIFFERENT DIRECTION. NOT TO FEAR. BUT TO YIELD FULLY TO MY LEADING AND NOT TO DIGRESS, BUT TO PREPARE MY PEOPLE FOR MY COMING SAITH THE LORD. "I WILL HOLD YOU ACCOUNTABLE FOR THE MASSES! NO ONE CAN ACCOMPLISH THIS THAT I AM GIVING YOU TO DO! WAGE WAR! ESTABLISH MY KINGDOM!!! GIVE DIRECTION TO MINISTRIES THAT HAVE NO FOCUS. THAT DO NOT HAVE THE VISION! I WILL HOLD YOU ACCOUNTABLE SAITH THE LORD! REST IN ME!!! I AM THE AUTHOR! AND I AM THE FINISHER!!!"

August 23, 2001

Prophecy

REVIVE MY PROPHETS! REVIVE MY PROPHETS SAITH THE LORD! REVIVE MY APOSTLES! REVIVE MY APOSTLES! IT IS TIME FOR THEM TO GO FORTH. IT IS HIGH TIME SAITH THE LORD! ONLY THE THINGS OF THE LORD ARE PROFITABLE! ONLY THE THINGS OF THE LORD REMIT SIN, HEAL THE SICK AND RAISE THE DEAD! STONE ALL ELSE SAITH THE LORD. CAST ASIDE THE IMMATERIAL! REFUTE THE INSENSITIVE! CASTIGATE THE UNPROFITABLE! REUSE WHAT I REUSE, BUT DISPOSE OF WHAT I DISPOSE! CLAIM THE UNADULTERATED WORD OF GOD! PUT TO USE THE BENEFITS OF FAITH AND FORTITUDE! REVAMP THE DORMANT VICISSITUDES OF CALLING THINGS THAT BE NOT AS THOUGH THEY ARE!!! TELL THE DEVIL TO BEHAVE AND LEAVE YOU ALONE BECAUSE HIS EFFORTS ARE FRUITLESS! THAT YOU WILL NOT BE DENIED THE BEATITUDES OF FAITH BECAUSE YOUR ATTITUDES ARE COMING INTO LINE WITH THE AUTHOR AND FINISHER OF YOUR FAITH! AND HE, THE ALL-KNOWING, ALL-POWERFUL ONE IS GROOMING YOU FOR GLORY AND DOMINION! HE IS TAKING YOU THROUGH TORMENTS AND TRIUMPHS. HE IS CHARACTERIZING HIS OWN CHARACTER IN THE PSYCHE OF YOUR SOUL. HE GIVES YOU ALL HIS ATTRIBUTES AS YOU ALLOW HIM TO BECOME THE CUSTODIAN OF YOUR TEMPLE. THE ENGRAFTED WORD TAKES RESIDENCE AFTER THE HOUSE IS CLEANED THROUGH AND THROUGH. REIGNING RESERVOIRS OF INFALLIBLE, LIMITLESS POWER AND AUTHORITY FILL THE FIBERS OF YOUR BEING! HOUSE-CLEANING TAKES PLACE WHEN WE SURRENDER OUR INTEGRITY TO THE INTEGRITY OF THE ALMIGHTY, TRULY MAKING HIM GOD AND GUARDIAN OF OUR INNERMOST BEING. LETTING <u>HIM</u> DOMINATE OUR THINKING AND OUR FEELING. LETTING THE BISHOP OF OUR SOUL TRULY LEAD US TO THE ULTIMATE GOAL OF PURITY OF PURPOSE AND MANDATE OF MIND. GIVING OUR DESTINY ITS DOMINION!!! SETTLING FOREVER ISSUES OF SURROGACY. FATHERING OUR PROGENY! BRINGING FORTH OUR POSTERITY. GIVING GRACE TO ALL WHO PARTAKE OF HIS HOLINESS. <u>GO SATAN</u>!!! RETALIATE

NO MORE AGAINST WHOLENESS OF PURPOSE AND PURITY OF PLAN! REVIVE MY PEOPLE SAITH THE LORD!

MARCH IN LINE! DO NOT BREAK RANK. BE SUBJECT ONE TO ANOTHER! LET THE APOSTLES BE COUNTED WORTHY OF DOUBLE HONOR AS THEY BLAZE THE TRAILS TO FULFILLMENT AND OPEN DOORS OF DESTINY!!! STAY THE HAND OF THE ENEMY!!! JUDGE NOT SAITH THE LORD! THERE IS ONE JUDGE! WHO ART THOU THAT JUDGES ANOTHER? HAVE YOU NOT YOUR OWN PAST FAILURES AND MISTAKES??? DARE YOU JUDGE ANOTHER FOR THEIRS? WHO HAS MADE YOU A JUDGE??? IMPART DIGNITY, RATHER THAN DIVISION!!! DIGNITY INCLUDES ALL PEOPLE OF ALL RACES, ALL BACKGROUNDS, ALL PAST EXPERIENCES! NO ONE IS LEFT OUT! KINGS ARE SEATED WITH SIMPLETONS, EVEN AS SOME KINGS ARE SIMPLETONS, SO SOME PENNILESS ARE PROMINENT IN FAITH AND FORTITUDE!!! JUDGE NOT BY CIRCUMSTANCE OR OUTWARD APPEARANCE! ONLY WALK IN MY SPIRIT, AND GRACE WHOM I GRACE AND GLORY IN WHAT I GLORY! I DO NOT GLORY IN ABUNDANCE OF MATERIAL THINGS THAT ONE POSSESSES!

I GLORY IN BONDAGES OF ADDICTIONS BEING BROKEN OFF DESTITUTE HUMANITY! I GIVE HONOR UNTO WHOM HONOR IS DUE AND I GIVE DOMINION UNTO WHOM DOMINION IS DUE!!! I RAISE UP THE POOR OUT OF THE DUST AND I LIFT UP THE NEEDY OUT OF THE DUNGHILL THAT HE MAY SIT WITH PRINCES. WHO ART THOU THAT JUDGES ANOTHER MAN'S POWERS AND PURPOSES? STAY ROOTED IN THE SOUL OF THE SAVIOR AND ALL YOUR DEEDS WILL BE LIKENED UNTO HIM! NOT MARKETED WITH CALLOUSNESS AND CALUMNY! PERVERTED PROVISIONS ARE BEING USED FOR SIGNS OF HONOR AND DESTINY, BUT MIGHT DOES NOT ALWAYS MAKE RIGHT! RIGHTEOUSNESS IS SOWN IN PEACE OF THEM THAT MAKE PEACE! NOT DIVISION! PEACE IS FOUNDED ON TRUTH OF MY WORD!!! ALL ELSE IS SINKING SAND!

August 27, 2001

PREPARE! PREPARE TO BE CAUGHT UP!

August 28, 2001

I GIVE YOU A PORTION OF MY SPIRIT EVEN NOW TO RAISE THE DEAD! SOON YOU WILL RAISE THE DEAD SAITH THE LORD. YOUR PERFECTION IS IN ME. YOUR PERFECTION IS IN ME SAITH THE LORD. I GO WITH YOU AND I BREAK DOWN EVERY BARRIER. I AM RESTORING MARRIAGES. I AM RESTORING MARRIAGES SAITH THE LORD. STOP BREAKING MY LAWS SAITH THE LORD! STOP BREAKING MY LAW OF LOVE AND FORGIVENESS! UN-FORGIVENESS IS SIN! LACK OF LOVE AND KINDNESS IS SIN! STOP NAME CALLING! STOP JUDGING! STOP CALLING THINGS THAT ARE! START CALLING THINGS THAT ARE NOT AS <u>THOUGH</u> THEY ARE! CALL FORTH ABUNDANCE OF RAIN! CALL FORTH OUTPOURINGS OF MY SPIRIT! I BREAK THE BARRIERS OF MAN AND MEN-WORSHIP! I STABILIZE HOMES AND HEARTS TO SUBMIT TO CROSSES AND CROWNS! THERE IS ONLY ONE CHRISTIANITY! IT IS THE WAY OF THE CROSS! IT IS FIRST, SUBMISSION TO ME AND THEN, SUBMISSION TO EACH OTHER! IT IS BEARING ONE'S CROSS DAILY, HOURLY, MINUTE BY MINUTE IN FASHION OF THE HOLY ONE! I BREAK THE BONDAGES OF FALSE CHRISTIANITY AND FALSE CHRISTS! I STAY THE HANDS OF POWER STRUGGLES AND THE SPIRIT OF PREEMINENCE! I AM THE <u>ONLY</u> ONE TRUE LIVING GOD!!! WORSHIP AND SERVE ME!!! SERVE NOT THE IDOL OF HIERARCHY WORSHIP AND WORSHIP OF LEADERS AND ANGELS! JUSTIFICATION IS BY FAITH! <u>FAITH IN THE LORD JESUS CHRIST WHO BLED AND DIED ON CALVARY!</u> ALL ELSE IS MAN MADE IDOL WORSHIP!!! SERVE <u>ME</u>!!! THE ONE TRUE LIVING GOD! PROSTRATE YOURSELF BEFORE ME! LAY IN MY PRESENCE UNTIL I SPEAK! I SPEAK AND SO SHALL IT BE SAITH THE LORD, THE GOD OF ALL FORCES!!!

EXTINGUISH ALL FIRES BUT THE FIRE OF THE HOLY GHOST! LET THE TRUTH BE THE DETERMINING FACTOR IN <u>ALL</u> DECISIONS AND DECREES! I AM THE CONSUMING FIRE!!! EXTINGUISH ME

NOT! GUARD YOUR HEART! ALLOW NOTHING INTO IT EXCEPT PURITY! MY WORD IS PURE! EAT IT! PURIFY YOURSELVES WITH THE WASHING OF THE WORD AND RENEWING OF THE HOLY SPIRIT, NOT MIXED WITH IDEAS AND OPINIONS! MY WORD AND MY SPIRIT AGREE AS ONE! <u>WHEN MY PEOPLE WILL ALLOW SPIRIT AND WORD ONLY TO DOMINATE, I CAN ACCOMPLISH ALL THINGS THAT I HAVE PURPOSED!</u> THE WORD TO BE FULFILLED, CONFIRMED AND MY RETURN TO CATCH AWAY MY BRIDE! I AM NOT COMING BACK AFTER A HALF-DRESSED BRIDE OR A BRIDE WHOSE WEDDING GARMENT IS SPOTTED, STAINED OR WRINKLED! THE ONLY WAY MY BRIDE WILL BE GLORIOUS IS TO BE <u>FULLY</u> SUBMITTED TO <u>MY</u> WORD AND TO <u>MY</u> SPIRIT! THERE IS NO OTHER WAY! AS IT IS WRITTEN, IF YOU ARE LUKEWARM I WILL SPEW YOU OUT OF MY MOUTH! WRESTLE NOT AGAINST ONE ANOTHER, AGAINST FLESH AND BLOOD! BUT WRESTLE AGAINST SPIRITUAL WICKEDNESS IN HIGH PLACES, AGAINST CORRUPT CHURCH GOVERNMENT, AGAINST PRINCIPALITIES AND POWERS, AGAINST RULERS OF THE DARKNESS OF THIS WORLD!!! STAND AGAINST ALL THAT DO NOT STAND FOR THE FULL TRUTH OF MY WORD AND MY SPIRIT!!! PRAYING <u>ALWAYS</u> WITH ALL SUPPLICATION IN THE SPIRIT AND WATCHING WITH <u>ALL</u> PERSEVERANCE FOR ALL SAINTS!!! WITHOUT RESPECT OF PERSONS WHICH IS SIN!

SEEK DILIGENTLY TO MAKE YOUR CALLING AND ELECTION SURE, FOR NOT EVERYONE THAT CALLS ME LORD WILL BE RECEIVED OF ME! FOR WITHOUT ADDING VIRTUE, MORAL EXCELLENCE OF GOODNESS, TO YOUR FAITH, WITHOUT ADDING THE KNOWLEDGE OF THE HOLY, WITHOUT BECOMING PROFICIENT IN MODERATION AND PATIENCE AND GODLINESS AND BROTHERLY KINDNESS AND CHARITY, YOU ARE BARREN AND UNFRUITFUL IN THE KNOWLEDGE OF WHO I REALLY AM!!! IF YOU ARE DEFICIENT, LACKING IN THESE ATTRIBUTES, YOU ARE BLIND AND CANNOT SEE! GIVE <u>ALL</u> DILIGENCE TO ADD THESE ATTITUDES TO YOUR LIFE OF FAITH FOR THEREBY YOU ARE CALLED TO GLORY AND VIRTUE!!! NOT TO RESPECT OF PERSONS, TRIBALISM, SECTARIANISM, JUDGMENTALISM,

RACISM AND DISDAIN! I AM LORD OF ALL!!! GIVE HEED TO MY EXAMPLE!!!

August 28, 2001

I HAVE CALLED YOU FOR THREE THINGS:

1) PROPHET TO THE NATION

2) APOSTLE TO THE WORLD

3) TEACHER TO TEACHERS

GOD DIDN'T SAY BE POPULAR. HE SAID, BE HOLY!!! HE SAID TO ME, YOU PROPHESIED TONIGHT WHEN YOU RAN AND SHOOK AND DEMONSTRATED IN THE SPIRIT. HE SAID, YOU SAID, "FOR WHICH OF THESE GOOD WORKS DO YOU STONE ME?"

August 29, 2001

Prophecy

HE IS COMING INTO PERFECTION. HE IS COMING INTO MATURITY. I AM RECONDITIONING HIM. I AM REMOLDING HIM. I AM GIVING HIM MY PERFECTION. I AM CALLING HIM INTO POWER. ALL MIGHT MUST BE FILTERED FROM MY THRONE. AS HE SURRENDERS HIS MIGHT, HIS AUTHORITY, HIS POWER UNTO ME, THE ALMIGHTY, I WILL UTILIZE HIS OTHER ATTRIBUTES FOR DISTRIBUTION TO THE MASSES. I AM RESTORING IMAGE. IMAGE IS PERCEPTION. PERCEPTION IS NEEDED TO ELEVATE MY PEOPLE TO PURITY. WITHOUT PURITY ONE IS NOT READY TO MEET THE LORD. WITHOUT PURITY YOU WILL BE LEFT BEHIND WHEN THE RAPTURE TAKES PLACE!!! PERCEPTION IS NEEDED TO UNDERSTAND THE WORK OF THE CROSS. JESUS BEING SLAIN FOR THE SINS OF THE WORLD WAS NOT ONLY TO WASH AWAY THE SINS OF HUMANITY, BUT ALSO TO ALLOW EACH HUMAN BEING TO WALK IN SON-SHIP OF WHOLENESS AND PURITY! AFTER JESUS DIED ON THE CROSS HE RETURNED TO THE FATHER SO THAT HE COULD LIVE IN YOU EACH DAY BY SENDING HIS SPIRIT, THE HOLY GHOST, TO ABIDE IN YOU THAT YOU WOULD HAVE NO LACK! JESUS ABIDING IN YOU GIVES YOU ACCESS TO ALL AUTHORITY, ALL POWER, ALL DOMINION, ALL KNOWLEDGE, ALL UNDERSTANDING, ALL TEACHING, ALL PERCEPTION, ALL ABILITY, ALL LOVE, ALL COUNSEL, ALL PURPOSE, ALL COMMUNION, ALL WILL AND ALL PURITY AND WHOLENESS AND COMPLETION AND ALL ONENESS WITH THE 'I AM', THE INTELLIGENCE OF ALL TIME AND VICISSITUDE. ALTHOUGH WE KNOW IN PART AND PROPHESY IN PART, WHATEVER PART OF THE WHOLE, THE ALL-KNOWING GOD THAT IS NEEDED FOR ONENESS WITH GOD AND WITH THE SAINTS IS AVAILABLE TO YOUR SPIRIT BY THE RELEASE OF YOUR AUTHORITY OF HEADSHIP TO THE HEADSHIP OF THE CHRIST! GOD RELEASES YOUR NEEDS, AS YOU RELEASE YOUR AUTHORITY TO HIS AUTHORITY AND SUBMIT YOUR WILL TO HIS WILL AND YOUR UNDERSTANDING AND PERCEPTION TO THE WILL AND PURPOSE OF THE ALMIGHTY!

August 30, 2001

Prophecy

I AM CALLING YOU TO PREACH WHERE I SEND YOU. BE SURE TO GO WHEN I SAY TO GO. I WILL HOLD YOU ACCOUNTABLE. I AM HOLDING YOU ACCOUNTABLE! I AM GOING TO GIVE YOU A SIGN. A SIGN OF SIGNIFICANCE. DON'T BE ALARMED AT EVILS THAT WILL COME AGAINST YOU. SHAKE IT OFF! PREACH THE WORD! RAISE THE DEAD! CAST OUT DEVILS! GO WHERE I SEND YOU! STAY COOL, CALM AND COLLECTED. LET ME LEAD YOU. YOU ARE PURE. YOU HAVE MANY TRIALS AND HURTS, BUT YOU DO NOT LET ANYTHING STAND IN THE WAY OF OBEDIENCE TO ME. I AM PROUD OF YOU. CARMAN NEEDS YOUR PRAYERS. INTERCEDE FOR HIS MINISTRY. I AM GIVING YOUR SISTER AND BROTHER-IN-LAW A MIRACLE IN THE FALL. IT WILL REJUVENATE THEIR FINANCIAL BASE. I AM HEALING HER. I AM GIVING HER A MIRACLE. I AM CALLING HER AND HER HUSBAND TO PRAY. I AM CALLING THEM INTO TOTAL OBEDIENCE ... NOTHING HELD BACK.

August 31, 2001

Wisdom

WHEN PRAISE IS NOT GOING UP TO GOD IN A SERVICE, JUST HANDCLAPPING, NOT THE FRUIT OF THE LIPS, YOU ARE HONORING THE GIFT OF THAT MAN MORE THAN YOU ARE HONORING THE GOD OF THAT GIFT!!!

August 5, 2001

SOMETIMES YOUR OWN THINKING THAT IS NOT FULLY SURRENDERED AND SANCTIFIED BECOMES YOUR SEED. AND WE YET WONDER WHY WE ARE NOT GLORIOUSLY OVERCOMING. BECAUSE THE SEED, MINED WITH OUR OWN INADEQUACIES, SHORTCOMINGS, WEAKNESSES, FAILURES, BECOMES OUR OWN DEPORTMENT, INSTEAD OF THE MANIFESTATION OF GOD AND HIS GLORY IN THE POWER OF A SANCTIFIED LIFE. ONE FILLED WITH HIM ALONE! WITHOUT A REVELATION OF GOD YOU WILL HAVE ISSUES. THINGS YOU DO NOT FULLY SUBMIT. WITH A REVELATION OF JESUS CHRIST YOU BECOME ONE WITH HIM AND HE LIVES IN YOU AND WALKS THROUGH YOU AND YOU OVERCOME THROUGH HIM!

August 20, 2001

IT IS TIME TO TAKE THE MASK OFF! DETAILS DETERMINE DESTINIES JUST AS LITTLE FOXES SPOIL THE VINE. THE CONTROL CENTER OF YOUR LIFE IS YOUR WILL. <u>THE PROCESS OF SANCTIFICATION IS TO CHANGE YOU, NOT YOUR CIRCUMSTANCES!</u> WE WANT GOD TO CHANGE OUR CIRCUMSTANCES. GOD WANTS TO CHANGE OUR LIVES. IF OUR LIVES DO NOT CHANGE, WE WILL BE BACK IN THE SAME CIRCUMSTANCES. THE PROCESS OF SANCTIFICATION CHANGES <u>US</u>, SO THAT WE REMAIN LIKE THE LORD, PATIENT, LONG-SUFFERING, PERSEVERING, FORGIVING, KIND, NO MATTER WHAT THE CIRCUMSTANCES!!!

August 22, 2001

Wisdom

THE REASON THAT PEOPLE KILL THE PROPHETS IS THAT THEY CANNOT GET RID OF THEM ANY OTHER WAY! THEY CAN'T HATE THEM AWAY! THEY CAN'T REBUKE THEM AWAY! THEY CAN'T REJECT THEM AWAY! TODAY PEOPLE KILL THE PROPHETS BY SETTING THEM ASIDE.

August 23, 2001

IT TAKES THE SAME ANOINTING TO ALLOW OTHERS TO BE OBEDIENT TO THE HOLY SPIRIT. SOME PEOPLE THINK THE GREATEST ANOINTING IS TO GO FORTH AND PREACH THE WORD WITH POWER. IT TAKES THE SAME POWERFUL ANOINTING TO ALLOW OTHERS TO GO FORTH AND PREACH WITH POWER. IT IS THE SAME AUTHORITY THAT RELEASES THE ANOINTING WHETHER YOU MINISTER OR WHETHER YOU ALLOW SOMEONE ELSE TO MINISTER. ANOINTINGS ARE BEING TOUCHED, SET ASIDE, HELD BACK BY PASTORS WHO REFUSE TO ALLOW OTHERS TO FLOW AND MOVE IN THEIR GIFTING AND CALLING!!!

August 24, 2001

COUNSELING DOES NOT BRING UNITY OF PURPOSE. ONLY SUBMISSION TO THE AUTHORITY OF THE AUTHOR BRINGS UNITY OF PURPOSE! DOMINION IS AUTHORITY INCARNATE!

August 30, 2001

Word of Faith

DO YOU KNOW HOW YOU KNOW THAT YOU ARE HEALED???
WHEN ALL THE PAIN IS GONE?????????? NO! WHEN ALL THE
SYMPTOMS ARE GONE? NO! YOU ARE HEALED BECAUSE GOD'S
WORD SAYS YOU ARE HEALED!!! YOU ARE HEALED BECAUSE
GOD SAID SO! <u>YOU ARE HEALED WHEN YOUR WORD LINES UP
WITH GOD'S WORD!!!</u> WHEN YOU SAY WHAT GOD SAYS, YOU
GET WHAT GOD HAS! YOU GET WHAT GOD SAYS!!! YOU CAN
HAVE WHAT GOD SAYS INSTEAD OF REPEATING WHAT THE
SYMPTOMS SAY!!!   IF YOU ARE STILL SAYING WHAT YOUR
SYMPTOMS SAY, GOD CANNOT HEAL YOU! HE OBEYS HIS WORD!
HE DOES NOT OBEY SYMPTOMS! HE OBEYS <u>FAITH</u>! <u>FAITH IS
ACTIVATED BY WORDS</u>! WORDS OF FAITH! FAITH IS NOW! NOT
WILL BE! FAITH IS PRESENT TENSE! YOU ARE HEALED BECAUSE
THE WORD SAYS YOU ARE!   JESUS, THE WORD, SAYS YOU ARE
HEALED! WHAT DO YOU SAY? IF YOU ARE NOT SAYING YOU ARE
HEALED IN THE PRESENT TENSE, CALLED CONFESSING GOD'S
WORD, YOU ARE NOT IN FAITH! FAITH IS NOW! NOT WILL BE!
WILL BE IS FUTURE. BUT FAITH IS NOW! PRESENT TENSE! WHEN
YOU GET YOUR DECLARATION IN LINE WITH WHAT THE WORD
SAYS, YOU WILL RECEIVE WHAT GOD'S WORD SAYS YOU CAN
HAVE! HOW CAN GOD HEAL YOU WHEN YOU KEEP CONFESSING,
I'M HURTING INSTEAD OF CONFESSING, I'M HEALED? WHEN
YOU CONFESS SYMPTOMS INSTEAD OF GOD'S WORD YOU ARE
DENYING HIS WORD! YOU ARE HEALED BECAUSE GOD'S WORD
SAYS YOU ARE HEALED! WHEN YOUR FAITH TOUCHES GOD'S
WORD BY CONTINUALLY CONFESSING GOD'S WORDS YOU WILL
RECEIVE THE MANIFESTATION OF TRUTH, WHICH IS GOD'S
WORD! HEALING! GOD DOES NOT DO ANOTHER THING THAN
WHAT JESUS ALREADY DID WHEN HE SUFFERED THE STRIPES
FOR YOUR HEALING! WHEN YOU GET HEALED GOD DOES NOT
DO ANYTHING! HIS SON JESUS ALREADY DID THE WORK 2000
YEARS AGO! YOU RECEIVE THE FINISHED WORK WHEN YOUR
FAITH TOUCHES GOD'S WORD! THE WORD <u>ALWAYS</u> WORKS
WHEN FAITH TOUCHES IT. FAITH TOUCHES THE WORD BY

SPEAKING WHAT THE WORD SAYS INSTEAD OF WHAT THE SYMPTOMS DO!

August 1, 2001

THE ORDER OF THE DAY IS OR IN MAN'S VERNACULAR ... THE QUESTION OF THE DAY IS CAN GOD SPEAK TOO MUCH TO US? GOD'S ORDER SAYS, YOU MAY ALL PROPHESY!!! ONE BY ONE! THAT <u>ALL</u> MAY LEARN AND <u>ALL</u> BE COMFORTED. GOD WANTS EVERYONE TO BE USED IN THE GIFTS OF THE SPIRIT, SO THAT WHENEVER AND WHEREVER THERE IS A NEED, THAT NEED CAN IMMEDIATELY BE FILLED BECAUSE WE ARE EXERCISED BY FAITH IN THE MOVING OF THE SPIRIT! THE SCRIPTURE STATES THAT <u>ALL</u> MAY BE COMFORTED! HOW ARE WE COMFORTED? BY GOD SPEAKING TO US! IT IS CALLED <u>PROPHECY!</u> IT IS WRITTEN, LET <u>ALL</u> THINGS BE DONE UNTO EDIFYING! IT IS WRITTEN, HE THAT PROPHESIES SPEAKS UNTO MEN TO EDIFICATION AND EXHORTATION AND COMFORT! I Corinthians 14:3 THIS IS HOW CLOSE WE ARE TO BE IN THE SPIRIT. LINE UPON LINE AND PRECEPT UPON PRECEPT!!! NOT OPINIONS UPON OPINIONS! NOR PREFERENCES UPON PREFERENCES! BUT THE PRECEPTS OF OUR LORD UPON THE PRECEPTS OF OUR LORD! NOTHING ADDED AND NOTHING TAKEN AWAY! PRECEPT UPON PREFECT! FOUNDATION OF THE APOSTLES AND PROPHETS, JESUS CHRIST THE CHIEF CORNERSTONE!

August 5, 2001

September 2001

Love is a matchless gram
of gold and diamonds
Ruby-redness perches
on luster-laden prayers.
Blood stains of countless martyrs
Paint the stairs to heaven's glory!

Part XI

Cast Down
Your Idols

My son, keep thy father's commandment and forsake not the law of thy mother: Bind them continually upon thine heart and tie them about thy neck. When thou goest, it shall lead thee: When thou sleepest, it shall keep thee and when thou awaken, it shall talk with thee. For the commandment is a lamp and the law is light and reproofs of instruction are the way of life to keep thee from evil.

Proverbs Six Twenty Through Twenty-four

Prophecy

I WANT YOU TO STAY CONSECRATED AT <u>ALL</u> TIMES. HARBOR NO RESENTMENT AT ANY TIME ABOUT ANYTHING!!! STAY VERY CALM WHEN YOU ARE REPROACHED OR SEEMINGLY CORRECTED! NO ONE CAN TAKE WHAT I HAVE GIVEN YOU. SOME THINK THEY ARE CALLING YOU TO TASK, BUT THEY ARE BRINGING CORRECTION TO THEMSELVES.

September 5, 2001

I SAY UNTO YOU: SURFACE, SURFACE, SAITH THE LORD. THE REAL YOU I AM BRINGING TO THE SURFACE SO THAT ALL OF YOUR INADEQUACIES AND INEPTITUDES CAN BE MORALIZED AND MADE NEW! I FASHION YOU INTO ONE HELD FAST BY WORD ALONE. ALL ELSE IS SINKING SAND!!!

September 6, 2001

ARE YOU PREGNANT WITH PEACE?

September 7, 2001

IT IS DONE!!!

September 8, 2001

THE CHURCH HAS BEEN HIJACKED!!! THE LORD SPOKE "TWIN TOWERS," "TWIN TOWERS," TO ME WHILE RETURNING HOME FROM PRISON MINISTRY!

September 9, 2001

Note: When 9/11 took place, I reflected, was I to have done something that could have changed the outcome? No, God only allowed me to be aware.

Prophecy

BEWARE, MY SERVANT! BEWARE SAITH THE LORD! DO NOT LET ANYTHING HINDER YOU! PRIDE IS OUT AND MIRACLES ARE IN! IN FOUR DAYS I WILL SHOW YOU A GREAT MIRACLE! I WILL RAISE ONE UP WHO IS ALMOST IN THE GRAVE!

September 10, 2001

Note: Of course, so it was at Ground Zero on September 14, 2001! One Thought to be dead, but yet found Alive under the rubble!

Prophecy

THE LORD AWAKENED ME AT 7 am SAYING: <u>BEWARE!</u> <u>BEWARE!</u>
<u>EVIL FORCES ARE ABOUT TO STRIKE!</u>

September 11, 2001

Note: I called my daughter, Tamah, about forty minutes before the first plane struck the World Trade Center in New York. When I awakened her, she was dreaming that she was on a tactical airplane! I told her what the Lord had spoken to me. She said, This is eerie. We prayed. Soon another daughter, Vicki, called and said, Turn on the TV! A little later, Tamah called and we prayed again, now on conference call with my son, Nathan, interceding for the hijacked plane that was still in the air! The plane on which Americans sacrificed themselves for others as they foiled the attempt of the hijackers in not allowing them to take the plane into another building, but made the ultimate sacrifice forcing the plane down in a field in Pennsylvania! Thank God, there are still True Americans!!! I had waited an hour before I called my daughter because she worked nights.

THE ACCOUNT OF MY DAUGHTER, TAMAH:

"I WOKE UP TO THE PHONE RINGING. IT WAS MY MOTHER. I TOLD HER, IN MY DREAM I WAS ON A TACTICAL AIRPLANE THAT HAD BEEN HIJACKED BY WHAT APPEARED TO BE ARABS. PEOPLE WERE FRANTICALLY SCRAMBLING FOR THEIR SEAT-BELTS, OXYGEN MASKS AND CELL PHONES. I SAW AND HEARD PEOPLE CRYING AND PRAYING AND CALLING THEIR LOVED-ONES FOR WHAT APPEARED TO BE THE LAST TIME. I HEARD A MAN TELL HIS WIFE THAT HE LOVED HER IN A CALM RESOLVED MANNER. WHILE THE ARAB WITH THE MACHINE RIFLE WAS DISTRACTED, ON INSTINCT, I GOT UP TO CHARGE HIM. WHILE I WAS GOING TOWARDS HIM, OTHERS CHARGED FORWARD WITH ME. THEN THE PHONE RANG WAKING ME. THIS DREAM WAS ALL BEFORE I EVEN KNEW THE TWIN TOWERS HAD BEEN ATTACKED."

LITERALLY, HER DREAM <u>WAS</u> <u>BEFORE</u> THE FIRST PLANE HIT!

Prophecy

PEACE. PEACE. I GIVE YOU MY PEACE. THERE IS LITTLE TIME.
THERE IS LITTLE TIME. I AM SHOWING MY AUTHORITY. I AM
GIVING MY JUDGMENT. ALL ELSE IS RHETORIC! MAN SHALL YET
KNOW AND UNDERSTAND THAT I AM GOD AND BESIDES ME
THERE IS NONE OTHER. WHEN I SAY TO STOP KILLING MY
PROGENY THAT IS EXACTLY WHAT I MEAN!!! PEOPLE ARE SEEING
A PORTION OF MY WRATH! I PRACTICE WHAT I PREACH. WHAT I
SAY, I DO! I AM GOING TO SHOW MY PEOPLE WHICH ARE CALLED
BY MY NAME THAT I CAN BE TRUSTED TO KEEP MY WORD. THERE
IS NO OTHER FAITH. I AM THE ONLY TRUE LIVING GOD! ALL ELSE
ARE IDOLS AND IMPOSTERS. I CAN MAKE ALIVE. AND I CAN
TAKE LIFE. ALL THAT I DO IS IN ACCORDANCE WITH MY
WRITTEN WORD. I DO NOT SEND JUDGMENTS WITHOUT
WARNING! I DO NOT OFFICIATE IN PLACE OF THE REAL THING!
THIS IS IT! THE ONE TRUE LIVING FAITHFUL GOD. WHAT YOU
KNOW IS WHAT I PROVE! I DO NOT SAY FALSELY! WHATEVER I
HAVE SAID, I BACK UP WITH PROOF AND AUTHORITY! REST IN
MY WILL AND IN MY WORD! DO NOT TRY TO GAINSAY OR
FALSIFY MY WRITTEN WORD! IT SHALL STAND IN EVERY
SITUATION. IT SHALL DOMINATE IN THESE LAST DAYS BEFORE I
APPEAR IN THE EASTERN SKY.

MAKE NO MISTAKE. I AM KEEPING RECORD OF ALL THAT IS
TAKING PLACE! I KNOW EVERY THOUGHT AND EVERY WORD,
NOT JUST WHAT IS EVIDENT BUT EVERY INTENTION, AS WELL AS,
EVERY ACTION! DO NOT SEEK TO COVER YOUR DEEDS, BUT GIVE
TO ME YOUR HEART SO THAT I CAN MAKE IT HOLY! WHAT ARE
ALL THESE THINGS THAT YOU LIVE FOR IF THEY ARE NOT
PREPARING YOU FOR ETERNAL LIFE??? DEATH ... ETERNAL
DEATH IS FOREVER! IT NEVER ENDS. THE TORMENTS OF
ETERNAL DAMNATION NEVER EVER STOP!!! CHOOSE THE ONE
TRUE LIVING GOD! THE ONE WHO GAVE HIS ONLY BEGOTTEN
SON TO DIE FOR YOUR SINS! LET ME WASH AWAY THE CURSES
AND THE ABUSES! LET ME SPEAK PEACE TO YOUR WEARY SOUL!
LET ME MAKE NEW YOUR TROUBLED MIND! LET ME SHOW YOU

THE POWER OF MY GLORY!!! REST. SURRENDER YOUR SEARED SOLACE. LET ME REPLENISH YOUR HOPE. LET ME GIVE POWER TO COPE. LET ME TAKE RESIDENCE IN YOU AND SHOW YOU THE GRANDEUR OF MY POWER AND MY GLORY! JUST ONE TOUCH IGNITES THE SPLENDOR. IT ONLY TAKES SURRENDER.

I AM RELEASING MY PROVISION FOR THOSE WHO WILL COMPLETELY TRUST IN ME. I AM GIVING THEM PERSEVERANCE. I AM GOING TO SHOW THEM THE GLORY AS OF THE ONLY BEGOTTEN OF THE FATHER! DO NOT TRY IN YOUR OWN ABILITY TO UNDERSTAND ALL THE THINGS THAT ARE TAKING PLACE, BUT REST ASSURED THAT I AM STILL IN CONTROL! THE LAST DAY EVENTS BEFORE THE RAPTURE OF THE CHURCH ARE TAKING PLACE ONE BY ONE! I CANNOT CATCH AWAY A LUKEWARM, DISOBEDIENT BRIDE! ALL THINGS ARE BRINGING INTO ALIGNMENT THE FINISHING TOUCHES OF TRUTH!!!

I WILL NOT WASTE PROSPERITY ON THE WILLFUL AND DISOBEDIENT! I AM GIVING MY TREASURES TO THOSE WHO WILL USE THEM FOR MY GLORY AND THE FULFILLMENT OF MY WILL AND PURPOSE. LET NOT GRACE PASS YOU BY. ONE IS SAVED FROM THE TERROR OF FUTILITY AND DISGRACE BY TAKING ME AS THEIR SAVIOR, BELIEVING ON MY NAME, THE LORD JESUS CHRIST! BY BELIEVING THAT I DIED FOR THEIR SINS AND THAT I ROSE AGAIN TO GIVE THEM POWER OVER DEATH AND HELL AND THE GRAVE! BELIEVE! PRAYER: I AM SORRY FOR MY SINS. I RENOUNCE THEM. I BELIEVE YOU DIED FOR ME THAT I MAY LIVE ETERNALLY. I ACCEPT YOU AS MY SAVIOR AND LORD! THANK YOU FOR MAKING ME WHOLE AND WASHING ME CLEAN! I AM A NEW CREATURE!!! I RECEIVE MY RIGHTFUL CITIZENSHIP. I TAKE MY PLACE IN THE KINGDOM OF THE LORD! I REFUSE TO BE LOST AND TO SUFFER ETERNAL TORMENT. I ACCEPT YOU, LORD!!! LEAD ME INTO TRUTH! GIVE ME UNDERSTANDING AND KNOWLEDGE. HELP ME TO ACCEPT MY RIGHTFUL PLACE TO FULFILL MY DESTINY! EACH DAY I SUBMIT TO YOUR GRACE AND THE RENEWING OF MY SPIRIT WITH THE WORD OF GOD AND THE HOLY SPIRIT! AMEN.

DOMINIONS HAVE DEPARTED. I AM IN FULL CONTROL OF THIS END TIME PARODY. NO ONE SUBJUGATES ME. I AM RULER OF THIS UNIVERSE. ALL THINGS ARE IN PLACE FOR THE FULFILLMENT OF THE WORD OF GOD! THE REVELATION OF MY GLORY IS FORTHCOMING. *I AM BRINGING INTO ALIGNMENT THE KINGS AND KINGDOMS FOR THE LAST BIG BATTLE. I AM GIVING INSTRUCTIONS FOR SEQUENCES AND SEVERITIES. NOTHING IS HID FROM MY JURISDICTION.* I REIGN. MAN IS MY CREATION. I DO NOT BOW TO HIS AUTHORITY. HE NOW BOWS TO MINE!!! DO NOT BE BLINDED BY MONEY OR BY POWER! THERE WILL BE MANY RICH FOOLS IN HELL. THERE WILL BE MANY EDUCATED FOOLS, AS WELL. RIGHTEOUSNESS ONLY COMES BY ME. ALL ELSE IS FUTILITY. *MY DOMINION SHALL PRECEDE MY GLORY.* DO NOT BE MISLED BY THE SHREDS OF THIS EXISTENCE. LIFE AS YOU NOW KNOW IT SHALL SOON BE NO MORE. ONLY THOSE WHO ARE IN ME SHALL LIVE ETERNALLY. WITH PEACE AND WITH PROSPERITY. THE DRUNKARD. THE FEARFUL. AND THE UNBELIEVING. THE ABOMINABLE. AND MURDERERS. THE PERVERTED. AND WHOREMONGERS. AND DRUG-MONGERS. AND IDOLATROUS. AND ALL LIARS SHALL HAVE THEIR PART IN THE LAKE OF FIRE WHICH BURNS WITH FIRE AND BRIMSTONE FOREVER AND FOREVER.

September 12, 2001

Prophecy

DO NOT WAIT ANY LONGER SAITH THE LORD! REESTABLISH <u>FULL</u> PRAYER TIME. ALL THE HOURS THAT I AM SPEAKING TO YOU ABOUT. WAIT NOT ON OTHERS. I AM WITH YOU. I SHALL SPEAK TO YOU HOURLY IN THE DAYS AHEAD. ESTABLISH WHAT I SPEAK. GIVE IT TO THE ADMINISTRATION. I AM GOING TO GIVE YOU CRITICAL, VITAL INFORMATION CONCERNING AMERICA'S FUTURE. DO NOT SPEAK TO OTHERS EXCEPT I BID YOU. DO NOT LET OTHERS MANDATE MY WILL FOR YOUR LIFE. I HAVE YOU AT STRATEGIC POSITIONING. REST, SAITH THE LORD, FOR I SHALL SPEAK TO YOU IN PEACE, NOT IN FEAR OR FRUSTRATION. *I AM REESTABLISHING MY HIERARCHY AND MY DOMINION. <u>I SEVER ALL TIES WITH ISLAM.</u> AMERICA IS TO BREAK OFF ALL COMMUNICATIONS WITH KNOWN TERRORIST LOVERS AND DEFENDERS! COMMISERATING WITH THE ENEMY DOES NOT BRING PEACE. ONLY LIES. LIARS SPEAK LIES. THEY DO NOT ACCEPT LOGICAL PEACE MEASURES! THEY MAIM! AND THEY KILL! STOP THE KILLING!!! I AM GIVING THE AMERICAN PEOPLE A LITTLE GLIMPSE AND EXPERIENCE OF WHAT I EXPERIENCE WHEN BY THE MILLIONS THEY INTENTIONALLY KILL MY BABIES!!!*

September 13, 2001

TODAY IS A SPECIAL DAY. TODAY IS A SPECIAL DAY. BEWARE, MY CHILD. I AM CALLING UP TROOPS! THIS IS NOT MAN'S WAR. <u>THIS IS MY WAR!!!</u> I AM BATTLING AGAINST EVIL! SOME DO NOT UNDERSTAND MY MODUS OPERANDI. SOME WOULD SAY, "NO WAY. GOD DOES NOT SEND EVIL." I AM CALLING OUT TO MAN TO CHANGE AND TO TURN TO ME WHILE THERE IS YET TIME! SOME RESIST ME BECAUSE THEY DO NOT UNDERSTAND A LOT OF THINGS THAT TAKE PLACE. EVEN THOUGH I ALLOWED THESE ATTACKS ON AMERICAN SOIL, I DID NOT INITIATE THEM! I ALLOWED THEM AS WARNING OF WHAT IS TO COME. I CAN NO LONGER ALLOW THE EVILS THAT PERVADE AMERICAN SOCIETY! YES, ABORTION IS THE MOST HEINOUS FOR THE ACTUAL INTENTIONAL PREMEDITATED TAKING OF LIFE OF THE INNOCENT, BUT I DESTROYED WHOLE

CITIES FOR THE SIN OF SEXUAL PERVERSION OF SAME SEX UNION!
<u>*JUDGMENTS ARE COMING TO CALIFORNIA!*</u> *I CAN NO LONGER*
ALLOW THIS SIN TO DOMINATE AND PREVAIL!!! I WILL TAKE
ACTION VERY SOON IN AMERICA! AMERICA WAS TO LEAD!!! TO BE
A BEACON FOR RIGHTEOUSNESS! SHE IS NO LONGER A BRIGHT
LIGHT IN THE DARKNESS OF DECEIT AND WICKEDNESS!!! <u>*I AM*</u>
<u>*SENDING JUDGMENTS TO CHASTISE AND BRING CORRECTION! I*</u>
<u>*AM CALLING AMERICA BACK TO TRUTH! AMERICA'S FUTURE*</u>
<u>*DEPENDS UPON AMERICA'S CHOICES!!!*</u>

September 15, 2001

Prophecy

I HAVE GIVEN YOU MANY SOULS! PREPARE. PREPARE. PREPARE SAITH THE LORD! LEAVE ALL PREJUDICES AT THE ALTAR. I AM CALLING ON THE TROOPS OF THIS NATION TO BEGIN TO ASSEMBLE! TO MAKE THEMSELVES READY TO ESTABLISH BEACHHEADS AND PORTS OF AUTHORITY! I AM GIVING COMMANDS TO SET THE BATTLES IN ARRAY! TO FORGE AHEAD AND NOT TO GIVE AMNESTY TO DIABOLICAL, DEVIOUS, DEVILISH, DECAPITATION OF MY DOMINIONS! I DO NOT MARKET BLOODSHED, NEITHER DO I ALLOW BLOODY MARKETS OF WHOLESALE SLAUGHTER TO GO UNCHECKED!!! THE DEVIL HAS UNLEASHED HIS DEMONS. NOT A SURPRISE TO THE COMMANDER OF END TIME ARMIES! BE FILLED NOW WITH THE INTEGRITY OF THIS ADMINISTRATION! TRUTH SHALL PREVAIL! BUT AGAIN I SAY, ABORTION SHALL NOT GO UNCHECKED EITHER!!!

SPEAK MY SERVANT! TODAY IS A MIRACLE DAY! I AM JUXTAPOSING! *I AM PARADING TYRANNY OF HATRED AND PREJUDICE BEFORE THE EYES OF HUMANITY! I AM EXPOSING RADICAL ISLAMIC DASTARDLY DEEDS!* I AM ENLIGHTENING A SPECTRUM OF FUNDAMENTALIST BELIEFS. I AM ALSO SHOWING A MEASURE OF FORGIVENESS FROM THOSE WHO WERE PERPETRATED AGAINST. FORGIVENESS, IN THE ESSENCE OF HATRED NOT BEING A MOTIVATING FACTOR IN THE DETERMINATION OF RETRIBUTION. WE FORGIVE THOSE INDIVIDUALS WHO HATE US BUT WE <u>PROTECT</u> OUR GENERATION AND OUR CHILDREN'S CHILDREN BY CURTAILING THE ACTS OF WAR AGAINST OUR OWN CITIZENS!!! THE ONLY WAY TO STOP THE ESCALATING ATTACKS OF TYRANNY IS TO FIGHT! BLOOD FOR BLOOD. SOME WOULD SAY, NOT CHRISTIAN. IT IS WRITTEN, <u>THE LAW IS NOT MADE FOR A RIGHTEOUS MAN, BUT FOR THE LAWLESS AND DISOBEDIENT, FOR THE UNGODLY AND FOR SINNERS, FOR UNHOLY AND PROFANE, FOR MURDERERS OF FATHERS AND MURDERERS OF MOTHERS, FOR MANSLAYERS!</u> I Timothy 1:9 BE NOT DECEIVED! I HAVE PUT IN THE WHITE HOUSE, THE DAVID, FOR THIS TIME OF BATTLE! I CURTAIL EVEN NOW

ALL DISRUPTION OF GOVERNMENT. DO NOT TAKE YOUR LIFE INTO YOUR OWN HANDS BY FIGHTING THIS ADMINISTRATION! *I AM IN CONTROL OF THE EVENTS OF THE FUTURE.*

MAN SHALL YET SEE THE TOP DOGS OF DIVISIVE, UNDERHANDED EXPLOITS BE REMOVED FROM POWER! STOP SAYING ONE THING WITH YOUR MOUTH WHILE DOING ANOTHER. *ISRAEL SHALL YET BE DELIVERED FROM SIEGE OF BIGOTRY AND ARBITRATION. I SHALL RAISE HER UP IN THE LAST DAY!* I AM NOT INUNDATED BY MAN'S ARROGANCE AND PERPETRATION OF HEINOUS ACTS OF DESTRUCTION! *ALL THINGS ARE IN ALIGNMENT TO FULFILL THE PROPHECIES OF EZEKIEL!*

I AM TRAVELING THROUGH THIS NATION BY MY SPIRIT TO SHOW MYSELF STRONG IN BEHALF OF THOSE WHO WILL HEED TO CHRISTIANITY!!! IT IS NOT BY MIGHT NOR BY POWER BUT BY MY SPIRIT SAITH THE LORD OF HOSTS!!! *JUXTAPOSITION OF POWERS IS COMING INTO ALIGNMENT! THE GOOD POWERS AND THE EVIL POWERS! I AM ALIGNING THE HEADS OF STATE.* SOME WILL FALL SOON FOR THEY REGARD NOT HUMAN LIFE ... BUT THEIR OWN POPULARITY! SOME WILL CURTAIL THEIR CONNECTIONS WITH WASHINGTON. I AM SANCTIONING NOTHING BUT TRUTH! DO NOT BE MISLED BY DOUBLE TALK. DO NOT TAKE INTO ACCOUNT RAMIFICATIONS OF ACTIONS THAT I GIVE YOU TO TAKE BUT PROCEED WITH OPERATION NOBLE EAGLE! DO NOT DELAY IN PUTTING INTO PLACE THE FORCES THAT ARE NEEDED TO EXECUTE THE PROCEDURES OF OPERATION. DO NOT HESITATE TO WITHHOLD SECURITY INFORMATION! THE ELEMENT OF SURPRISE IN EXECUTING STRIKES IS MANDATORY! RELEASE NO INFORMATION TO THE MEDIA UNTIL ALL TROOPS ARE CLEAR OF REPRISAL! THIS IS TO BE A MAJOR INFILTRATION OPERATION RATHER THAN WHOLESALE SLAUGHTER.

WAR IS NOT MEANT TO BE BROADCAST BLOW BY BLOW! DISCLOSING ANOTHER'S COVER IS KILLING YOUR OWN TROOPS! STAY COOL IN YOUR COMMITMENT TO FOLLOWING ORDERS! LIFE IS PRECIOUS. SOME WILL BE TAKEN. BUT CAUTION IS

CLEARLY TO BE A WAY OF LIFE FOR YOUR OWN AND FOR THOSE UNDER YOUR COMMAND AND ALSO FOR THOSE IN HARM'S WAY. I AM LEADING THIS ATTACK! I DO HAVE ANSWERS AND OPERATIONS FOR EXECUTION. PROPEL NO ONE INTO AUTHORITY THAT HAS NOT BEEN PROVEN! USE MEN OF INTEGRITY, NOT JUST WARRIORS!!! THERE ARE THOSE WHO FIT BOTH BILLS. STAY IN CONSTANT COMMUNICATION AT ALL ... FRONTS. I WILL CHANGE SOME DEPLOYMENTS IN MIDSTREAM. EVEN THIS IS ... TO COUNTERATTACK SPY INTERCEPTION AND LEAKS. I AM GIVING BUSH PREEMPTED PROMOTION OF SOME WHO FILL OTHERS SHOES. STAY CLEAR OF 'TIT' FOR 'TAT' AND 'RUB MY BACK AND I'LL RUB YOURS'! <u>THIS IS WAR!!!</u> <u>NOT POLITICS!!!</u>

September 16, 2001

Prophecy

THE LORD AWAKENED ME WITH: I AM GIVING BIN LADEN THREE
DAYS TO TURN HIMSELF IN BEFORE AIR STRIKES TAKE PLACE.

September 17, 2001

NEW YORK IS STILL UNDER SIEGE. A TERRORIST IS IN NEW YORK.
WAGE WAR. IT IS BEGUN. THE FULFILLMENT OF THE TIMES. MAN
NO LONGER DEEMS ME RELEVANT FOR THE MOST PART. EVEN
THOSE WHO ESTEEM ME DO NOT REALLY COMPREHEND THE AGE
OR THE DESTINY. ENLIGHTENMENT COMES AS SURRENDER
GIVES WAY. PRAYER IS THE ISSUE OF REALLY BEING SUBMITTED
TO AUTHORITY. MY VESSELS OF MIGHT AND WONDER ... SHALL
BEGIN TO EMERGE! I AM CALLING FORTH SPIRITUAL ARMIES AS
WELL AS MILITARY ONES! I AM GIVING BACK MILITARY MIGHT
TO SPIRITUAL LEADERS IN AMERICA! I AM BRINGING MY
SOLDIERS TO FIGHT FOR TRUTH! FIGHT FOR TRUTH AT <u>ALL</u>
COSTS! I <u>AM</u> TRUTH! I GAVE ALL! MY FOLLOWERS DO LIKEWISE.
IT WILL NOT BE FOR NAUGHT! EVERY VICTORY HAS A PRICE!
AMERICA HAS ALWAYS PAID WITH BLOOD! AMERICA IS MINE!
THAT IS REASON SHE MUST BE TRIED AS BY FIRE. MIGHT DOES
NOT MAKE RIGHT! RIGHTEOUSNESS MAKES RIGHT!!! CURTAIL
ALL SPECULATION OF THE COST. IT WILL COST EVERYTHING!
WHAT ARE THINGS WITHOUT TRUTH? WHAT IS MONEY
WITHOUT INTEGRITY? WHAT IS A NAME ... WITHOUT WHAT
THAT NAME STANDS FOR? WHAT IS FREEDOM WITHOUT REALLY
BEING FREE? WHAT IS ... COURAGE WITHOUT ACTION? WHAT IS
LOVE WITHOUT DEMONSTRATION?

WAR IS DEMONSTRATION OF LOVE! LOVE OF TRUTH PROPELS
MEN OF STEEL TO BEACON THE LIGHT IN THE DARKNESS OF
NIGHT!!! TO STAND IN THE HOLY PLACE. I AM HOLY. BE YE
ALSO!!! WAR MAKES MEN FREE. FREEDOM DEMONSTRATES
LOVE. GOD IS LOVE!!! WHEN MEN ARE TRULY FREE THEY
DEMONSTRATE <u>MY</u> LOVE. WHEN LOVE IS DEMONSTRATED I AM
IN CONTROL! FREEDOM IN THE SPIRIT COST MY SON HIS LIFE'S

BLOOD. THE LIVES THAT WILL BE LOST WILL RISE AGAIN, EVEN AS MY SON AROSE FROM DEATH!!! THE LIVES THAT DIE IN FAITH IN ME WILL LIVE ETERNALLY!!!

September 18, 2001

Prophecy

*THE WRATH OF GOD IS WORSE THAN ANY TERRORIST STRIKE!!!
HELL IS ETERNAL DAMNATION THAT NEVER ENDS!!! YES, YOU
ARE ATTACKED BY A WICKED ENEMY! AND THAT ENEMY IS SIN!
AND NOWHERE IN THE WORLD IS SIN MORE RAMPANT THAN IN
THE VERY SHORES AND PORTALS OF AMERICA!!! AMERICA,
REPENT!!! IF DRASTIC CHANGES ARE NOT EXECUTED IN THE
COURTS TO REPEAL KILLING BABIES, AMERICA WILL SEE NOT ONLY
THESE FEW BUILDINGS AND THESE THOUSANDS DESTROYED ... BUT
STRIKES IN EVERY TERRITORY AND STATE!!! I WILL GET THE
ATTENTION OF THE SUPREME COURT!!!*

September 19, 2001

I SAY UNTO THEE, MY CHILD, I AM GOING TO DO A QUICK
WORK! MAN WILL YET SEE THAT I AM THE LORD!!! I AM
CALLING IN AUTHORITIES AND DOMINIONS! I AM GOING TO
SHOW YOU IN THE DAYS AHEAD THE THINGS THAT I SHALL DO
TO PROTECT MY PEOPLE! I AM GUARDING MANY EVEN NOW
AND PUTTING SHIELDS OF POWER AROUND MANY WHO IT IS
NOT THEIR APPOINTED TIME! I WILL USE ALL THINGS IN THIS
END TIME, EVEN FOOLISH THINGS THAT OTHERS DO NOT SEE AS
VERY IMPORTANT! I ESTABLISH EVEN NOW BEACHHEADS IN
ASIA, IN AFGHANISTAN, AND EVEN AFRICA SAITH THE LORD! I
WILL DO NOTHING ... WITHOUT REVEALING IT TO MY
SERVANTS THE PROPHETS.

*I CANNOT HOLD BACK THE JUDGMENTS FROM AMERICA! I MUST
BRING HER INTO CHECK BEFORE I RETURN! SHE IS IN SIN FOR THE
MOST PART BECAUSE EVEN THOSE WHO NAME MY NAME HAVE YET
BIGOTRY, CLASS DISTINCTION, PREJUDICES AND RAPES OF CAUSES
AND CULTURES! I CAN NO LONGER TOLERATE THIS BIGOTRY OF
ECONOMIC DISTINCTION! CHRISTIANS ARE NOT RATED IN MY
EYES BY HOW MUCH STOCK THEY CAN ACCUMULATE! THEY
JUDGE ONE ANOTHER BY WHO HAS THE BIGGEST BANK ROLLS.
THAT ISN'T EVEN ON MY LIST AS HOW TO EVALUATE MAN'S*

MEASURE OF SUCCESS. I EVALUATE YOU BY HOW MUCH YOU VALUE OTHERS!!! CLASS DISTINCTION IS COMING DOWN IN THE UNITED STATES! *I AM NOT GOING TO TOLERATE ANY LONGER CLOUT AND SPECIAL INTEREST GROUPS. CURTAIL NOW YOUR DOUBLE STANDARDS!* YOU WILL NOT SUCCEED IN ELECTING OFFICIALS THAT SERVE YOUR HIDDEN AGENDAS! I AM PUTTING IN PEOPLE WHO SERVE MY PURPOSES!!! REGARD NOT THE JUDGES THAT REFUSE TO JUDGE RIGHTEOUSLY. I SHALL TAKE SOME OUT BY DEATH BECAUSE THEY REFUSE TO ACKNOWLEDGE MY AUTHORITY AND MY POWER! I CANNOT USE THE FEARFUL AND THE DISOBEDIENT! THE ONES THAT I WILL USE IN GOVERNMENT AND MILITARY ARE THE ONES WHO STAND FOR TRUTH!!! HONOR STILL MEANS SOMETHING TO MY CHOSEN FEW! I STAND ERECT WITH MIGHT AND POWER FOR THOSE WHO WILL NOT DENY MY MANDATES, JUDGMENTS AND AUTHORITIES!!! I COUNSEL YOU TO BUY OF ME NOW ... GOLD TRIED IN THE FIRE!!! FUTILITY SHALL CONSUME THE REST!

September 22, 2001

Prophecy

BEWARE! BEWARE, MY CHILD, ANOTHER STRIKE ON AMERICAN SOIL!!! TALIBAN IS INFILTRATING THE UNITED STATES! IT IS THREE DAYS BEFORE MORE BLOODSHED. I HAVE SPOKEN REPEATEDLY THROUGH MY PROPHET THAT JUDGMENT HAS COME TO AMERICA FOR THE FILTHY LAW THAT MAKES IT LEGAL TO DESTROY THE PRE-BORN!!! I HAVE ALREADY SPOKEN THAT JUDGMENTS WOULD CONTINUE UNTIL THIS DECREE IS EXTRICATED FROM THIS GOVERNMENT! IF YOU DO NOT HEAR ME SOON AND MOVE TO STRIKE IT FROM YOUR RECORDS, I WILL STRIKE IN PLACES THAT YOU FEEL THAT YOU ARE SAFE! LIFE IN THE WOMB FEELS SAFE! YET YOU TAKE IT FROM ITS SAFETY NET! I SHALL BEGIN TO TAKE LIFE OUT OF YOUR SAFE PLACES EVEN ATTEMPTING TO GET YOUR ATTENTION THAT KILLING THE PRE-BORN IS MURDER!!! COLD-BLOODED, DIABOLICAL! MURDER IS PUNISHABLE BY JUSTICE! DO NOT BE DECEIVED!!! I AM NOT MOCKED! YET, NOT WITHOUT GRAVE CONSEQUENCES!!!

ABORTION IS MOCKERY AGAINST THE GOD OF ALL LIFE! WHO ART THOU TO TAKE THE LIFE OF ANOTHER HUMAN BEING? WHO MADE YOU A JUDGE? LIFE AS YOU KNOW IT SHALL DRASTICALLY CHANGE IN THE MONTHS AHEAD! I WILL NO LONGER TOLERATE YOUR REFUSAL TO HEAR ME!!! I CANNOT STOP THE BLOODSHED WHEN YOU REFUSE TO STOP THE WHOLESALE SLAUGHTER OF INFANTS IN THEIR SAFETY ZONE!!! PREPARE FOR ALL OUT WAR!!! WHEN YOUR MEN AND WOMEN OF MIGHT BEGIN TO COME HOME IN BODY BAGS, EXAMINE YOURSELVES AND WHAT YOU ARE DOING LEGALLY EACH DAY!!! KILLING AMERICANS!!! THOSE WHO CANNOT DEFEND THEMSELVES!!!!! AS I HAVE ALREADY SAID I USE ALL THINGS! I DO NOT INITIATE ACTS OF TERRORISM, BUT I COULD STOP THEM AND I HAVE PREVENTED MANY SAITH THE LORD!!! BUT IN AMERICA'S PROSPEROUS TIMES SHE DOES NOT RECEIVE CORRECTION AND CHANGE!!!

WORRY NOT ABOUT ANYTHING, MY SERVANT. I AM IN CONTROL. I AM WELL PLEASED. YOU ALWAYS OBEY ME. YOU WALK IN MY

SPIRIT. YOU TALK IN MY SPIRIT. YOU ACT IN MY SPIRIT. YOU REACT IN MY SPIRIT.

September 22, 2001

The Prophecies of September were faxed to President Bush, Vice President Dick Cheney, Attorney General John Ashcroft, Defense Secretary Donald Rumsfeld, National Security Adviser Condolezza Rice, FBI Director Robert Mueller. The September 22 Word that there would be an attack in three days was faxed to Washington three days before the Anthrax invasion. And, of course, to the host of Spiritual Leaders across our Nation!

Prophecy

TODAY IS A MEETING IN THE GOVERNMENT. GEORGE BUSH WILL TELL THE TROOPS TO SECRETLY INVADE THE BORDERS OF AFGHANISTAN. I AM TELLING GEORGE TO PROCEED WITH INFILTRATION WITHIN THE ENEMY LINES! *I WILL NOT TOLERATE THIS EVIL DOCTRINE OF HATRED AGAINST MANKIND!!!* PEOPLE HAVE HAD FREEDOM TO WORSHIP WHO AND WHAT THEY WANTED TO WORSHIP. BUT FREEDOM DOES NOT GIVE ONE THE RIGHT TO KILL OTHERS WHEN THEIR BELIEFS ARE DIFFERENT! ONE DOES HAVE THE RIGHT TO DEFEND ONE'S BELIEFS AND CITIZENS AGAINST ATTACK, AS WELL AS, TO SEEK JUSTICE!!! OSAMA BIN LADEN IS IN HIDING, BUT SOON HE WILL BE CAPTURED AND TAKEN ALIVE. HE WILL BE TRIED IN A COURT OF LAW FOR HIS CRIMES AGAINST SOCIETY! HE WILL BE EXECUTED! ALL OTHER TERRORISTS WILL BE PUT ON NOTICE THAT THEY ARE NEXT. CAPITAL CRIMES AGAINST SOCIETY ARE PUNISHABLE BY DEATH! I WILL RESTORE AMERICA'S DIGNITY. BUT WAR IS INEVITABLE. I SPOKE AND SO SHALL IT BE!

TIME IS RUNNING OUT FOR PEOPLE TO PRAY AND TO GET IT RIGHT. I TAKE ALL DEATHS SERIOUSLY!!! EVEN THE SMALLEST OF HUMAN BEING LIFE! AS IT IS WRITTEN, I FORMED THEM IN THE WOMB! SO WHEN YOU INTENTIONALLY ABORT A LIFE YOU ARE KILLING ONE THAT IS MADE IN MY LIKENESS AND IN MY IMAGE! I CANNOT STOP THE BLOODSHED ON THESE SHORES UNTIL YOU STOP TAKING THE LIVES OF THE INNOCENT! AGAIN, AS IT IS WRITTEN, BE NOT DECEIVED! GOD IS NOT MOCKED: FOR WHATSOEVER A MAN SOWS THAT SHALL HE ALSO REAP! AMERICA HAS SHED THE BLOOD OF MILLIONS OF INNOCENT LIVES! SO DO NOT BE DISMAYED AT THE LIVES OF MANY THAT HAVE BEEN TAKEN AND WILL YET BE TAKEN. MANY THAT HAD NO PART IN THE SHEDDING OF INNOCENT BLOOD. AS IT IS WRITTEN, SUPPOSE YOU THAT THE GALILEANS WHOSE BLOOD PILATE HAD MINGLED WITH THEIR SACRIFICES WERE SINNERS ABOVE ALL THE GALILEANS BECAUSE THEY SUFFERED SUCH THINGS, I TELL YOU, NAY: BUT EXCEPT YOU REPENT, YOU SHALL ALL LIKEWISE

PERISH! OR THOSE EIGHTEEN, UPON WHOM THE TOWER IN SILOAM FELL, AND SLEW THEM, THINK YE THAT THEY WERE SINNERS ABOVE ALL MEN? I TELL YOU NAY: BUT EXCEPT YOU REPENT YOU SHALL ALL LIKEWISE PERISH!!!

AS I HAVE ALREADY SAID, BECAUSE OF THE LAW OF THIS LAND IN DECREEING WHOLESALE SLAUGHTER UPON THE PRE-BORN MANY INNOCENT LIVES WILL SUFFER BECAUSE OF THIS DECREE! AMERICA WILL SUFFER MUCH LOSS OF LIFE IN THE DAYS AHEAD UNTIL THIS DECREE IS ABOLISHED!!! MURDER IS MURDER! IN THE WOMB OR OUT OF THE WOMB!!! LAWS CAN BE REPEALED! LIVES ARE NEVER REPLACED! SET YOUR HOUSE IN ORDER, AMERICA! IT IS TIME TO STAND FOR TRUTH! FOR RIGHT! DO YOU NOT HAVE THE GUTS TO DO SO??? YOUR POSITION CAN BE REPLACED BY THOSE WHO WILL!!!

September 23, 2001

Long before Osama bin Laden was captured and inadvertently executed on May 2, 2011 in a private residential compound in Abbottabad, Pakistan by the United States Navy Seals, CIA Operatives had his known whereabouts in earlier times.

Prophecy

HOLD NOT BACK ANYTHING I BID YOU TO DO. I AM GIVING
GRACE TO GO FORWARD AND PORTRAY MY DIGNITY! I STIR UP
EVEN NOW HEZBOLLAH TO INFILTRATE THE FORCES OF GOOD. I
AM BRINGING ALL THINGS TO THE FOREFRONT. ALL THINGS
SHALL BE BROUGHT INTO THE OPEN. HAVE I NOT EVEN SAID IN
MY WORD THAT MY PEOPLE SHALL JUDGE ANGELS? HOW MUCH
MORE THINGS THAT PERTAIN TO THIS LIFE!!! DO YOU NOT KNOW
THAT THE SAINTS SHALL JUDGE THE WORLD? SEVERAL PEOPLE
OF UNNAMED ORIGIN SHALL STRIKE AGAINST THE CAPITOL IN
WASHINGTON. I WILL NO LONGER HOLD BACK JUDGMENT. I DO
NOT PROTECT UNREPENTANT MURDERERS. THE BLOOD ON
AMERICA'S HANDS DRIPS OVER THE CASKETS OF THE INNOCENT
THAT ARE SLAIN. WILL YOU NOT ARISE AMERICA? AMERICA
WHO IS NO LONGER FREE. ARE YOU BRAVE ENOUGH TO STAND
UP AGAINST THE EVIL SURGERY DONE ON INNOCENT LIVES? I
WILL NOT RESTRAIN THE TERROR FROM YOUR SHORES, YOU
WHO MADE IT LEGAL TO BUTCHER YOUR OWN BABIES!!! YOU ARE
REAPING WHAT YOU HAVE SOWN! STOP THE KILLING AND I WILL
RESTRAIN THE TERROR!!! AMERICA HAS SINNED AND KEEPS ON
SINNING AND KEEPS ON TRANSGRESSING MY COVENANT: THOU
SHALT NOT KILL!!! ABORTION IS PREMEDITATED PLANNED
MURDER OF THE MOST INNOCENT!!!!!

September 26, 2001

On October 8, 2001, a letter filled with Anthrax was sent to Senator Tom
Daschle's office, with billions of spores, enough to kill a thousand people.
Nearly forty workers had to be treated with antibiotics. It is no small thing
that the then majority leader in the Senate refused to allow the Partial Birth
Abortion Bill to <u>even</u> come to the floor to be voted on. Although the
legislation has since been passed and signed into law by President Bush, it
is non-effective for it is on appeal! When Bill Clinton was president, the
bill passed <u>both</u> Houses of Congress <u>twice</u> and he <u>vetoed</u> it <u>both</u> times! <u>It
is a sad commentary that one man can VETO what the grass roots BOTH</u>

<u>PARTY elected officials representing the views and opinions of Every Day Ordinary Americans voted into law!!!</u>

O CONGRESS! CONGRESS! WILL YOU NOT STRIKE DOWN THE TERROR OF THE WOMB?

September 27, 2001

Prophecy

EVIL ATTACKERS ARE COMING THIS WAY!!! DO NOT FEAR MY CHILD. I AM SENDING YOU FORTH SAITH THE LORD. BE STILL AND KNOW THAT I AM GOD!

I AM TELLING HER TO BEHAVE, BUCK UP, AND TAKE TELLING! EVERYTHING I GIVE YOU TO TELL HER IS NOT WELL RECEIVED, BUT SOON I SHALL GIVE HER A DOUBLE PORTION OF MY SPIRIT! I SHALL TOPPLE <u>ALL</u> OF HER MENTAL IDOLS AND I SHALL MAKE HER INTO MY IMAGE! I SHALL GIVE HER MANY INSTRUCTIONS THAT SHE DOES NOT APPRECIATE, BUT AS SHE OBEYS THEM SHE WILL BECOME MIGHTY IN ME! MIGHT IN ME IS NOT FAME AND FORTUNE. MIGHT IN ME IS SETTING THE CAPTIVES FREE AND DELIVERING THE SICK AND THE OPPRESSED!!!

I WANT YOU TO LEARN TO NOT DO ANYTHING BUT BY PRAYER! PRAY FIRST! LET ME SPEAK! I WANT YOU TO TELL HER TO STOP SAYING ANYTHING WHEN SHE IS IN DISAGREEMENT WITH YOU. TO PRAY ONLY AND TO NOT SPEAK OUT AT YOU. IT IS NOT MY WILL FOR HER TO CORRECT YOU. SHE IS TO PRAY IN THE SPIRIT ONLY! I WANT YOU TO SPEAK CORRECTION TO HER. TAKE HEED WHAT I AM TELLING YOU. TAKE HEED WHAT I AM TELLING YOU SAITH THE LORD! IT IS WRITTEN, <u>REBUKE NOT AN ELDER</u>!!!

September 30, 2001

Spiritual Warfare

I BREAK EVEN NOW THE FORTITUDES OF FILTH AND DEPRAVITY!!!
I REGURGITATE THE PUTRIDNESS OF PAST ADMINISTRATIONS! I
UPROOT THE SEED OF FILTHINESS AND ARBITRATION OF MEN'S
LAWS OVER THE LAWS OF GOD!!! I CURTAIL NOW ALL
SEDIMENTS OF FILTH AND DEGRADATION! I THROW OUT THE
JUDGES OF PURTRIDNESS AND POWER DEMAGOGUES! I
CASTIGATE EVEN NOW THOSE IN AUTHORITY WHO WOULD RID
THE HALLS OF TRUTH AND DECENCY! COME OUT IN THE NAME
OF JESUS! BE BROKEN, YOU RUTHLESS PRODIGALS OF
PORNOGRAPHY AND PETULANCE!!! BE THOU CAST DOWN AND
DESTROYED, YOU IDOLATROUS LIARS AND PEDOPHILES OF
PUTRIDNESS! I CALL YOU BY NAME! COME OUT, LIQUOR LOVERS,
SEX SOULS, HELLHOLE REPROBATES! I BAR YOU EVEN NOW FROM
CONTAMINATING MY HALLS OF JUSTICE AND TABERNACLES OF
GLORY!!! I RID YOU EVEN NOW OF YOUR GAMBLING CASINOS
THAT HAVE TAKEN RESIDENCE IN MY TEMPLES!!! I BREAK DOWN
EVERY FETTER OF VICE THAT LIES IN THE HALLS OF JUSTICE!
COME OUT, DEMONS OF DIVORCE, PERJURY, ABORTION, GRAFT,
BRIBERY, SEDUCTION, LICENTIOUSNESS, DRUNKENNESS, DRUG
CARTELLING AND LICENSE SELLING! YOU FOUL PUTRID DEMON
OF GRAFT AND BRIBERY, I CAST YOU OUT OF THE HALLS OF
JUSTICE!!! COME OUT IN THE NAME OF JESUS! TEMPLES OF GOD,
I FREE YOU EVEN NOW OF YOUR LIES AND GAMBLING, OF YOUR
DESECRATION OF MY HOLY PLACES THAT ARE TO BE FILLED
WITH <u>MY</u> GLORY AND <u>MY</u> DOMINION!!! COME OUT, IN THE NAME
OF JESUS, SERPENTS OF DECEIT, SPIRITS OF LUST, VANITY AND
TRADITION!!! RITUALISTIC SANCTIMONY, I CALL YOU BY NAME,
COME OUT OF MY CHURCHES!!! NOW!!! I FREE MY HOLY PLACES
NOW TO RECEIVE THE GRACE AND GOODNESS OF MY SPIRIT AND
MY PRESENCE TO PREPARE MY HOLY PEOPLE FOR MY RETURN TO
CATCH AWAY THE CHURCH OF THE LORD JESUS CHRIST!!!

<u>PREPARE YE THE WAY OF THE LORD!!! MAKE STRAIGHT PATHS
FOR YOUR FEET!</u> NO LONGER WILL YOU DENY THE TRUTH OF
<u>MY</u> WILL AND OF <u>MY</u> WORD! I SEND YOU EVEN NOW TO THE

PITS OF HELL, YOU FILTHY SPIRITS OF RAGE, MURDER AND OBSCENITY!!! DESECRATE MY TEMPLES NO LONGER! AND YOU PRIESTS THAT HARBOR AND HIDE THESE FUGITIVES OF JUSTICE, YOU WILL RECEIVE A DOUBLE PORTION OF MY WRATH FOR ALLOWING THESE EVILS TO CONTINUE TO FOMENT AND MULTIPLY! <u>DEVILS ARE TO BE CAST OUT OF THE PEOPLE!!! NOT TO BE PROTECTED BY THE CHURCH</u>!!! CAST THE SPIRITS OUT OF THE PEOPLE AND FREE MY PEOPLE TO LIVE HOLY, HONESTLY AND SOBERLY! DIVISIONS AND STRIFES THAT HAVE INFILTRATED MY CHURCHES, I CAST YOU OUT EVEN NOW!!!!! JEALOUSY, BE BROKEN IN JESUS NAME!!! I SEND EVEN NOW, MICHAEL, TO SUBDUE ALL WRATH AND ALL CLAMOR AND ALL EVIL SPEAKING! HELL HAS ENLARGED ITSELF TO BE ABLE TO CONTAIN ALL WHO WILL NOT TURN FROM THEIR WICKEDNESS!!!

This word of the Lord was sent to Pope John Paul II at the Vatican in 2001 and to the Cardinals in the United States, <u>before</u> the pedophilia atrocities and abuses in the Catholic Church were exposed across the United States in 2002.

September 3, 2001

Wisdom

MAJOR IN WHAT JESUS MAJORED IN! MAJOR IN WHAT THE LORD MAJORS IN! SOME PEOPLE ARE SITTING IN THE CHURCH PEWS TODAY THAT THE CHURCH HIERARCHY HAS ALREADY CAST OUT, SET ASIDE, SILENCED! YET THEY STILL SPEAK! THEIR PRESENCE CRIES OUT FOR THE FULLNESS OF GOD'S GLORIES! THEY ARE ACTUALLY HOLDING BACK THE JUDGMENTS OF THE LORD! WHEN GOD SENDS THEM FORTH, JUDGMENTS WILL COME IN THE SANCTUARY! BECAUSE YOU WOULD NOT HEAR, THUS SAITH THE LORD! WHEN YOU REFUSE TO HEAR, THUS SAITH THE LORD, YOU ARE REJECTING GOD ALMIGHTY HIMSELF! YOU CANNOT BREAK THE LAWS OF GOD. YOU BREAK YOURSELF UPON THEM!

September 9, 2001

A STRONGHOLD FORMS WHEN ONE GIVES STRENGTH TO ANOTHER HOLD OTHER THAN THE LORD. WHEN YOU HOLD TO SOMETHING ELSE AND MEDITATE ON THAT RATHER THAN THE WORD OF GOD! PEOPLE NEED TO GET OVER *THEMSELVES!* TO GET OUT OF THE WAY AND TO *LET* GOD! SPEAK TO YOUR PROBLEMS! CONFESSING THE WORD OF GOD OVER YOUR CIRCUMSTANCES!!! CHANGE THE ATMOSPHERE!!! WORDS DO THAT! WORDS MAKE YOU ONE WITH GOD WHEN YOU SPEAK *HIS* WORD! HOW MUCH GREATER CAN YOU GET??? THAN TO BE ONE WITH GOD! GOD IS THE *ORIGINAL* CALLER I D!!!

September 10, 2001

GOD IS NOT MOVED BY THOUSANDS OF DEATHS WHILE AMERICA HAS BEEN SLAUGHTERING MILLIONS OF HER OWN PEOPLE FOR DECADES, MANY THOUSANDS EACH AND EVERY DAY, YEAR AFTER YEAR! IT IS NOT BY CHANCE THAT OUR OWN FATALITIES WERE CAUSED BY OUR OWN PLANES. DAILY WE KILL AMERICANS LEGALLY BECAUSE OF THE LAW ON OUR BOOKS!

September 11, 2001

Wisdom

DURING THE TEN MONTHS BEFORE 9/11 I SENT NUMEROUS FAXES AND LETTERS AND E-MAILS TO THE WHITE HOUSE WARNING OF COMING DESTRUCTIONS BECAUSE OF THE MANMADE LAW OF SLAUGHTERING BABIES IN THE WOMB! THESE SAME WARNINGS WERE SENT TO FORTY GOVERNMENT AND SPIRITUAL LEADERS ACROSS THE NATION!

IT IS THE HEIGHT OF ARROGANCE TO CONTINUE TO BE LESS THAN ADAMENT IN EXECUTION OF THE STRICTEST SECURITY MEASURES TO PROTECT OUR OWN CITIZENS! IT IS ARROGANCE OR STUPIDITY THAT CAUSES PEOPLE NOT TO BE PRUDENT IN PROTECTING THEIR OWN.

September 12, 2001

Wisdom

I called the FBI in Washington, D.C.: "I DO NOT BELIEVE IT IS IN THE BEST INTERESTS OF OUR COUNTRY TO TELL THE WHOLE WORLD TWENTY-FOUR HOURS BEFORE HAND WHERE THE PRESIDENT IS GOING TO BE THE NEXT DAY AND WHEN. I AM NOT SAYING THAT HE SHOULD NOT GO. THE TERRORISTS ARE STILL HERE."

September 13, 2001

IF YOU ARE DISOBEDIENT YOU ARE NOT FILLED WITH GOD. (WORD) IF YOU ARE FILLED WITH GOD YOU ARE OBEDIENT! IF YOU ARE FILLED WITH GOD (WORD) THERE IS NO ROOM FOR DISOBEDIENCE!

September 13, 2001

PROPHETS ARE A FORM OF TERRORIST BECAUSE THEY _FEAR_ THE WRATH OF GOD!

September 19, 2001

THE REAL TRAGEDY IS TO EXPERIENCE A DEFINING MOMENT AND TO NOT KNOW WHAT IT MEANS. AMERICA IS YET UNAWARE THAT THE REASON GOD DID NOT PROTECT US FROM THE TERRORIST ATTACKS IS THAT AMERICA TERRORIZES AND ATTACKS AND MURDERS HER OWN CITIZENS BY THE THOUSANDS DAILY IN THE WOMB!

September 20, 2001

AMERICA'S WAKE UP CALL COULD HAVE BEEN MUCH MORE DEVASTATING! ANTHRAX OR SMALLPOX COULD HAVE BEEN STREWN OVER THE FIELDS, BUT FOR THE GRACE OF GOD!!! AMERICA, GET UP! WHY ARE YOU LAYING ON YOUR FACE? GET THE ACCURSED THING, ABORTION, OFF OF YOUR LAW BOOKS!!! WILL YOU NOT NOTICE THAT THE KING OF THE REAL NEW WORLD ORDER, NOT THE IMPOSTERS BUT THE REAL KING OF THE

REAL NEW WORLD ORDER, PUT MURDER AT THE TOP OF THE LIST AS TO WHAT IS TRULY EVIL!!!!! Matthew 10:18 THOU SHALT DO NO MURDER!!! YOU CAN PRAY UNTIL YOU ARE BLUE IN THE FACE BUT IF YOU KEEP MURDERING YOUR OWN CHILDREN, GOD IS NOT GOING TO STOP THE DESTRUCTION!!!

September 26, 2001

IT IS ALMOST BEYOND BELIEF TO ME THAT IT IS EVEN BEING SAID, JUDGMENT HAS COME TO AMERICA BECAUSE WE TOOK PRAYER OUT OF SCHOOLS. NOT A WORD ABOUT THE BUTCHERING OF OUR OWN CHILDREN, EXCEPT THROUGH A FEW THAT TONED IT DOWN AFTER BEING ATTACKED BY THE LIBERAL MEDIA.

September 28, 2001

Submission and Death to Self

NO OTHER GRAVE HAVE I THAN THIS GHOST OF BEING HOLY! PERPETUAL PAIN IS NOT KNOWING THE DEATH OF DIGNITY. WHEN ONE IS SOLDERED, ENMESHED, INGRAINED, ENGRAFTED ... THERE IS NO PAIN ... JUST GLORY! LETTING HIM BE THE STORY! THE STAR! THE CZAR! THE MAN! THE ONE WHO IMPREGNATES MY SOUL WITH HIMSELF!!! I POSITION MYSELF TO RECEIVE THE FLOW OF HIS MAGNITUDE, NOT RATIONALIZING, NOR FANTASIZING, NOT CRITICIZING, NOR COMPROMISING ... BUT PROSTRATING MY POWER TO RECEIVE THE GRACE OF HIS GLORY!!!

September 3, 2001

Prophetic Teaching: PENANCE

YOU CANNOT REPENT OF A SIN UNTIL YOU ARE SORRY FOR IT. SPEAKING WORDS DOES NOT METE REPENTANCE. GODLY SORROW GRIEVES UNTO REPENTANCE. II Corinthians 7:10 WITHOUT GODLY SORROW THERE IS NO REPENTANCE. THERE CAN BE NO GODLY SORROW WITHOUT FIRST SURRENDERING TO GOD! IF YOU DO NOT SURRENDER WHOLEHEARTEDLY YOU ARE UNGODLY. TO BE GODLY ANYTHING OR GODLY EVERYTHING, YOU MUST FIRST PROSTRATE YOUR FEELINGS, FANTASIES, FRAGMENTS OF YOUR IMAGE, FORTITUDES, FALSEHOODS, FLAILINGS, FLOUNDERINGS, FAVORITES, FUTILITIES, FINANCES, FEUDS, FOMENTATIONS, FOCUSES, FORCES, FREEDOMS, FLAWS, FLARE-UPS, FLAKINESS, FINESSE, FIRES, FIGHTINGS, FILES, FICTIONS, FEIGNINGS, FAULTS, FASTS, FAMILIES, FABLES, FACTIONS, FRACTURES, FAITH. SOME PEOPLE NEED TO BE OFFENDED!!! THEY NEED TO BE OFFENDED UNTIL THEY ARE DEAD! WHEN THEY ARE DEAD UNTO THEMSELVES, THEY CAN'T BE OFFENDED ANYMORE! Psalms 119:165 WHEN YOU ARE DEAD, GOD USES YOU FOR HIS GLORY!!!!! I Corinthians 10:32-33, II Corinthians 6:1-3 GIVING NO OFFENSE IN ANYTHING!!!!! PEOPLE ARE NOT COMING TO CHRIST, ARE NOT STAYING IN THE FAITH BECAUSE YOU ARE OFFENDING THEM AND THE MINISTRY IS BLAMED!!! THE MINISTRY: APOSTLES, PROPHETS, EVANGELISTS, PASTORS AND TEACHERS IS CLEAN. CLEAN UP YOUR FILTHY SELF SO THAT THE MINISTRY BE NOT BLAMED! YOU ARE NOT APPROVED OF GOD BY MUCH PREACHING AND TEACHING. YOU ARE APPROVED GOD BY SUFFERING! Hebrews 2:10, 5:8-9 HOW DID CHRIST LEARN OBEDIENCE? BY THE THINGS WHICH HE SUFFERED! OH, BUT YOU'RE GONNA GET YOURS SOME OTHER WAY. HOW DID THE CAPTAIN, JESUS, BECOME PERFECT, MATURE, FULLY GROWN? THROUGH SUFFERING! BUT, OF COURSE, YOU THINK YOU'RE GONNA GET YOUR STRIPES, YOUR BARS, YOUR PROMOTION, SOME OTHER WAY! AIN'T NO OTHER WAY, CHILD! JUST SUBMIT AND GO THROUGH THE MANEUVERS! TAKE TELLING! BOW TO AUTHORITY! Hebrews 2:9 WE SEE NOT ALL THINGS PUT UNDER HIM? Ephesians 1:22 WHY? 'CAUSE PEOPLE

WON'T DIE! THEY WON'T PUT EVERYTHING THEY'VE GOT UNDER HIM! UNDER THE CROSS!!! TO DIE THE DEATH OF THE SELF-LIFE! BUT! BUT WE SEE JESUS! YOU AIN'T GONNA TRULY SEE JESUS UNTIL YOU ARE MADE CONFORMABLE TO HIS DEATH AND SUFFERING! YOU CANNOT ENTER INTO HIS REST UNTIL YOU KNOW HIS WAYS! II Corinthians 1:4-10 YOU AIN'T GOING TO SEE ALL THINGS PUT UNDER HIM UNTIL YOU SEE HIM! SEE JESUS! FIRST GRADE 101! SEE JANE! SEE JESUS! DO WHAT JESUS DID IF YOU WANT THE RESULTS THAT JESUS HAD! AND YOU CAN'T SEE JESUS, KNOW JESUS, UNTIL YOU <u>SUFFER</u> WITH HIM! FOLLOWING IN HIS FOOTSTEPS! FORSAKING THE SELF-LIFE! AND PUTTING ON THE LIFE OF CHRIST! YOU AIN'T GONNA RECONCILE THE WORLD WHEN YOU WON'T EVEN BE A PART OF THE RECONCILIATION OF THE CHURCH WORLD! COME DOWN OFF YOUR THRONE! AND <u>LET</u> THE CHRIST HAVE THE LAST WORD! THAT IS THE ONLY WORD THAT WILL BREAK EVERY BONDAGE AND LOOSE THE POWER OF DOMINION AND THE AUTHORITY TO BREAK THE YOKES OVER LOST HUMANITY!

YOU HAVE TO GIVE UP IN ORDER TO GO UP!!! YOU HAVE TO GROW UP SO THAT CHRIST WON'T THROW UP! AS HE HAS ALREADY STATED SO SUCCINCTLY, YOU ARE LUKEWARM AND NEITHER HOT NOR COLD, I WILL SPEW YOU OUT OF MY MOUTH! Revelation 3:16 JOHN 3:16 WILL WORK FOR BABES IN CHRIST. IF YOU ARE NOT STILL YOUNG IN THE LORD, YOU BETTER BE WORKING ON REVELATION 3:16: BECAUSE YOU SAY, I AM RICH AND INCREASED WITH GOODS AND HAVE NEED OF NOTHING AND KNOWEST THOU NOT THAT YOU ARE WRETCHED AND MISERABLE AND POOR AND BLIND AND NAKED! I COUNSEL YOU TO BUY OF ME GOLD TRIED IN THE FIRE (THAT'S CALLED SUFFERING) THAT YOU MAY BE RICH, CLOTHED IN WHITE RAIMENT AND THAT THE SHAME OF YOUR NAKEDNESS DOES NOT APPEAR!!! ANOINT YOUR EYES WITH EYE-SALVE THAT YOU MAY SEE! THE ANOINTING OF THE WORD AND THE SPIRIT OF GOD! IF YOU AIN'T DEAD OR IF YOU HAVEN'T BLASPHEMED THE HOLY GHOST, JESUS IS STANDING WITH OUTSTRETCHED HANDS AND OPEN ARMS! COME INTO THE GLORIES OF THE LORD!

<u>CASTING ALL OF YOUR CARE UPON HIM FOR HE CARES FOR YOU!!!
LET HIM SOOTHE YOUR SOUL AND WIPE AWAY YOUR TEARS!</u> LET
JESUS LEAD YOU <u>ALL</u> THE WAY 'CAUSE HE'S A MIGHTY GOOD
LEADER! LET JESUS LEAD YOU ALL THE WAY! ALL THE WAY FROM
EARTH TO HEAVEN, LET JESUS LEAD YOU ALL THE WAY!!! GIVE
GOD YOUR F'S! ALL OF YOUR F'S FOR FAILURE!!! YOUR FAINT-
HEARTEDNESS, YOUR FAITHLESS WAILS, YOUR FALTERING
FACTS, YOUR FALLACIOUS ACTS, FAMILIAR SPIRIT TACKS, YOUR
FANGED ATTACKS, YOUR FARCE CONTRACTS, YOUR FAMED
PACTS, YOUR FASCIST PROPHYLACTS! YOU BETTER FACE THE
FACTS, BEFORE THE AX DROPS ON YOUR ROOTS! AND YOU GET
CUT OFF FROM THE TRUE VINE! AND THE LORD SAYS YOU ARE
NONE OF MINE!!! THE SWEETNESS OF THE GLORY IS SUBMITTING
TO THE FATHER! FATHERS FEEL THE FAILURES OF THEIR SONS
AND DAUGHTERS! THEY DESIRE TO BE RECONCILED! WITHOUT
RECONCILIATION THERE IS NO PEACE! WITHOUT PEACE THERE IS
NO POWER! WITHOUT POWER THERE IS NO REVIVAL! WITHOUT
REVIVAL THERE IS NO COMING OF THE LORD! RECONCILIATION
BRINGS REVIVAL! REVIVAL PRECEDES HOLINESS! HOLINESS
PREPARES THE WAY OF THE LORD!!!!! EVEN SO, COME LORD
JESUS! COME INTO ME SO THAT REVIVAL CAN ULTIMATELY
BRING BACK THE KING! AMEN AND AMEN! SO BE IT!

JESUS DIED FOR EVERY SITUATION KNOWN TO MAN!!!!! WHEN IN
DISAGREEMENT OR OFFENSE, SHUT UP AND LET THEM TALK AND
QUIETLY SAY, "WE MAY NOT AGREE ABOUT THIS SITUATION IN
ALL THE DETAILS, BUT JESUS DIED FOR EVERY SITUATION
KNOWN TO MAN! I AGREE WITH YOU NOW TO GIVE IT ENTIRELY
OVER TO THE MAN JESUS, WHO HAS ALL THE ANSWERS TO BRING
PEACE TO THIS SITUATION. I LOVE YOU. BE AT PEACE." Matthew
18 SOME OF YOU DON'T FEAR GOD ENOUGH! THAT IS WHY YOU
LET LITTLE FOXES NIP AT THE VINE! EATING AWAY THE TRUTH!
IF YOU TRULY FEARED GOD, YOU WOULD DO HIS BUSINESS <u>HIS</u>
WAY! GO TO THE ONE WHO OFFENDED YOU. HIM ALONE! YOU
DON'T FEAR GOD! YOU JUST KEEP LETTING DISCORD MAIM THE
MINISTRY WHILE YOU GO THROUGH YOUR LITTLE RITUALS
OF DOING GOD'S BUSINESS YOUR WAY! TEARING DOWN

FOUNDATIONS AND BLASTING A LOT OF PEOPLE THAT DO NOT DESERVE TO BE BLASTED.

JUDGMENT IS COMING. GOD HAS BEEN LOOKING ON AT ALL THE TURMOIL AND DISSENSION! YOU COULD HAVE STILLED SOME STORMS BUT YOU CHOOSE TO BE A BIG HEAD INSTEAD OF SUBMITTING TO THE HEAD!!!!! NOW YOU WILL SUFFER CORRECTION! GET IN LINE WITH THE WORD AND THE SPIRIT OF THE ALMIGHTY. HE DOES NOT CONTRADICT HIMSELF AT ANYTIME. WHY DO YOU? YOU PURPORT TO BE GOD'S PERSON OF FAITH AND POWER? BUT AT TIMES YOU KNOW NOT WHAT MANNER OF SPIRIT YOU ARE OF! GOD IS SAYING: MY SPIRIT DOES NOT BLAST AT PEOPLE WHO ARE DOING MY WILL! WHY DO YOU? IF THINGS ARE OUT OF ALIGNMENT, CHECK YOURSELF BEFORE ACCUSING ANYONE ELSE! Psalms 39:1 NO MATTER WHO IS BEFORE YOU! HOLD YOUR PEACE! HOLD YOUR PEACE 'CAUSE IF YOU DON'T SOMEBODY IS GOING TO TAKE IT AWAY FROM YOU!!! YES, KING DAVID MESSED UP, BUT HE HAD SENSE ENOUGH TO OWN UP TO IT!!! EXODUS 14:14: THE LORD SHALL FIGHT FOR YOU AND YOU SHALL HOLD YOUR PEACE!!! DISAPPOINTMENT IS ATTACHED TO EXPECTATION, NOT TO REALITY! SURRENDER TO COMMITMENT! APPRECIATE WHAT YOU HAVE! FEAR NOT!!! STAND STILL, AND SEE THE SALVATION OF THE LORD!!! Verse 13 BE NOT AS THE MULE OR HORSE WHICH HAVE NO UNDERSTANDING, WHOSE MOUTH MUST BE HELD IN WITH BIT AND BRIDLE!!!!! WHO HAVE TO BE MADE TO OBEY!!!!! Psalms 32:9

MAN THAT IS IN HONOR AND UNDERSTANDS NOT IS LIKE THE BEASTS THAT PERISH!!!!! Psalms 49:20 A FOOL'S WRATH IS PRESENTLY KNOWN, BUT A PRUDENT MAN COVERS SHAME! THERE IS THAT SPEAKS LIKE THE PIERCING OF A SWORD, BUT THE TONGUE OF THE WISE IS HEALTH! THE WAY OF A FOOL IS RIGHT IN HIS OWN EYES: BUT HE THAT HEARKENS UNTO COUNSEL IS WISE! Proverbs 12:15-18 WE EXHORT YOU, BRETHREN, WARN THEM THAT ARE UNRULY: UNGOVERNABLE, TURBULENT, UNRESTRAINED, UNCONTROLLABLE, STUBBORN, OBSTINATE, RESISTANT TO ADVICE, DEFIANT TO AUTHORITY, INFLEXIBLE, UNYIELDING,

UNBENDING, MULISH, OFTEN PERVERSELY ADHERING TO ONE'S OWN OPINION, REBELLIOUS, INSUBORDINATE!!! BE <u>PATIENT</u>: CALM, UNCOMPLAINING, QUIETLY ENDURING STRAIN, ANNOYANCE, PAIN, MISFORTUNE OR DELAY, ENDURING PROVOCATION UNTO ALL MEN! SEE THAT NONE RENDER EVIL FOR EVIL UNTO ANY MAN, BUT EVER FOLLOW THAT WHICH IS GOOD, BOTH AMONG YOURSELVES AND TO <u>ALL</u> MEN!!!

<u>REJOICE EVERMORE! PRAY WITHOUT CEASING! IN EVERYTHING GIVE THANKS: FOR THIS IS THE WILL OF GOD IN CHRIST JESUS CONCERNING YOU! QUENCH NOT THE SPIRIT! DESPISE NOT PROPHESYINGS!!! PROVE ALL THINGS! HOLD FAST THAT WHICH IS GOOD! ABSTAIN FROM ALL APPEARANCE OF EVIL! AND THE VERY GOD OF PEACE SANCTIFY YOU WHOLLY AND I PRAY GOD YOUR WHOLE SPIRIT AND SOUL AND BODY BE PRESERVED BLAMELESS UNTO THE COMING OF OUR LORD JESUS CHRIST!!! FAITHFUL IS HE THAT CALLETH YOU, WHO ALSO WILL DO IT!!! BRETHREN PRAY FOR US! I Thessalonians 5:14-25 FOR UNTO US A CHILD IS BORN, UNTO US A SON IS GIVEN: AND THE GOVERNMENT SHALL BE UPON HIS SHOULDER: AND HIS NAME SHALL BE CALLED WONDERFUL, COUNSELOR, THE MIGHTY GOD, THE EVERLASTING FATHER, THE PRINCE OF PEACE! OF THE INCREASE OF HIS GOVERNMENT AND PEACE, THERE SHALL BE NO END, UPON THE THRONE OF DAVID AND UPON HIS KINGDOM, TO ORDER IT, AND TO ESTABLISH IT WITH JUDGMENT AND WITH JUSTICE FROM HENCEFORTH EVEN FOR EVER! THE ZEAL OF THE LORD OF HOSTS WILL PERFORM THIS!!! Isaiah 9:6-7 FOR IT PLEASED THE FATHER THAT IN HIM SHOULD ALL FULLNESS DWELL AND HAVING MADE PEACE THROUGH THE BLOOD OF HIS CROSS, BY HIM TO RECONCILE ALL THINGS UNTO HIMSELF, BY HIM, I SAY WHETHER THEY BE THINGS IN EARTH OR THINGS IN HEAVEN! AND YOU WHO WERE SOMETIMES ALIENATED AND ENEMIES IN YOUR MIND BY WICKED WORKS, YET NOW HE WILL RECONCILE!!! IN THE BODY OF HIS DEATH, TO PRESENT YOU HOLY AND UNBLAMEABLE AND UNREPROVEABLE IN HIS SIGHT: IF YOU CONTINUE IN THE FAITH GROUNDED AND SETTLED AND BE NOT MOVED AWAY FROM THE HOPE OF THE GOSPEL WHICH</u>

YOU HAVE HEARD AND WHICH IS PREACHED TO EVERY
CREATURE WHICH IS UNDER HEAVEN!!! Colossians 1:19-23

THEREFORE BEING JUSTIFIED BY FAITH, WE HAVE PEACE WITH
GOD THROUGH OUR LORD JESUS CHRIST! BY WHOM ALSO WE
HAVE ACCESS BY FAITH INTO THIS GRACE WHEREIN WE STAND
AND REJOICE IN HOPE OF THE GLORY OF GOD! AND NOT ONLY IN
THIS, BUT WE GLORY IN TRIBULATION ALSO: KNOWING THAT
TRIBULATION WORKS OUT PATIENCE! AND PATIENCE WORKS
OUT PROVEN CHARACTER. AND PROVEN CHARACTER HOPE!!!
AND THE HOPE DOES NOT PUT US TO SHAME. Romans 5:1-4

September 6, 2001

October
2001

The Richness of Lives Attuned to Tragedies
Transformed by Meek n' Lowly ... Sparkle
Brightly ... in SONset Guises. ... Gems ...
Glowing out Beneath the Mortarboards of Life.

Part XII

The
Spirit of Man
Is the
Candle of the Lord

The spirit of man is the candle of the Lord,
searching all the inward parts of the belly.

Proverbs Twenty Twenty-Seven

There is a spirit in man: and the inspiration of the
Almighty gives them understanding.

Job Thirty-Two and Eight

Prophecy

BECAUSE OF YOUR OBEDIENCE TO ME I HAVE RELEASED ALL POWER INTO YOUR SPIRIT! I HAVE RELEASED THE PROVISION OF POWER AND AUTHORITY!!! REGARD NOT CIRCUMSTANCES, BUT CONTINUE TO SEEK MY FACE FOR EVERY DECISION AND ACTION!!! I WILL RESTORE ALL THINGS THAT HAVE BEEN STRIPPED FROM THE MINISTRY! I AM GIVING YOU GRAVE APOSTLESHIPS. I AM CALLING INTO POSITION JEWISH MEN AND WOMEN OF PURPOSE!!! I WILL REINSTATE THE NATION OF ISRAEL!!! I AM GIVING MANDATES!!! I AM CALLING FORTH GENERALS EVEN NOW!

I SEE YOU, MY SERVANT. AND I KNOW ABOUT THE BOOK. IT IS MY WORDS SAITH THE LORD. YOU HAVE A MANUSCRIPT THAT IS MY WORDS. I WILL SHOW YOU WHAT YOU MUST DO. RESPECT LEADERS. REBUKE TROUBLE MAKERS. REVIVE MY PEOPLE TO RIGHTEOUSNESS AND PURPOSE! ALLOW MY ANOINTED ONES TO COME FORTH TO SPEAK FOR ME! TEACH IT. TELL IT. STAND IN THE GAP! OPEN THE FLOODGATES AND ALLOW MY GLORY!

I HAVE PUT YOU HERE TO DISPERSE EVIL! CALAMITIES ARE COMING! DECLARE THIS WORD: OSAMA BIN LADEN IS DECEIVED. HIS CULTURE HAS BEEN DECEIVED. HE KNOWS ONLY WHAT IS PUT INTO HIM BY WAR AND INJUSTICE. FALSE TEACHING IS RAMPANT DURING DIFFICULT TIMES. DO NOT FINE TUNE TRIBULATION. IT COMES WHEN IT IS LEAST EXPECTED. I HAVE CALLED BUSH TO THE FOREFRONT TO RECAPTURE THE SPIRIT OF AMERICA! AMERICA IS JUSTICE, AMERICA IS INTEGRITY! AMERICA IS FAITH! AMERICA IS PRIDE IN COUNTRY AND CREED! I HAVE COME THAT YOU MIGHT HAVE LIFE AND HAVE IT MORE ABUNDANTLY! ABUNDANT LIFE IS NOT KILLING THE FRUIT OF YOUR OWN WOMB! ABUNDANT LIFE IS NOT CONCEIVING BABIES AND THEN KILLING THEM! AMERICA DISTRIBUTES FREE BIRTH CONTROL! ABOLISH KILLING THE FRUIT OF YOUR WOMB! YOU ARE TAKING LIFE WHEN YOU DESTROY THE PRE-BORN! LIFE IN THE WOMB IS FORMED BY THE

ALMIGHTY! WHEN YOU DESTROY IT YOU ARE PLAYING GOD!!! WILL YOU NOT SHAKE YOURSELF AND REALIZE THIS TRUTH BEFORE MORE DESTRUCTION COMES NOW TO THESE UNITED STATES OF AMERICA??? MAN IS NOT GOD! STOP ACTING IN BEHALF OF THE ALMIGHTY! IF YOU DO NOT WANT CHILDREN, STOP CONCEIVING THEM!!! WHEN YOU KILL THEM AFTER CONCEPTION YOU ARE A MURDERER! MURDERERS, EXCEPT THEY REPENT AND TURN AWAY FROM THEIR WICKEDNESS, SHALL HAVE THEIR PART IN THE LAKE OF FIRE WHICH BURNS WITH FIRE AND BRIMSTONE WHICH IS THE SECOND DEATH!

Note: It did come to pass. But the worst is not yet over. On April 1, 2004, Special Agent to the Capitol Building in Washington, D.C. phoned me to inform me that he is sending a recommendation to the Assistant Attorney General's Office that I be arrested and prosecuted because of the warnings of more and greater destructions that I continue to send to the officials in the government.

October 2, 2001

Prophecy

I SEE YOUR NEEDS. I KNOW EVERYTHING THAT YOU NEED RIGHT NOW! NOTHING IS HID FROM ME! I SEE YOUR DESIRES. I KNOW YOUR HEART IS TO OBEY ME AT ALL COSTS. I WILL SEE TO YOUR DESIRES. I KNOW YOUR HEART IS TO OBEY ME AT ALL COSTS. I WILL CURTAIL SOON YOUR BEING HELD BACK FROM YOUR CALLING AND YOUR DUTIES. I HAVE PLACED YOU IN THE WORLD TO PUT INTO POSITION MY AGENDA, MY PRIORITIES, MY PURPOSE. I WILL SCHEDULE SOON A MEETING WITH PEOPLE WHO WILL PROMOTE ME INSTEAD OF THEMSELVES!!! WHEN I AM PROMOTED, GIVEN THE RIGHT AWAY TO PERFORM, I EJECT EVIL, PRIDE, PROGRAMS AND PUTRIDNESS! I EMIT HEALING, HEALTH, HOPE AND HARVEST! I EJACULATE THE PROVISION TO BRING FORTH THE FRUIT FROM THE WOMB OF ZION! I PUT INTO THE WOMB OF MY CHURCH FERTILE SEED THAT BRINGS FORTH THE FRUIT OF RIGHTEOUSNESS! SHOW WITHOUT SUBSTANCE, NOISE WITHOUT PROVISION, WORD WITHOUT CONFIRMATION, IS LIFELESS! LIFE IS MANIFESTED BY SIGNS FOLLOWING THE BELIEVER!!! THE WORD IS CONFIRMED WITH SIGNS FOLLOWING!

CONFIRM MY WORD WITH HEALINGS, MIRACLES, DELIVERANCES AND PROVISION!!! MAKE ROOM! GIVE ROOM TO THE PROPHETS TO PERFORM MY MIGHTY ACTS SAITH THE LORD! THE FIRST AND THE LAST! THE HOLY AND THE RIGHTEOUS! THE TRUTH! THE WHOLE TRUTH! AND NOTHING BUT THE TRUTH!!! THE WHOLE TRUTH! WHICH IS <u>ALL</u> OF MY BODY PARTS! AND <u>ALL</u> OF MY MINISTRIES!!! NOT JUST TEACHING AND PREACHING! BUT PROPHESYING AND WORKING OF MIRACLES, SIGNS AND WONDERS!!! HOLD THEM BACK NO LONGER LEST MORE JUDGMENTS COME TO THE HOUSE OF GOD! RIDICULE NO LONGER THE ONES WHO HAVE BEEN SENT TO PERFORM MY DUTIES AND MY PURPOSES!!!!! PROPEL MY PEOPLE FORWARD!!! NOT BACKWARD TO TRADITIONS OF MEN!!! WHEN JOHN SENT MEN TO JESUS TO ASK IF HE WAS THE CHRIST, HIS ANSWER WAS: <u>THE BLIND RECEIVE THEIR SIGHT! THE LAME WALK! THE LEPERS ARE CLEANSED! THE DEAF HEAR! THE DEAD ARE RAISED!</u> AND

LASTLY THE POOR HAVE THE GOSPEL PREACHED TO THEM!!! AS IT IS WRITTEN, JESUS OF NAZARETH WAS APPROVED OF GOD AMONG THE PEOPLE BY MIRACLES AND SIGNS WHICH GOD DID THROUGH HIM!!! AS IT IS WRITTEN, THE PEOPLE WITH ONE ACCORD GAVE HEED UNTO THOSE THINGS WHICH PHILIP SPAKE, <u>AFTER</u> HEARING AND SEEING THE MIRACLES WHICH HE DID!!! IF THE MIRACLES, SIGNS AND WONDERS WERE NOT NECESSARY, JESUS AND HIS DISCIPLES WOULD NOT HAVE PERFORMED THEM!!! AS IT IS WRITTEN BY THE APOSTLE PAUL: I HAVE <u>FULLY</u> PREACHED THE GOSPEL OF CHRIST THROUGH MIGHTY SIGNS AND WONDERS BY THE POWER OF THE SPIRIT OF GOD!!!!!!!

October 2, 2001

Prophecy

I CONFIRM MY WORD WITH SIGNS FOLLOWING WHEN MY PEOPLE WHICH ARE CALLED BY NAME ARE GIVEN FREEDOM TO ABIDE IN THEIR CALLING!!! WHEN THEY ARE RESTRAINED AND HELD IN CHECK, I DO NOT FALTER AND I DO NOT FAIL. I AWAIT UPON THE MERCIES. WHEN THEY HAVE FINISHED THEIR COURSE I ADMINISTER MY JUDGMENTS AND MY DOMINIONS! <u>ALL</u> THINGS ARE TO BRING MY PEOPLE TO THE FULFILLMENT OF MY WORDS! MAN HAS ESTABLISHED BEACHHEADS AGAINST MY PROPHETS, BUT SOON I SHALL HAVE DOMINION IN THE SANCTUARY FOR I SHALL CLEAN HOUSE THUS SAITH THE LORD! MY MIGHT *IS* POWER. AND MY DOMINION IS AUTHORITY! KNOW YOU NOT THAT IT IS I WHO HAS MADE YOU AND NOT YOU YOURSELVES? I PREPARE ALL THINGS FOR MY WILL AND FOR MY PURPOSE!!! I DO NOT BOW TO THE AUTHORITY OF MAN OR MEN WORSHIP. QUIT SETTING ASIDE MY PROPHETS LEST I SET YOU ASIDE IN GRAVE CLOTHES. POWERS AND AUTHORITIES AND DOMINIONS AND MIGHTS ARE TO BE EXCLUSIVELY IN ALIGNMENT WITH THE WORDS OF MY PROPHESIES IN THE WRITTEN HOLY SCRIPTURES! IS IT NOT WRITTEN, <u>DESPISE NOT, DO NOT SET ASIDE PROPHESYINGS?</u> IS IT NOT WRITTEN, <u>COVET, DESIRE UNRESTRAINEDLY, TO PROPHESY!!!</u> <u>IS IT NOT WRITTEN, DO MY PROPHETS NO HARM!!!</u> <u>NONE!</u> <u>NIL!</u> <u>NOT ANY HARM!</u> <u>IS IT NOT WRITTEN, LET THE PROPHETS SPEAK!!!</u> IS IT NOT WRITTEN, THEY THAT ARE IGNORANT OF MY AUTHORITY IN USING THE WOMEN IN THESE LAST DAYS ARE IGNORED! IS IT NOT WRITTEN, THESE DEFILE THE FLESH, DESPISE DOMINION AND SPEAK EVIL OF DIGNITIES! IS IT NOT WRITTEN, THEY SPEAK EVIL OF THOSE THINGS WHICH THEY HAVE NOT KNOWLEDGE OF BUT WHAT THEY KNOW NATURALLY, IN THESE THINGS THEY ARE CORRUPTED! JEALOUSIES HAVE BEEN ALLOWED TO RUN RAMPANT IN THE DISGUISE OF DECENCY AND IN ORDER! I'LL GIVE YOU ORDER! <u>ORDER IS MY WORD!!!</u> <u>ORDER IS MY DOMINION!</u> ORDER IS MY SPIRIT RULING AND REIGNING!!! STOP THE KILLING OF MY ANOINTED PROPHETS! STAY THE JURISDICTION OF MAN!!! MAN IS NOT THE AUTHORITY OVER MY

CHURCH!!! *I AM!!!* IS IT NOT WRITTEN, THEY THAT LOVE TO HAVE THE PREEMINENCE DO NOT RECEIVE THE GIFT OF GOD WHICH I SEND! IS IT NOT WRITTEN, I WILL REMEMBER THEIR DEEDS, PRATING, GOSSIPING, CONDEMNING WITH MALICIOUS WORDS, NOT RECEIVING THE BRETHREN AND FORBIDDING THEM THAT WOULD, CASTING THEM OUT! IS IT NOT WRITTEN, FOLLOW NOT THAT WHICH IS EVIL BUT THAT WHICH IS GOOD? BUT WHOSOEVER DOES NOT RIGHTEOUSNESS IS NOT OF GOD, NEITHER HE THAT DOES NOT LOVE HIS BROTHER!!! IS IT NOT WRITTEN, GRUDGE NOT ONE AGAINST ANOTHER LEST YOU BE CONDEMNED! BEHOLD, THE JUDGE STANDS AT THE DOOR!!! <u>IS IT NOT WRITTEN, TAKE MY BRETHREN THE PROPHETS WHO HAVE SPOKEN IN THE NAME OF THE LORD FOR AN EXAMPLE OF SUFFERING AFFLICTION AND OF PATIENCE!!! IF YOU KNEW THE GIFT OF GOD YOU WOULD NOT CONTINUE TO CRUCIFY THE LORD OF GLORY FOR IS IT NOT WRITTEN AS MUCH AS YOU HAVE DONE IT UNTO ONE OF THE LEAST OF THESE MY BRETHREN YOU HAVE DONE IT UNTO ME!!!</u>

IS IT NOT WRITTEN, WITHHOLD NOT GOOD FROM THEM TO WHOM IT IS DUE WHEN IT IS IN THE POWER OF THINE HAND TO DO IT! IS IT NOT WRITTEN, RENDER THEREFORE TO ALL, THEIR DUES: TRIBUTE TO WHOM TRIBUTE IS DUE, CUSTOM TO WHOM CUSTOM, FEAR TO WHOM FEAR, HONOR TO WHOM HONOR! IS IT NOT WRITTEN, OWE NO MAN ANYTHING BUT TO LOVE ONE ANOTHER! IS IT NOT WRITTEN, DESPISE NOT GOVERNMENT! KNOW YOU NOT THAT THE GOVERNMENT OF THE CHURCH IS SET IN ORDER BY GOD: APOSTLES, PROPHETS, EVANGELISTS, PASTORS AND TEACHERS!

IS IT NOT WRITTEN, THEY THAT DESPISE THE GOVERNMENT OF GOD ARE PRESUMPTUOUS (ARROGANT, FOOLHARDY) SELF-WILLED (OBSTINATE, PERVERSE: WILLFULLY DETERMINED TO GO COUNTER TO WHAT IS RIGHT) NOT AFRAID TO SPEAK EVIL OF DIGNITIES!!! IS IT NOT WRITTEN, THAT A GREAT DOOR AND EFFECTUAL IS OPENED UNTO ME AND THERE ARE MANY ADVERSARIES! AND IF MY BROTHER COME UNTO YOU, SEE THAT

HE MAY BE WITH YOU WITHOUT FEAR, FOR HE WORKS THE WORK OF GOD! LET NO MAN THEREFORE DESPISE (SET ASIDE) HIM, BUT CONDUCT HIM IN PEACE!!! IS IT NOT WRITTEN, LET <u>ALL</u> THINGS BE DONE WITH CHARITY!!! IS IT NOT WRITTEN, THAT THEY HAVE ADDICTED THEMSELVES TO THE MINISTRY OF THE SAINTS! IS IT NOT WRITTEN, THAT YOU SUBMIT YOURSELF UNTO THEM AND TO EVERYONE THAT HELPS AND LABORS WITH US!!! THEY REFRESH YOU IN THE SPIRIT, THEREFORE ACKNOWLEDGE THEM!!! YOU SERPENTS OF FILTH, WHY DO YOU YET KILL THE PROPHETS WITH YOUR WORDS OF DENIAL? DENYING THE PROPHETS BRINGS DESTRUCTION UPON YOURSELVES!!! IS IT NOT WRITTEN, REBUKE THEM SHARPLY THAT THEY MAY BE SOUND (FIRM, ORTHODOX, UNIMPAIRED, UNBROKEN) IN THE FAITH!!! NOT GIVING HEED TO COMMANDMENTS OF MEN THAT TURN FROM THE TRUTH!!! THEY PROFESS THEY KNOW GOD BUT DENY HIS TESTIMONY WHICH IS PROPHECY!!! RIGHTEOUSNESS IS BEING ALIGNED PROPERLY WITH AUTHORITY!!! HOLINESS IS PURE (NOT MIXED) INTEGRITY INSIDE AND OUT!!!

October 2, 2001

Prophecy

I LOVE YOU, MY SERVANT. YEA, SEEK TO DO WHAT I WOULD HAVE YOU TO DO!!! I GIVE YOU COUNSEL EVEN NOW. I AM CALLING YOU FORTH INTO DOMINION AND POWER!!! OTHERS SHALL REALIZE THAT YOU ARE A PROPHET OF GOD. THEY SHALL UNDERSTAND YOUR LEADING AND APOSTLESHIP. SOME ARE BRACING THEMSELVES NOW FOR CORRECTION. THEY KNOW THAT THEY HAVE COME AGAINST YOU. I AM GIVING THEM SPACE TO REPENT. THIS BLANKET APOLOGY THAT PEOPLE GIVE IN A GROUP IS NOT ACCEPTABLE. PEOPLE MUST GO TO THE PEOPLE PERSONALLY THAT THEY HAVE OFFENDED, AND ASK FOR FORGIVENESS FOR THEIR ERRORS. I AM CALLING PEOPLE TO PURITY AND TO SANCTIFICATION NOT TO RITUALS, PAGANISM! I CALL PEOPLE NOW TO REPENTANCE, TO HUMILITY, TO WALK IN MY SPIRIT AND TO STOP MAKING ERRORS WITH THEIR WORDS!!! IS IT NOT WRITTEN, HE THAT BRIDLES HIS TONGUE IS THE SAME AS A PERFECT MAN, ABLE ALSO TO BRIDLE THE WHOLE BODY? WHY DO YOU NOT RESIST THE TEMPTATION TO SPEAK YOUR MIND? WHY? I WILL TELL YOU WHY. YOU ARE NOT RENEWING YOUR MIND DAILY WITH MY WORD AND BY PRAYING IN THE HOLY GHOST! WHEN YOU PRAY IN THE SPIRIT ENOUGH, YOU WILL WALK IN THE SPIRIT! WHEN YOU WALK IN THE SPIRIT, YOU WILL SPEAK MY WORDS AND NOT YOUR OWN OR ANOTHER'S!!! BE SURE YOUR SINS WILL FIND YOU OUT, FOR OUT OF THE ABUNDANCE OF THE HEART, THE MOUTH WILL SPEAK! TO SAY RIGHT ONE MUST PRAY RIGHT, IN TONGUES, AND KEEP THE HEART PURE!

WHEN YOU DO WRONG, SAY YOU ARE SORRY! IF YOU ARE TOO PROUD TO SAY YOU ARE SORRY, YOU ARE IN SIN!!! THE REASON GODLY SORROW IS NOT WORKING REPENTANCE IN THOSE THAT DO ERR IS THAT THEY ARE NOT SUBMITTING TO GOD! REPENTANCE, TRUE REPENTANCE, COMES FROM SORROW! IF THERE IS NOT SORROW, THERE IS NO REPENTANCE. EVEN SAYING YOU ARE SORRY IS NOT TRUE REPENTANCE IF THERE IS NOT <u>GODLY</u> SORROW! SORROW FOR BEING WRONG!

SORROW FOR GRIEVING THE HEART OF GOD! SORROW FOR OFFENDING THE ANOINTING! SORROW FOR TOUCHING THE ANOINTING! SORROW FOR HINDERING THE ANOINTING! SORROW FOR NOT REALLY UNDERSTANDING THE ANOINTING! SORROW FOR NOT RECOGNIZING THE ANOINTING OF GOD! HIS ANOINTED ONES! SORROW FOR MISJUDGING THE ANOINTING AND GOD'S ANOINTED!!!

REPENT, CHURCH! REPENT! POSITION AND TITLE DO NOT MAKE YOU RIGHT! CARING FOR THE THINGS OF GOD ENABLES ONE TO WALK CORRECTLY AND NOT TO SIN WITH THE LIPS! BE SWIFT, QUICK TO HEAR, SLOW TO SPEAK AND SLOW TO ANGER AS IT WRITTEN!!! NEITHER DOES MIGHT MAKE RIGHT! MANY ARE WRONG WHO HAVE STOOD AGAINST THE FEW!!! ONE, IN THE RIGHT WITH ME IS A MAJORITY! STAND NOT AGAINST TRUTH!!! FOR TRUTH WILL STAND WHEN THE WORLD IS ON FIRE! BE SURE YOUR SINS WILL FIND YOU OUT! NOTHING IS HID FROM ME! WHEN YOU ARE WRONG, JUST ADMIT IT! UNTIL YOU DO, YOU WILL NOT PROSPER. THAT IS MINGLED SEED AND WILL BE EXPOSED! TRUTH IS NOT TO BE TAINTED WITH ERROR OR COMPROMISE! I AM HOLY! BE YE HOLY, ALSO! HOLY IS NOT MIXED WITH OPINIONS. HOLY IS PURE UNADULTERATED WORD!!! WHATEVER IS WRITTEN. NOT OPINIONS, PREFERENCES, PUNDITS OR PLAUDITS! HOLY IS BEING LED BY MY SPIRIT AND MY WORD! THEY AGREE! <u>WHY DON'T YOU?</u>

October 3, 2001

Prophecy

MANY HAVE TRIED TO ENSNARE YOU. MANY HAVE TRIED TO HIJACK YOUR GIFT, BUT I HAVE HELD THEM IN CHECK, FOR MY GLORY SHALL HAVE DOMINION IN THIS LAST AND EVIL DAY. TODAY IS A MIRACLE DAY, MY CHILD. I WILL SHOW FORTH MY DOMINION AND MY GLORY. MAN IS A PUPPET IN THE HANDS OF THE ALMIGHTY. HE TAKES HIS TIME IN GETTING READY TO HOUSE MY GLORY. BUT <u>ALL</u> THINGS ARE ON MY TIME TABLE. I TABLE THE TIMES! I BREAK THE CHAINS OF DOMINION AND POWER OF ALL FORCES THAT TRY TO TAKE DOMINION FROM THE DOMINATOR! MY POWER IS NOT GAINSAYED BY MERE MEN. SOME THINK THEY HAVE IN CHECK THE ANOINTED OF THE ALMIGHTY. THEY BRING DESTRUCTION UPON THEMSELVES WHEN THEY HOLD BACK THE ANOINTING OF THE ANOINTED ONE! I WAIT. I GIVE AMPLE TIME TO LEADERSHIP. BUT IT IS WRITTEN, BE NOT DECEIVED, WHATSOEVER A MAN SOWS, THAT SHALL HE ALSO REAP! MY WORDS ARE <u>MY</u> WAY! WHEN YOU SET ASIDE MY WRITTEN WORD, YOU ARE ON DANGEROUS GROUND!!!

October 9, 2001

Prophecy

THE WORD OF THE LORD GIVEN THIS DAY OF OCTOBER 9, 2001 WHILE PRAYING WITH BENNY HINN, JAN CROUCH, AND OTHERS AS THEY PRAYED TO GOD ON TRINITY BROADCASTING NETWORK FOR OUR NATION:

TODAY IS A MIRACLE DAY! I AM REALIGNING MY CHURCH HIERARCHY. I AM SANCTIONING NOTHING BUT POWER AND DOMINION! I WILL NO LONGER TOLERATE PRIDE AND PREJUDICE, GREED AND GLORIES OF MAN! IF MY PLACES OF WORSHIP WHICH ARE CALLED BY NAME WILL NOT ALLOW MY GLORIES ONLY, I SHALL BEGIN TO POUR OUT MY VIALS OF WRATH UPON THE ALTARS OF POMP AND RESPECT OF PERSONS!!! MY SPIRIT IS ME! WHEN YOU REJECT ME IN WHOMEVER I SEND, YOU STOP THE FLOW OF MY PRESENCE AND YOU GRIEVE MY HOLY SPIRIT! I SHALL NO LONGER RESTRAIN THE JUDGMENTS COMING TO THE SANCTUARIES. THEY ARE NO LONGER SANCTUARIES. THEY ARE PODIUMS OF POWERS OF FLESH AND RECOGNITION!!!!! WHEN MY PROPHETS ARE RESTRAINED, MY GLORIES ARE WITHHELD. RELEASE MY PROPHETS!

STOP THE SLAUGHTER OF THE INNOCENTS!!! I HEAR NOT AMERICA REPENTING OVER THE MILLIONS OF INFANTS SLAUGHTERED IN HER NAME! ALL OF THESE THAT YOU HAVE SLAUGHTERED WERE *CHILDREN OF GOD, MY SEED, MY PROGENY!!!* YET YOU WEEP NOT FOR THESE SLAIN, THESE MILLIONS! UNTIL MY PEOPLE WHICH ARE CALLED BY MY NAME DEMAND THE ABORTION DECREE TO BE ABOLISHED, I WILL NOT HEAR YOUR PLEAS FOR PROTECTION AND FOR REVIVAL! DID I NOT EVEN SAY TO MY SERVANT, JOSHUA, AS HE CRIED UNTO ME FOR THE LIVES OF HIS ENEMIES, GET UP AND DESTROY THE ACCURSED THING AMONG YOU!!!!! *THE ACCURSED THING IN AMERICA IS HER NATIONAL SIN OF ABORTION! OPEN AND BLATANT SLAUGHTER OF THE INNOCENTS!!! DEMAND THIS FILTHY DECREE TO BE RIPPED FROM THE PAGES OF YOUR STATUTES!!! UNTIL IT IS, TERROR WILL*

CONTINUE TO MANIFEST EVEN AS YOU, YES, YOU AMERICA, THE HOME OF FREEDOM, NOW CONTINUE TO TERRORIZE THE WOMB!!!

SHUT UP, AMERICA! SILENCE YOURSELF! UNTIL YOU CAN RECOGNIZE THAT YOUR HANDS ARE BLOODY WITH THE SOULS OF THE DEAD AND THE DYING, UNTIL YOU CAN REALIZE THAT YOUR MINISTRY IS ONLY AS FRUITFUL AS HOW MUCH SALT AND LIGHT THAT YOU ARE IN YOUR OWN CULTURE, SHUT UP!!! MY SONS, PARSLEY AND KENNEDY CRIED OUT AND WARNED YOUR GOVERNMENT AGAINST THIS HOLOCAUST OF BABY BLUDGEONING! AS DID MANY OTHERS! BUT EVERY PULPIT AND PROGRAM ON THE AIRWAVES SHOULD HAVE SOUNDED THE ALARM UNTIL THE BREACH WAS BROKEN!!! MONEY IS NOT MIGHT! FAVOR WITH ME IS MIGHT!!! CRY IT FROM YOUR PULPITS! SEND ENTOURAGES AND COUNSELORS TO THE GOVERNMENT! BLOOD WILL SPILL UNTIL YOU STOP MURDERING THE CREATION THAT I GOD CREATED IN YOUR OWN WOMB THUS SAITH THE LORD!!!

October 9, 2001

Prophecy

I AM GOD AND BESIDES ME THERE IS NONE OTHER! WHY CALL YE ME LORD, LORD, AND DO NOT THE THINGS WHICH I SAY??? I CANNOT ASCRIBE TO THE COUNSELS THAT DO NOT ASCRIBE TO MY WRITTEN WORD! MY WRITTEN WORD *IS* ME! MY SPIRIT AGREES WITH MY WRITTEN WORD! DOES YOURS? DOES YOUR SPIRIT ASCRIBE TO MY WRITTEN WORD? HOW CAN YOU REJECT MY WORD AND PROCLAIM ME? I *AM* MY WRITTEN WORD! *ALL* OF IT! NOT ONE JOT NOR ONE TITTLE SHALL PASS AWAY TILL *ALL* BE FULFILLED! THESE ARE WELLS WITHOUT WATER. THOSE WHO ASCRIBE TO KNOW ME AND YET DO NOT KNOW MY ANOINTED SERVANTS! AND YOU SET ASIDE MY ANOINTED VESSELS. I WILL REMEMBER THIS AND WILL HOLD SOME ACCOUNTABLE FOR BLASPHEMY SAITH THE LORD. WHEN YOU REJECT MY SPIRIT IN MY ANOINTED YOU ARE REJECTING ME! STOP IT! MY SPIRIT AND I ARE ONE! I WILL BEGIN TO TAKE VENGEANCE UPON THOSE WHO REJECT AND SET ASIDE THE ANOINTING OF MY ANOINTED ONES!!! DO YOU ACTUALLY PURPORT TO GAINSAY THE SPIRIT OF THE ALMIGHTY? WHY WOULD YOU BRING DESTRUCTION UPON YOURSELVES? GET THE FILTHINESS OUT OF YOUR SPIRIT! WHY WOULD YOU TROUBLE THOSE WHO SPEAK FOR ME? WHO TELL YOU THE THINGS WHICH I SAY! WHO LAY BEFORE ME AT THE MIDNIGHT HOUR AND THE BREAKING OF DAY! WHO SET ASIDE THEIR NECESSARY FOOD IN ORDER TO RECEIVE THE COUNSELS OF THE ALMIGHTY! JUDGMENT SHALL DESCEND SOON UPON THE NAY SAYERS! I SHALL TAKE VENGEANCE UPON THOSE WHO SHOW NO MERCY. WHO WALK AS BUSYBODIES IN OTHER MEN'S MATTERS! WHO STUMBLE AT THE STUMBLING-STONE AND THOSE WHO REJECT THE MAJESTY OF MIGHT, I AM PROPELLING INTO ETERNITY!!!

I AM RESCUING OTHERS WHO REGARD NOT THE COUNSEL OF THE WICKED, BUT WHO DESIRE TO WALK IN HOLINESS! WHO ARE SEEKING ME FOR TRUE RICHES!!! THE HIDDEN RICHES! BLASPHEME NO LONGER MY HOLY ANOINTED VESSELS FOR YOU SHALL NOT ESCAPE THE FURY THAT SHALL DESCEND IF YOU

CONTINUE TO REJECT AND CONDEMN THE SPIRIT OF COUNSEL IN MY VESSELS OF INTEGRITY! THEY ARE SIGNS AND ENSIGNS. THEY ARE MARSHALLING THE MURKY WATERS OF THE SPIRITS OF THE BLACKNESS AND THE DARKNESS! MANGLED MAJESTIES DO NOT STOP MY AUTHORITIES AND DOMINIONS! I STILL HAVE DOMINION THOUGH YOU EVEN KILL MY PROPHETS! I SHALL HAVE THE LAST SAY AT THAT GREAT AND NOTABLE DAY WHERE THE RECORD ALONE WILL SPEAK! THERE WILL BE NO COUNSELS, NO TUMULTS, NO SWELLINGS, NO LIARS, AND NO SURMISINGS. NO BACKBITERS. NO FAULTFINDERS. NO WHISPERERS. NO JEALOUSIES. NO POINTING OF THE FINGER. MY HAND ALONE SHALL RULE AND JUDGE!!!

REJECT NOT MY COUNSEL, YOU SERPENTS OF CRAFTINESS! YOU WHO SEEK TO HARBOR OUGHT AGAINST THE ANOINTED OF THE ANOINTED ONE! REJECT NOT THE CORRECTIONS!!!!! SILENCE YOUR WRANGLINGS. SPEAK PEACE. NOT LIES! ALL LIARS WILL HAVE THEIR PART IN THE LAKE OF FIRE! YOU WHO HAVE STRAINED AT A GNAT AND SWALLOWED THE CAMELS OF JUDGMENTALISM, CRITICISM, CALLING GOOD EVIL! TEARING DOWN THE WALLS, BREAKING THE FELLOWSHIP OF THE SPIRIT! YOU SHALL NOT GO UNPUNISHED!!! EXCEPT YOU REPENT AND TURN FROM THIS WICKEDNESS I SHALL REWARD YOU WITH SNARES AND PLAGUES! YOU CANNOT CONTINUE TO SMITE THE INNOCENT AND BE BLAMELESS! I WILL UNCOVER YOUR DECEITFULNESS AND YOU SHALL BE MARKED FOR CORRECTION!!!

October 10, 2001

Prophecy

I SAY UNTO YOU, MY CHILD, MY CHILD, I AM JEALOUS OVER YOU.
YOU HAVE BEEN FAITHFUL AND HENCEFORTH THERE IS LAID UP
FOR YOU A CROWN OF RIGHTEOUSNESS!

October 15, 2001

BEWARE! BEWARE! SOME SPEAK WITH A DOUBLE TONGUE!!! I
ADJURE YOU BY THE AUTHORITY AND POWER OF THE ALMIGHTY,
STAND DOWN! LET THE PROPHETS SPEAK TO MY PEOPLE! I HAVE
ENCOURAGEMENT AND I HAVE STABILITY OF PURPOSE! I HAVE
THE ORACLE BY WHICH THE FUTURE SHALL BE SPOKEN FORTH! I
HAVE GIVEN MY DOMINION OF MIGHT! I SPEAK AND SO SHALL
IT BE! NO ONE STANDS ME DOWN! WHEN YOU CONTINUE TO DO
SO, I BRING YOU DOWN! THERE IS ONE ALMIGHTY AND IT'S ME!
MY DOMINION! MY AUTHORITY! MY POWER! MY MODUS
OPERANDI! MY ORDER OF SERVICE!!! MY ALIGNMENT OF POWER!
MY CHAIN OF COMMAND! STEP ASIDE, LIEUTENANTS AND LET
THE CAPTAIN OF THIS ARMY SPEAK THROUGH THE PROPHETS
ORDAINED BY ALMIGHTY GOD!!!!!!! PROVISIONS ARE BEING
MADE FOR ALL OF MY MINISTRY OFFICES!!! NOT JUST PASTORS
AND EVANGELISTS! APOSTLES, PROPHETS AND TEACHERS ARE
WORTHY OF THEIR HIRE!!! I AM ESTABLISHING FUNDS FOR MY
PEOPLE OF POWER AND AUTHORITY TO GO FORWARD IN ME! IN
DIVINE ORDER OF PURPOSE AND DESTINY!!! I HAVE HEADS OF
STATE THAT YOU ARE PUTTING IN JEOPARDY, CAUSING MANY TO
REJECT THEM BECAUSE YOU WANT YOUR ORDER INSTEAD OF
MINE!!! CEASE THIS MUTINY! I ESTABLISH ORDER IN MY
CHURCH: APOSTLES, PROPHETS, EVANGELISTS, PASTORS AND
TEACHERS! WHEN YOU STEP OUT OF LINE, REJECTING OFFICERS
THAT I PLACED IN MY BODY, YOU ARE NOT COMING AGAINST
MEN! YOU ARE COMING AGAINST THE ALMIGHTY! STAND
DOWN, SAITH THE LORD!!!

October 15, 2001

Prophecy

THE CHURCH DOES NOT BELONG TO A DENOMINATION! TO A MAN! IT'S MY CHURCH! THE CHURCH DOES NOT BELONG TO PASTORS! IT'S MY CHURCH! THE CHURCH OF THE LORD JESUS CHRIST!!! RELEASE THE PROPHETS OR I WILL RELEASE JUDGMENT!!! I AM GIVING SOME THEIR LAST CHANCE BEFORE GRAVE JUDGMENTS FALL!!!

October 16, 2001

IT IS NOT MY WILL FOR YOU TO PONDER. ONLY TO TRUST!!! YEA, THE DAY IS COME SAITH THE LORD, I WILL NO LONGER TOLERATE THE SETTING ASIDE OF MY TRUE PROPHETS! SOME HAVE COME IN MY NAME THAT HAVE REFUTED MY CAUSE! SOME SAY WHEN I HAVE NOT SAID, BUT WHEN I SAY IT, IT BETTER BE HEARD FOR I WILL HOLD ACCOUNTABLE THE WORDS THAT I SPEAK! REGARD NOT THOSE WHO HOLD THEIR NOSES AND REJECT MY PROPHECIES! THEY SHALL NOW TOPPLE AS THE TOWERS. I AM MARCHING THROUGH THIS LAND. IT IS MY LAND, DESECRATED, BUT STILL MY LAND!!! I AM GIVING DOMINION AND I AM GIVING POWERS TO THE ONES WHO STAND IN MY NAME WITH ALL MY GLORY!!! THOSE WHO WITHSTAND MY GLORY SHALL BE REPLACED! TOPPLE NOT YOUR OWN STANDING!!! STAND FOR TRUTH AND YOU SHALL SURELY STAND INDEED! FIGHT NO LONGER THE TRUTHS OF MY APOSTLES AND PROPHETS LEST YOU BE CUT DOWN AND WITHER AS THE GRASS! WHAT I HAVE SPOKEN IS MY DOCTRINE! THERE IS NO OTHER! STAY YOUR HAND! LET THE PROPHETS SPEAK! WHEN YOU REJECT THEM YOU ARE REJECTING ME!!! MY TESTIMONY IS THE SPIRIT OF PROPHECY!!! I HAVE STATIONED PROPHETS HERE FOR A PURPOSE! I WILL RELEASE THEM SOON TO THIS NATION!!!

October 17, 2001

SPEAK MY SERVANT. WRITE THE VISION. KNOW YOU NOT THAT THE DESTRUCTION IS JUDGMENT EVEN THOUGH I DO NOT

INITIATE THE ATTACKS, I USE THEM! I AM TELLING MY PEOPLE WHICH ARE CALLED BY NAME TO REEVALUATE THEIR POSITION. TO DISENGAGE ALL ACTIVITY THAT I AM NOT IN CHARGE OF. <u>TO ESTABLISH PRAYER AS NUMBER ONE PRIORITY! TO HEAR MY VOICE AS THE NUMBER TWO! TO THEN DO MY WILL ACCORDING TO WHAT I SPEAK! I AM NOT TO BE SET ASIDE AS SANTA CLAUS, COMING OUT ON A YEARLY BASIS!!!</u> I AM TO BE FEARED, REVERED AND OBEYED DAILY! MY MISSION IS MEN!!! MY GOAL IS GLORY! MY PRIORITY IS POWER! THE POWER OF MY SPIRIT! RETALIATE FOR NO SLIGHT. RETURN GOOD FOR EVIL! BE HEALTHY! BE WHOLE! BE CIRCUMSPECT! BE ON ONE ACCORD! THE ACCORD OF MY WORD!!! UNTIL MY PEOPLE ACCEPT, RECEIVE, APPLY, PUT INTO ACTION ALL OF MY WRITTEN WORD, THE FULL MANIFESTATION OF SIGNS, WONDERS AND MIRACLES IS HINDERED!!!!!

DO NOT RESTRAIN PROPHECY, OR THE PROPHETS!!! WHY DO YOU THINK IT IS WRITTEN, DESIRE SPIRITUAL GIFTS, BUT <u>RATHER THAT YOU MAY PROPHESY???</u> <u>BECAUSE THAT IS MY ORDER!!!</u> PAUL SPOKE FOR ME!!! HE SPOKE THIS ORDER BECAUSE THAT IS WHAT I COMMISSION!!! <u>I AM THE HEAD OF THIS ARMY! AND THAT IS MY COMMAND!</u> I DO NOTHING WITHOUT REVEALING IT TO MY SERVANTS, THE PROPHETS!!!!! JUDGMENT HAS ALREADY BEGUN IN THE CHURCH! AND IN THE SECULAR SOCIETY! WHAT SAY YE, MEN AND WOMEN OF GOD? DO YOU SAY WHAT I SAY??? OR DO YOU SIDE WITH MAN AND COMPROMISE??? WHO IS ON THE LORD'S SIDE? <u>LET</u> THE WILL AND WORDS OF GOD COME FORTH! <u>LET</u> THE MIRACLES BE PROCLAIMED IN ABUNDANCE! <u>LET</u> THE WOMEN AND THE MEN MOVE INTO POSITION!!! <u>LET</u> THE GIFTS BE DEMONSTRATED IN THE SERVICES! IT IS NOT TO BE A PREACHING ONLY SERVICE! <u>IT IS TO BE A MANIFESTATION OF MY GLORY SERVICE!!!</u> THIS TAKES PLACE WHEN FLESH MOVES OUT OF THE WAY AND GIVES ME FREE REIGN TO USHER IN WHATEVER IT IS THAT I WANT TO DO IN EACH PARTICULAR GATHERING! I WANT TO MANIFEST MY GLORY! I WANT TO DO EXCEEDINGLY ABUNDANTLY ABOVE ALL THAT YOU ASK OR THINK! I DO THIS

WHEN I AM GIVEN FREE REIGN TO USE WHOMEVER I WILL <u>THAT NO FLESH SHOULD GLORY!!!</u>

I HAVE MEN AND WOMEN I DESIRE TO USE IN THE SERVICES!!! LET ME BRING THEM FORTH! LET ME SHINE THROUGH WHOMEVER I DESIRE! IF YOU REALLY DESIRE ME AS YOU SAY AND SING, YOU WILL RELEASE <u>ALL</u> OF MY BODY PARTS FOR I AM A MANY-MEMBERED BODY! NOT JUST PREACHING! <u>READ THE BOOK</u>! FOR YOU MAY <u>ALL</u> PROPHESY THAT ALL MAY LEARN AND ALL MAY BE COMFORTED! I WILL GET YOUR ATTENTION VERY SOON!!! EVEN AS IN THE GOVERNMENT! DEATH HAD TO COME TO GET THE ATTENTION OF LEADERS! YOU CAN NO LONGER KILL YOUR OWN! SO LIKEWISE IN THE CHURCH, YOU CAN NO LONGER KILL, SET ASIDE, DISMEMBER CREATIVE BODY PARTS AND CONTINUE TO RECEIVE MY GRACE AND MY GLORY!!! MY BODY IS MADE UP OF <u>ALL</u> MY BODY PARTS! EVANGELISTS, PROPHETS AND APOSTLES!!! NOT JUST PASTORS AND TEACHERS! MY MINISTRY GIFTS OF HEALINGS, MIRACLES, PROPHECIES, TONGUES AND INTERPRETATION, WORDS OF WISDOM AND WORDS OF KNOWLEDGE ARE TO BE MANIFESTED THROUGH MANY! ACTUALLY THE CHURCH IS TO BE THE SCHOOL OF MANIFESTATION!!! THE CHURCH IS TO BE THE TESTING GROUND FOR ALL MINISTRY! SURELY IT IS WRITTEN, THE SPIRITS OF THE PROPHETS ARE SUBJECT TO THE PROPHETS! BUT THE VERSE BEFORE THAT SAYS, <u>YOU MAY ALL PROPHESY,</u> ONE BY ONE, THAT <u>ALL</u> MAY LEARN, AND <u>ALL</u> MAY BE COMFORTED! THE VERSE BEFORE THIS SAYS, IF ANYTHING BE REVEALED TO ANOTHER THAT SITS BY, <u>LET THE FIRST HOLD HIS PEACE!!!</u> THE VERSE PRIOR TO THAT SAYS, <u>LET THE PROPHETS SPEAK!!!</u> YES, THERE IS AN ORDER OF SERVICE! BUT PART OF THE ORDER IS, <u>LET THE PROPHETS SPEAK!!!</u> <u>PASTORS ARE IN DANGER IF THEY DO NOT RELEASE THE PROPHETS!!!</u>

October 18, 2001

Prophecy

I BREAK THE FETTERS OF DARKNESS OFF THE MINDS OF ALL LIVING!!! I CURTAIL EVEN NOW THE INSIDIOUS FALSIFYING OF MY DOMINION AND MIGHT! I CURTAIL THE COPYCAT RITUALS OF CHURCH LEADERS WHO ARE GOING THROUGH THE MOTIONS AND DECLARING MY DIGNITY AND INTEGRITY WITHOUT MY GLORY AND MY DOMINION! I STOP THE ONES WHO SIT ON MY SPOKESPERSONS AND DO NOT ALLOW THEM TO PROPHESY, EXHORT AND REBUKE!!! I STOP GAME PLAYING AND SÉANCE SAYING! I STOP BLACK MAGIC, WHITE MAGIC AND THE SELLING OF SEXUAL INTERCOURSE!!! INTERCOURSE IS TO BE WITHIN THE BONDS OF HOLY MATRIMONY! WITHOUT IT YOU ARE ADULTERERS AND ADULTERESSES, FORNICATORS AND WHOREMONGERS!!! I BREAK THE BONDS OF PORNOGRAPHY, X-RATED MOVIES!!! I CLOSE DOWN STRIP CLUBS! I DISBAR CORRUPT JUDGES! I BRING INTO ACCOUNTABILITY THOSE WHO ARE SELLING THEIR SOULS FOR A MESS ... SOME A MESS OF DOPE, SOME A MESS OF FUTILITY, SOME A MESS OF SCARS AND AGONIES!!!

COME OUT OF MY CHURCH, YOU RUTHLESS DEMONIC ACTIVISTS!!! I QUENCH YOUR FIRES OF GREED AND GRANDEUR! I TEAR DOWN THE STRONGHOLDS OF MAN WORSHIP, PUPPET PULLING! I BAN EVEN NOW ALL FORMS AND REFORMS OF SO-CALLED CHURCH AUTHORITY!!! I AM IS THE AUTHORITY! WHAT I SAY *IS* LAW! IS IT MY CHURCH OR YOURS? SOME HAVE ALREADY CLOSED. OTHERS OPEN AGAIN IN ANOTHER PLACE. BUT EXCEPT THE LORD BUILD THE CHURCH, YOU LABOR IN VAIN!!! I ESTABLISH MY CHURCH ON THE FOUNDATION OF THE APOSTLES AND PROPHETS! JESUS CHRIST THE CHIEF CORNERSTONE! HAVE I NOT EVEN SAID IN MY HOLY WRIT, HE THAT IS LEAST ESTEEMED SHALL JUDGE A MATTER? WHY DOES NO ONE TEACH OR PREACH THIS??? IT IS TIME TO SET THE CHURCH IN ORDER BY THE TENETS OF THE APOSTLES' DOCTRINE, WHICH IS MY ORDER! OBLIGATE NO ONE TO BE OTHER THAN WHAT I SPEAK THAT THEY ARE TO BE! TANGLED WEBS OF MEN'S

CREEDS AND DISTORTIONS SHALL BE REPLACED WITH MY ESTABLISHED ORDER! READ THE BOOK! NOT THE CHURCH MANUAL. WHAT DOES THE <u>BIBLE</u> SAY? THAT IS WHAT YOU ARE TO DO!!!

I AM TELLING SOME NOW TO PULL OFF THEIR ROBES OF ROBBERY AND DISSENSION AND PREEMINENCE!!! IT IS TIME FOR MY COMING OUT PARTY! EVEN AS I SPOKE TO THE CHURCH AT LAODOCEA: KNOW YOU NOT THAT YOU ARE WRETCHED AND BLIND? WHAT MAKES A GLORIOUS CHURCH??? ONE THAT IS DOING <u>ALL</u> THE TENETS OF THE FAITH IN ACCORDANCE WITH MY WILL THAT IS ESTABLISHED IN THE BIBLE!!! EAT YE <u>ALL</u> OF IT! EAT I CORINTHIANS CHAPTERS TWELVE AND FOURTEEN. IF YOU CAN'T STOMACH IT, ALL OF AT ONCE, SANDWICH IT BETWEEN LARGE PORTIONS OF CHAPTER THIRTEEN!!! EAT YE <u>ALL</u> OF IT!!!

BLASÉ DOES NOT CUT IT WITH ME! IF YOU CONTINUE TO BE INDIFFERENT TO MY TENETS OF THE FAITH YOU WILL NOT BE INDIFFERENT WHEN THE JUDGMENTS COME!!! THE CURSES CAUSELESS DO NOT COME!!!

October 20, 2001

Prophecy

GRAVE, GRAVE DAYS AHEAD! BATTLES!!! SPIRITUALLY AND MILITARILY!!! I AM CALLING YOU TO FOCUS! BE PREPARED!!! KNOW EACH DAY EXACTLY WHAT I WANT YOU TO ACCOMPLISH! NEEDS ARE BEING MET. NO ONE STOPS MY MOVE. LET ME USE YOUR TEMPLE TO DISPLAY MY GLORY!!! I KNOW THE CESSPOOLS THAT HAVE STAGNATED!!! I SEE THE STREAMS WHICH ARE POLLUTED! CRY ALOUD AND SPARE NOT! NO MAN RULES MY SPIRIT!!! I AM IN CONTROL!!! MY SPIRIT IS THE MEDIATOR! NOT MAN'S MIND!!! PUT ON MY MIND! LET MY MIND RULE YOU DAILY, NOT JUST ON SPECIAL OCCASIONS! I AM GOD <u>ALL</u> DAY, EVERY DAY! DAY IN AND DAY OUT!!! I NEVER TIRE! I NEVER GO ON VACATION! I STAY THE HAND OF <u>ALL</u> SOURCES THAT ARE NOT OF ME! I AM MOVING IN THE POLITICAL ARENA! I AM GIVING MY JURISDICTIONS! STAY IN LINE WITH MY DISCOURSES, MY STIPULATIONS, MY MANDATES, MY PRIORITIES, MY PURPOSES!!! AM I THE MAN? WELL, ACT LIKE IT!!!!! NOT JUST WHEN THINGS ARE GOING YOUR WAY! I'M THE SAME! BOMBINGS OR NO BOMBINGS! WAR OR NO WAR! GOOD DAYS OR NO GOOD DAYS!!! HELL DON'T MOVE ME!!! I RULE!!!!! LET ME RULE YOU AND YOU CAN RULE! I AM MEEK AND LOWLY OF HEART! I KILL AND I MAKE ALIVE! I AM ALL THINGS TO ALL MEN! LET ME BE YOUR REGULATOR! YOUR THERMOSTAT! YOUR PRESSURE GAUGE! I AM EVERYTHING!!! WHATEVER YOU NEED IN ANY AND EVERY SITUATION! LET ME!!! THE LAST MISSION OF THE CHURCH IS *SUBMISSION*!!!!! THAT MEANS YOU SUBMIT TO ME! TO DO THIS YOU HAVE TO *KNOW ME! TO KNOW ME YOU MUST COME INTO MY PRESENCE! TO REALLY KNOW ME IS TO LET ME COME INSIDE YOU!!! THAT IS SUBMISSION!* WHEN I AM PERMITTED TO COME INSIDE YOU! WHEN I AM PERMITTED TO MAKE MY ABODE, TAKE MY RESIDENCE, CAST MY SEED INTO YOUR WOMB, YOU BECOME PREGNANT WITH MY OFFSPRING! WHEN MY SEED, MY WORD, IS ALLOWED TO REMAIN IN YOU, I NOURISH YOUR REPRODUCTIVE ORGANS!!! I NEVER STOP FILLING YOU UP!!! YOU STAY SATISFIED! YOUR CONTENTMENT IS A MOTIVATOR! THE SMILE ON YOUR FACE IS ADVERTISEMENT

OF HOW GOOD I AM! IT CAUSES OTHERS TO WANT WHAT YOU'VE GOT. IT DRAWS THEM TO COME UNTO ME SO THAT I CAN COME INSIDE OF THEM SO THAT I CAN PRODUCE MORE CHILDREN!!!

SUBMIT, MY CHILD! I SATISFY! WHEN NOTHING AND NOBODY CAN PUT THAT SMILE ON YOUR FACE, I CAN!!! I'M THE MAN!!! LET ME MAKE YOU! LET ME TAKE YOU! STAY STRONG! IN ME! IN THE POWER OF MY MIGHT!!! I WANT YOU TO LOVE ME BACK! I WANT YOU TO PUT PASSION IN THIS LOVE RELATIONSHIP!!! WITH THE SAME MEASURE THAT YOU METE, IT WILL BE METED UNTO YOU!!!!! WHATEVER YOU ARE EXPERIENCING IN ME, IT IS COMMISERATE WITH THE LOVE THAT YOU HAVE SHOWN TO ME!!! I CAN ONLY GIVE TO YOU IN THE MEASURE THAT YOU GIVE TO ME! WHATEVER YOU HOLD BACK, YOU MAKE YOUR OWN LACK!!! WHATEVER YOU WITHHOLD FROM ME HINDERS OUR LOVE RELATIONSHIP!!!!!

<u>LOVE IS SUBMISSION</u>! WITH THE SAME MEASURE THAT YOU SUBMIT TO ME, I IN TURN SUBMIT TO YOU LIKEWISE!!! MMM! MMM! WHAT AN EXCHANGE! WHATEVER IS MISSING IN OUR RELATIONSHIP, THAT IS PART OF YOU THAT IS NOT SUBMITTED UNTO ME! YOU SEE, I MOVE ACCORDING TO WHATEVER IS FULLY SUBMITTED TO MY WILL AND MY PURPOSE! THE WAY I WANT TO MOVE! NOT YOUR PREFERENCE! I MOVE AND I KEEP ON MOVING! I DON'T GET TIRED!!! NEITHER AM I WEARY! I AM ONLY WAITING FOR SUBMISSION! I'M THE MAN!

October 26, 2001

Prophecy

I AM JEALOUS OVER YOU WITH GODLY JEALOUSY. I AM TELLING PEOPLE TO LEAVE YOU IN MY HANDS! THAT I SPEAK DIRECTLY TO YOU. POWER STRUGGLES ARE CEASING. I THE LORD HAVE SPOKEN IT! REMOVE ALL GLOSS FROM POSITIONS OF POWER! I AM THE BRIGHT AND MORNING STAR!!! THAT IS ENOUGH! I SANCTION MY ANOINTED TO SHINE FOR ME ONLY, NOT IN THEIR OWN MIGHT! I LOVE YOU, MY CHILD. ARISE AND GLITTER FOR ME. GLEAM WITH MY HOLINESS AND MY DOMINION! SPARKLE WITH MY GLORY AND MY PROVISION. SPEAK MY AUTHORITY AND MY POWER!!! GLISTEN WITH HEALINGS AND DELIVERANCES! GROSS NEGLECT IS BEING ERADICATED FROM MY MINISTRY AND GOVERNMENT. I AM EMPOWERING SOLDIERS OF FORTUNE TO EMBARK INTO MY GLORIES AND MY DOMINIONS!!! I SANCTION ALL POWER AND MIGHT TO COME FROM MY THRONE ONLY! I WILL QUICKLY SET ASIDE GLORY SEEKERS AND THOSE WHO WANT THE PREEMINENCE! AGAIN, I SAY, I AM THE ONLY PREMIER!!! SHUT YOUR MOUTH AND LET ME SPEAK SAYS THE GOD OF ALL FORCES!!! I AM THAT I AM! WHAT IS DOMINION AND MIGHT AND POWER AND AUTHORITY??? ME!!!!! AND DON'T YOU FORGET IT!!!

October 27, 2001

Prophecy

BEHOLD, THE I AM *IS* COMING TO INSTILL THE BASIC TENETS OF TRUTH!!! WOULD YOU NOT HEAR THE WORD OF THE LORD? WOULD YOU NOT TAKE COUNSEL WITH ME? DO YOU NOT ESTEEM MY WORD ABOVE YOUR NECESSARY FOOD? IS IT NOT WRITTEN, WHOSOEVER HE BE OF YOU THAT FORSAKES NOT ALL THAT HE HAS HE CANNOT BE MY DISCIPLE! IS IT NOT WRITTEN, THAT WHOSOEVER DOES NOT DENY HIMSELF AND TAKE UP HIS CROSS AND FOLLOW ME CANNOT BE MY DISCIPLE! IS IT NOT WRITTEN, IF ANY MAN COME TO ME AND LOVE FATHER OR MOTHER OR SPOUSE OR CHILDREN OR BROTHERS OR SISTERS, YEA, AND EVEN HIS OWN LIFE MORE THAN ME IS NOT WORTHY OF ME AND CANNOT BE MY DISCIPLE!!! IS IT NOT WRITTEN, HE THAT RECEIVES YOU RECEIVES ME? IS IT NOT WRITTEN, HE SCATTERS THE PROUD IN THE IMAGINATION OF THEIR HEARTS! IS IT NOT WRITTEN, HE PUTS DOWN THE MIGHTY FROM THEIR SEATS AND EXALTS THEM OF LOW DEGREE! IS IT NOT WRITTEN, HE THAT IS NOT WITH ME IS AGAINST ME AND HE THAT GATHERS NOT WITH ME SCATTERS ABROAD! IS IT NOT WRITTEN, THAT THIS IS A REBELLIOUS PEOPLE, LYING CHILDREN, CHILDREN THAT WILL NOT HEAR THE LAW OF THE LORD!!! WHICH SAY TO THE SEERS, SEE NOT! AND TO THE PROPHETS, PROPHESY NOT!!! IS IT NOT WRITTEN, I BESEECH YOU BRETHREN TO MARK THEM WHICH CAUSE DIVISIONS AND OFFENSES CONTRARY TO DOCTRINE AND TO AVOID THEM! FOR THEY THAT ARE SUCH SERVE NOT OUR LORD JESUS CHRIST, BUT THEIR OWN DESIRES AND BY GOOD WORDS AND FAIR SPEECHES DECEIVE THE HEARTS OF THE UNLEARNED! IS IT NOT WRITTEN, BRETHREN, I BESEECH YOU BY THE NAME OF THE LORD JESUS CHRIST THAT YOU ALL SPEAK THE SAME THING AND THAT THERE BE NO DIVISIONS AMONG YOU, BUT THAT YOU BE PERFECTLY JOINED TOGETHER IN THE SAME MIND AND IN THE SAME JUDGMENT!!! IS IT NOT WRITTEN, LET YOUR CONVERSATION BE AS IT BECOMES THE GOSPEL OF CHRIST, THAT YOU STAND FAST IN ONE SPIRIT WITH ONE MIND STRIVING TOGETHER FOR THE FAITH OF THE GOSPEL!!!

STRIVING TOGETHER FOR WHAT? FOR THE FAITH OF THE GOSPEL!!! NOT YOUR OWN POPULARITY!!!

IS IT NOT WRITTEN, THAT IS THE PURPOSE FOR THE FIVE-FOLD MINISTRY, ALL FIVE OFFICES, APOSTLES, PROPHETS, EVANGELISTS, PASTORS, TEACHERS??? DID I NOT SET THEM ALL IN THE BODY FOR THE PERFECTING OF THE SAINTS, FOR THE WORK OF THE MINISTRY, FOR THE EDIFYING OF THE BODY OF CHRIST? TILL YOU ALL COME TO THE UNITY OF THE FAITH AND OF THE KNOWLEDGE OF THE SON OF GOD UNTO A PERFECT MAN UNTO THE MEASURE OF THE STATURE OF THE FULLNESS OF CHRIST!!! HENCEFORTH, BE NO LONGER CHILDREN, TOSSED TO AND FRO BY THE SLEIGHT OF MEN AND CUNNING CRAFTINESS!!!!! BUT SPEAK THE TRUTH IN LOVE AND GROW UP INTO CHRIST IN ALL THINGS!!! HE IS THE HEAD!!! FROM WHOM THE WHOLE BODY IS FITLY JOINED TOGETHER AND COMPACTED BY THAT WHICH EVERY JOINT SUPPLIES! ACCORDING TO THE EFFECTIVE WORKING IN THE MEASURE OF EVERY OFFICE! MAKING INCREASE OF THE BODY, EDIFYING ITSELF IN LOVE! THIS I SAY, THEREFORE, THAT YOU HENCEFORTH WALK NOT AS OTHERS WALK, IN THE VANITY OF THEIR MINDS!!!!! BUT WALK IN MY SPIRIT! AND OBEY MY VOICE EACH DAY!!!!!

October 31, 2001

Spiritual Warfare

EVERY SPIRIT OF INSANITY, MURDER, FLAGRANCY, INORDINATE AFFECTION, LUST, PERVERSION, ALCOHOLISM, DRUG DEPENDENCY, PEDOPHILIA, PEDERASTY, LESBIANISM, INCEST, HOMOSEXUALITY, BESTIALITY, PORNOGRAPHY, SADISM, SATANISM, BLACK MAGIC, VOODOO, PRIDE, ARROGANCE, LYING, COVETOUSNESS, EMULATION, SORCERY, HUMAN SACRIFICES, CULTS, FORTUNE TELLING, WITCHCRAFT, THIEVERY, SEDITION, HERESY, HATRED, MALICE, ENVY, CARNALITY, BLASPHEMY, REBELLION, I BIND YOU NOW AND I BREAK YOUR DOMINIONS IN THE NAME OF JESUS CHRIST!!! I RENDER YOU NULL AND VOID!!!

I TEAR DOWN THE STRONGHOLDS OF PRIDE, PREJUDICE, RACISM, INFIDELITY, FORNICATION, ADULTERY, DIVORCE, COVENANT BREAKING, PANDERING, PROSTITUTION, ANTI-SEMITISM, INFANTICIDE, ABORTION, ASSISTED SUICIDE, GENOCIDE, EUTHANASIA, SLAVERY, RESPECT OF PERSONS, BIGOTRY, ISOLATIONISM, PATRICIDE, MATRICIDE, KIDNAPPING, RAPE, TORTURE, BRAIN-WASHING, DISMEMBERMENT, TREASON! COME OUT IN THE NAME OF JESUS!!! BE DELIVERED AND BE SET FREE FROM BONDAGE!!!!!

IN THE NAME OF JESUS WE SURRENDER TO GOD'S GUIDANCE AND DIRECTION! WE LISTEN FOR YOUR LEADING!!! WE ACCEPT OUR DUTY, OUR OBLIGATION TO PRAY WITHOUT CEASING AND TO FAST AND TO COME ASIDE AND TO WAIT UPON YOU!!! IN THE NAME OF JESUS, WE PROCLAIM VICTORY AND AUTHORITY OVER THE ENEMY OF OUR SOULS!!! SATAN, LOOSE YOUR HOLD OVER OUR NATION!!! WE TAKE AUTHORITY OVER YOUR STRONGHOLDS!!! WE BREAK THEM DOWN NOW!!! WE TEAR DOWN YOUR EVIL INFLUENCES OVER OUR GOVERNMENT, THE MEDIA, OUR HOMES AND OUR SCHOOLS AND OUR CHURCHES!!! WE BREAK YOUR DOMINION IN COMMERCE, IN OUR CIVIL LIBERTIES, OUR CULTURE, OUR HUMANITIES!!! WE DRIVE OUT

THE VICES, ALL SATAN'S DEVICES, LYING WONDERS, LUSTS AND PERVERSIONS!!!!!

October 22, 2001

Wisdom

A SIN IS WHAT YOU DO IN PLACE OF THE WILL OF GOD! A WEIGHT IS WHAT HINDERS YOU FROM INSTANTLY DOING GOD'S BIDDING. A WEIGHT IS WHAT YOU HAVE TO ATTEND TO, DO, OR MOVE OUT OF THE WAY BEFORE YOU CAN OBEY YOUR LORD!!! WHEN HE REALLY DOES BECOME YOUR MASTER, HE CALLS THE SHOTS, THE PRIORITIES, <u>AND</u> THE AGENDA!!!!!

October 2, 2001

DO YOU KNOW WHAT AMERICA MEANS? AMERICA MEANS: I <u>AM</u> 'ER I <u>CAN</u>! IT MEANS NEVER GIVE UP! IT MEANS FIGHT TO THE FINISH! IT MEANS TRUTH IS INDISPENSABLE AT <u>ANY</u> COST!!!

October 3, 2001

HE KNOWS THE HAIRS OF YOUR HEAD! HE KNOWS HOW MANY OF YOUR HAIRS FELL OUT THIS MORNING! AND YOU THINK IF HE KNOWS THE HAIRS OF YOUR HEAD, HAIRS THAT DIDN'T CAUSE YOU ANY PAIN, NO AGONY, THAT HE DOESN'T SEE <u>ALL</u> THESE BABIES BEING TORTURED BY SUCTIONING OUT THEIR BRAINS? BEING CHEMICALLY CREMATED!!! BREAKING THEIR LITTLE BONES AND CRUSHING THEIR SKULLS! HE IS ALMIGHTY GOD AND DON'T YOU FORGET IT!!! AND IF HE GIVES YOU SOME OF HIS MIGHT, HE WANTS YOU TO BE A GOOD STEWARD OF IT! NOT LORDING IT OVER OTHERS! NOT TAKING A HIGH SEAT AND DESIRING PREEMINENCE! HE'S THE ONLY PREMIER!!! I ADJURE YOU TO BEHOLD THE GLORY OF GOD AND TO OBEY THE GOD OF <u>ALL</u> GLORY!!!

October 13, 2001

Exhortation

HONOR TO WHOM HONOR IS DUE. CUSTOM TO WHOM CUSTOM IS DUE. TRIBUTE TO WHOM TRIBUTE IS DUE. I KEEP TELLING PEOPLE, THIS LIFE IS NOT SUPPOSED TO BE PERFECT! THAT IS WHY WE ARE STRIVING FOR ANOTHER ONE. HELL IS MEANT TO BE FELT ONCE IN A WHILE TO REMIND YOU TO BE SURE OF WHERE YOU DON'T WANT TO GO! 'CAUSE TROUBLE HERE IS ONLY A MINISCULE INFINITESIMAL TASTE OF TYRANNY IN THE LAKE OF FIRE ... NEVER EVER GETTING OUT OR EXPERIENCING RELIEF OR RESPITE! <u>FIGHT THE GOOD FIGHT OF FAITH!</u> LAY HOLD ON ETERNAL LIFE! PUT YOUR MONEY WHERE YOUR MOUTH IS! THAT IS WHAT FASTING INCORPORATES! MANDATES! IF YOU ARE NOT HUNGERING AND THIRSTING AFTER RIGHTEOUSNESS, YOU ARE IN DISOBEDIENCE! <u>HAPPY ARE YOU WHEN YOU ARE REPROACHED FOR THE NAME OF CHRIST FOR THE SPIRIT OF GLORY AND OF GOD RESTS UPON YOU! I Peter 4:14 DOES IT? IF THE SPIRIT OF GLORY AND OF GOD RESTS UPON YOU, YOU ARE EVEN TEMPERED, TENDERHEARTED AND HAVE LOVING-KINDNESS!</u> THE ONLY WAY TO BE HAPPY IF YOU ARE REPROACHED, IS TO BE DEAD!!! OR TO BE IN THE PROCESS OF CRUCIFYING THIS FLESH! Galatians 2:29, 5:19-26, 6:14 Romans 6:6 John 12:23-25 THE ONLY WAY TO STAY DEAD IS TO BE IN FASTINGS OFTEN.

FASTING GIVES PROPER PERSPECTIVE TO EVENTS, SITUATIONS, REPROACHES, PERSECUTIONS IN THE LIGHT OF THE GOSPEL. WHY ARE YOU HAPPY WHEN YOU ARE SUFFERING? BECAUSE THE SPIRIT OF GLORY AND OF GOD RESTS UPON YOU! ON THE PART OF BUSYBODIES, CRITICAL JUDGMENTAL PEOPLE, SAINTS AND SINNERS, HE, THE CHRIST IS EVIL SPOKEN OF, FOR THE HOLY ONE SAID, AS MUCH AS THEY DO IT UNTO THE LEAST OF THESE MY BRETHREN, THEY DO IT UNTO ME! Luke 17:1-4 SO IT IS WITH THE WITHHOLDING OF GOOD TO WHOM IT IS DUE, AS WELL AS, SPEAKING EVIL AND NOT RECEIVING THE GIFT OF GOD, THE VESSELS THAT GOD HAS SENT TO BLESS HIS PEOPLE. VERILY I SAY UNTO YOU, INASMUCH AS YOU DID IT NOT TO ONE OF THE

LEAST OF THESE YOU DID IT NOT UNTO ME! Matthew 25:40,45 HE
THAT RECEIVES YOU RECEIVES ME! Matthew 10:40 IT IS
IMPOSSIBLE BUT THAT OFFENCES WILL COME BUT WOE UNTO
HIM THROUGH WHOM OFFENCE COMES! Verses 2-4 (AND THERE IS
AN EXCLAMATION MARK IN THE HOLY WRIT!) IT WERE BETTER
FOR HIM THAT A MILLSTONE WERE HANGED ABOUT HIS NECK
AND HE CAST INTO THE SEA, THAN THAT HE SHOULD OFFEND
ONE OF MINE! Luke 17:1-4

BUT YOU NEED TO KNOW THAT EVERY TIME YOU THINK
SOMEONE IS OUT OF LINE THEY ARE NOT. SOMETIMES IT IS YOU
WHO ARE OUT OF LINE BECAUSE YOU DO NOT OBEY THE
SCRIPTURES. THE SCRIPTURES ARE CORRECT! LIKE IT OR LUMP
IT! EVEN AS IT IS WRITTEN CONCERNING WOMEN AND
CONCERNING THE MOVING OF THE SPIRIT THROUGH PROPHECY
AND THE PROPHETS! I Corinthians 14:38 IF ANY MAN BE IGNORANT
CONCERNING THESE THINGS, HE IS IGNORED OF GOD! SO SAYS
THE ORIGINAL GREEK. GOD IGNORES PEOPLE WHO DO NOT
RECEIVE HIS HOLY MEN AND WOMEN OF GOD AND HE
CONTINUES TO GO RIGHT ON USING THEM BECAUSE HE'S GOD.
EVEN AS HE HAS SAID, COVET TO PROPHESY! Verse 39 COVET
DOES NOT MEAN TO SET IT ASIDE AND TO SHUT IT UP!!! COVET
TO PROPHESY MEANS TO DESIRE, LONG FOR AND ASPIRE TO
PROPHESY!!! DESIRE IS A STRONG FEELING THAT IMPELS ONE TO
THE ATTAINMENT AND POSSESSION WHICH IS WITHIN REACH!
TO CRAVE: TO DESIRE INTENSELY, LONG FOR, TO ASK FOR
EARNESTLY, BEG, YEARN: STRONG TENDERNESS, ASPIRE: TO SEEK
AMBITIOUSLY, EAGERLY, ARDENTLY: GLOWING WITH FEELINGS,
PASSIONATE, FERVENT ZEAL! FERVENT: SHOWING GREAT
WARMTH AND EARNESTNESS OF FEELING. EARNEST: SERIOUS IN
INTENTION, PURPOSE, EFFORT, SINCERELY ZEALOUS WITHOUT
CRACKS, SERIOUS ATTENTION, STEADILY AND SOBERLY EAGER
IN PURSUING IT, FIRM, STABLE. SINCERE: GENUINENESS,
TRUSTWORTHY, RELIABLE, ABSENCE OF DECEIT: THE HABIT OR
PRACTICE OF INTENTIONALLY CONCEALING THE TRUTH OR
PERVERTING THE TRUTH, THUS MISLEADING: LEADING INTO
ERROR OF CONDUCT, THOUGHT, JUDGMENT, GUIDING

WRONGLY, LEADING ASTRAY, OR SUPERFICIALITY: SHALLOW, FRIVOLOUS. TO LEAD AWAY FROM PROPHECY WHEN IT IS WRITTEN TO COVET TO IT IS FALSE TEACHING!!! DESIRE EARNESTLY THE BEST GIFTS, *BUT RATHER* THAT YOU MAY PROPHECY! WHY? BECAUSE PROPHECY EDIFIES! AND IF GOD IS ALLOWED TO EDIFY YOU ENOUGH BY SPEAKING HIS LIFE GIVING WORDS TO YOU, YOU BECOME EMPOWERED TO DO WHATEVER IT IS THAT YOU NEED, DESIRE OR ARE SUPPOSED TO DO, EVEN THE IMPOSSIBLE WHICH HE SAID IS POSSIBLE WITH HIM!!!!! WITH HIS WORD! AND HIS SPIRIT! AND WITH HIS MIRACLE WORKING POWER OF THE GIFTS OF THE SPIRIT!!! LET'S JUST DO IT! IN THE FLOW! IN ALIGNMENT! UNDER THE AUTHORITY OF THE HOLY GHOST OF GOD! ZEAL ACCORDING TO KNOWLEDGE AND UNDERSTANDING! PROPER ORDER! CHECK YOUR SPIRIT! EVERY TIME YOU FEEL SOMETHING, IT AIN'T GOD! SOMETIMES IT'S YOUR FLESH WANTING TO BE NOTICED! SOMETIMES IT IS GOD, AND YOUR FLESH IS STILL WANTING TO BE NOTICED! GET THAT FILTHY FLESH UNDER SUBJECTION SO THAT THE GLORIOUS POWER OF ALMIGHTY GOD CAN BE MANIFESTED WITH CLARITY AND PURITY!!!!! EARNEST IMPLIES HAVING A PURPOSE AND BEING STEADILY AND SOBERLY EAGER IN PURPOSING IT. RESOLUTE ADDS MORE OF A QUALITY OF DETERMINATION, VERY DIFFICULT TO SWAY OR TURN ASIDE FROM THE PURPOSE. SERIOUS IMPLIES HAVING DEPTH AND A SOBERNESS OF ATTITUDE WHICH CONTRASTS WITH GAIETY AND FRIVOLITY.

WHY DOES GOD'S WORD TELL US TO DO SOMETHING THAT CHURCH HIERARCHY FROWNS UPON? WHY DOES CHURCH HIERARCHY FROWN UPON SOMETHING THAT GOD ALMIGHTY HAS SPOKEN FOR US TO DO????? IT'S CALLED DISOBEDIENCE. IT IS BETTER TO OBEY GOD THAN MAN. Acts 5:29 MAN SHALL NOT LIVE BY BREAD ALONE BUT BY <u>EVERY</u> WORD THAT PROCEEDS OUT OF THE MOUTH OF GOD! Matthew 4:4

October 5, 2001

November 2001

You Cannot Silence ... The Faith in Me.
For Oracles Speak ... While Cowards Flee.
If You Will Not ... Let Truth Be ...
The Martyr's Soul ... Shall Set It Free!

Part XIII

Keep
Ye Judgment
and
Do Justice

Therefore turn thou to thy god: Keep mercy and judgment, and wait on thy God continually.

Hosea Twelve and Six

Thus saith the Lord, Keep ye judgment and do justice: for my salvation is near to come and my righteousness to be revealed.

Isaiah Fifty-Six and One

Prophecy

GRACE, MY CHILD. YOU SHALL SEE MANY STRANGE THINGS IN THE DAYS AHEAD. BUT I WILL SUSTAIN YOU. I WILL BREAK DOWN THE WALLS THAT HAVE SEPARATED MY PEOPLE. I WILL BEGIN TO BRING TOGETHER THE RACES AND CAUSE MANY TO SEE THAT THERE IS JUST ONE CULTURE. THE CULTURE OF THE HUMAN RACE! MANY CUSTOMS, BUT ONLY ONE CULTURE. I AM GIVING YOU A SMATTERING OF MY PROGRAMS THAT I WANT IMPLEMENTED IN THESE LAST DAYS: GIFTS OF THE SPIRIT SCHOOL. A RELEASING OF THE PROPHETS. CASTING OUT DEVILS. DISCERNING OF SPIRITS. RELEASING PAST HURTS AND FORGIVENESS OF INJUSTICES.

November 2, 2001

TODAY IS A MIRACLE DAY. PREPARE TO GO.

November 3, 2001

YEA, I LOVE YOU, MY CHILD. YEA, I KNOW YOUR HEART! AND I SEE YOUR PAIN. I WILL SHOW YOU WHAT I WOULD HAVE YOU TO DO. I AM COUNSELING MANY NOW. I AM BRINGING SUBMISSION INTO THE HOUSE. I WAGE WAR AGAINST ALL DIVISION! THOSE WHO ARE SUPPLANTING I AM SEVERELY CHASTISING THEM! WHAT I HAVE CLEANSED CALL NOT THOU COMMON OR UNCLEAN! I SET MY HOUSE IN ORDER! TERMINAL CANCER IS COMING UPON SOME WHO SET ASIDE THOSE WHO I HAVE ANOINTED FOR MY GLORY AND FOR <u>MY</u> DOMINION! MY DOMINION! I AM RESCUING OTHERS WHO WILL SUBMIT TO MY JURISDICTION OF LOVE!!!

I SEE <u>ALL</u> DIVISION, <u>ALL</u> STRIFE, <u>ALL</u> JEALOUSIES AND I AM SETTING ASIDE NOW SOME WHO WERE SCHEDULED FOR PROMOTION! I WILL NO LONGER ALLOW EVIL TO TAINT MY SANCTUARY!!! SOME WILL BE KILLED INSIDE THE WALLS OF THE TABERNACLE FOR THEY HAVE DESECRATED MY CHURCH FOR

THEIR LAST TIME. DO NOT HARBOR OUTRAGE AGAINST ANYONE FOR JUDGMENT COMES FROM ME! NOT MAN. I AM GOD ALL BY MYSELF. I REFUSE TO ALLOW OTHERS TO TAINT MY HOLINESS AND MY DOMINION!

RELEASE THE PROPHETS!!! SOME WILL COME SOON FROM ANOTHER COUNTRY! I WILL BE MISALIGNED NO LONGER! PROPHETS ARE PART OF MY BODY! MY BODY WILL NO LONGER BE FRAGMENTED! I WILL SAY WHO SPEAKS AND WHO IS DENIED! NOT MAN! MAN IS NOT GOD! I AM!!!!!

I WILL HOLD BACK NO LONGER THOSE APPOINTED FOR DOMINION AND MIGHT. MY AUTHORITY IS THE LAST SAY! NOT MAN'S! PERPETUATE YOUR OWN AGENDA NO LONGER! STEP ASIDE INTO MY GLORY!!! MY POWER AND AUTHORITY! IT IS ALL WRITTEN IN THE HOLY SCRIPTURES! PREPARE FOR SPLENDOR AND GLORY! LET ME BE GOD IN MY SANCTUARY! I DO NOT HAVE RESPECT OF PERSONS! WHY DO YOU? DO YOU NOT FEAR THE JUDGMENTS OF THE ALMIGHTY? WILL YOU NOT RECEIVE, IT IS WRITTEN, "THE WHOLE BODY FITLY JOINED TOGETHER AND COMPACTED (CLOSELY AND FIRMLY UNITED, SOLID, MADE FIRM AND STABLE) BY WHAT? BY THAT WHICH *EVERY* JOINT SUPPLIES, ACCORDING TO THE EFFECTIVE WORKING IN THE MOVEMENT OF EVERY PART OF THE BODY! INCREASING THE EDIFICATION OF ITSELF BY LOVE!!!" "THE PROPHET THAT HATH MY WORD *LET* HIM SPEAK MY WORD FAITHFULLY!!! WHAT IS THE CHAFF TO THE WHEAT, SAITH THE LORD??? *LET* NO MAN GLORY IN MEN!!! IS CHRIST DIVIDED? WAS A MERE MAN CRUCIFIED FOR YOU? OR WERE YOU BAPTIZED IN THE NAME OF A MAN?" THERE ARE CONTENTIONS AMONG YOU, BUT I SAY UNTO YOU, SPEAK WHAT MY WORD SAYS, THAT YOU BE PERFECTLY JOINED TOGETHER IN THE SAME MIND AND IN THE SAME JUDGMENT! ALL THINGS ARE YOURS! AND YOU ARE CHRIST'S! AND CHRIST'S IS GOD'S! AND MY WORD IS ME!!!

November 5, 2001

Prophecy

MY PEOPLE WHICH ARE CALLED BY MY NAME ARE HUMBLING THEMSELVES AND I AM CALLING FORTH MY GLORY AND MY DOMINION!!! STAY FOCUSED IN WHAT I WOULD HAVE YOU TO DO SAITH THE LORD! I AM GIVING YOU A MANDATE! I AM CALLING YOU FORTH SAITH GOD! IT IS TO BE A DEMONSTRATION OF LOVE AND RACE CULMINATION. I AM BRINGING MY PEOPLES INTO ONENESS WITH ME AND WITH ONE ANOTHER!!! STAY FOCUSED!!! MEDITATE CONTINUOUSLY UPON MY MISSION! MY COMMISSION FOR YOU IS TO BRING UNITY INTO THE BODY, TO BRING FEARLESSNESS OF EXECUTION TO MY WILL AND DIVINE PURPOSE!!! MY PURPOSE FOR THE BODY OF CHRIST IS TO MEET THE NEEDS OF MY PEOPLE! TO BECOME ONE IN UNITY OF PURPOSE! BY THIS SHALL ALL MEN KNOW THAT YOU ARE MY DISCIPLES IF YOU HAVE LOVE ONE TO ANOTHER! TO ANOTHER! IF YOU REALLY HAVE MY LOVE, THE GOD KIND OF LOVE, IT WILL BURST FORTH ONE TO ANOTHER!!! THE ENEMIES OF THE CROSS DO NOT PORTRAY LOVE ONE TO ANOTHER!!! GOD IS LOVE!!! IF LOVE IS NOT FLOWING ONE TO ANOTHER THROUGHOUT THE WHOLE BODY, MY BODY, MY CHURCH, I CANNOT DO MY MIGHTY ACTS IN ALL THEIR FULLNESS!!!

TRUE FAITH WORKS BY LOVE! BUT WHERE THERE IS ENVY AND STRIFE THERE IS CONFUSION AND EVERY EVIL WORK!!! IF YOU HAVE STRIFE IN YOUR HEART OR ENVY, DO NOT GLORY IN ME AND PRAISE MY HOLY NAME! DO NOT LIE AGAINST TRUTH!!! DO NOT SPEAK EVIL ONE OF ANOTHER!!! WHEN YOU SPEAK EVIL, DOUBT, UNKINDNESS AGAINST YOUR BROTHER OR SISTER AND JUDGE THEM YOU ARE SPEAKING EVIL OF THE LAW AND JUDGING THE LAW! THERE IS ONE LAWGIVER WHO IS ABLE TO SAVE AND TO DESTROY! WHO ARE YOU TO JUDGE ANOTHER? WHO IS WISE AMONG YOU AND ENDUED WITH KNOWLEDGE? LET HIM SHOW OUT OF A GOOD CONVERSATION HIS WORKS WITH MEEKNESS OF WISDOM!!! THEREFORE, BLESS YOU GOD, EVEN THE FATHER AND THEN CURSE YOU MEN, WHO ARE MADE

IN THE IMAGE OF GOD? THESE THINGS OUGHT NOT TO BE! I PUT
DOWN ONE AND SET UP ANOTHER!

I <u>KNOW</u> THE HEARTS OF MEN!!! I <u>SEE</u> EVERY MOTIVE! I <u>HEAR</u>
EVERY WORD SPOKEN IN THE HEART! I <u>KNOW</u> EVERY THOUGHT!
I <u>KNOW</u> THE REASONING FOR EVERY ACTION TAKEN! MAN
LOOKS ON THE OUTSIDE AND THE PAST! I KNOW THE <u>DAILY</u>
HEART CRIES AND THE VERY DESIRES OF THE INNERMOST BEING!
I CANNOT BE FOOLED, GAINSAYED, <u>OR</u> CONFUSED! WHAT I HAVE
CLEANSED CALL NOT COMMON OR UNWORTHY! CRUCIFY YOUR
FLESHLY THOUGHTS AND JUDGMENTS! CARNAL MINDS DO NOT
<u>DISCERN</u> THE MOVING OF MY SPIRIT! THINGS OF THE SPIRIT ARE
SPIRITUALLY DISCERNED! KEEP YOUR IDEAS AND OPINIONS TO
YOURSELF! BETTER YET GET THEM SANCTIFIED!!! <u>IF</u> ANYONE
SPEAKS, <u>LET</u> THEM SPEAK AS THE ORACLE OF GOD! IF YOU DO
NOT HAVE THE MIND OF CHRIST, CEASE YOUR CHATTER AND
VAIN JANGLING AND CONDEMNATION! I <u>AM</u> THE JUDGE! HE
THAT IS SPIRITUAL JUDGES ALL THINGS BUT THE NATURAL MAN
DOES NOT RECEIVE THE THINGS OF GOD BECAUSE THEY ARE
SPIRITUALLY DISCERNED. THE HOLY GHOST TEACHES,
COMPARING SPIRITUAL THINGS WITH SPIRITUAL, NOT IN THE
WORDS WHICH MAN'S WISDOM TEACHES! RECEIVE THE SPIRIT
WHICH IS OF GOD, NOT THE SPIRIT OF THE WORLD, THAT YOU
MAY KNOW THE THINGS THAT GOD GIVES!!!

THE FOOLISHNESS OF GOD IS WISER THAN MEN AND THE
WEAKNESS OF GOD IS STRONGER THAN MEN! UNDERSTAND
YOUR CALLING, CHURCH, HOW THAT NOT MANY WISE MEN
AFTER THE FLESH AND NOT MANY MIGHTY, NOT MANY NOBLE
ARE CALLED, BUT I HAVE CHOSEN THE FOOLISH THINGS TO
<u>CONFOUND</u> THE WISE! I HAVE CHOSEN THE THINGS WHICH ARE
OF LOW ESTEEM AND THINGS WHICH ARE DESPISED, YEA, AND
THINGS WHICH ARE NOT, TO BRING TO NOTHING THINGS THAT
ARE: <u>THAT NO FLESH (NOT ANY) SHOULD GLORY!!!!!</u> HE THAT
GLORIES, LET HIM GLORY IN ME ALONE!!! <u>THAT YOUR FAITH</u>

STAND NOT IN THE WISDOM OF MEN, BUT IN THE POWER OF GOD!!! IN THE DEMONSTRATION OF MY SPIRIT AND MY POWER!!!

November 9, 2001

Prophecy

*I AM GIVING THEM THEIR MARCHING ORDERS. MARCH IN LINE TO
MY WILL AND TO MY WORD OR BREAK RANKS AND STEP ASIDE
UNTIL YOU ARE READY TO KEEP IN STEP, IN LINE WITH <u>MY</u> ORDERS
AND <u>ALL</u> MY COMMANDMENTS. I DO NOT CHANGE MY WORD TO
ACCOMMODATE YOUR WEAKNESSES. SPEAK PEACE AND ENSUE IT.
CLEANSE YOUR HANDS, YOU SINNERS AND PURIFY YOUR HEARTS
YOU DOUBLE-MINDED. I DO NOT ESTABLISH ORDERS TO
ACCOMMODATE YOUR PERSONALITY. IF YOU ARE <u>FULLY</u>
SUBMITTED UNTO ME AND TO <u>MY</u> WORD, YOU ARE TAKING,
PUTTING ON <u>MY</u> PERSON. <u>MY</u> PERSONALITY. WHEN MY
PERSONALITY IS IN CHARGE IT GETS THE JOB DONE!* DO NOT BE
DECEIVED BY HOW GREATLY I HAVE USED YOU IN TIMES PAST.
PEOPLE DO NOT GET TO HEAVEN BY HOW GREATLY I HAVE USED
THEM IN THE GIFTS OF THE SPIRIT OR ANOINTED PREACHING.
THEY GET TO HEAVEN BY ABIDING IN MY WORD, OBEYING IT
EVERY DAY AND WALKING EACH DAY IN MY SPIRIT!!! WHEN YOU
DO THIS DAILY, YOU DO NOT OPERATE IN THE FLESH, THE
CARNAL NATURE. I DO NOT BEHAVE UNSEEMLY, RUDELY, IN
OBSTINACY, REBELLION, STRIFE AND ENVY. I DO NOT SPEAK
EXCEPT BY THE SPIRIT OF GOD. IS IT NOT WRITTEN, DEATH AND
LIFE ARE IN THE POWER OF THE TONGUE? IS IT NOT WRITTEN,
THE TONGUE IS A FIRE, A WORLD OF INIQUITY, DEFILING THE
WHOLE BODY AND SETTING ON FIRE THE NATURE OF MAN! IT IS
SET ON FIRE OF HELL, FULL OF DEADLY POISON! YOU PUT BITS IN
THE HORSES' MOUTHS SO THAT THEY WILL OBEY. WILL YOU NOT
ALLOW THE HOLY SPIRIT TO BE YOUR BRIDLE? IS IT NOT
WRITTEN, HE THAT PUTS A BRIDLE ON HIS TONGUE, REFUSING
TO OFFEND IN WORDS IS THE SAME AS A <u>PERFECT</u> MAN ABLE
ALSO TO BRIDLE THE WHOLE BODY? IS IT NOT WRITTEN, TO BE
QUICK TO HEAR AND SLOW TO SPEAK AND SLOW TO WRATH?
FOR WHAT PURPOSE DOES THIS SERVE? AS IT WRITTEN, HE
BEGAT US WITH THE WORD OF TRUTH SO THAT WE COULD BE
<u>FIRST</u> FRUITS OF HIS CREATURES! <u>IF</u> ANY MAN WILL FULFILL THE
ROYAL LAW OF CHRIST, TO LOVE THE LORD WITH <u>ALL</u> YOUR
HEART AND <u>ALL</u> YOUR SOUL AND <u>ALL</u> YOUR MIND AND <u>ALL</u>

YOUR STRENGTH AND LOVE YOUR NEIGHBOR AS YOURSELF, YOU WILL <u>HOLD YOUR PEACE</u> AND <u>LET THE LORD GOD ALMIGHTY FIGHT YOUR BATTLES</u>! AS IT IS WRITTEN, <u>THE BATTLE IS NOT YOURS BUT THE LORD'S</u>! REFRAIN YOUR LIPS FROM SPEAKING GUILE AND YOUR TONGUE FROM EVIL! FOR BY YOUR WORDS YOU SHALL BE JUSTIFIED AND BY YOUR WORDS YOU SHALL BE CONDEMNED!!! LET NONE OF YOU SUFFER AS AN EVILDOER OR AS A BUSYBODY IN OTHER MEN'S MATTERS! FOR THE TIME IS COME THAT JUDGMENT MUST BEGIN AT THE HOUSE OF GOD!!!

November 12, 2001

Prophecy

GET UP AND BIND THE STRONG MAN THAT HAS HELD CAPTIVE MY AUTHORITIES AND DOMINIONS AND MIGHTS! STABILIZE MY PROPHETS AND PRIESTS. REFUSE TO ALLOW FLESH TO DOMINATE AND DISGUISE THE TRUTH. ALLOW NO ONE TO IMPEDE MY PROMINENCE AND MY SPLENDOR! GLORY IS TO COME FROM <u>MY</u> THRONE ALONE, NOT MAN'S. HAGGLE NO LONGER. USE THE DOMINION THAT I HAVE GIVEN YOU! SPEAK CORRECTION TO THE PULPIT AND RELEASE JUDGMENTS SAITH THE LORD! SPEAK CORRECTION TO THE PRAISERS OF MEN. <u>MY PRAISE IS TO BE THE FRUIT OF THE LIPS WITH UPLIFTED HANDS!</u> WITHOUT <u>HOLINESS</u> NO MAN SHALL SEE THE LORD!

I HAVE OPENED A GREAT DOOR FOR YOU, MY CHILD. I HAVE GIVEN YOU MANY SOULS. NO ONE CONDEMNS YOU WITHOUT CONDEMNING ME. I WILL SOON TAKE VENGEANCE ON THE SCORNERS. THE SCOFFERS AND REJECTERS OF MY MANDATES!!!!! AND MY PROVISIONS! I HAVE SPOKEN AND NOT ONE WORD OF MY PROVISION SHALL RETURN UNTO ME VOID!!! I AM NOW ESTABLISHING ALL CIRCUITRIES WITH ALL POSITIONS OF MY MINISTRIES IN PLACE FOR DOMINIONS AND MIGHTS AND AUTHORITIES! NO COUNSEL SHALL STAND AGAINST TRUTH! MY TRUTH SHALL PREVAIL IN THE FACE OF ALL! ALL OPPOSITIONS! MAN SHALL NO LONGER STOP THE DISPLAY AND DEMONSTRATION OF ALL OF MY GLORY! I SHALL BEGIN TO REMOVE PEOPLE BY DEATH BECAUSE THEY REFUSE TO ACCEPT MY MAJESTIES AND MY DOMINIONS!!! MY AUTHORITIES SHALL PREVAIL IN THE MIDST OF TURMOILS AND GRIEFS!!!!! I SHALL NO LONGER STAND BY AND ALLOW MAN WORSHIP AND DOMINION BUT I SHALL GIVE TO MY PEOPLE OF INTEGRITY THEIR PROPER PLACES FOR THE FULFILLMENT OF THEIR DUTIES AND PURPOSES!!! SOME SHALL NOT BE ABLE TO STAND, SOME BECAUSE OF DEATH AND SOME BECAUSE OF MY GLORY! FOR MY MIGHT SHALL BE DISPLAYED IN THE SANCTUARIES!!! SOME SHALL FALL AND NOT RISE! SOME WILL BE TAKEN OUT BEFORE THEIR EXPECTED TIME. THOSE WHO REFUSE TO ALLOW MY

PROPHETS AND MY APOSTLES TO PERFORM THEIR PURPOSES SHALL BE REMOVED!

November 13, 2001

Prophecy

YEA, I AM GIVING YOU MANY SOULS. I DO SEE ALL THE
OBSTACLES THAT HAVE STOOD IN YOUR WAY. I KNOW ALL THE
SACRIFICES. I WILL NOT LET ANYTHING HINDER THE END RESULT.
I AM GOING TO GIVE YOU A MIGHTY MIRACLE VERY SHORTLY.
STAY CONSECRATED. REAP THE HARVEST. YOUR LABORS ARE
NOT IN VAIN. I LOVE YOU, MY CHILD. STAY FOCUSED AND BE LED
BY MY HOLY SPIRIT AS YOU HAVE BEEN DOING. YOUR CHILDREN
ARE MINE AND ALSO YOUR GRANDCHILDREN. I AM WELL
PLEASED SAITH THE LORD. BE AT PEACE.

November 20, 2001

I SAY UNTO THEE, IT IS NOT MY WILL FOR YOU TO WORRY ABOUT
YOUR SON AT ALL FOR SURELY HE IS MINE!

November 22, 2001

I SAY UNTO THEE, MY CHILD, I HEAR YOUR CRIES FOR YOUR SONS
AND FOR YOUR DAUGHTERS. FOR ALL YOUR CHILDREN AND
YOUR GRANDCHILDREN. I KNOW ALL THE SPECIAL THINGS YOU
HAVE DONE AND ALL THE THINGS THAT YOU WANTED TO DO
FOR THEM. I SEE THE TIMES YOU WERE EXHAUSTED AND YOU
PRESSED ON TO TRY TO PLEASE. I KNOW ALL THE FAILURES YOU
HAVE EXPERIENCED IN THE EYES OF OTHERS. BUT I TOUCH EVEN
NOW HEARTS THAT RIDICULE AND SET ASIDE MY ANOINTED. I
WILL NOT ALLOW THE BLUDGEONING OF MY WORD.

I WILL CALL TO REPENTANCE THOSE WHO JUSTIFY GREED AND
GAIN AS GODLINESS. THE HOLINESS OF MY WILL AND MY WORD
IS WHAT IS GODLY. PERFECTION COMES THROUGH THE POWER
OF SUBMITTING ONE'S LIFE TO MY PRIORITIES ... WHETHER IN
BUSINESS, FINANCE, THE CLERGY OR THE HOMEMAKER. I DO
NOT EVALUATE ONE'S WORTH BY HOW BIG THEIR BANK
ACCOUNTS ARE OR THEIR STOCK PORTFOLIO. I GAUGE ONE'S
GREATNESS BY THEIR SUBMISSION TO MY AUTHORITY AND MY

PURPOSE FOR THEIR LIFE'S WORK WHETHER IT BE ON THE MISSION FIELD OR IN A KINDERGARTEN CLASS. PURPOSE IS DETERMINED BY ATTITUDE. STOCKS AND BONDS MAY DETERMINE THE SIZE OF MONEY ACCOUNTS WHICH ARE EVER CHANGING AND TEMPORAL, BUT FULFILLMENT OF DESTINY OF PURPOSE IS WHAT TRULY IS ETERNAL. STRIVE TO ENTER IN AT THE STRAIT GATE, FOR I TESTIFY TO YOU TRULY THAT MANY SHALL SEEK TO ENTER IN AND WILL NOT BE ABLE!!!

November 23, 2001

Prophecy

SPEAK, MY CHILD! SPEAK! GRAVE, GRAVE DESTRUCTIONS. GRAVE, GRAVE DESTRUCTIONS IN THE CAPITOL. DEATH IS IMMINENT.

YOU ARE UNDER MY UMBRELLA, MY JURISDICTION. I LEAD YOU BY MY EYE. I AM GUIDING YOU. HEED TO MY CALL. LET NOTHING HINDER YOU. MY GRACE ALLOWS YOU TO ENDURE ALL THINGS. MY GRACE ALLOWS YOU TO BELIEVE ALL THINGS. MY GRACE ALLOWS YOU TO FLEE THE WRATH WHICH IS TO COME, BY TOTALLY SURRENDERING TOTALLY UNTO ME, TO OBEY ALL MY PRECEPTS AND MY COMMANDMENTS. I AM COMING SOONER THAN MOST PEOPLE BELIEVE. I WILL NOT RECEIVE UNTO MY SELF THOSE WHO REFUSE TO OBEY MY WORDS. THOSE WHO KNOWINGLY THWART MY WILL AND REFUSE TO BE LED BY MY SPIRIT.

MY WORDS ARE SPIRIT AND THEY ARE LIFE! WITHOUT TAKING THE TIME TO STUDY MY WORD AND TO BE LED BY MY SPIRIT, YOU WALK IN DEATH AND DEGRADATION. I WILL SPEAK CORRECTION THIS ONE LAST TIME BEFORE MANY ARE TURNED OVER TO SATAN'S DEVICES TO BELIEVE A LIE AND BE DAMNED. DO NOT ALLOW YOUR CONSCIENCE TO BE SEARED BY SATAN'S LIES.

THE WORD OF GOD IS THE RULE BOOK FOR ETERNAL LIFE. IF YOU REFUSE TO ABIDE IN IT AND TO LET MY WORDS LIVE IN YOU, YOU ARE ACCEPTING ETERNAL DAMNATION AS YOUR ETERNAL HABITATION, WHERE THE PAIN NEVER DIES AND THE FIRE IS NEVER QUENCHED. YOUR TORMENT LASTS FOREVER. WHY DO YOU THINK I CONTINUALLY WARN THE PEOPLE BY SENDING MY SERVANTS TO TELL YOU OVER AND OVER AND OVER AGAIN, FLEE THE WRATH WHICH IS TO COME!!! IT IS NO FAIRY TALE! IT IS A BEST SELLER!!! AND IT IS THE EVERLASTING TRUTH FROM THE THRONE OF GOD!

November 28, 2001

Deliverance

I BREAK THE CHAINS THAT BIND YOU! I FREE YOU NOW FROM YOUR HOMO-SEXUALITIES, FROM YOUR ADULTERIES, FROM YOUR FORNICATIONS, FROM YOUR DRUNKENNESS, FROM YOUR CRACK AND COCAINE, FROM YOUR ECSTASY AND LSD, FROM YOUR SPEED AND MARIJUANA, FROM YOUR NICOTINE AND REBELLION, FROM HEROIN, FROM GAMBLING, AND FROM EVERY OTHER EVIL ADDICTION, FROM PRESCRIPTION DRUGS, FROM GLUE SNIFFING AND EVERY OTHER FAD HIGH! I TAKE AUTHORITY OVER THE GAMBLING CAPITOLS AND I ABOLISH THE SLAVE TRADE! SEX FOR HIRE, I CURSE YOU TO THE ROOTS! YOU EVIL SPIRIT OF CONCUPISCENCE, I BREAK YOUR DOMINION! PORN QUEENS AND KINGS, I CURSE YOUR DIABOLICAL INSIDIOUSNESS TO THE ROOTS! SELF-INDULGENT THIEVERY, BE LOOSED FROM YOUR LUCRATIVE LYING LECHERY! AMERICA, BE SET FREE FROM YOUR BONDAGES OF LIQUOR AND LIES AND SEX ADDICTIONS! I CURSE TO THE VERY ROOTS <u>ALL</u> SEX PERVERSIONS AND HOUSES OF PROSTITUTION!!! BE SET FREE FROM THE LIES OF THE WICKED ONE! BE MADE WHOLE IN YOUR MIND AND IN YOUR WILL AND IN YOUR EMOTIONS!!! I SUBDUE SELF-WILL, PRIDE, ANGER, BITTERNESS, UN-FORGIVENESS, SEXUAL ABUSE, VERBAL ABUSE, EMOTIONAL ABUSE, GANG RAPE AND MOLESTATION! I BREAK THE STONY HEARTS OF HARDHEARTED KILLERS AND ABUSERS! BE LOOSED FROM YOUR MENTAL DECAY! BE SET FREE FROM ATROCITIES AND MURDER FOR HIRE!!! I BREAK THE <u>CHAINS</u> OF <u>ALL</u> EVIL CRACK HEADS AND PERVERSIONS OF SOCIETY! STAY LOOSED BY SUBMITTING YOURSELF TO THE AUTHORITY OF MY WORD! I AM GOD! DO NOT BE DECEIVED AS MANY ARE, THAT ARE BURNING IN HELL AT THIS MOMENT!

THE MOMENT YOU DIE YOU WILL BE IN TORMENT OR TREASURE. DO NOT BE SO FOOLISH AS TO THINK YOU CAN ESCAPE THE RIGHTEOUSNESS OF GOD. THAT IS WHY I SEND MY SERVANTS TO WARN THE PEOPLE DAY AND NIGHT! TO ESCAPE THE TORMENTS OF ETERNAL DEATH! IT NEVER STOPS! DO NOT BE DECEIVED, BUT OPEN YOUR HEART TO KNOW THE TRUTH FOR

THE TRUTH WILL MAKE YOU FREE WHEN YOU ACCEPT IT WITH <u>ALL</u> YOUR HEART!

I LOOK AT THE HEART OF MAN. THAT IS WHY I DIED ON THE TREE ... TO SET YOU FREE FROM THE FORCES OF EVIL THAT HAVE HELD YOU IN BONDAGE! COME OUT OF THE CAGE NOW INTO THE FREEDOM OF THE GLORIOUS LIGHT OF THE GOSPEL! IT IS GLORY UNSPEAKABLE, FULL OF GLORY AND THE HALF HAS NEVER YET BEEN TOLD! I AM GLORY AND HONOR AND PRAISE. AND MY MAGNIFICENCE FILLS YOU UP TO OVERFLOWING! AND YOU WALK IN THE LIGHT AND DO NOT TREMBLE AT THE DARKNESS BECAUSE YOU KNOW THAT I KEEP YOU!!! AND LET ME TELL YOU, IF YOU HAVE NEVER BEEN KEPT BY A KING, A TRUE SOVEREIGN, YOU DO NOT KNOW THE FULL MEANING OF BEING KEPT! THE RAPTURE OF MY DOMINION, THE MAGNIFICENCE OF MY PROVISION AND PEACE AND PRESENCE AND POWER AND PRAISE AND ... AND I FILL YOU AND I THRILL YOU DAY AND NIGHT! I AM NOT AS AN EARTHLY LOVER WHO MUST REST TO RECOVER HIS VIGOR AND PROWESS. I STAY IN YOU FROM MORNING TILL NIGHT, COURSING THROUGH YOU TO KEEP YOU ALIVE WITH MY GLORY AND POWER AND ENERGY AND LOVE MAKING!

<u>I AM THE MAN</u>! MY POWER INVIGORATES YOUR WOMB TO COME ALIVE AND TO PRODUCE CHILDREN AFTER MY KIND! ONES WHO KNOW WHO THEY ARE! <u>MY</u> KIND! WHO DO NOT TRY TO BE SOMETHING ELSE. WHO DO NOT TAKE FALSE PRIDE IN BOASTING IN WHAT THEY HAVE MADE OF THEMSELVES. BUT WHO ALLOW ME TO BE BIG INSIDE OF THEM THUS RELEASING UNENDING VICTORY, SUCCESS AND SATISFACTION! COME ON, YOU FOOLISH ONES! QUIT TRYING TO BE THE KING AND QUEEN OF JOCK AND LET THE REAL JOCK PUT HIS SEED INTO YOUR OPEN SOUL!!! IT THRILLS. AND CHILLS. AND GOSPEL FILLS. AND THIS HIGH DON'T COME DOWN. IT JUST KEEPS GETTING BETTER. NOT BITTER. BETTER. HOLINESS IS AN ANCHOR. AN ANCHOR OF THE HEART OF GOD. HOLINESS MEANS TO HOUSE THE HEART OF GOD! HIS TEMPLE YOU ARE!

If Christ expressing his intimacy to His Bride, the Church, is too much for the carnal mind, please read THE SONG OF SOLOMON in the HOLY BIBLE. It is a Spiritual Allegory, representing the holy affections existing between God and his chosen People, and Christ and His Church. It is an Oriental Poem, the ardent expressions of which can only be properly interpreted by a mature spiritual mind. The Jewish interpretation represented the poem as setting forth Jehovah's love for Israel. To the Christian, it represents Christ's love for His Church. Furthermore, both the Old and New Testament set forth the Lord's relation to His people by the figure of marriage! Isaiah 54:5 Hosea 2:19-23 Romans 7:4 II Corinthians 11:2 Ephesians 5:21-33 Revelation 19:5-9

November 28, 2001

Discerning of Spirits

IF GOD ISN'T <u>BIG</u> ENOUGH, ACTUALLY, YOU ARE NOT SMALL ENOUGH TO <u>LET</u> HIM BE BIG IN YOU! IF YOU ARE NOT SMALL ENOUGH TO LET HIM BE BIG ENOUGH TO ERADICATE ALL YOUR FEARS OF THE PAST, ACCIDENTS, HORRORS, HELLS AND WOES, YOU ARE NOT GETTING SMALL ENOUGH YET! <u>YOU MUST DECREASE SO THAT HE CAN INCREASE</u>!

MOST OF OUR PERCEPTION IS BUILT UPON HOW MUCH WE FEEL GOD LOVES US. FEAR IS A DEFICIENCY OF LOVE SOMEWHERE. YOU HAVE NOT BEEN FEEDING YOUR FAITH IN THAT AREA! FAILURE IS TO FAIL IN BEING CONSISTENT. THE WORD OF GOD WORKS ~ EVEN IN THE MOST DIFFICULT OF CIRCUMSTANCES! WE HAVE TO SPEAK IT, WORK IT, AFFIRM IT TO OUR SPIRIT IN ORDER TO DRIVE OUT FEAR!!!

November 12, 2001

REBELLION IS A SIGN OF WEAKNESS!!! ADMITTING TO THOSE THAT CARE: THAT YOU DON'T CARE! THAT WHAT YOU FEEL TO BE IMPORTANT IS NOT THE SAME. AND THAT WHAT OTHERS ESTEEM TO BE IMPORTANT IS NOT REALLY VALID TO YOU. ESTEEMING YOURSELF BETTER THAN OTHERS, RATHER THAN THE BIBLICAL RESPONSE OF ESTEEMING OTHERS BETTER THAN YOURSELF! TRUE HUMILITY IS TO DEFER TO OTHERS! TRUTH WILL BE MANIFESTED FOR THE SAKE OF TRUTH. BUT BIBLE DEFERENCE IS TO BE THE GUIDELINE FOR INTERACTION. EVEN AS IN THE COURT OF LAW, INNOCENCE IS TO BE RELEGATED UNTIL PROVEN OTHERWISE. COMPASSION FOR ALL IS THE TRUE MARK OF CHRISTIANITY. NOT TRIBALISM OR SECTARIANISM. GOD IS NOT BIGOTED. THE LAST WORD WILL BE HIS. NOT MAN'S!

November 16, 2001

Prophetic Teaching

WHY DO YOU THINK IT IS WRITTEN, FOR THIS CAUSE SHALL A MAN LEAVE HIS FATHER AND MOTHER AND SHALL BE JOINED TO A WIFE AND THEY TWO SHALL BE ONE FLESH? THIS IS A GREAT MYSTERY: BUT I SPEAK CONCERNING CHRIST AND THE CHURCH! AS A MAN AND WOMAN BECOME ONE FLESH IN HOLY MATRIMONY, PLEASING AND FULFILLING ONE ANOTHER IN THE MARRIAGE BED. WHEN YOU SUBMIT YOURSELF UNTO ME, TO BECOME ONE WITH ME, I TAKE UP MY RESIDENCE IN YOU, CONTINUING TO THRILL YOU AND FULFILL YOU WITH MY PEACE, MY JOY, MY DELIGHT, MY PROVISION, MY SATISFACTION! ALL THAT I HAVE IS YOURS! EVEN AS IT IS WRITTEN IN THE SONG OF SOLOMON, A SPIRITUAL ALLEGORY, REPRESENTING THE HOLY AFFECTIONS BETWEEN GOD AND HIS CHOSEN PEOPLE, CHRIST AND HIS CHURCH. THE AMOROUS LANGUAGE BRINGS HEIGHTENED AWARENESS OF THE PROPOSED INTIMACY THAT CHRIST SEEKS WITH THE CHURCH. FOR WHEN YOU BECOME ONE FLESH TRULY IN THE ATTRIBUTES OF HONORABLE MARRIAGE, THE DISPLAY IS TO PORTRAY THE CHURCH OF THE LORD JESUS CHRIST, TO BE THE EXAMPLE OF MAN LAYING DOWN HIS LIFE FOR HIS WIFE AND GIVING HIMSELF FOR HER, EVEN AS CHRIST ALSO LOVED THE CHURCH AND GAVE HIMSELF FOR IT EVEN TO THE DEATH ON THE CROSS! AND WIVES SUBMIT YOURSELVES UNTO YOUR OWN HUSBANDS, EVEN AS UNTO THE LORD, FOR THE HUSBAND IS THE HEAD OF THE WIFE, EVEN AS CHRIST IS THE HEAD OF THE CHURCH: AND HE IS THE SAVIOR OF THE BODY! THEREFORE AS THE CHURCH IS SUBJECT UNTO CHRIST SO LET THE WIVES BE SUBJECT TO THEIR OWN HUSBANDS IN EVERYTHING!!! Ephesians Five

WHY DOES THE LORD SAY, HUSBANDS, LOVE YOUR WIVES AS CHRIST LOVED THE CHURCH AND GAVE HIMSELF FOR IT? WHY DID CHRIST LOVE THE CHURCH ENOUGH TO DIE FOR IT? SO THAT HE MIGHT <u>SANCTIFY</u> IT AND <u>CLEANSE</u> IT! SO OUGHT MEN TO LOVE THEIR WIVES AS THEIR OWN BODIES! HE THAT LOVES HIS WIFE, LOVES HIMSELF. WE ARE MEMBERS OF <u>HIS</u> BODY, OF <u>HIS</u>

FLESH AND OF <u>HIS</u> BONES. FIRST NATURAL. THEN SPIRITUAL. <u>LET</u> EVERYONE OF YOU SO <u>LOVE</u> HIS WIFE EVEN AS HIMSELF AND THE WIFE SEE THAT SHE <u>REVERENCE</u> HER HUSBAND. IN SO DOING THE PORTRAYAL OF CHRIST'S CHURCH IS MADE VISIBLE TO THE WORLD. AND HUMANITY IS GIVEN INSIGHT INTO CONCEIVING A RELATIONSHIP WITH THE GOD OF SUCH STABILITY AND HARMONY.

TO NOURISH AND CHERISH YOUR WIFE AS YOUR OWN BODY IS TO LOVE YOUR WIFE AS CHRIST LOVES THE CHURCH. SUBMITTING YOURSELVES ONE TO ANOTHER IN THE FEAR OF THE LORD! YOU WIVES, BE IN SUBJECTION TO YOUR OWN HUSBANDS THAT IF ANY OBEY NOT THE WORD, THEY MAY BE WON BY THE CONVERSATION, ATTITUDES AND THE GODLY SUBMISSION TO BIBLICAL AUTHORITY. WHILE THEY BEHOLD YOUR GENTLE CONVERSATION THAT SHOWS PATIENCE, KINDNESS AND TENDERNESS COUPLED WITH THE FEAR OF THE LORD! WHOSE ADORNING, LET IT NOT BE THE OUTWARD SHOW, BUT LET IT BE THE INWARD ADORNING OF THE HEART, IN GRACIOUSNESS AND THANKSGIVING, THE ORNAMENT OF A MEEK AND QUIET SPIRIT, WHICH IS IN THE SIGHT OF THE GOD OF GREAT PRICE! FOR AFTER THIS MANNER IN TIMES PAST, THE HOLY WOMEN WHO TRUSTED IN GOD ADORNED THEMSELVES, BEING IN SUBJECTION UNTO THEIR OWN HUSBANDS.

LIKEWISE, YOU HUSBANDS, LIVE WITH THEM ACCORDING TO <u>KNOWLEDGE</u> (WHAT PLEASES AND BLESSES AND CHERISHES <u>THEM</u>) GIVING <u>HONOR</u> UNTO YOUR WIVES, AS BEING HEIRS TOGETHER OF THE GRACE OF LIFE, THAT YOUR PRAYERS BE NOT HINDERED. YEA, ALL OF YOU HAVE <u>COMPASSION</u> WITH ONE ANOTHER, LOVING EACH OTHER AS YOU WOULD A BELOVED BROTHER OR SISTER! BE <u>EMPATHETIC</u> TO ONE ANOTHER, UNDERSTANDING EACH OTHER'S THOUGHTS AND FEELINGS. BE <u>CONSIDERATE</u>! BE <u>POLITE</u>! YES, TO SPOUSES AND FAMILY MEMBERS, TO ALL AS YOU ARE TO OTHERS NOT IN YOUR INNER CIRCLE. MARKED BY GOOD MANNERS, <u>TACTFUL</u> BEHAVIOR, <u>CIVIL</u>, <u>GENTLE</u> MINDFUL OF THE NEEDS AND FEELINGS OF YOUR LOVED

ONES. I Peter 3 BE <u>KINDLY</u> AFFECTIONED ONE TO ANOTHER WITH BROTHERLY LOVE IN HONOR PREFERRING ONE ANOTHER.

BLESS THEM WHICH PERSECUTE YOU: BLESS AND CURSE NOT. Romans 12 WHO IS A WISE MAN AND ENDUED WITH KNOWLEDGE AMONG YOU? LET HIM SHOW OUT OF A GOOD CONVERSATION HIS WORKS WITH MEEKNESS OF WISDOM. BUT IF YOU HAVE BITTER ENVYING AND STRIFE IN YOUR HEARTS, GLORY NOT AND LIE NOT AGAINST THE TRUTH. THIS WISDOM DESCENDS NOT FROM ABOVE, BUT IS EARTHLY, SENSUAL, DEVILISH. FOR WHERE ENVYING AND STRIFE IS, THERE IS CONFUSION AND EVERY EVIL WORK. <u>BUT THE WISDOM THAT IS FROM ABOVE IS FIRST PURE, THEN PEACEABLE, GENTLE AND EASY TO BE ENTREATED, FULL OF MERCY AND GOOD FRUITS, WITHOUT PARTIALITY AND WITHOUT HYPOCRISY. AND THE FRUIT OF RIGHTEOUSNESS IS SOWN IN PEACE OF THEM THAT MAKE PEACE.</u> James 3

WE SOW, MAKE, PLANT, SEEK AFTER RIGHTEOUSNESS WITH PEACE! FOR THE FRUIT OF RIGHTEOUSNESS IS SOWN IN PEACE! James 3:18 IF THE FRUIT OF RIGHTEOUSNESS IS SOWN IN PEACE, THUS, THE REASON IT IS WRITTEN, LET EVERY MAN BE SWIFT TO HEAR AND SLOW TO SPEAK, SLOW TO WRATH! FOR THE WRATH OF MAN DOES NOT WORK THE RIGHTEOUSNESS OF GOD! RECEIVE WITH MEEKNESS THE ENGRAFTED WORD WHICH IS ABLE TO SAVE YOUR SOULS AND LAY ASIDE ALL FILTHINESS: ABOMINATION, IDOLATRY, MORAL AND SEXUAL UNCLEANNESS, FORNICATION, ADULTERY, EFFEMINATE, ABUSERS OF THEMSELVES WITH MANKIND, SAME SEX UNIONS, GIVING THEMSELVES UP UNTO VILE AFFECTIONS, CHANGING THE NATURAL USE, BURNING IN THEIR LUST, ONE TOWARD ANOTHER, MEN WITH MEN, AND WOMEN WITH WOMEN, DISHONORING THEIR OWN BODIES BETWEEN THEMSELVES THROUGH THE LUSTS OF THEIR OWN HEARTS, CHANGING THE TRUTH OF GOD INTO A LIE, BEING FILLED WITH ALL UNRIGHTEOUSNESS! THE WRATH OF GOD IS REVEALED FROM HEAVEN AGAINST ALL UNGODLINESS AND UNRIGHTOUSNESS

OF THOSE WHO HOLD THE TRUTH IN UNRIGHTEOUSNESS SO THAT THEY ARE WITHOUT EXCUSE! Romans One

NOT ONLY THESE SAITH THE LORD SHALL BE CAST INTO THE LAKE OF FIRE WHICH BURNS WITH FIRE AND BRIMSTONE FOREVER AND FOREVER, BUT ALSO THIEVES, DRUNKARDS, THE COVETOUS, REVILERS AND EXTORTIONERS! I Corinthians Six

PEACE IS A TOOL. ACTUALLY IT IS THE SOIL FOR WHICH RIGHTEOUSNESS CAN BE SOWN. RIGHTEOUSNESS IS SOWN WHERE? IN PEACE! SO WHAT IS THE FIRST REQUIREMENT IN ATTAINING RIGHTEOUSNESS? PEACE!!! FOLLOW PEACE WITH ALL MEN AND HOLINESS WITHOUT WHICH NO MAN SHALL SEE THE LORD! Hebrews 12:14

FOR UNTO US A CHILD IS BORN, UNTO US A SON IS GIVEN: AND THE GOVERNMENT SHALL BE UPON HIS SHOULDERS. AND HIS NAME SHALL BE CALLED WONDERFUL, COUNSELOR, THE MIGHTY GOD, THE EVERLASTING FATHER, THE PRINCE OF PEACE! OF THE INCREASE OF HIS GOVERNMENT AND PEACE THERE SHALL BE NO END, UPON THE THRONE OF DAVID, AND UPON HIS KINGDOM, TO ORDER IT, AND TO ESTABLISH IT WITH JUDGMENT AND WITH JUSTICE FROM HENCEFORTH EVEN FOR EVER! THE ZEAL OF THE LORD OF HOSTS WILL PERFORM THIS! Isaiah Nine

November 26, 2001

Acknowledgement and Submission

GOD USES FAILURES, BECAUSE THEY UNDERSTAND THE <u>TRUE</u> MEANING OF THE CATCHING AWAY! THEY KNOW, BUT FOR THE GRACE OF GOD!!! THEY KNOW, THERE IS NO OTHER FOUNTAIN! THEY <u>KNOW</u> IN WHOM THEIR STRENGTH LIES! THEY GLORY IN NOTHING SAVE IN THE LORD JESUS CHRIST!!! THEY KNOW THAT NOTHING BUT THE BLOOD OF JESUS!!! THEY RELY ON NOTHING ELSE THAN JESUS CHRIST AND HIS RIGHTEOUSNESS! THANK YOU, LORD! FOR YOUR HOLINESS! I LIVE AND MOVE AND HAVE MY BEING IN YOU! THANK YOU FOR YOUR GRACE! YOUR LOVING-KINDNESS! NO OTHER HOPE HAVE I BUT IN THEE! <u>ALL</u> MY GOODNESS IS IN YOU! <u>ALL</u> MY HOPE AND STAY! I GIVE ALLEGIANCE TO THE GLORY OF YOUR MAJESTY AND DOMINION! I SUBMIT TO YOUR FORTITUDES AND TO YOUR FAITHFULNESS! I AM YOUR LOVE SLAVE!

November 26, 2001

Exhortation

THERE IS LOVE INSIDE OF YOU THAT IS TRYING TO COME OUT TO MANIFEST! GOD IS LOVE AND HE WANTS TO LIVE IN YOU. PRACTICE THE PEACE OF GOD IN YOUR LIFE IN EVERYTHING. JESUS WAS REJECTED MOST OF HIS LIFE! THE APOSTLES AND PROPHETS WERE AND ARE REJECTED! ANYONE WHO IS GREATLY USED OF THE LORD IS REJECTED IN SOME DEPTH OF MEASURE. GOD WANTS US TO LIVE A CRUCIFIED LIFE! ASKING IN PRAYER BRINGS HUMILITY, MAKING US DEPENDENT ON GOD! NO ONE LEAVES THE PRESENCE OF THE LORD EMPTY EXCEPT THOSE WHO ARE FULL OF THEMSELVES, WHO REFUSE TO ALLOW THEMSELVES TO BE DUG OUT AND EMPTIED OF THEIR OWN SELF-SEEKING! GOD DOES NOT REJECT US. PEOPLE DO. THE REJECTED STONES OF THE BUILDING CAN MAKE THE BEST, LIVELIEST HOLY GHOST HEARTS!!! GOD CANNOT FILL YOU WITH HIMSELF IF YOU ARE NOT EMPTIED OF YOURSELF!!! GOD WANTS YOU TO BE THOROUGHLY FURNISHED, LACKING NOTHING! THE ONLY WAY TO BE READY FOR THE WORK OF THE LORD IS TO BE FILLED WITH THE LORD AT ALL TIMES! GOOD AND BAD! YOUR ATTITUDE DETERMINES YOUR PROGRESS!!!!! YOU ARE CONSTANTLY BEING DELIVERED TO THE MINISTRY OF THE HOLY GHOST WHICH IS TO PERFECT YOU! TO CAUSE YOU TO SET YOUR AFFECTIONS ON THE THINGS OF GOD! GREEK FOR SET IS: "DRIVE IN LIKE A NAIL!!!" THIS LAND WAS ESTABLISHED UPON THE DOCTRINE OF JESUS CHRIST!

Acknowledgement and Submission

WHAT IS A DOCTRINE WORTH WITHOUT THE PRINCIPLES AND
PRECEPTS OF THAT DOCTRINE??? BECAUSE WE DO NOT READILY
COMMUNICATE IN DEPTH OF THOUGHTS AND FEELINGS WE
PERCEIVE THINGS AS THOUGH THEY ARE NOT AND WE MUST
DEAL WITH THEM AS THOUGH THEY ARE. PERCEPTION IS NINETY
PERCENT OF LIFE. BUT SO MUCH OF OUR LIFE IS MADE UP OF
ALTERED REALITY. WORD AND SPIRIT ARE TRUE REALITY. TO
RECEIVE FROM GOD YOU HAVE TO TOUCH THE ANOINTING. TO
TOUCH THE ANOINTING, YOU MUST TOUCH ONE ANOTHER. TO
REALLY TOUCH ONE ANOTHER YOU MUST TOUCH AT THE POINT
OF PRESSURE. TO CARE ENOUGH TO RESOLVE CONFLICTS AND
MISUNDERSTANDINGS! TO LOVE THE HEART OF ANOTHER IS TO
TOUCH GOD FOR GOD IS LOVE! I John 4

YOUR OWN SOUL, YOUR MIND, YOUR WILL AND YOUR EMOTIONS
ARE NOURISHED WHEN YOU ARE KIND!!! BUT THEY ARE
DESTROYED WHEN YOU ARE CRUEL!!! WRATH IS CRUEL AND
ANGER IS OUTRAGEOUS! Proverbs 17:4 THEY THAT ARE CHRIST'S
HAVE CRUCIFIED THE FLESH (THOUGHTS, FEELINGS, OPINIONS
CONTRARY TO GOD'S) WITH THE AFFECTIONS AND LUSTS!
Galatians 5:24 SO IT IS UP TO YOU WHETHER YOU ARE REALLY IN
CHRIST! WHETHER HE IS REALLY IN YOU! II Corinthians 5:17 IF
YOU ARE NOT CRUCIFYING YOUR OWN THOUGHTS, FEELINGS,
OPINIONS AND ALLOWING YOUR FLESH TO BE MADE
CONFORMABLE TO THE IMAGE OF CHRIST, ARE YOUR REALLY
HIS??? TO BELONG TO CHRIST MEANS TO SURRENDER OUR
AFFECTIONS AND PLEASURES! IF WE LIVE IN THE SPIRIT LET US
ALSO WALK IN THE SPIRIT!

LET US NOT BE DESIROUS OF VAIN GLORY, PROVOKING ONE
ANOTHER, ENVYING ONE ANOTHER! Galatians 5:25-26 THE FUEL OF
FAITH IS TO GO THE DISTANCE TO REAP THE HARVEST. GOD
DETERMINES WHEN IT IS HARVEST TIME. THOU HAST GIVEN ME
THE SHIELD OF THY SALVATION AND THY RIGHT HAND HATH
HOLDEN ME UP AND THY GENTLENESS HAS MADE ME GREAT!

Psalms 18:35 IF SO BE THAT YOU HAVE HEARD HIM AND HAVE BEEN TAUGHT BY HIM AS THE TRUTH IS IN JESUS: THAT YOU PUT OFF CONCERNING THE FORMER LIFESTYLE THE OLD MAN WHICH IS CORRUPT ACCORDING TO THE DECEITFUL AFFECTIONS! AND BE RENEWED IN THE SPIRIT OF YOUR MIND AND PUT ON THE NEW MAN WHICH IS CREATED IN RIGHTEOUSNESS AND TRUE HOLINESS! WHEREFORE PUT OFF THE LIE (DECEIT), SPEAK EVERY MAN TRUTH WITH HIS NEIGHBOR FOR WE ARE MEMBERS ONE OF ANOTHER! DO NOT LET YOUR ANGER CAUSE YOU TO SIN WITH YOUR LIPS OR YOUR ACTIONS. BE RECONCILED DAILY!

<u>GIVE NO PLACE TO THE DEVIL!</u> <u>LET NO UNKIND COMMUNICATION PROCEED OUT OF YOUR MOUTH BUT THAT WHICH IS GOOD TO THE IMPROVEMENT OF THE NEED AND GRIEVE NOT THE HOLY SPIRIT OF GOD!</u> LET <u>ALL</u> BITTERNESS AND WRATH AND ANGER AND CLAMOR AND BLASPHEMY BE PUT AWAY FROM YOU WITH <u>ALL</u> EVIL AND <u>BE KIND</u> TO ONE ANOTHER, TENDERHEARTED, FORGIVING ONE ANOTHER, EVEN AS GOD FOR CHRIST'S SAKE HAS FORGIVEN YOU! Ephesians 4 BE THEREFORE IMITATORS OF GOD AS BELOVED CHILDREN! AND WALK IN LOVE AS CHRIST ALSO HAS LOVED US AND HAS GIVEN HIMSELF FOR US AN OFFERING AND A SACRIFICE TO GOD FOR A SWEET-SMELLING SAVOR!!! <u>BUT FORNICATION AND ALL SAME SEX LUST, OR GREEDINESS LET IT NOT ONCE BE NAMED AMONG YOU AS BECOME SAINTS! NEITHER FILTHINESS, NOR FOOLISH TALKING, NOR RAILING, WHICH ARE NOT BECOMING, BUT RATHER GIVING OF THANKS! BE NOT PARTAKERS WITH THEM!</u> BUT YOU WERE THEN IN DARKNESS, BUT NOW ARE YOU LIGHT IN THE LORD: WALK AS CHILDREN OF LIGHT: FOR THE FRUIT OF LIGHT IS IN ALL GOODNESS AND RIGHTEOUSNESS AND TRUTH! PROVING WHAT IS WELL-PLEASING UNTO THE LORD! <u>AND HAVE NO FELLOWSHIP WITH THE UNFRUITFUL WORKS OF DARKNESS, BUT RATHER EVEN REPROVE THEM!</u> WHEREFORE, RISE UP YOU SLEEPING ONES, OUT OF THE DEAD ONES AND CHRIST WILL SHINE ON YOU! SEE THAT YOU WALK CAREFULLY NOT AS UNWISE, REDEEMING THE TIME BECAUSE THE DAYS ARE EVIL! THEREFORE BE NOT FOOLISH, BUT UNDERSTAND WHAT

THE WILL OF THE LORD IS!!! <u>AND BE NOT DRUNK WITH ALCOHOL WHICH IS WANTONNESS, BUT BE FILLED BY THE SPIRIT!!!</u> BEING SUBJECT TO ONE ANOTHER IN THE FEAR OF CHRIST!!! Ephesians 5 THE ULTIMATE SACRIFICE OF SHOWING LOVE! NO HUMAN CAN FILL THE VOID, ABUSE, ABANDONMENT, HURTS! ONLY GOD! ONLY HIS SPIRIT AND HIS GRACE CAN FILL ALL THE HOLES IN THE HEART! IT WAS COMMON IN SECOND CENTURY CHRISTIANITY FOR CHRISTIANS TO SELL THEMSELVES INTO SLAVERY IN ORDER FOR SOMEONE ELSE TO COME OUT OF SLAVERY SO THAT THEY COULD HEAR THE GOSPEL!!! THE ULTIMATE SACRIFICE OF SHOWING LOVE!!! IN FIRST, SECOND AND THIRD CENTURIES, CHRISTIANS EXPERIENCED CHANGE IN <u>EVERY</u> AREA OF THEIR LIVES! COVENANT IS NOT JUST IN COMMANDMENTS, IN PERFORMANCE! COVENANT IS IN RELATIONSHIPS!

COVENANT IS HEART TO HEART COMMUNICATION! COVENANT MUST BE BASED ON TRUST AND LIVED OUT IN LOVE! WE BECOME ONE SO THAT THE WORLD MAY KNOW THAT THE KINGDOM IS COME! THOSE WHO NAME THE NAME OF CHRIST NEED TO REALIZE THAT WHEN JESUS WAS CRUCIFIED, THEIR OLD MAN WAS CRUCIFIED WITH HIM!!! IF IT HURTS, IT ISN'T DEAD YET! LOVE IS HAVING A VISION FOR OTHERS!!! POURING YOURSELF OUT SO THAT YOU MAY STAY FILLED UP WITH HIM!!! LOVE IS PUTTING YOURSELF IN ANOTHER'S PLACE! <u>PAY THE PRICE OF SACRIFICE!</u> YOU ARE ENOUGH WHEN BROKEN ENOUGH! YOU WILL BE JUDGED BY THE SAME STANDARD BY WHICH YOU JUDGE OTHERS!!!!! JUDGE YOURSELF IN FORGIVING OTHERS! UNDERSTAND THE PRINCIPLES OF MERCY!!! EDUCATION DOES NOT BRING REVELATION! ILLUMINATION THROUGH THE ANOINTING OF THE HOLY SPIRIT BRINGS REVELATION! IN THE SCRIPTURES, I CAN DO <u>ALL</u> THINGS THROUGH CHRIST WHICH STRENGTHENS ME! THE GREEK TRANSLATION OF STRENGTHEN IS: <u>WHO FUSES HIS STRENGTH WITH MINE!</u> EACH CELL OF OUR SPIRIT MAN IS FILTERED THROUGH THE HOLY GHOST SO THAT WE CAN BE BALANCED AND THOROUGHLY FURNISHED WHEN WE FUSE OUR STRENGTH WITH THE LORD'S! YOU MAY BE WISE IN

INTELLECT, BUT ARE YOU WISE ENOUGH <u>NOT</u> TO BE DUMB? EXPECT A PROBLEM WHEN YOU WALK IN OBEDIENCE! ALL LIFE HAS PROBLEMS! THE HOLY SPIRIT IS A PROBLEM SOLVER! WHY DO YOU THINK IT IS WRITTEN, <u>BE FILLED WITH THE SPIRIT</u>? SO THAT YOU CAN FULFILL YOUR PURPOSE! <u>IF YOU ARE FULL OF THE INFILLING OF THE SPIRIT OF GOD, YOU CAN BE A PROBLEM SOLVER!</u> CHRISTIANS ARE TO BE PROBLEM SOLVERS! NOT GLORIOUS CONTAINERS OF EASE AND LAZINESS! <u>LOVE IS A SYMBOL OF RIGHTEOUSNESS WHICH MEANS TO HAVE A VISION FOR OTHERS, POURING YOURSELF OUT IN ORDER TO BE FILLED UP! PUTTING YOURSELF IN THE OTHER PERSON'S PLACE, ALWAYS INITIATING PROTECTION AND PROVISION!!!</u> PEACE IS THE <u>PRESENCE OF RIGHTEOUSNESS! PEACE COMES FROM ALLOWING YOUR LIFE TO FLOW OUT TO OTHERS AS YOU CONTINUE SUBMITTING TO THE LIFE OF THE LORD FLOWING INTO YOU!!! OH, HALLELUJAH!!!!!</u>

November 26, 2001

JOURNEY TO PEACE ~ PHILIPPIANS 4:1-7

1) <u>STAND</u> FAST IN THE LORD!

2) BE OF <u>ONE</u> MIND!

3) <u>HELP OTHERS</u>, EVEN WOMEN LABORERS!

4) <u>REJOICE</u> IN THE LORD <u>ALWAYS</u>!

5) LET YOUR <u>MODERATION</u> BE KNOW UNTO <u>ALL</u> MEN!

6) BE ANXIOUS ABOUT NOTHING, BUT IN EVERYTHING BY <u>PRAYER</u> AND <u>SUPPLICATION</u> (WITH THE KNOWLEDGE THAT HIS GRACE, SUPERNATURAL ABILITY, IS ALWAYS GOOD) WITH <u>THANKSGIVING</u> LET YOUR REQUESTS BE MADE KNOWN UNTO GOD!!!!

7) AND (AFTER DOING ALL OF THE ABOVE) <u>THE PEACE OF GOD</u>, WHICH PASSES <u>ALL</u> UNDERSTANDING SHALL KEEP YOUR HEARTS AND MINDS THROUGH CHRIST JESUS!!!!!

STEPS TO KEEP PEACE ~ EPHESIANS 4:8-9

1) THINK ON THINGS THAT ARE TRUE! GOD'S WORD! THE LOGOS AND THE RHEMA!

2) THINK ON THINGS THAT ARE HONEST! GOD'S WORD! THE LOGOS, THE RHEMA!!!!

3) THINK ON THINGS THAT ARE JUST! GOD'S WORD! THE LOGOS AND THE RHEMA!!

4) THINK ON THINGS THAT ARE PURE! GOD'S WORD! THE LOGOS AND THE RHEMA!!!!!

5) THINK ON THINGS THAT ARE LOVELY! GOD'S WORD! THE LOGOS, THE RHEMA!!!!!

6) THINK ON THINGS THAT ARE OF GOOD REPORT! GOD'S WORD! THE LOGOS AND THE RHEMA!

7) THINK ON THINGS THAT ARE VIRTUOUS! GOD'S WORD! THE LOGOS AND THE RHEMA!!!!

THINK ON THESE THINGS AND PRAISE THE LORD!!! THOSE THINGS WHICH YOU HAVE LEARNED, AND HEARD, RECEIVE AND DO <u>AND</u> THE GOD OF PEACE SHALL BE WITH YOU!!!!!

November 23, 2001

Wisdom

THUS AGAIN, THOUGHTS UNDER-GIRD THE THEMES OF LIFE. THOUGHTS ESTABLISH STABILITY, REALITY! SO WHY THINK YOU OTHERWISE! TO DO SO TRULY IS NOT BEING WISE! YOU ARE THE <u>AUTHOR</u> OF YOUR OWN <u>REALITY</u>! ONLY YOU CAN TRULY STABILIZE DIGNITY. <u>ONLY YOU CAN DICTATE WHAT YOU CHOOSE TO THINK UPON, MEDITATE UPON</u>! YOU ARE A PRODUCT OF YOUR OWN INTEGRITY! WHAT YOU ARE AND ARE BECOMING IS THE RESULT OF YOUR <u>OWN</u> CHOICES! CHOOSE CAREFULLY WHAT GOES INTO YOUR THINKING! FOR TRULY AS YOU DO SO, YOU DEVELOP YOUR PERCEPTION OF TRUTH! REALITY! BUILD YOUR REALITY ON <u>LIFE</u> HIMSELF! THE <u>REAL</u> TRUTH! <u>THE TRUTH</u>! THE <u>WHOLE</u> TRUTH! <u>AND NOTHING BUT THE TRUTH</u>! IF YOU WILL USE <u>ALL</u> TRUTH THAT IS AVAILABLE TO YOU, INSTEAD OF BITS AND PIECES, YOU CAN HAVE WHAT GOD'S WORD SAYS THAT YOU CAN HAVE! WORRY IS CAUSED BY PAIN OR FEAR! SOME PAIN OR FEAR IS INEVITABLE, BUT MISERY IS A CHOICE! JOY AND PEACE ARE NOT DEPENDENT ON CIRCUMSTANCES! JOY IS DEPENDENT ON OUR LORD AND SAVIOR JESUS CHRIST!!! CHOOSE LIFE AND PEACE IN THE MIDST OF PAIN! THE SOURCE OF YOUR STRENGTH IS JOY! THE JOY OF THE LORD <u>IS</u> YOUR STRENGTH!!! Nehemiah 8:10

WITH <u>JOY</u> YOU SHALL DRAW WATER OUT OF THE WELLS OF PROVISION! Isaiah 12:3 LAUGHTER AND EXERCISE INCREASE ENDORPHINS IN THE BODY WHICH RELIEVE PHYSICAL PAIN! EXERCISE IN THE HOLY SCRIPTURES AND IN HEALTHY ATTITUDES RELIEVE EMOTIONAL PAIN! PRACTICE JOY AND PEACE! IT IS A DELIBERATE AND INTENTIONAL CHOOSING! SIMPLE, BUT NOT TO BE CONFUSED WITH EASY! PAIN FORCES YOU TO MAKE HARDER CHOICES, THUS PAIN FORCES YOU TO GROW! THE CHOICE OF JOY BRINGS THE ABILITY TO COPE WITH PROBLEMS! A LIFESTYLE! COMMIT TO DISCIPLE-HOOD! FOUNDATION ROOTS MUST DEEPEN!

WOE UNTO THEM THAT CALL EVIL "GOOD" AND GOOD "EVIL!" THAT PUT DARKNESS FOR LIGHT AND LIGHT FOR DARKNESS! THAT PUT BITTER FOR SWEET AND SWEET FOR BITTER! WOE UNTO THEM THAT ARE WISE IN THEIR OWN EYES! AND PRUDENT IN THEIR OWN SIGHT! WOE UNTO THEM THAT ARE MIGHTY TO DRINK WINE AND MEN OF STRENGTH TO MINGLE STRONG DRINK! WHICH JUSTIFY THE WICKED FOR REWARD AND TAKE AWAY THE RIGHTEOUSNESS OF THE RIGHTEOUS FROM HIM! THEREFORE AS THE FIRE DEVOURS THE STUBBLE AND THE FLAME CONSUMES THE CHAFF SO THEIR ROOT SHALL BE AS ROTTENNESS AND THEIR BLOSSOM SHALL GO UP AS DUST: <u>BECAUSE THEY HAVE CAST AWAY THE LAW OF THE LORD OF HOSTS AND DESPISED THE WORD OF THE HOLY ONE OF ISRAEL!!!</u> Isaiah 5:20-24

November 23, 2001

Exhortation

ALL SIN COMES ABOUT FROM NOT HATING EVIL! WE DO NOT PARTAKE OF THAT WHICH WE HATE! THE ONLY WAY TO BE DELIVERED FROM UN-FORGIVENESS OR ANY OTHER SIN IS TO SURRENDER IT UNTO THE LORD GOD ALMIGHTY BECAUSE AS AN ACT OF YOUR WILL YOU CHOOSE TO HATE WHAT GOD HATES!!! FORGIVENESS AND POWER OVER SIN ONLY COME WHEN ONE'S WILL IS TOTALLY SURRENDERED UNTO OUR LORD AND TO THE COMMAND OF HIS WORD! Matthew 6:14-15 FORGIVE TO ESCAPE HELL WHEN IT IS TOO DIFFICULT TO FORGIVE FOR ANY OTHER REASON!

A MATURE SERVANT (MIND YOU, I DID STATE SERVANT) OF GOD IS FILLED WITH LOVE AT ALL TIMES AND IN EVERY SITUATION. DO YOU KNOW THE REASON WHY THEY ARE? THERE IS ONLY ONE. THEY ARE FILLED WITH <u>HIS WORD</u>! WORD WILL OBLITERATE SIN! UN-FORGIVENESS AND ANY OTHER EVIL! WHAT IN HELL IS WORTH GOING THERE FOR? SINCE GOD <u>IS</u> ALMIGHTY, SINCE HE DOES HAVE <u>ALL</u> MIGHT, HE CAN SUBDUE, OBLITERATE <u>ALL</u> PAIN OF THE PAST <u>AND</u> PRESENT WHEN WE ALLOW <u>HIM</u> <u>ONLY</u> TO BE THE LORD OF OUR LIFE, BREATH AND BEING!!! WHATEVER WE <u>FULLY</u> SUBMIT TO HIM HE WILL BE LORD OVER! WHEN HE IS LORD OVER SOMETHING, IT SUBMITS!!! PAIN AND AGONY AND TORMENTED FEELINGS ARE SUBDUED, ABSOLVED AND <u>HE</u>, BECAUSE WE MAKE HIM LORD OF OUR LIFE, PUTS INTO US <u>HIS</u> FEELINGS, ATTITUDES, FORGIVENESSES, MERCIES AND PASSIONS! O, HALLELUJAH! GLORY TO THE LORD AND KING OF <u>ALL</u> MERCIES AND DOMINIONS AND POWERS AND AUTHORITIES AND MIGHTS!!!

November 23, 2001

Reflection

MY EXPERIENCE IN LIFE HAS BEEN THAT THE CIRCUMSTANCES ... THE SO-CALLED NORMS OF LIFE DO NOT ALWAYS GET BETTER. FOR ME THE SO-CALLED NORMS IN MY LIFE HAVE ALWAYS GOTTEN WORSE WHEN MEASURED BY MEN'S STANDARDS. BUT GOD. THE CALL OF PROPHET IS A UNIQUE CALL. NOT ALWAYS MEASURED NOR UNDERSTOOD BY LOGIC AND PATTERN. NOT MAN'S ANYWAY. BUT A GOOD ANALOGY OF LIFE, EVEN AS I CONTINUE TO WORK ON THE LAYOUT OF THIS MANUSCRIPT ... IT WAS GOOD BEFORE ... BUT IT GETS BETTER THE MORE TIME I COMMIT TO THE WORK. GOD'S.

November 25, 2001

I MUST REMEMBER TO TELL MY SON THE IMPORTANCE OF LAYING ON ONE'S FACE BEFORE THE LORD! FOR TRULY GOD IS KING OF KINGS AND THE LORD OF LORDS! AND THERE IS NONE LIKE HIM IN DOMINION AND MIGHT AND BEAUTY AND AUTHORITY! HE TRULY CAN MAKE THE CROOKED PLACES STRAIGHT! HE BRINGS DOWN THE HIGH PLACES AND BRINGS UP THE LOW PLACES SO THAT WE CAN FULFILL OUR DESTINIES AND OUR DOMINIONS! THERE IS NOBODY LIKE JEHOVAH! THERE IS NONE TO COMPARE!

November 26, 2001

Affirmations of Faith

I AM STRONG IN YOU, LORD, AND IN THE POWER OF YOUR MIGHT! I SUBMIT MY WILL TO YOUR AUTHORITY AND TO YOUR PROVISION! I SEE CLEARLY MY OBLIGATIONS AND MY RESPONSIBILITIES. AND I DO NOT DENY MY DUTIES NOR DO I FAIL TO PERFORM ALL MY NECESSITIES. I TAKE PLEASURE IN BEING A SERVANT OF THE LORD. I CAST DOWN NATURAL REASONING, MEN'S LOGIC AND EVERYTHING THAT WOULD SEEK TO EXALT ITSELF ABOVE THE KNOWLEDGE OF GOD. I AM MORE THAN A CONQUEROR THROUGH HIM THAT LOVES ME. I PRAISE HIS WONDERFUL AND GLORIOUS NAME. I CAST OUT ALL PRIDE, SLOTHFULNESS AND DESIRE FOR PREEMINENCE. I AM BEING CONFORMED TO THE IMAGE OF MY LORD. I DO THOSE THINGS ALWAYS THAT ARE PLEASING IN HIS SIGHT. I DO NOT FEAR MAN. I DO NOT SEEK THE APPROVAL OF THE MASSES. I STAY SUBMITTED TO THE PRECEPTS OF MY LORD EVEN IN TIMES OF STRUGGLE AND STRESS. ALL DOMINIONS AND MIGHTS AND POWERS AND AUTHORITIES BOW BEFORE THE FATHER. I TAKE ORDERS FROM THE THRONE OF HEAVEN.

I AM OBEDIENT IN THE SMALL THINGS. FOR HE THAT WOULD KNOW THE GREATNESS OF DOMINION AND THE HEART OF THE FATHER COMES TO UNDERSTAND THAT THERE ARE NO SMALL DUTIES. FOR IT IS WRITTEN, HE THAT IS FAITHFUL IN THE LEAST WILL BE FAITHFUL ALSO IN MUCH. AND HE THAT IS UNJUST IN THE LEAST WILL BE UNJUST IN MUCH. FOR TRULY AS IT IS WRITTEN, THE LITTLE FOXES SPOIL THE VINE. THEREFORE, I ABIDE, LIVE AND MOVE AND HAVE MY BEING IN HIM, THE TRUE VINE, THE LIVING WATER, THE FOREVER FAITHFUL, THE FIRST AND THE LAST, THE MIGHTY AND THE MAGNIFICENT, MY ALL IN ALL, MY WHOSOEVER WILL LET HIM COME AND DRINK OF THE WATER OF LIFE FREELY! COME WITHOUT MONEY AND WITHOUT PRICE! JESUS GIVES UNTO ME HIMSELF! THE LIVING WATER! THE NEVER ENDING FOUNTAIN! THE LORD CHERISHES ME AND SUSTAINS ME. HE IS NOT ONLY THE GOD OF <u>ALL</u> FORCES, BUT HE

ACTUALLY <u>LIVES</u> IN ME!!! HE TAKES UP HIS ABODE INSIDE OF ME! WHY DO YOU THINK IT IS WRITTEN, FOR THIS CAUSE SHALL A MAN LEAVE HIS FATHER AND MOTHER AND SHALL BE JOINED TO A WIFE AND THEY TWO SHALL BE <u>ONE</u> FLESH. THIS IS A GREAT MYSTERY: BUT IS SPEAKING CONCERNING CHRIST AND THE CHURCH!

November 26, 2001

Affirmations of the Name of the Lord

- WE REJOICE IN THY SALVATION AND IN THE NAME OF OUR GOD WE SET UP OUR BANNERS! THE LORD FULFILLS <u>ALL</u> OF OUR PETITIONS! Psalms 20:5 I PRAISE THE LORD FOR HIS GOODNESS AND FOR HIS WONDERFUL WORKS TO THE CHILDREN OF MEN! I DECLARE HIS WORKS WITH REJOICING! Psalms 107:15, 22

- THE NAME OF THE GOD OF JACOB DEFENDS US! HE HEARS US IN THE DAY OF TROUBLE! Psalms 20:1 RIGHTEOUSNESS AND JUDGMENT ARE THE HABITATION OF HIS THRONE! Psalms 97:2

- WE STAND UP AND BLESS THE LORD OUR GOD FOREVER AND EVER! BLESSED BE THY GLORIOUS NAME, WHICH WE EXALT ABOVE <u>ALL</u> BLESSING AND PRAISE! THOU EVEN THOU ART LORD ALONE! THOU HAST MADE HEAVEN, THE HEAVEN OF HEAVENS, WITH ALL THEIR HOST, THE EARTH, AND ALL THINGS THAT ARE THEREIN AND THOU PRESERVEST THEM ALL, AND THE HOST OF HEAVEN WORSHIPS THEE! Nehemiah 9:5-6 THE LORD IS RIGHTEOUS IN <u>ALL</u> HIS WAYS AND HOLY IN <u>ALL</u> HIS WORKS! BLESS HIS HOLY NAME FOREVER AND EVER! Psalms 145:17, 21

- FROM THE RISING OF THE SUN UNTO THE GOING DOWN OF THE SAME WE PRAISE THY HOLY NAME! Psalms 113:3 WE SHALL SPEAK OF THE GLORY OF THY KINGDOM AND TALK OF THY POWER! Psalms 145:11

- THE NAME OF THE LORD IS MY STRONG TOWER! I RUN INTO IT AND I AM SAFE! Proverbs 18:10 I WILL SPEAK OF THE GLORIOUS HONOR OF THY MAJESTY AND OF THY WONDROUS WORKS! Psalms 145:5

- I PRAISE THE NAME OF GOD WITH SONG AND I MAGNIFY HIM WITH THANKSGIVING! Psalms 69:30

- WE PRAISE THY GREAT AND TERRIBLE NAME FOR IT IS HOLY! Psalms 99:3 HOLY AND REVEREND IS THY NAME! Psalms 111:9

- BLESSED BE THE NAME OF GOD FOREVER AND EVER FOR WISDOM AND MIGHT ARE HIS! HE CHANGES THE TIMES AND SEASONS! HE REMOVES KINGS AND SET UP KINGS! HE GIVES

WISDOM UNTO THE WISE AND KNOWLEDGE TO THEM THAT KNOW UNDERSTANDING! THE KNOWLEDGE OF THE HOLY IS UNDERSTANDING! HE IS REVEALING THE DEEP AND SECRET THINGS UNTO US! I THANK THEE AND PRAISE THEE, O THOU GOD OF MY FATHERS WHO GIVES ME WISDOM AND MIGHT AND HAS MADE KNOWN UNTO ME NOW THE THING I HAVE DESIRED! Daniel 2:20-23

- I OBSERVE TO DO ALL THE WORDS THAT ARE COMMANDED ME SO THAT I MAY FEAR THE GLORIOUS AND FEARFUL NAME OF THE LORD MY GOD! Deuteronomy 28:58
- WE WALK IN THE NAME OF THE LORD OUR GOD FOREVER AND EVER! Micah 4:5
- I STRETCH FORTH MY HANDS TO HEAL AND SIGNS AND WONDERS ARE DONE BY THE NAME OF THY HOLY SERVANT JESUS! FOR GOD HAS GRANTED UNTO ME THAT WITH ALL BOLDNESS I SPEAK HIS WORD! Acts 4:29-30
- BLESSED BE THE LORD GOD, THE GOD OF ISRAEL, WHO ALONE DOES WONDROUS THINGS! AND BLESSED BE HIS GLORIOUS NAME FOREVER AND LET THE WHOLE EARTH BE FILLED WITH HIS GLORY! AMEN AND AMEN. Psalms 72:18-19
- WHATSOEVER I ASK IN HIS NAME, THAT WILL HE DO, THAT THE FATHER MAY BE GLORIFIED IN THE SON! John 14:13, 15:16
- I PREACH REPENTANCE AND REMISSION OF SINS IN HIS NAME AMONG ALL NATIONALITIES THAT THEY MAY BELIEVE THAT JESUS IS THE CHRIST, THE SON OF GOD AND THAT BELIEVING THEY MAY HAVE LIFE THROUGH HIS NAME! Luke 24:47 John 20:31
- I SING UNTO THE LORD AND BLESS HIS NAME! I SHOW FORTH HIS SALVATION FROM DAY TO DAY! I DECLARE HIS WORK AMONG THE HEATHEN! HIS WONDERS AMONG ALL PEOPLE! FOR THE LORD IS GREAT AND GREATLY TO BE PRAISED! I FEAR HIM ABOVE ALL GODS! FOR ALL THE GODS OF THE NATIONS ARE IDOLS BUT THE LORD MADE THE HEAVENS! I GIVE UNTO THE LORD THE GLORY DUE UNTO HIS NAME! I WORSHIP THE LORD IN THE BEAUTY OF HOLINESS! Psalms 96
- SILVER AND GOLD HAVE I NONE, BUT SUCH AS I HAVE GIVE I THEE IN THE NAME OF JESUS CHRIST OF NAZARETH, RISE UP

AND WALK! BE HEALED OF <u>ALL</u> MANNER OF SICKNESS AND DISEASE! I AM HEALED! Acts 3:6

- HIS NAME THROUGH FAITH IN HIS NAME IS MAKING ME STRONG! I BEHOLD AND KNOW AND MAKE FIRM HIS NAME! FAITH IN HIS NAME GIVES ME PERFECT SOUNDNESS AND STRENGTH! Acts 3:16 I RECEIVE MY SIGHT, MY HEALING, MY DELIVERANCE, MY MIRACLE, THROUGH FAITH IN HIS NAME! GLORY TO THE LAMB OF GOD WHO TAKES AWAY MY SIN AND PAIN! O, HALLELUJAH!

- TEACH ME THY WAY, O LORD. I WILL WALK IN THY TRUTH! UNITE MY HEART TO FEAR THY NAME! I WILL PRAISE THEE, O LORD MY GOD, WITH <u>ALL</u> MY HEART AND I WILL GLORIFY THY NAME FOR EVERMORE! Psalms 86:11-12

- I OPENED MY MOUTH AND PANTED FOR I LONG FOR THY COMMANDMENTS! LOOK THOU UPON ME AND BE MERCIFUL UNTO ME, AS THOU USED TO DO UNTO THOSE THAT LOVE THY NAME! Psalms 119:131-132

- I WILL PRAISE THEE WITH MY <u>WHOLE</u> HEART! BEFORE THE GODS WILL I SING PRAISE UNTO THEE! I WILL WORSHIP TOWARD THY HOLY TEMPLE AND PRAISE THY NAME FOR THY LOVING-KINDNESS AND FOR THY TRUTH FOR THOU HAST MAGNIFIED THY WORD ABOVE ALL THY NAME! Psalms 138:1-3

- I BLESS THE LORD, O MY SOUL AND <u>ALL</u> THAT IS WITHIN ME BLESSES YOUR HOLY NAME! Psalms 103:1

- I GLORY IN YOUR HOLY NAME, REJOICING AND SEEKING YOUR FACE EVERMORE! I SEEK THE LORD AND HIS STRENGTH! I SEEK YOUR FACE EVERMORE! REMEMBERING YOUR MARVELOUS WORKS THAT YOU HAVE DONE, YOUR WONDERS AND THE JUDGMENTS OF YOUR MOUTH! Psalms 105:3-5

Appendix

LET NO MAN DECEIVE HIMSELF! IF ANY MAN AMONG YOU SEEM TO BE WISE IN THIS WORLD, LET HIM BECOME A FOOL, THAT HE MAY BE WISE! FOR THE WISDOM OF THIS WORLD IS FOOLISHNESS WITH GOD!!! AS IT IS WRITTEN, HE TAKES THE WISE IN THEIR OWN CRAFTINESS!!! AND AGAIN, THE LORD KNOWS THE REASONINGS OF THE WISE, THAT THEY ARE USELESS!!! THEREFORE, LET NO MAN BOAST IN MEN! FOR ALL THINGS ARE YOURS! AND YOU ARE CHRIST'S! AND CHRIST IS GODS! LET A MAN SO ACCOUNT OF US AS UNDER-SERVANTS OF CHRIST AND STEWARDS OF MYSTERIES OF GOD. BUT TO ME IT IS A VERY SMALL THING THAT I AM JUDGED BY YOU, OR OF MAN'S JUDGMENT: YEA, I JUDGE NOT MY OWN SELF!!! FOR I KNOW NOTHING BY MYSELF; YET AM I NOT HEREBY JUSTIFIED! BUT HE THAT JUDGES ME IS THE LORD! WHO WILL BRING TO LIGHT BOTH THE HIDDEN THINGS OF DARKNESS, AND WILL REVEAL THE COUNSELS OF THE HEARTS!!! AND OF THESE THINGS, BRETHREN, I HAVE EXHORTED YOU FOR YOUR SAKES, THAT YOU MIGHT LEARN NOT TO THINK OF MEN MORE HIGHLY THAN YOU OUGHT, THAT NO ONE OF YOU BE PUFFED UP FOR ONE AGAINST ONE ANOTHER!!!

I Corinthians

Chapters Three and Four

THE LORD SPOKE THAT I SHOULD BEGIN A FAST ON CHRISTMAS DAY. ON DECEMBER 29, 1999, THE LORD SAID THAT HE WAS GOING TO REVEAL SOME THINGS TO ME. ONE WAS WHY HE HAS HELD ME BACK FOR SUCH A LONG TIME SINCE HE EQUIPPED ME OVER 30 YEARS AGO. HE SAID, "IT HAS SEEMED CRUEL." I CRIED.

LATER, HE SPOKE, "IF I HAD BROUGHT YOU FORTH BEFORE THIS END-TIME YOU WOULD HAVE BEEN KILLED BEFORE YOUR TIME AND I NEEDED YOU FOR THIS HOUR."

Gloria - Servant of the Lord

Background: Can any good thing come out of Harlan, Kentucky?

Born: August 19, 1941 to Boyd and Ilena Saylor. Named Gloria Dean.

Age 2:   Parents divorced. Hit in head with hammer. Scar on forehead.

Early Childhood: Shuffled from parent to parent, relative to relative, aunts, uncles, cousins, grandparents.

Age 5:   Lived with elderly paternal grandparents, Dan and Frances Saylor, who were eighty years old, and brother Edgar. Hit by a truck. Fractured skull, broken bones, unconscious. Given up to die by doctors. Grandmother prayed.

Age 8:   Father had nervous breakdown. Beloved maternal grandfather, John P. Saylor, died in prime of life. Reunited with Mother and sister Betty. Took violin lessons.

Age 10:   Was converted. Hit in head with baseball bat. Father killed by gangsters. Had attended 7 different schools. Took piano lessons.

Teens: Continuous battle for her soul!

Age 22:   Lord let her know if she did not answer the call of God on her life, a spirit of suicide would take her out of this world!

But God: Impartation, mentoring and hands-on training from A .A. Allen, R. W. Schambach, and Lester Sumrall. Bible College, Dallas, Texas 1964-1968: W. V. Grant, Sr. Correspondence School.

Now: Mother of six children and their beloved spouses plus ten grandchildren!!! Traveled extensively throughout the United States, the former Soviet Union, Russia, Communist China, India, Japan, Africa, Thailand, Jamaica, Mexico, etc. Dead have been raised, the sick healed, souls regenerated! Demons cast out!

And God is not finished yet! It ain't over till God says it's over!
BE READY FOR IN AN HOUR THAT YOU THINK NOT THE SON OF MAN COMETH!!!

Currently: Intercessory prayer and fasting for America. Faxing Government and Spiritual Leaders with God's Truth. Overseeing Five-Fold Ministry Convocations in various cities. Gloria is ordained under World Harvest Ministries with Pastor Rod Parsley, Under World Harvest Fellowship Ministries and as a member of International Covenant Ministries under Dr. Creflo Dollar she is in covenant with ministry brethren worldwide.

Author Contact Information

If you would like to write please let us know if you are experiencing a change in your life. If we can be of any assistance to you as you journey towards TRUTH. Let us hear your needs, concerns and your praise reports. We love you and will pray for you.

To order, write or call:
Gloria B Daulton
2119 Trapp Court
Cincinnati, Ohio 45231-2163
(513) 542-4156 (phone and fax)
gloriadaulton@yahoo.com

Gloria is available for meetings, seminars, conferences and retreats. The Ministry God has given her is a full spectrum of preaching, teaching, sign, gift, word Ministry in demonstration of the Spirit and of Power.

HER PREVIOUS BOOK, <u>SPIRIT OF PROPHECY</u>, IS ALSO AVAILABLE. THANK YOU FOR YOUR PRAYERS AND PARTNERSHIP. IN HIS LOVE.

CPSIA information can be obtained at www.ICGtesting.com
Printed in the USA
BVOW020041120112

280121BV00006B/6/P

9 781932 503258